Andrew Marr was born in Glasgow in 1959. He studied English at the University of Cambridge and has since enjoyed a long career in political journalism, working for the *Scotsman*, the *Independent*, the *Daily Express* and the *Observer*. From 2000 to 2005 he was the BBC's Political Editor. He has written and presented TV documentaries on history, science and politics, and presents the weekly *Andrew Marr Show* on Sunday mornings on BBC1 and *Start the Week* on Radio 4. He lives in London with his family.

Andrew Marr

THE DIAMOND QUEEN

Elizabeth II and Her People

PAN BOOKS

First published 2011 by Macmillan

First published in paperback 2012 by Pan Books
an imprint of Pan Macmillan, a division of Macmillan Publishers Limited
Pan Macmillan, 20 New Wharf Road, London N1 9RR
Basingstoke and Oxford
Associated companies throughout the world
www.panmacmillan.com

ISBN 978-0-330-54416-0

Typeset by SetSystems Ltd, Saffron Walden, Essex
Printed and bound by CPI Group (UK) Ltd, Croydon, CR0 4YY

Visit www.panmacmillan.com to read more about all our books
and to buy them. You will also find features, author interviews and
news of any author events, and you can sign up for e-newsletters
so that you're always first to hear about our new releases.

For my mother, Anne Valerie Marr,

sometimes mistaken for . . .

Contents

Preface and Acknowledgements

The Diamond Jubilee of Queen Elizabeth II will make millions of people reflective. It will give the British, and the Queen's subjects overseas, a chance to look back at sixty years of changing politics, fashions, dramas, successes and failures. As she has grown from the willowy dark-haired young mother of the 1950s into the shrewd great-grandmother of today, so we have all grown older, watching her, hearing her, thinking about her. Her family's ups and downs are reflected in the stories of millions of families. Her record of service is rather more unusual. For many people, the Queen still stalks their dreams; frank conversations with her are the stuff of reverie and fiction. This book is an attempt to tell her life story, looking at the influences on her, and trying to explain why she does what she does. Though the well-known tales of her children's trials and tribulations are included, as they have to be, this is not a particularly gossipy life story. I am more interested in trying to explain what monarchy now means; why the Windsor dynasty behaves as it does; and what having a Queen for all these years, rather than a succession of presidents, might mean.

The book was written while writing and filming a three-part BBC television series about the Queen, which will be broadcast for the anniversary of her accession, in February 2012. It is not, however, 'the book of the series' but a separate endeavour. Nor is it in any way officially authorized. The text has been read by the Palace to correct errors of fact but there has been no access to the Royal Archive, nor any restrictions about what I could say. I would, however, like to record my profound thanks to the Queen's helpful, sensible and friendly staff at Buckingham Palace who have opened doors and corrected mistakes. I would like to thank members of the royal family, past and present royal servants, family friends, Whitehall officials, many politicians and journalists for their candid help too. Many of them did not want to be identified by name and I have tried to respect all promises of confidentiality. I have not splattered the text with knowing asterisks and the irritating footnote 'private information'. What follows is based on my best efforts to record facts and views given to me by people in a position to know, and based as well, of course, on some of the vast pyramid of books about the Queen, her reign and her family that already exist. (Published sources are referenced in the endnotes.)

I could not have written this without the help of the London Library, which is the nearest thing I have to a spiritual home. Nor without the expert help of Gilly Middleburgh or the help and encouragement of the BBC team, including Nick Vaughan-Barratt and Sally Norris. Of the many people who have been particularly kind, I would like to mention the team at the Buckingham Palace press office who have been unfailingly pleasant and helpful; Lord Janvrin and Lord Fellowes, the Queen's former private secretaries; the Earl of Airlie, Lord Luce, Charles Anson; Peter Hennessy, friend and pinnacle of modern British history-writing; Sir Gus O'Donnell, Lord Wilson, Lord Armstrong of Ilminster, Lord Turnbull, Mary Francis, Philip Astor; my terrifyingly successful agent Ed Victor; my wife Jackie Ashley; Philippa Harrison, who expertly edited the rough manuscript; and the team at Macmillan headed by Jon Butler and Georgina Morley.

Many years back, I would have confidently described myself as a republican. This was mainly because I thought it would make me seem clever. As a strategy it was doomed. 'Get over yourself,' I thought, and long ago jettisoned the elitism of anti-monarchism in a profoundly pro-monarchy country. The majority are not always right, God knows; but when they raise a glass or a mug to the stability and reassurance Queen Elizabeth II has brought during difficult decades, they express genuine common sense. I have followed the Queen during some of her many duties, and talked to those closest to her, from ladies-in-waiting to friends of the family and members of the royal family too. And honestly, the more you see of her in action, the more impressed you are. She has been dutiful, but she has been a lot more than dutiful. She has been shrewd, kind and wise. Britain without her would have been a greyer, shriller, more meagre place.

Andrew Marr
September 2011

'She is never – you know – *not* the Queen.' A friend

'There's a lot of nonsense talked about what a terrible life she has. Nonsense! I think she loves it.'

A senior politician

'Constitutional monarchy is a subtle device which enables us, anthropologically speaking, both to adore and kill our Kings; by dividing supreme authority into two, we can lavish adulation upon the Crown and kick out the government when we choose.'

Kingsley Martin, editor of the *New Statesman*, 1953

'I would earnestly warn you against trying to find out the reason for and explanation of everything . . . To try and find out the reason for everything is very dangerous and leads to nothing but disappointment and dissatisfaction, unsettling your mind and in the end making you miserable.'

Queen Victoria to a granddaughter, 1883

'Well . . . She knows what's going on. She has – a *good nose for a story*. She would have been a good journalist.'

A senior member of the Royal Household

What the Queen Does

She is a small woman with a globally familiar face, a hundred-carat smile – when she chooses to turn it on – and a thousand years of history at her back. She reigns in a world which has mostly left monarchy behind, yet the result of her reign is that two-thirds of British people assume their monarchy will still be here in a century's time. She is wry and knowing, but she feels a calling. All this is serious. She can brim with dry observations but she seems empty of cynicism. She is not a natural public speaker.

But there she is, in May 2011 and dressed in emerald green, arriving for her first visit to the Republic of Ireland. Aged eighty-five, she makes one of the most politically significant speeches of her life. 'It is a sad and regrettable reality that through our history our islands have experienced more than their fair share of heartache, turbulence and loss. These events have touched many of us personally . . . To all those who have suffered as a consequence of a troubled past I extend my sincere thoughts and deep sympathy.' This is a highly emotional trip, recalling the murder of her relative Lord Mountbatten by the IRA in 1979, and centred on a visit to Croke Park, the stadium and headquarters of the Gaelic Athletic Association where, in 1920, fourteen innocent people were shot by police and auxiliaries loyal to the Crown – to her grandfather – at the beginning of the bloody struggle for Irish independence.

It had been a long time coming and security bosses on both sides of the Irish Sea had been pale-faced with worry. The visit had been announced well in advance, and the Queen does not cancel. As it happened, the vast majority of Irish people welcomed the visit; the Queen even shook hands with a representative of the diehard republican Sinn Fein. So this was a small but significant page-turn in history, recognizing that by 2011 what mattered to Irish and British were their family, business, emotional and sporting links, not the bloodied past. The Queen impresses on the Irish prime minister, the Taoiseach, Enda Kenny, that this is a visit she has waited much of her life to make; what he calls 'a closing of the circle'. In private she sits under the portrait of the Irish military leader Michael Collins. In public she bows her head in memory of the Irish rebels who died fighting the Crown.

Her grandson and the future King, Prince William, said afterwards it had meant a huge amount to her: 'It's like a door that has been locked to her for a long time, and she's been dying to see what's on the other side of it.' Many people would not understand quite what it had been like for her. Ireland was 'off limits' despite her fond connections, particularly with Irish racing, and she had always wanted to go, 'almost like a child not allowed to go into a certain room . . . so I think it was a huge turning-point for her.'[1] Her twelfth Prime Minister, David Cameron, admitted: 'I was nervous about it. But I was hugely admiring of the fact that the royal family wanted to go ahead with this visit relatively quickly after the finalizing of the last bits of devolution of power to Northern Ireland. They didn't want to wait and play it a little bit longer . . . and it was an extraordinary success.'

Nobody else from Britain could have made such a visit of high-profile reconciliation, covered by more than a thousand journalists and reported all round the world. No British politician has been around for long enough, or been personally touched so closely, or could claim to speak for Britain itself. Ireland's President Mary McAleese speaks for her people warmly and well, the first Northerner and the second woman to serve in the job. But no Briton other than the Queen could speak in that way for the British.

There she is again, just a few days later, welcoming President Barack Obama to stay at Buckingham Palace. In the gusty sunshine overlooking the lawn there is picture-postcard pomp – a guard of Household Cavalry, marching soldiers, bagpipes, national anthems, the reverberations of artillery salutes. On the eve of his visit, speaking in Washington, Obama had gone out of his way to praise the Queen in lavish if not entirely politically accurate terms as 'the best of England'. His earlier visit had gone spectacularly well. Even so, this is a relationship which is also, in a gentler and more personal way, about friendship and reconciliation.

For when Obama first became US president there had been unease in London. Here was a man who seemed cool about the (exaggerated) 'special relationship' with Britain. He had no personal ties – or rather, just one, which was unhappy and about which he had written himself. His grandfather had been arrested, imprisoned and tortured in Kenya. The early years of the Queen's reign had been marked by a brutal war against the nationalist Mau Mau there. Obama is a supremely professional politician, very unlikely to allow personal history to influence his decision-making, but the unease was there. Once the pomp was over the Queen did her level best to make him and his wife Michelle feel especially welcome, showing the couple to their bedroom.

There was on show a very shrewdly chosen selection of

memorabilia from the Royal Archive – as there always is for a state visit. These are worth dwelling on. There was a note in George III's handwriting, from around 1780, lamenting 'America is lost! Must we fall beneath the blow?' but going on to speculate about a future of trade and friendship. There were letters from Lincoln, Obama's hero, and from Queen Victoria to his widow; and diary entries by Victoria showing her sympathy for black slaves, recording her excitement in meeting one, Josiah Henson, who she said had 'endured great suffering and cruelty' before escaping to British Canada. There were records of a visit by the then Prince of Wales to Obama's home city of Chicago in 1860, and a handwritten note by the Queen Mother to the then Princess Elizabeth recording their visit to President Roosevelt in 1939 when they ate under the trees 'and all our food on one plate ... some ham, lettuce, beans and HOT DOGS too!' Homely – but a reminder of the vital wartime alliance which followed King George VI's most important overseas visit. There were details and a flag from Hawaii, Obama's birthplace.

This is worth mentioning at the start of a biography of the Queen because in a small way it contains the essence of the case for monarchy. First, this is a constitutional job but it is also a personal one. From American independence, through the story of slavery and places of particular interest to Obama, the job was to make an emotional connection – to find points of contact. In return, Obama gave the Queen a book of photographs of her parents' 1939 visit, on the eve of war. He would set off for important and potentially tricky talks with Prime Minister David Cameron about Libya, Afghanistan and their different approaches to economics in the warmest possible mood. This is what the Queen is for. As with the Irish visit, nobody else could do it. Second, though, she can only work effectively because plenty of other people (such as the Royal Librarian Lady Roberts) work very hard behind the scenes, unknown to the public. This is their story too.

But it is hers first. The best antidote to weariness or hostility about the Queen is to try to follow her about for a few months. From trade-based missions overseas to visits to small towns and hospitals, it is a surprisingly gruelling routine. It includes grand ceremonial occasions and light-footed, fast-moving trips to meet soldiers, business people, volunteers and almost every other category one can imagine. It eats up evenings, where at one palace or another thousands of people have been invited to be 'honoured' for their work or generosity. It involves the patient reading of fat boxes of heavily serious paperwork, oozing from the government departments who work in her name. In Whitehall, where they assess the most secret intelligence as it arrives, the Queen is simply 'Reader No. 1.'

It has been a life of turning up. But turning up is not to be underestimated. The Queen has a force-field aura that very few politicians manage to project. There is an atmospheric wobble of expectation, a slight but helpless jitter. When she turns up, people find their heart-rate rising, however much they try to treat her as just another woman. Somehow, despite being everywhere – in news bulletins, on postage stamps, cards and front pages – she has managed to remain mysterious. Her face moves from apparently grumpy to beaming, and back. Her eyes flicker carefully around. She gives little away.

After the rapids of family crisis and public controversy, she is in calmer waters. British royalty has become surprisingly popular around the world. She watched with great interest and some pleasure a recent film about her father's struggle against his stutter and the man who helped him, the Australian Lionel

Logue. She remembers Logue very vividly. Her father was played by the actor Colin Firth. She herself was the subject of a blockbuster film, starring Helen Mirren. Her illustrious ancestress Elizabeth I was potrayed by Judi Dench in a film about Shakespeare. Firth, Mirren and Dench all won Oscars, as one of the Queen's children wryly notes.

She is not an actor. But the popularity of the monarchy owes a lot to the way she performs. Life has taken her around the world many times and introduced her to leaders of all kinds, from the heroic to the monstrous; and to seas of soapy faces; and to forests of wiggling hands. Since she was a small girl, she has known her Destiny. All the accounts of her childhood agree that she was a calm, thoughtful child, with a passion for animals. Though shy, she regards being Queen as a vocation, a calling which cannot be evaded. She has borne four children, seen three of them divorced, has eight grandchildren and – take a bow, Savannah Phillips – one great-granddaughter.

Like any eighty-five-year-old she has been bereaved and suffered disappointment as well as enjoying success. She has lost a King, a Queen and Princesses – her father, mother, sister and the remarkable Diana – as well as friends. Yet she can be satisfied. She knows that her dynasty, unlike so many others, is almost certain to survive. Her heir and her heir's heir are waiting. With her, and her kind of monarchy, most of her people are content.

Those who can remember her as a curly-headed little girl are now a small platoon. On 12 May 2011 she became the second-longest-serving monarch in British history, having reigned for 21,645 days, beating George III's record. In September 2015, if she is still alive, she will outlast even Queen Victoria's record too. Her husband, now ninety, still has the gimlet stare and suspicious bearing of a man's man cast adrift in a world of progressives and wets. He could have scaled most ladders. He chose to spend his life as 'Consort, liege and follower'.

The Duke's life and the Queen's life have been lived in lock-step, through an annual circle of ritual and tradition, swivelling from palace to palace as the seasons change; dressing up, often several times a day, for lunches, openings, speeches, military parades, investitures and dinners. The Queen's mornings begin as they have for most of her life, with BBC radio news, Earl Grey tea, the *Racing Post* and the *Daily Telegraph* and, while having breakfast toast with her husband, enjoying the music (ignorant people would call it noise) of her personal bagpiper in the garden. Near her are the last truly dangerous members of the British monarchical system, the Queen's dogs – four corgis and three dorgis (a dachshund–corgi cross).

A discreet, protective staff she calls by their first names come and go; a typed diary sheet of engagements is waiting; soon the first of the boxes of official papers, containing everything from minor appointments to alarming secret service reports, will arrive. There may be a visit upstairs to the domain of Angela Kelly, her personal assistant and senior dresser, who has rooms off a narrow corridor just below the Buckingham Palace roof. A genial and down-to-earth Liverpudlian, she is one of the people closest to the Queen, family apart. She works with huge bolts of cloth, dummies and scissors to create many of the Queen's outfits. Before overseas or long domestic visits, she has planned in detail the dresses, hats, bags and shoes with the Queen. Outside designers are brought in from time to time. One Scottish designer insisted on a full personal fitting. As she crouched down nervously with a tape-measure, the Queen exclaimed: 'leg out! Arm out! Leg out!'and giggled as the measurements were taken. A floor below Angela Kelly, the old-fashioned leather suitcases and trunks for a Royal progress, each stamped simply with 'The Queen', are waiting. They have had a lot of use; the monarch is not a fan of the throwaway society.

Down in her office, the contents of the various official boxes have been sorted out by her private secretary and carried upstairs to be scrutinized. She alone reads these; the Duke maintains a careful constitutional distance from some parts of her life, though he runs the estates and remains a very active nonagenarian, still often weaving through the London traffic at the wheel of his own, usefully anonymous taxi. She is the longest-lived monarch in her country's history. Like anyone who has followed routines for so long, she hopes there will be a surprise today; just a small one. Now what? What will happen today?

The Job

Today, the Queen will dress, and go out and do her job. Angela Kelly will have laid out clothes which will, they both hope, make the Queen stand out in a crowd and will be appropriate to whatever jobs lie ahead that day. At certain times of the year, of course, she will not be working. There are quiet family weekends and a long summer break, mostly at Balmoral in Scotland. But if you totted up the hours she puts in, the European health and safety people would itch to prosecute – well, who? There is the problem. There is no trade union or employment contract for a Queen. The expectations of civil servants and politicians, tourists, presidents and the passing crowd are so great that her duties never end.

Take a breath. As head of state, Queen Elizabeth is the

living symbol of nations, above all that of the United Kingdom of Great Britain and Northern Ireland – though another fifteen besides, including Australia, Canada, New Zealand and smaller countries, down to Tuvalu. She is not like most other constitutional monarchs. The British state has no single written constitution nor any founding document. About a third of the Dutch constitution, by contrast, explains what the Dutch monarch's duties are. Spain's king is part of one of Europe's oldest and grandest royal houses, the Bourbons; but his job is strictly limited in the careful prose of the Spanish constitution.

The British Queen's authority is more like a quiet growl from ancient days, still quietly thrumming and mysterious. She stands *for* the state – indeed, in some ways, at least in theory, she *is* the state. She is the living representative of the power-structure that struggles to protect and sustain some 62 million people, and another 72 million in her other 'realms'.

She is not the symbol of the people. How could she or anyone represent the teeming millions of different ethnic groups and religions, of every political view, shape, bias and age? Her enthusiasm for the Commonwealth of nations, which is not the private passion of many British politicians, has made her more interested in the lives of the new black and Asian Britons than one might expect. Receptions at Buckingham Palace are generally more socially and ethnically mixed than they are at Downing Street, or in the City. She is at her most relaxed and smiling with young people, nervous people and unflashy people. Watching her at official occasions, it is clear that the chores are the grand dinners and speeches.

Yet, like it or not, she is the symbol of the authority which drives the state servants and laws – the elections, armies, judges and treaties which together make modern life possible. For sixty years she has appeared to open *her* Parliament, to

remember *her* nation's war dead, to review *her* troops or
to attend services of *her* Church. 'Britain' cannot go to the
Republic of Ireland to finally heal a political breach that goes
back to the Irish struggle for independence in the 1920s – but
the Queen can. 'Britain' cannot welcome a pope or a president.
She can.

She has great authority and no power. She is a brightly
dressed and punctual paradox. She is the ruler who does not
rule her subjects but who serves them. The ancient meaning
of kingship has been flipped; part of the purpose of this book
is to explain how, and why, that has been done. Modern
constitutional monarchy does not mean subjection, the hand
pressed down on an unruly nation. Instead it offers a version
of freedom. For the Crown is not the government. There is a
small, essential space between them. It would be rude to say
that ministers are squatters in the state – for governments
come from parliaments which are elected, the ultimate bastions
of our liberty. Nevertheless, ministers are lodgers in the state.
They are welcome for a while, but have no freehold rights.

The Queen stands for continuity. This is a dull word, but
when asked what the Queen is really about, 'continuity' is the
word used most often by other members of the royal family,
by prime ministers, archbishops and senior civil servants. What
do they mean? Not simply the continued existence of the
country or the state. It is true that the state is a living and
valuable presence before and after any one government. People
look back to the past and imagine a future that outlives them:
monarchy takes a real family and makes it the rather blatant
symbol of that existential fact. So a constitutional monarchy
claims to represent the interests of the people before they
elected this government, and after it has gone. It remembers.
It looks ahead, far beyond the next election.

The distinction between state and government is an essential foundation of liberty. In Britain a pantomime of ritual has grown up to express it. At the annual State Opening of Parliament, once in a year, the Queen reads out her prime minister's words, ventriloquizing for her government. She speaks with deliberate lack of emphasis or emotion: nobody must be able to hear her own feelings break through. A junior minister is taken hostage at Buckingham Palace to guarantee her safety and underline the separation of politics and state. When she leaves Westminster, he is released (after a decent drink) and normal politics resumes. The state and the government have come together, touched hands, and gone their separate ways. Other countries have a similar distinction, expressing it through written documents or powerless elected presidents; the British have long preferred a person.

This is the job. In practice it is a little harder than it looks. When the most important foreign leaders arrive for a state visit, the Queen greets them in the country's name with a smile and a gloved handshake and small-talk, again deliberately designed never to offend. She offers house-room and pays kind attention to people she may privately regard as abominable or merely hideous bores. Guests at Buckingham Palace or at Windsor will be guided around by the Queen in person. She will have checked the rooms first herself, trying to make sure suitable books are left by the bed, that the flowers look good, and that everything is welcoming. At the grand dinners she will have overseen the food, flowers and place-settings: will everybody be satisfied with where they are seated, and get on with the people put beside them?

When the guests arrive and the conversation starts she has to remember to dodge anything that might cause her ministers a headache. One former foreign secretary, Douglas Hurd, has watched her do it: 'She's got quite an elaborate technique. When a visiting head of state, or whatever it is, begins to talk politics, begins to explain what's happening in his country, she says, "That's very interesting Mr President . . . and I'm sure the foreign secretary would very much like to discuss that with you." And so you're shunted. The points change, and you're shunted onto a different line.' Others talk about how she uses polite silence to deflect trouble; and it is very noticeable that when you ask people about their conversations with the Queen, they bubble about her wit and insight – and then tell you exactly (and only) what *they* said to *her*. Clever.

Much the same seems to happen in her weekly audiences with her prime ministers, of whom there have been a dozen to date. Though these meetings are completely private (no note-takers, no secretaries, no microphones), former premiers and civil servants talk about them as a kind of higher therapy, rather than a vivid exchange of views. For sixty years she has listened to whatever they have said – self-justifying explanations, private whinges, a little malice about their rivals – without letting any of them know whose side she is on except, in the broadest sense, the side of the continuing government of the country. Sir Gus O'Donnell, a cabinet secretary who has worked with four prime ministers – Sir John Major, Tony Blair, Gordon Brown and now David Cameron – says: 'They go out of their way not to miss it. It's a safe space where prime ministers and sovereigns can get together, they can have those sorts of conversations, which I don't think they can have with anybody else in the country . . . they come out of them better than they went in, let's put it that way.'

Cameron himself agrees. 'She's seen it all and heard it all.' She is immensely knowledgeable about policy, was particularly interested in how a coalition government was working and 'wants to be in a position where she knows everything that's going on', cross-questioning him closely. What did it mean for a prime minister? Was it worth all the time he spent traipsing up to Buckingham Palace? 'Apart from seeing Mrs Cameron at the end of the day, it's about the only meeting where there's no one else in the room, and I feel the responsibility as prime minister to try to explain my perspective on the big issues going on in the world and the country that week.' So it made him think harder? 'Absolutely. I'm suddenly having to explain in a hopefully clear and concise way . . . our deep, innermost thinking and worries and concerns.' Because there was no one else there, nor any minutes taken, 'I think you reveal both to her, but also to yourself your deepest thinking and deepest worries . . . and sometimes that can really help you to reach the answers.'

It is a subtle point made independently by Tony Blair, one of her more controversial prime ministers, who went through many crises and found his audiences with her equally useful. She is someone, he says, who keeps her ear to the ground and reads closely. 'Although conventionally it's supposed to be the prime minister briefing the Queen, I would find it was a genuine exchange . . . There is nobody who had a better idea of crisis, what it's like, how it is, and how it also doesn't go on forever, even though when you're in the middle of it, you think it does. So she was somebody who would give you a very clear historical perspective of what a premiership was like.' He had discussed his own side too, 'all sorts of cabinet ructions and difficulties.' Prime ministers, he points out, have to learn to deal with crises psychologically as well as politically, 'and I always found it really useful to talk to her. I often used to talk to her about the past, about previous prime ministers, how it was, how they handled things.' And, he added, that in the context of the audience, 'she was very frank, and open, and informative.' This is more than previous prime ministers have admitted publicly about this mysterious 'holy of holies' in the heart of the British system.[2]

She knows almost every state secret of the past sixty years. Every day she works her way through state papers, sent in red boxes to her desk. Gus O'Donnell again: 'We give the Queen the minutes of cabinet, for instance, so she's up to date on the discussions, the decisions that have been made. She gets a lot of material about what the government's actually doing, in her red boxes.' The Queen is very interested in issues involving the constitution – Sir Gus singles out current controversies about Britain's switch to fixed-term parliaments and the future of the House of Lords – and anything to do with Britain's military. She works hard too, to support the civil service, who, like her, have to be neutral but get very little applause from the public or press. In public, in her Christmas broadcasts and many speeches, she generally takes great care to stay on the safe ground of general expressions of goodwill, although at Christmas she often touches on issues of the day. For decade after decade she has dodged traps that could have led the monarchy into serious danger. She has made mistakes, of course. She is only human. But she has managed this dance of discretion so adroitly that many people have concluded that she is herself almost without character – neutral, passive, even bland.

She is not. She is capable of sharp asides, has a long memory, shrewd judgement and is a wicked mimic. She has been very frank about her children's scrapes. She has closely observed and dryly described the oddities of foreign leaders and famous politicians. She has done it sitting playing patience during the evening at Balmoral, or with her legs tucked up under her on a sofa on the Royal Yacht, a glass of something cheerful in hand, or walking on beaches and hillsides. In private she has hugged and laughed; and been sharp with bores, dawdlers and slow eaters. Though she does not like confrontation, and has often sub-contracted that out to her husband, she has strong views about people. It is just that her job means she has to hide all this. Other people, celebrities and actors, are paid to have a 'personality'. She is required to downplay hers.

This does not mean her life is dull. 'We're in the happiness business,' whispers one of her ladies-in-waiting as the Queen heads for yet another line of shouting, waving children. It must be wonderful to cheer people up without cracking jokes, or telling odd stories. She can do it simply by arriving, smiling, nodding and taking a posy or two. No one who has followed this now slightly stooping lady in her mid-eighties as she walks through small towns, foreign hotels, cathedrals and military barracks, casting sharp glances all around, and observed the grinning, pressing lines of people waiting for her, can doubt it. But there is 'the tough stuff' too – a huge amount of ceremonial, religious and social business to be dealt with, week in, week out. (Some say, too much, particularly for a woman of her age.)

She is a woman of faith. She stands atop the Anglican Church, that national breakaway from Rome hurriedly set up by her Tudor ancestor, the beef-faced and priapic Henry VIII. So she is called Defender of the Faith and Supreme Governor of the Church of England. The former title is technically absurd since it was given to Henry by Pope Leo X before he rebelled. But the latter one certainly counts: the Queen appoints bishops and archbishops and takes her role as the fount of Anglican respectability very seriously, addressing the General Synod and talking regularly to its leading figures.

The current Archbishop of Canterbury, Rowan Williams, says she is formally the final court of appeal, the place where arguments stop. In practice, of course, she does not intervene in rows about the ordination of women priests or gay marriage, any more than she does in parliamentary arguments. But, says the Archbishop, 'She believes that she has some responsibility for keeping an eye on the business of the church, some responsibility to support it, to get on the side of those who are administering the church and she is herself very committed as a Christian.' Williams says she was profoundly affected by being given a book of private prayers by a predecessor shortly before her Coronation, which she still uses. For her the Coronation was a vocation, 'a calling, not a privilege but a calling. If it's costly, it's costly.' As we shall see, at times it certainly has been.

The Queen is also 'the fount of honours'. She bestows medals, crosses, knighthoods and ribbons, mostly (but not always) on the advice of politicians, to those who are worthy (and sometimes not so worthy). Each one requires conversation, eye-contact, briefing and time. She has so far bestowed 404,500 honours and awards, and personally held more than 610 Investitures (the grand honour-giving ceremonies) since becoming Queen in 1952.

Then there are the services: the Queen is Head of the Armed Forces. It is to the Queen that new soldiers, airmen and sailors pledge allegiance, and in whose name they fight and die. She has a special relationship with some regiments – her first official job was as a colonel-in-chief – and a general one with all. This means many more visits and ceremonies. She is also a patron of huge numbers of charities. They too lobby and plead for her time, often to encourage fundraising. From time to time the royal family settles down together to try to organize their charitable work. After the death of her mother and sister, the family sat down at Sandringham around a card-table and shared out the work they would have to take on. They discovered some charities had rather too many Royals associated with them, and others none at all; so some switching-around was agreed.

Beginning to feel tired? What about Abroad? The Queen never forgets that she is Head of the Commonwealth, a title invented in 1949 to allow the newly independent republican India to keep its association with Britain. This involves her in a huge amount of travel, in addition to visiting her other realms and the diplomatic and trade-boosting visits her government tells her each year she must make. In the Foreign Office they draw up their wish list for state visits and other visits, arguing about which trading partner has priority over which, and which leader would be particularly gratified if the Queen arrived. And then another negotiation about her diary begins.

These visits are not jaunts. They involve a lot of planning and travel, endless changes of dresses and hats and, above all, a huge amount of listening, nodding and smiling. Most trying of all, there are the speeches. The Queen is a naturally shy and quiet person who even now, after all these years, gets no pleasure from public speaking whether the event is grand or modest. One journalist who has followed her for decades says, 'Whether it is the Great Hall of the People, or the Girl Guides' Association, she gets nervous before the speech. And yet afterwards, once she's completed that speech and she's got marvellous congratulation and applause, then she's . . . really buzzing because it's out of the way. I've never seen her change once.' As the Queen and Duke get older, they find these visits more tiring and trying. So far, they keep agreeing to go, in general twice a year.

Beyond all this, the Queen has run the monarchy as a national adhesive, making constant visits around the country to be seen, to greet and to thank people who are mostly ignored by the London power-brokers and commercial grandees. She holds parties, lunches and charity gatherings at Buckingham Palace and Edinburgh's Palace of Holyroodhouse to thank or bring together other lists of good-doers, civic worthies and business strivers. At special themed receptions she honours all sorts of disparate groups – they might be Australians in Britain, or young people in the performing arts, or campaigners for the handicapped, or the emergency services. These events are meticulously planned. The Queen hangs over the lists of who may be invited, and why. She plans the evenings and the choreography, and manages to remember at least many of the names. Only by watching the delight of elderly volunteers whom nobody else had thought to make much of or struggling young musicians, can one understand the quiet power of this mostly unreported monarchical campaign.

Finally, there are the mass celebrations, the royal jubilees and marriages, which get most of the attention. The jubilees are an invented tradition, which allow the monarchy to dominate the crowded news agenda of a busy country and enable people to look back at the last twenty-five, fifty or sixty years, and to look forward too: a kind of national pause-for-thought. The marriages may turn out well or not, but allow the most fanatically royalist, and many others, to go briefly mad. Anyone who has paid any attention to public life in Britain sort of knows all this. Not many of us think about it much. By now, I hope the reader is feeling a little exhausted. We have not yet talked about the extra little jobs of mother, grandmother, wife, aunt, horse-owner, manager of farms and estates, employer and overall accountant-in-chief that fill in the quiet moments.

For most of us the Queen seems always to have been there. She has done her job so well it has come to seem part of the natural order of things, along with the seasons and the weather. One day, of course, she won't be there. Then there will be a gaping, Queen-sized hole in the middle of British life.

Part One

DYNASTY IS DESTINY

How the British Monarchy Remade Itself

The Queen is only the fourth head of a fairly new dynasty. If you put brackets around her uncle, Edward VIII, who lasted less than a year, she is only the third of the Windsors. Yet the British monarchy itself is one of the world's oldest and the Queen can trace tiny flecks of her bloodline back to famous Anglo-Saxons and ancient Scottish warlords. More recently, Hanoverian ancestry remains a strong influence. Both she and her eldest son have faces that recall monarchs of the eighteenth century, the solemn early Georges. But like other families, monarchies can reinvent themselves. Today's House of Windsor created itself less than a century ago, leaping away from the Hanoverians and their German connections in 1917.

The previous British monarchy, of Victoria the fecund Queen-Empress and her son Edward, the louche and shrewd King-Emperor, had been at the centre of a spun golden web of royalty stretching across Europe and Russia. Monarchy was a family club, largely closed to outsiders. Britain's segment of the web had particularly close connections with German royal houses, connections that went back to the eighteenth century and the Hanoverians. Kaisers came to tea and joined parades dressed in British military uniform. They raced their yachts against those of their British cousins at Cowes. There might be mutual suspicion, but it was family rivalry rather than political. The closeness was symbolized by the last visit King George and Queen Mary made to Germany before the war. Arriving in Berlin in May 1913 for the wedding of the Kaiser's daughter to their cousin, the Duke of Brunswick-Lüneburg, they had been greeted by Queen Mary's aunt, the Grand Duchess of Mecklenburg-Strelitz – a very old English-born lady who remained in her north German estate until 1916. They went on to meet the Kaiser, Tsar Nicholas II, endless other dynastic cousins and what the family called simply 'the royal mob'. The mob noted the presence of film cameras, or what they called 'those horrid Kino-men', but felt themselves a family, whose connections remained essential to the future of the 'civilized' world.

George V was particularly fond of his Austro-Hungarian fellow Royals, and of numerous princely German relatives. Fritz Ponsonby, the King's private secretary, noted of the visit, 'whether any real good is done, I have my doubts. The feeling in the two countries is very strong . . .' and George's biographer rightly said that, in the coming of the Great War, 'King George V was no more than an anguished and impotent spectator.'[1] Others at the time took the opposite view, or diplomatically pretended to: the British ambassador to Berlin Sir Edward Goschen said he thought the visit would prove 'of lasting good'.[2] Queen Mary had a lovely time in Berlin. Interestingly, by contrast, she dreaded a visit to Paris the following year, primarily because France was to her above all an alien republic and there were no friendly family faces to welcome her.

By 1917, however, deep into the bloodied mud of total war, this royal web seemed likelier to choke the British monarchy to death than to protect it. Germans had become loathed in Britain, their shops destroyed, their brass bands expelled, even their characteristic dogs put down. To be a monarch with German connections was uncomfortable. Rising radical and revolutionary feeling across Europe had made monarchs generally unpopular too. King George was already well aware of it. During 1911–12 Britain had faced mass strikes and great unrest. At times it felt like a revolution, in which London would be starved of food by militant dockers. Radical Liberals struck at the aristocratic principle when the House of Lords blocked their radical budget. In the streets, a more militant socialism was being taught, with the earliest Labour politicians often defining themselves as anti-monarchists. Labour's much loved early leader, Keir Hardie, was a lifelong republican who was particularly hated by the Palace. Though an MP, he had been banned from the Windsor Castle garden-party list for attacking Edward VII's visit to see his cousin Tsar Nicholas in 1908. Later, he described George V as 'a street corner loafer ... destitute of ordinary ability'. The King responded by calling him simply 'that beast'. For monarchs, even before the war came, these were unsettling times.

George, however, was lucky in his advisers, one above all. Lord Stamfordham's story began colourfully. As Arthur Bigge, the son of a Northumberland parson, he was an artillery officer who fought in the Zulu War of 1879. One of his friends was the son of France's deposed Emperor Napoleon III and when this young man was killed by a Zulu, Bigge was chosen to show his bereaved mother where it had happened, and to visit Queen Victoria to tell her the story. Queen Victoria liked Bigge so much that she immediately appointed him her assistant private secretary. He spent the rest of his life working for the monarchy. When Edward VII became king, Bigge served his son, first as Duke of Cornwall, then Prince of Wales, then as King George V, when Bigge became Lord Stamfordham. He had a huge influence on George, who said he could hardly write a letter without his help, but to start with Stamfordham did not get everything right. George and Stamfordham both had instinctively strong conservative views, and in the constitutional crisis of 1910–11 he advised George to face down the Liberal prime minister Herbert Asquith. The Liberals were confronted by the Tory-dominated House of Lords, which was blocking the 'People's Budget'. Asquith had had a promise from Edward VII to allow a deluge of Liberal peers to be created, as a last-resort way of swamping the upper house. George V instinctively hated the idea, which seemed an assault on the notion of aristocracy. Had the newly crowned George V gone with his instincts and backed the peerage rather than the elected government, he would have forced an immediate general election that would have been in part about the right of the monarch to interfere in politics – the very thing his granddaughter has spent her entire reign carefully avoiding.

Had George and Stamfordham stood and fought on the rights of the aristocracy and then lost the battle in the polling stations, the future of the British monarchy would have been in doubt. What we often now imagine as reassuring, golden-hazed 'Edwardian' Britain was a confrontational and seething nation. The Liberals, though more moderate than the rising Labour and socialist parties, were convinced Stamfordham was their implacable enemy, sitting at the centre of the imperial state. Feelings were running high. The then Liberal chancellor, later prime minister, Lloyd George, disliked him so much that when Stamfordham came for meetings in Downing Street during the war he made him wait outside on a hard wooden chair. Yet Stamfordham learned from his mistakes. Later King George said he was the man who had taught him how to be a king. He had done it by telling truth to power. Stamfordham was a dry and difficult man, but he prided himself on his honesty, and in particular telling his king the facts, however alarming they might seem. He now began to work hard to turn the sea-dog and countryman into a politically aware national leader. By the outbreak of the First World War, and then through its first hard years, George V had become a vivid and popular rallying point.

By the spring of 1917, however, the truths brought to him by his adviser seemed very alarming indeed. The war was going badly. There were strikes and growing complaints that the King was closer to his German cousin, the hated Kaiser, than to his own people. This was entirely untrue. But George V had made mistakes that gave the wrong impression.

He had been against stripping the Kaiser and his family of their honorary commands of British regiments and their British chivalric honours, not to mention their banners hanging at St George's Chapel, Windsor. Royal solidarity and ancient hierarchy apparently counted, even in the throes of an industrial war. Early in the war, King George had been furious at the campaign against Admiral Prince Louis of Battenberg, born German, but married to one of Queen Victoria's granddaughters and now British First Sea Lord. Battenberg had to quit, to the despair of his son, then a naval cadet himself, who wrote to his mother about the latest rumour 'that Papa has turned out to be a German spy . . . I got rather a rotten time of it.' (That boy grew up to be Lord Louis Mountbatten, and one of the most influential figures in the Queen's life; what seem remote historical footnotes to outsiders turn out to be significant family memories.)

These instinctive flinches against the rampant anti-Germanism of wartime Britain had allowed the King's critics to begin to paint him as not wholly patriotic. Lloyd George, summoned to Buckingham Palace in January 1915, wondered

aloud 'what my little German friend has got to say to me'.
London hostesses mocked the court's Hanoverian character.
Street-corner agitators warned about 'the Germans' in the
Palace. In fact, George was an exemplary wartime monarch,
carrying out hundreds of troop visits and cutting down heavily
on the expenses and living standards of the monarchy while
the country suffered. He even gave up alcohol when Lloyd
George asked him to, in order to set an example to drunkards
(not an example, it has to be said, that Lloyd George himself
followed). But the whispering went on. It grew louder. On
31 March 1917 there was a mass meeting at the Albert Hall
chaired by one of Labour's great heroes, George Lansbury, to
celebrate the fall of Tsar Nicholas II, with much cat-calling
against monarchy in general. Government wartime censors kept
news of this out of the papers, but George was given eyewit-
ness reports of what was said. Stamfordham had made it his
job to get as much information as possible and to pass it on.

Thus, when Ramsay MacDonald, later Labour prime minister, called for a convention to be held in Leeds 'to do for this
country what the Russian revolution had accomplished in
Russia', or the trade union leader Robert Williams called for a
'to let' sign to hang outside Buckingham Palace, George was
told about it. Stamfordham said a few weeks later, 'There is
no socialist newspaper, no libellous rag, that is not read and
marked and shown to the King if they contain any criticism,
friendly or unfriendly to His Majesty and the Royal Family.'[3]
In April 1917 the writer H. G. Wells had written to *The Times*
calling for the establishment of republican societies; he was
also reported to have complained that England suffered from
an alien and uninspiring court, to which George famously
retorted: 'I may be uninspiring, but I'm damned if I'm an
alien.' In the Marxist newspaper *Justice* the eccentric, top-hatted

editor Henry Hyndman argued that the royal family is 'essentially German' and called for a British Republic. At the other end of the political scale, the editor of the *Spectator* magazine, John St Loe Strachey, told Stamfordham that there was a spread of republican feeling among coalminers who 'feel kings will stand together' and that there was 'a trade union of kings'.[4] Lady Maud Warrender said that when George was told that it was whispered he must be pro-German because his family had German names, 'he started and grew pale'. Wells returned to the attack, this time in the *Penny Pictorial*, calling for the monarchy to sever its destiny 'from the inevitable collapse of the Teutonic dynastic system upon the continent of Europe . . . we do not want any German ex-monarchs here'. The file headed simply 'Unrest in the Country' had begun to thicken at the Palace.

More than ninety years on, it might seem that all this was mere hysterical fluff, and that George and his advisers were wrong to take it seriously. Small magazines, reported conversations in the coalfields, publicity-seeking authors . . . did it really add up to the beginning of the end for the British monarchy? The truth is that in 1917 British society was stretched to breaking point. People were ready to believe the wildest claims about German plots and secret networks of sexual blackmail, stretching right up to the court itself. The armies in France faced defeat and the Atlantic seabed was a graveyard of supply ships. Russia had been engulfed, Germany was next and there was rising militancy in British factories. In Britain the key war leader was not the King but the King-mocking Lloyd George, soon to be hailed as 'the man who won the war'. Aristocracy, which has always buttressed monarchy, was on its knees, its sons dead or maimed and its estates facing financial ruin. The monarchy, it seemed, had few powerful friends. King George and Queen Mary had thrown themselves into visits to regiments, naval bases, children's homes and voluntary organizations of all kinds. The King had clocked up 300 hospital visits alone, most of them emotionally draining. Yet none of it seemed to have made much difference. So George V decided that if the monarchy was to survive in Britain, it must be changed.

Advised by Stamfordham, King George made a series of reforms which have had a huge influence on the current Queen's reign. The first and most public was to change his name, and that of the dynasty. 'Saxe-Coburg-Gotha' was not only a mouthful but rather obviously German. It had to go. Tellingly, George did not know what his own original surname might be: it was lost in the tangled skeins of monarchical bloodlines and rampant hyphenation. Nor, it seemed, did anyone else know. The Royal College of Heralds was consulted. They told the King his surname was not Stuart. It might be Guelph. More probably it was Wipper or Wettin, neither of which sounded helpfully British. So the search began for an invented surname. Tudor, Stuart, Plantagenet, York and Lancaster were all discussed, as colourful history books were rummaged through. They were cast aside, as was the too obvious 'England', which would hardly have pleased the Scots, Irish or Welsh. More obscure suggestions included D'Este and Fitzroy. Finally, Stamfordham went back to the place-name of the King's favourite palace and chose 'Windsor'. It sounded good. It later turned out that Edward III had once used the name too, so there was even a slender historical connection.

Thus, on 17 July 1917, the Windsor dynasty was born. George V declared and announced 'that We for Ourselves and for and on behalf of Our descendants . . . relinquish and enjoin the discontinuance of the use of the degrees, styles, dignities, titles and honours of Dukes and Duchesses of Saxony and Princes and Princesses of Saxe-Coburg and Gotha, and all other German degrees . . .' A cascade of further name-changes followed which confuse many people even today about who was really who. There were the Tecks, for instance. George V's wife, Queen Mary, or May, was the daughter of Francis, Duke of Teck, who had married one of George III's granddaughters, the famously substantial Mary Adelaide, known in the family as 'fat Mary' and memorably described as being 'like a large purple plush pincushion'. So George V's in-laws included a lot of Tecks. For de-Tecking, mellifluous British place-names were at a premium. One of Queen Mary's brothers became the Marquis of Cambridge and another the Earl of Athlone. Similarly, the Battenbergs, descended from Queen Victoria and the Princes of Hesse, and connected to the Tsar's family, became Mountbattens, one being renamed Marquis of Milford Haven and another Marquis of Carisbrooke. Anything Germanic was briskly rubbed out.

For monarchy, names matter a great deal – but there were more substantial changes to come. George V and Queen Mary also announced that, in the King's words in his diary, they 'had decided some time ago that our children would be allowed to marry into British families. It was quite an historical occasion.'[5] Though less publicized than the name-change, this was indeed quite historical, and quite important too. As far back as the eighteenth century, politicians and much of the British public had not liked the Hanoverian habit of marrying German princesses and princelings since it seemed to mean British taxes subsidizing foreign families. Queen Victoria herself had pointed out that her family's dynastic marriage habits had caused 'trouble and anxiety and are of no good' when European countries went to war with one another: 'Every family feeling was rent asunder, and we were powerless.'[6] Yet the habit had continued. Now Victoria's instinct that 'new' blood – by which she meant, blood from non-royal British families – would strengthen the throne morally and physically became a settled policy.

In effect, the British monarchy was being nationalized. The Bishop of Chelmsford, an influential figure, had told Stamfordham that 'the stability of the throne would be strengthened if the Prince of Wales married an English lady . . . she must be intelligent and above all full of sympathy.' A little later, another churchman, Clifford Woodward, the Canon of Southwark, had said to Stamfordham that the Prince of Wales should live for a year or two in some industrial city, perhaps Sheffield, and marry an Englishwoman preferably 'from a family which had been prominent in the war'.[7] Though 'David', the Prince of Wales, would later follow a very different path, this 1917 announcement paved the way for Elizabeth Bowes Lyon, a Scotswoman whose family had indeed been prominent in the war, to marry 'Bertie', the Duke of York and later George VI. It meant Prince Charles could marry Diana, and later Camilla; and that Prince William could marry Kate Middleton. Now it seems so obvious as to be barely worth mentioning; but marrying their subjects had hardly occurred to the old House of Saxe-Coburg-Gotha.

The next move was more brutal, some say cowardly. George V cut off his 'Cousin Nicky', the deposed Tsar Nicholas II, and his entire family, leaving them to the tender mercies of Lenin's Bolshevik revolution. The Tsar, unlike the Kaiser, had been a loyal ally of Britain's until his empire collapsed. Though George cannot have known that the Romanovs would be assassinated in a cellar, he knew they were in serious danger, and that they hoped for refuge in Britain. Initially he agreed.

But as we have seen, left-wing opinion was violently hostile to the Tsar and supportive of the revolution. For a long time it was thought and put about by friends of the Windsors that Lloyd George was to blame for letting the Tsar down. He, it was said, had countermanded the original offer of asylum for the Romanovs.

A detailed trawl through the correspondence by George V's biographer Kenneth Rose revealed a different story. It was the King who panicked. At his request Stamfordham bombarded Number Ten with notes making it clear the Tsar was not welcome after all. Much was made of petty issues, such as the lack of suitably grand accommodation. This is a complicated story, for there was a fear at times that trying to get him out might actually put him more at risk – and even vague rumours of a secret British attempt to free him by force. But unless more evidence comes to light, it seems that George was at least willing to look the other way while Nicholas and his family were imprisoned and finally killed. The current Queen read the evidence and wrote with a flourish across a manuscript of Rose's book: 'Let him publish.'

Nothing could more eloquently show the radical change brought about by the war. Before it, in 1905, King George's father had refused the Tsar's plea for Britain to restore normal relations with Serbia, after the particularly brutal assassination of its king. In words that sound like those of George Bernard Shaw or even Oscar Wilde, Edward VII explained that his trade was simply 'being a king ... As you see, we belonged to the same guild, as labourers or professional men. I cannot be indifferent to the assassination of a member of my profession or, if you like, a member of my guild. We should be obliged to shut up our business if we, the Kings, were to consider the assassination of kings as of no consequence at all.'[8] And now his son had taken avoiding action which would result in the assassination of the Tsar himself. No evidence of private guilt on George V's part has emerged, merely his public expressions of regret at the murders. A revolution can focus the mind of a monarch as effectively as a judicial death sentence for lesser mortals. There were even discussions about whether or not he should attend a church memorial service for the Romanovs, though he did go in the end.

The next change was to the honours system. Most countries have some such system; Britain's was both limited and tightly entwined with royal history. There were the ancient orders. The oldest is the Order of the Garter, established by Edward III probably in 1344 and limited to the monarch, the heir and up to twenty-four other members or 'knights companions'. Membership is in the monarch's gift. Today's Knights and Ladies of the Garter, who parade each June at Windsor for a ceremony during Royal Ascot week, wearing Tudor caps with ostrich and heron feathers, blue velvet capes and blue garters, are a mix of aristocrats, former prime ministers and retired civil servants. There are also 'Stranger Knights' of the Garter who are foreign monarchs: in 1915 both Kaiser Wilhelm and the Austro-Hungarian emperor Franz-Joseph were stripped of their memberships. So, during the Second World War, was the Japanese Emperor Hirohito (though the honour was restored to his successor Akihito). Haile Selassie was a member, too. Other old orders include Scotland's Order of the Thistle, which goes back to 1687 and is limited to sixteen knights and ladies, and the Irish Order of St Patrick, now defunct. Apart from these, the grandest is the Order of the Bath, founded by the first of the Hanoverians, George I, in 1725. Though the name refers to the ancient medieval practice of new knights being bathed for purification, the order has a less elevated origin: it was created partly because the first and infamously corrupt prime minister Robert Walpole wanted a new form of patronage. It was extended after the Napoleonic wars and today is also used by Britain to honour eminent foreigners, from overseas generals to leaders. Two of them, the tyrants Nicolae Ceauçescu of Romania and Robert Mugabe of Zimbabwe, were eventually stripped of the honour.

For most of its history the British monarchy has been muttered at by artists and intellectuals for being insufficiently interested in the arts, writing or ideas generally. This was considered a problem even during the early years of Queen Victoria's reign, when it was noticed that Britain had nothing like the Prussian *Pour le Mérite* decoration, or the French honours for cultural and scientific achievement. Eventually Edward VII instituted the Order of Merit in 1902, to mark his Coronation. Unlike most other honours, it carries no aristocratic handle and has no connection with the government; it is in the gift of the king or queen alone and is limited to twenty-four members. Perhaps as a result it is one of the few British systems of award with an almost faultless record. Of all the figures in science, the arts and politics during the twentieth century one might have expected and hoped to be represented, a surprising proportion actually have been. From figures of the Victorian age still alive in the early days, such as Florence Nightingale, the co-discoverer of evolution by natural selection Alfred Russel Wallace, and Thomas Hardy, through the great composers – Elgar, Britten, Vaughan Williams, Walton – poets such as T. S. Eliot and Ted Hughes, the artists Henry Moore, Graham Sutherland, Lucian Freud, Anthony Caro, writers such as E. M. Forster, Isaiah Berlin, Henry James and Tom Stoppard and a vast range of scientists, many of them Nobel Prize-winners or world-changers, such as Paul Dirac and Tim Berners-Lee, the roll-call has been very impressive. Even the political choices, such as Attlee and Thatcher, have been well made. In general, it is a club for people who need only their surname to identify them. They get the occasional lunch or dinner, all together with the Queen, and they get their portraits painted; but OM has nothing to do with pomp or pageantry. It is the nearest Britain has to a gathering of 'the immortals' – though as one of them put it to the author, beaming happily, 'There are, I think, rather more immortals than there are of us.' In 1917, these, plus a special order for diplomats and another for personal service to the monarch, the Royal Victorian Order, comprised the entire honours system. There were military honours too, of course; but nothing for all those ordinary Britons who served in other ways – giving money, giving extraordinary service, doing something 'above and beyond'.

Until then it could be argued that being honoured and having 'an honour' were different things, and rightly so. Fellow citizens' approval and private marks of respect, together with the occasional gong from a charity or civic organization, were the most anyone would expect. George V changed that when he instituted the Order of the British Empire on 4 June 1917. It has five classes, running from the Knight Grand Cross to the more humble Member. The top two classes create Knights or Dames and the higher ones are limited in number – the simple OBEs and MBEs are not. The order is divided into military and civilian wings and the latter in particular has had, as it were, a huge influence on the influence of the monarchy. Many of the 404,500 honours conferred by the Queen are OBEs and MBEs: the twice-yearly lists of celebrities, sports stars and others have become a staple for newspaper comment, congratulation and disappointment. The notion of such an honour was almost certainly the idea of Lord Esher, a one-time Liberal MP whose long service as a courtier had started in Victorian times (he installed a lift for Queen Victoria at Windsor and pushed her wheelchair round Kensington Palace) and who had been heavily involved in Edward VII's reign. Esher was sinuous, bisexual and a bit too much of a crawler, as well as a pusher, for George's taste; but he was shrewd and saw the need for a more democratic honour.

The war had seen new military honours being distributed for the vast numbers of front-line heroes, while at home the idea was that the OBE would go to people involved in some way in the huge voluntary efforts being made. Since it was impossible for the Palace to find and assign those to be honoured, this became almost entirely in the gift of the government of the day. Among the first recipients were trade union officials, including the left-wing William Appleton of the General Federation of Trade Unions and Ben Turner of the textile workers. By the end of 1919, 22,000 OBEs had been awarded, many to factory workers and charitable campaigners. The monarchy was putting down new roots in the very areas where it felt threatened. Unfortunately, the post-war Lloyd George government not only sold peerages and knighthoods, but also treated the OBEs as a kind of bargain-basement offer, and they became known for a time as the Order of the Bad Egg. In the decades since then, however, the OBE has risen in status, rather than declined, and is now at least as important to the British honours system as the Légion d'honneur is in France. The similarly republican honours system in the USA is more complicated than the British one, not less.

The final founding act of the House of Windsor merely took a habit of earlier twentieth-century monarchy and pushed it further. Edward VII had known the importance of being seen by his people, and making regular visits to open hospitals, launch ships and inspect regiments. The Victorian Royals had had their names appended to almost anything built in brick, or granite, with a large door. But George and Mary were in a different league. During the industrial strife of the pre-war period they made major visits to industrial areas of England, Scotland and Wales. George went down a coal mine and visited bereaved miners' families. On a visit to poor housing in Kennington, he got into trouble in the home of a Labour MP when his party noticed a picture of 'the beast' Keir Hardie on the wall, and made a disparaging remark, only to be told by the spirited daughter of the house that Hardie was of 'one of the best men I know; and if anyone does not like him they need not stay in our house'.

But war brought a far greater drive to get out and visit ordinary people. Wartime Britain depended on voluntary organizations in a way that is hard to appreciate today; around 10,000 new ones were formed during 1914–18. Having a royal patron or connection, or even visit, helped raise money and the renamed Windsors put themselves at the centre of an endless flurry of fundraising and morale boosting. Those 300 hospital visits mentioned before were only part of the story.

Recently George V has not had a good press. He is remembered as a philistine, obsessed by outdated rules of dress and etiquette, and over-enthusiastic about his world-class stamp collection. He was certainly a naval martinet, equally capable of intimidating visitors and his children. His official biographer, while writing his life, gloomily confided to his wife that he had a 'down' on him: 'He is all right as a gay young midshipman. He may be all right as a wise old King. But the intervening period when he was Duke of York, just shooting at Sandringham, is hard to manage or swallow. For seventeen years in fact he did nothing at all but kill animals and stick in stamps.'⁹ But like others who waited long to become king, George greatly improved when he finally got the job. After his bumpy start, many of his later political interventions were well judged. His already short temper became shorter still following a bad fall from his horse during the Great War, after which he was often in great pain; but he coped well with a changed world in which socialist politicians arrived at Buckingham Palace and the aristocracy was losing its power.

On becoming king before the First World War he loathed having to side with the democratically elected radical Liberal government against the House of Lords. But he bit his tongue and grimly got on with it. He found young Winston Churchill an impudent puppy and never took to cocky Lloyd George, particularly when he began to debase the honours system by selling off titles. But there was no public protest: George sat them both out. Later he made a truly important intervention in Northern Ireland after the creation of the Irish Republic, which did much to soothe things when it seemed to many a wider war in Ireland was unavoidable.

Later in life, remembering the 'Great War' with horror, he was too soft on the subject of Hitler and too sceptical of Churchill as he began to rumble warnings; but he was hardly alone in that. For this story, what matters most is how he remade the monarchy itself. How the Queen reigns today; what she does; how she is seen and described, all have their origins in decisions taken by her grandfather when Europe was writhing in bloodsoaked turmoil, and Britain was facing starvation and defeat at the hands of U-boat captains. This is the first man who really matters in the Queen's story – the cigar-scented, bearded old naval officer with whom she played as a child and still remembers well. George V was the founder of 'the Firm'.

He was greatly helped by his wife. In press photographs and formal pictures Queen Mary looks about as grandly stony-faced as any Royal could be. She was born at Kensington Palace in the zenith of Queen Victoria's reign, surviving both her husband and her son King George VI and living, to see her grand-daughter Elizabeth become queen in 1952. Her birth had been communicated around the Royals of Europe in handwritten German letters; she watched her son's funeral on television. Queen Mary's influence on today's British monarchy is big, if mostly forgotten. For although she was imposing, like the frosted prow of some ancient warship, and over-enthusiastic about being given presents by those she visited, Mary was a keen social reformer. As her husband reshaped the monarchy she formed a close alliance with a radical female trade union leader called Mary Macarthur who had led campaigns to raise the wages of the 'sweated labour' of Edwardian women sewing blouses, working in jam factories or forging chains. Macarthur was married to the Labour Party chairman Will Anderson and was a notorious firebrand. When Queen Mary invited her to Buckingham Palace she, in Macarthur's own words, 'positively lectured the Queen on the inequality of the classes, the injustice of it'. She concluded, rightly or not, that 'The Queen does understand and grasp the whole situation from a Trade Union point of view.'[10]

The first 'situation' was the shock effect of the early days of the war on trade and business, which meant huge numbers of female workers losing their jobs. Queen Mary and her aristocratic friends had encouraged a great surge of knitting and needlework as war-work, which of course simply made life harder for female employees of the clothing industry.

Macarthur begged one friend to do everything in her power 'to stop these women knitting!' Queen Mary got the point and launched The Queen's Work for Women Fund to raise money to subsidize projects for unemployed women. An all-party committee was set up, and though the Queen herself did not join the MPs, she heckled it from the sidelines and interested herself in the problem, in ways new to royalty.

As the war dragged on, more and more women were recruited to replace fighting men, and the problems changed. Queen Mary, like the King, became a relentless visitor of food centres and hospitals, insisting always on seeing the worst wounded and those with the most distressing injuries, including the dying. She worked to raise money for relief funds and Christmas boxes for troops, and was affectionately described as 'a charitable bulldozer'. In her paperwork and replies to charitable requests she was equally tireless. She was later said to have retorted to an exhausted princess complaining about yet another boring hospital visit, 'We are the royal family – and we *love* hospitals.' And she noted in the margin of one biography of her, which said she was easily bored, 'As a matter of fact, the Queen is never bored.' It is an attitude the current Queen shares.

After the war ended, all this activity became part of the early Windsors' unending effort to demonstrate royal relevance. There was plenty of evidence of the need for change. Lord Cromer, a kind of ancient crocodile of public service, had warned that 'the Monarchy is not so stable now'. In November 1918, George V was visiting a rally of 35,000 ex-servicemen in Hyde Park and noted that he, with other members of the royal family, was duly cheered. But then men broke through to press round the King, complaining about their poor pensions, joblessness and lack of decent houses: he was mobbed, not in a particularly friendly way, and nearly pulled off his horse. Protest banners were raised and it was a narrow squeak for the police to get him safely out. After silently riding back to Buckingham Palace with the Prince of Wales, he dismounted and said: 'Those men were in a funny temper,' before shaking his head and striding into the building.

So, under political pressure, for the first time, the charitable and visiting parts of the monarchy became its most notable aspects, as important as its ceremonial state functions. The future King George VI was made president of the Boys Welfare Association and the Prince of Wales, later Edward VIII, became patron of the National Council of Social Services. He was sent on visits across the more depressed parts of Britain, showing the charisma he would become famous for.

George V began to compile a map showing the charitable public work being done by the family, almost like a military campaign, with flags to show where they had been; and later produced a chart, showing the productivity of its individual members, which would be brought to him each Christmas at Sandringham. One writer describes 'the King poring over his charts like a sea captain over his log books'.[11] Not all the early reform ideas were immediately accepted. Clive Wigram, a former Bengal Lancer who became equerry to George and later his private secretary, argued shortly after the war that it was time to open up Buckingham Palace and its garden to 'people of all classes' including schoolteachers and civil servants 'on the lines of the White House receptions'. With that idea, Wigram was too early by about eighty years. But in all this we can see what was, effectively, the creation of a new kind of monarchy. The crisis of 1917 produced a royal family, which cut itself off from its German origins and its Russian relatives, and which made determined efforts to dig itself into the subsoil of British life more snugly than before. Lord Stamfordham, apart from choosing its name, gave the House of Windsor its founding principle when he wrote in the same year, 'We must endeavour to induce the thinking working classes, socialist and others, to regard the Crown, not as a mere figurehead and an institution which, as they put it, "don't count", but as a living power for good . . . affecting the interests and well-being of all classes.' That was the job George set out to do, and which his son and granddaughter then took on. It is the most important sentence a British courtier has ever written, and remains the most influential.

The Windsors were still extremely rich, of course, attended by aristocratic servants and most of the time physically remote in their castles and palaces. At Buckingham Palace during the 1920s a brown Windsor silence descended, heavy curtains and country-life routines shutting out the febrile noise of the Jazz Age. After the war, George and Mary stayed in Britain, travelling abroad for just seven weeks during the sixteen years between the Armistice and the King's death. He preferred the company of his own immediate family to that of anyone else, a pious countryman whose day was run with clockwork precision, attended by a pet parrot and emotionally dependent on a daily phone call to his sister, Princess Victoria. (In one of the many good stories about George, she was put through to Buckingham Palace and began the conversation: 'Hello, you old fool,' only to be interrupted by the operator: 'Beg pardon, your Royal Highness, His Majesty is not yet on the line.'[12]) He was contemptuous of literary types and intellectuals generally, dismissing them as 'eyebrows' – until he discovered the word was highbrow.

Yet politically, the man Princess Elizabeth came to know as 'Grandpa England' had proved himself an astute operator, a master of the strategic retreat who was determined to win over working-class critics, if not eyebrows, and who was soon succeeding. When Britain's first, short-lived Labour government arrived in 1924, George speculated privately on what his grandmother Queen Victoria would have made of it (not much); but he went on to do his very best to make the new cabinet ministers – described by one as 'MacDonald the starveling clerk, Thomas the engine-driver, Henderson the foundry labourer and Clynes the mill-hand' – feel welcome at Buckingham Palace, Windsor and Balmoral.[13] He developed real friendships with several of them. Under George V the imperial pomp of the nineteenth century and the angry confrontations of Edwardian Britain had faded, and, despite all those predictions, the monarchy had again become a symbol of unity, easing itself away from the political fray.

That was no mean feat, and another monarch might not have pulled it off. Had George's weak, rackety elder brother Eddy, Duke of Clarence, not died of flu in 1892, the story of the British monarchy might have ended long ago. George V, who married the woman who had originally been betrothed to Eddie, had many traits which reappear in the current Queen's reign. He was quietly devout, emotionally reserved, with an utter belief in duty and family. More than seventy years ago the super-patriotic historian Sir Arthur Bryant said of George V that he and his Queen represented the secret convictions of every decent English person at a time when other more intellectual leaders of the nation were 'preaching the gospel of disintegration and many of its social leaders were making bad manners and loose living a social fashion'.[14] Despite the florid language it is a judgement which applies also to the Queen. This is not surprising. Grandpa England was part of her life for her first ten years, waving at her from his window in Buckingham Palace, playing with her as he had not with his own children, and delighting in her company. After his death, which moved her greatly, his widow, Queen Mary, was heavily involved in Elizabeth's education. She is her parents' child; but her grandparents' grandchild, too. When Elizabeth was born in 1926, she was joining not just a family, but a family campaign. Ten years later, it was a campaign being derailed.

Uncle David's Crisis

The Queen's 'Uncle David', as King Edward VIII was known in the family, was the Bad King, the Windsor Who Got It Wrong. He was the vain, self-indulgent celebrity who demonstrated that charisma, while useful in politics or entertainment, is a flimsy material from which to build a constitutional monarchy. King Edward was bored by duty and sought pleasure. For a senior Royal to be truly badly behaved wrecks everything. The dreadful warning of Edward VIII is one of the foundations of the Queen's world-view. She knew him quite well up to the time when she was nine as the engaging, cheerful Uncle David who would romp into her parents' home and play games. Then he stopped romping and vanished into newspaper headlines and exile.

The droll, immaculately dressed yet always sad-eyed prince had for a long time been the hope of the British Empire. He had been trained by the navy and struggled hard to be allowed to fight in the trenches, getting near enough to the front line to be shelled. After the war, he had been sent on ritual tours of the Empire, touching that vanished world at its grandest moment before it began to crumple, meeting and greeting adoring crowds from the highlands of India to the snowy wastes of Canada. He read out the speeches written with fluency and grace.

In the 1920s he was, for British newspaper-readers, the beau idéal of the modern man: informal, a keen dancer and pleasure-seeker who nevertheless said the right words at the right moments. Though a demon rider to hounds, he also sought out the new world of nightclubs and golf links. He was taken at face value by the masses, in Britain and overseas, as an attractive man of energy, advanced views and great charisma. Yet 'David' was, before Diana, the prime example of what can happen when a leading member of the royal family starts to behave like a celebrity. The little-people's rules did not count for him. He was bored by royal paperwork and he was privately contemptuous of the courtly world enclosing him.

One can sympathize. His own book, though self-serving and moany, is a convincing account of the stultifying life of George V's inter-war court, with its slow dinners, endless protocol and early nights. Edward was also tinged with the progressive ideas of the day. When his father, at the end of the Great War, called upon the eldest son to remember his position and who he was, he reflected: 'But who exactly was I? The idea that my birth and title should somehow or other set me apart from and above other people struck me as wrong . . . without understanding why, I was in unconscious rebellion against my position. That is what comes, perhaps, of sending an impressionable Prince to school and war.'[15] If republican readers perk up at this point and start to ask if Edward is a putative hero, they must remember that he was as haughty to those around him as the worst modern 'celeb'. He rebelled not by rethinking the role and rhythm of monarchy, or even declaring for its abolition (and thus all the comforts it brought him too, presumably), but by being selfish and wayward. He took married mistresses, then brutally dumped them. He danced into the small hours and infuriated his staff with his petulant demands. Behind the scenes, he was causing despair to the people on whom he depended, and no senior member of the royal family can afford to do that. Unlike the rest of us, they are attended on, followed and guided by a small army of their own. And as in any army, if the chief loses the support of the soldiers, everything goes.

'Tommy' Lascelles was the war-decorated and intensely patriotic assistant private secretary to the Prince of Wales. He later served George VI and – briefly – the present Queen. Like most people, he was star-struck by Edward when he first met him and as a fervent monarchist he was delighted by his new job. As time went on, though, he grew more and more alarmed by the playboy capriciousness of his 'Chief,' until he became thoroughly disillusioned. During their 1927 tour of Canada, he took counsel from the then prime minister, who was part of the British group:

> I felt such despair about him [the Prince of Wales] that I sought a secret colloquy with Stanley Baldwin one evening ... I told him directly that, in my considered opinion, the Heir Apparent, in his unbridled pursuit of wine and women, and whatever selfish whim occupied him at the moment, was rapidly going to the devil, and unless he mended his ways, would soon become no fit wearer of the British Crown. I expected to get my head bitten off; but Baldwin heard me to the end, and, after a pause, said he agreed with every word I had said. I went on, 'You know, sometimes when I sit in York House waiting to get the result of some point-to-point in which he is riding, I can't help thinking that the best thing that could happen

to him, and to the country, would be for him to break his neck.' 'God forgive me,' said Stanley Baldwin, 'I have often thought the same.'[16]

That is quite a moment: the prime minister and a private secretary to the heir to the throne agreeing it would be better for Britain if he accidentally killed himself. Lascelles considered resignation but was short of money and long on patriotism. Encouraged by his wife, he soldiered on. Yet only a year later, writing to her during another tour, this fervent monarchist was questioning whether monarchy was really such a 'flawless and indispensable institution' after all. The thoughtless behaviour of the Prince had made the life of a courtier with the slightest self-respect simply intolerable. Lascelles reflected: 'It is like being the right-hand man of a busy millionaire, when one is not at all certain that capitalism is a good thing . . . Why *should* I undo an hour's work just because another man suddenly decides he wants to play golf at three instead of five? Why *should* I continually hang about on one foot or the other because another man can't take the trouble to go and change his clothes in time?'[17] If you want a explanation as to why the Queen places such emphasis on behaving well to her staff (never her 'servants'), and expects her family to treat them with similar thoughtfulness and courtesy, look no further than Uncle David.

Lascelles – not the last senior courtier to grind his teeth about a Prince of Wales – finally exploded with Edward during their lion- and elephant-hunting expedition in East Africa in November 1928 when King George V fell seriously ill and Baldwin cabled repeatedly, begging the Prince to come home at once. Lascelles showed Edward the cables. The Prince, who was having far too much fun to want to leave Africa, replied that he didn't believe a word – it was 'just some election dodge of old Baldwin's. It doesn't mean a thing.' Lascelles recounted that after this 'incredibly callous behaviour', he lost his temper with the heir to the British Empire: ' "Sir," I said, "the King of England is dying; and if that means nothing to you, it means a great deal to us." He looked at me, went out without a word, and spent the remainder of the evening in the successful seduction of a Mrs Barnes, wife of the local Commissioner. He told me so himself next morning.'[18]

Not only Lascelles but two more of Edward's most senior staff were desperate to escape from him. Lascelles got in first, however, in January 1929, writing the Prince a blunt letter and later giving him a verbal dressing-down: 'I paced his room for the best part of an hour, telling him, as I might have told a younger brother, exactly what I thought of him and his whole scheme of life, and foretelling, with an accuracy that might have surprised me at the time, that he would lose the throne of England.' To their mutual credit the two men parted relatively affably. Lascelles returned to serve George V shortly before he died, and remained at Buckingham Palace through the next two reigns. He was not surprised by the abdication when it came, but he was appalled by what he saw as a dereliction of duty. Once exiled, the Duke of Windsor referred to Lascelles simply as 'the evil snake'.

Some people argue that the abdication crisis of 1936 was the defining moment of the Windsors, and there is a lot to be said for that. It was certainly their biggest shock. But the story itself need not keep us long here. It has been exhaustively described, from every possible angle, for seventy years. The wild rumours about the sexual hold Wallis Simpson had over the King; the brutal political battle between him and Stanley Baldwin; the arguments about a morganatic marriage (in which he would have been King but Wallis would not have been

Queen); and the tussle over money and status when the King finally did abdicate are interesting questions but have been exhaustively discussed by several generations of historians, novelists and journalists. What matters in the Queen's story is that, without the abdication, she would have led a quiet life, probably as a little-known royal countrywoman, enjoying her dogs and horses and supporting local charities. Her father would surely have lived longer since he would not have had to endure kingship during the world war to come. Her sister too would have had a happier and more private life. As it was, she seems to have watched which paths 'David' chose and in every way beetled as fast she could in the opposite direction.

The new dynasty had looked into the abyss. Had Edward fought to stay on as King and succeeded, it might well have meant the break-up of the Empire, with very great consequences for the war to follow. Even as it was, the institution of monarchy was exposed, sniggered at around the world, and had felt itself wobble. These things are not forgotten in the family. Almost as soon as Edward VIII abdicated and became the Duke of Windsor, going abroad to marry without the support of his brother or parents, he was vigorously erased from the story. His memory was expunged and the solid virtues were re-instated. The British court swiftly reverted to the style of the old king, George V. It returned to convention, family, duty.

Good King George

Except for her husband, the single biggest influence on the Queen was her father, George VI. If you want a measuring device for King George VI's service to his country, you should not turn first to the recent film about his struggle with his stammer. Good though it is, its unforgettable image is of Colin Firth bellowing four-lettered words. Look instead at a picture of the real man when he was Duke of York, such as the Philip de László portrait of 1931, and then compare it with a photograph of him after the war, such as the official portrait in RAF uniform of twenty years later. We all age. The King, like most of his generation, was a heavy smoker. Even so, the alteration is shocking. He goes from looking like an adult boy, with a smooth, sensitive, carefree face – big, dark eyes and full lips – to an image of exhausted decay, haggard, lined and sunken. By his mid-fifties, he has the hair of a young man and the face of someone in his seventies. It was being a wartime leader that did this to him. Another measure of the alteration is found in the fearlessly frank diaries of Harold Nicolson, the politician and writer responsible for the official life of George's father. In 1929 he found the Prince 'just a snipe from the Windsor marshes', but by 1940 was writing after meeting him that he was no longer 'a foolish loutish boy' but calm and reassuring: he and the Queen were 'resolute and sensible. WE SHALL WIN. I know that now.'[19]

George VI knew what being king would do to him. He felt he was horribly unequipped for the job. On the day 'David' finally made it clear to his younger brother that he was abdicating, after having left him hanging in suspense for days, the future king went to see his mother, Queen Mary, '& when I told her what had happened I broke down and sobbed like a child'.[20] She said he had sobbed for an hour on her shoulder. The next day, as he was watching his brother make his final preparations for departure, he told Mountbatten, one of Edward's closest friends, in great distress, 'Dickie, this is absolutely terrible. I never wanted this to happen; I'm quite unprepared for it. David has been trained for this all his life.

I've never even seen a State Paper. I'm only a Naval Officer, it's the only thing I know about.'[21] For once, Mountbatten's encyclopedic memory for royal anecdotage proved tersely useful: he happened to remember his father telling him that King George V had said just the same when his elder brother died, to be told: 'George, you're wrong. There is no more fitting preparation for a King than to have been trained in the Navy.'

Whether that is true or not – and there is a case for it, since the navy puts the trainee monarch alongside all types and classes of men in a confined place, and involves good time-keeping, practicality and dealing with stress – it was only part of the answer. 'Bertie' had been struggling all his life with a terrible stammer, perhaps derived from lifelong feelings of inadequacy prompted by comparisons with his glamorous and self-assured brother, whom he had once idolized. He had spent his early years with his siblings in York Cottage, a crowded home in the grounds of Sandringham, before going to the tough boarding environment of the Royal Naval College on the Isle of Wight, which had once been Queen Victoria's favoured southern retreat, Osborne. This must have been hard for a shy boy who had never mixed well with other children. He was bullied and struggled to make his mark, coming sixty-eighth out of sixty-eight in his final exams. He nevertheless went on to the next phase of his naval training at Dartmouth, did a year at Oxford and was commissioned as a junior midshipman a year before the beginning of the First World War. He had had bow legs and been forced to wear excruciatingly painful leg braces as a boy. His digestive system was badly impaired, perhaps partly as a result of neglectful feeding by an early nurse. During the war, he was repeatedly away from his ship in hospitals but managed to get back to fight at the extremely bloody, if indecisive, Battle of Jutland. Unable to speak well in public, untrained in statecraft, physically in poor shape, though a good rider and tennis player, he seemed about as badly suited to become King-Emperor as any man could be.

Yet he had shown another side to his character, a streak of determination and persistence which would change his reputation. After the war, he fell in love with a glamorous Scottish aristocrat. Elizabeth Bowes Lyon was only twenty when they met for the first time at a dance in 1920. She was besieged by confident and pushy admirers. Bertie paid court and made his first proposal through an emissary. It was rejected. He was then rejected in person. He refused to give up and was eventually accepted in January 1923. This was a side to Bertie his parents had not seen before, and they were delighted. Elizabeth was the first commoner to be ushered into the family since the 1917 Windsor revolution. ('Commoner' in this respect means only 'non-royal', since she came from a grand Scottish landowning family.) Winning her changed his life. As his brother went further and further off the rails, their father began to see his second son in a kinder light. When Bertie married, George V wrote that 'you have always been so sensible and easy to work with, and you have always been ready to listen to my advice and to agree with my opinions about people and things, that I feel we have always got on very well together (very different from dear David)'. Later, George was reported to have said he hoped his eldest son would not marry, so that Bertie and then little Elizabeth would succeed instead. 'Ready . . . to agree with my opinions' reads now as rather a double-edged compliment: Bertie, it implies, was doing well because he was complaisant and deferential, ready to go with the flow. There is some truth in that.

Between the wars he had settled into the quiet life of a

private gentleman, while not shirking the royal duties imposed by his father. He was interested in industry and public works, opening a summer camp for boys from very different backgrounds. His inclinations, however, were profoundly private and quietly conservative as he revelled in a warm family life, leaning on a wife who was, according to courtiers at the time, even more instinctively conservative than he was. He was deeply suspicious of socialists, Liberals and indeed any politicians who were not 'sound' Tories of the old school. He loathed public speaking and there was a deeply embarrassing moment in May 1925 when he struggled to complete a speech at the Empire Exhibition at Wembley. As the authors of a book on the King's speech defect put it, 'It would be difficult to overestimate the psychological effect that the speech had both on Bertie and his family, and the problem that his dismal performance threw up for the monarchy. Such speeches were meant to be part of the daily routine of the Duke, who was second in line to the throne, yet he had conspicuously failed to rise to the challenge.'[22]

Though he had tried almost every obvious speech-therapist in London, it was after this, in October 1926, that his wife persuaded Bertie to meet Lionel Logue, the Australian whose unorthodox skills would do so much to help him. Speech therapy was still in its infancy, a hit-or-miss affair which oscillated between psychology, physical work on the diaphragm, lungs and tongue, and exercises both useful and bizarre. Logue was not medically trained but was himself a good and self-confident public speaker whose optimism and energy won over his suspicious and pessimistic royal client. The most striking thing about the treatment, hard to convey in the cinema, is the sheer relentlessness and frequency of the sessions. In a little over a year, running through to December 1927, Bertie had eighty-two sessions with Logue in Harley Street and practised day after day at home, breaking engagements and leaving his beloved hunting field early to force himself through tongue-twisters, breathing exercises and reading practice. Little by little, the intense effort paid off, and audiences who had been expecting a monosyllabic, stuttering performance found themselves listening to relatively fluent royal addresses. Throughout, his wife was urging him on, sitting beside him, her knuckles white with tension. On foreign visits, during numerous home speeches and even broadcasts, Bertie got steadily better.

Speech defects do not disappear overnight, and absolute cures are very rare. The psychological pressures of his early upbringing could not be simply magicked away; like so many people, the future king lived with the scar tissue of those very hard years and learned to cope with the consequences. Once he became king there was vicious gossip about him, even before it was decided that he would take his father's name (he might have been the first King Albert). He was, it was said, too nervous and dim to manage the duties of kingship; he would barely make it through his Coronation. There is a theory, revealed by an authorized royal biographer called Dermot Morrah, that 'some men of authority in the state' had seriously considered hopping over Bertie during the December 1936 abdication crisis, and settling the Crown instead on his youngest brother, the more dashing and outgoing Duke of Kent, who also, unlike Bertie, had a son and heir.[23] Had that happened, there would have been no 'Diamond Queen' for the British to celebrate in 2012. Instead, her cousin, the current Duke of Kent, would have been king. Now twenty-fourth in line of succession, he has had a long military career and is a leading Freemason. The royal pack is constantly shuffled, by chance and half-forgotten choices.

So in his first years as King, George VI had to endure the kind of loud clubland muttering and drawing-room whispering that was the 1930s equivalent of a Twitter persecution. He did not visit India for the expected Durbar (and, despite being its last Emperor, never visited India at all). Unhelpfully, the somewhat cloddish Archbishop of Canterbury of the day openly discussed his stammer. His brother bombarded him with unwanted advice from his Austrian exile. When his first prime minister, Stanley Baldwin, who had been an avuncular source of support, soon resigned, George VI was forlorn. Yet he again showed the tenacity that had won him his wife and subdued his stammer, applying himself to royal business and duty with a grim vigour Edward VIII had been incapable of. King Edward had horrified the political establishment by ignoring boxes of official papers, sending them back with whisky-glass stains or, worse, showing them around, so that Whitehall officials began to censor what was sent to the Palace.

George read his papers and kept his counsel, and began to overcome his meagre constitutional education. The establishment responded, warily and then with relief. The British press, which had hushed up the Edward and Wallis affair almost until the last moment, returned to its former instincts for loyalty and discretion. In many ways, this was bad for the monarchy. Though it allowed George VI to grow into the role of king, it meant that the royal family reverted to past habits, including a knee-jerk preference for 'safe' aristocratic and Conservative politicians, just at the moment when they were to prove wanting. The court was deeply suspicious of Churchill in particular, who had been belligerently pro-Edward. More generally, Lascelles and his colleagues provided a protective crust of tradition and precedence around the four-strong family, which lasted until the 1950s.

In the run-up to the Second World War George VI was still an inexperienced monarch, finding his way. When his second prime minister, Neville Chamberlain, embarked on the policy of appeasement, the King backed him so enthusiastically some MPs believed he was behaving too politically, breaking his constitutional role. George wanted to make personal King-to-Führer appeals himself, and he insisted on Chamberlain joining him on the balcony at Buckingham Palace after his now notorious visit to Munich to show the royal family's support for appeasement. Today, the consensus is that this was a bad mistake, but at the time most British people were also delighted. The King issued a message to the Empire promising 'the time of anxiety is past' and thanking God and Mr Chamberlain for 'a new era of friendship and prosperity'. This was a family view. His mother, Queen Mary, wrote to him expressing her exasperation with the critics of Munich – why couldn't people simply be grateful that Chamberlain had come home bringing peace: 'It is always so easy for people to criticize when they don't know the ins and outs of the question.' When, after the war had started and Britain's early Norway campaign had failed, Chamberlain was forced to resign, the King was aghast and angry with the prime minister's critics. To replace Chamberlain the King wanted Lord Halifax, another arch-appeaser and a high Tory aristocrat. It was with great reluctance that he eventually accepted that the intemperate and unreliable Winston Churchill was the better choice, and he took quite some time to get used to him. Princess Elizabeth, hearing the news of Chamberlain's resignation, cried.

One eminent royal biographer concluded: 'George VI was

not a born leader. He could seem shy and harassed, aloof and even morose.'[24] He was also famous for his outbursts of temper, his 'gnashes', as the family called them. Yet the war made his reputation, as it was to make Churchill's and Mountbatten's. Underneath the thin skin was an intelligent and sensitive man with an iron sense of duty. The first real evidence that he might prove a good king came in his visit to America just before the war. George VI was on a long-planned visit to Canada. President Roosevelt invited him south. It was the first time a reigning British sovereign had stepped into the USA. Roosevelt had seized his moment. According to his wife, he believed 'we might all soon be engaged in a life or death struggle, in which Great Britain would be our first line of defence' and wanted 'to create a bond of friendship'.[25]

It worked. Both Queen Elizabeth and the King were greeted ecstatically and impressed American politicians, newspapers and crowds with their informality and warmth. The Queen wrote to her daughter revealing the informal excitements of dining outside, with all the food jumbled together, including 'HOT DOGS!' More is sometimes claimed for royal visits than can be properly measured or substantiated. This one certainly mattered. At his home on the Hudson River, President Roosevelt and George VI talked long into the night about such nitty-gritty issues as debts, steel exports, naval bases, the Soviet position and how to win round American opinion from isolationism. Roosevelt went far further than most Americans would have been comfortable with then: he promised, according to the King's note, that 'If London was bombed USA would come in.' All this was meticulously recorded by him the next day and sent back to the British government. When President Obama visited London in the spring of 2011, he brought as a present for the Queen a bound volume of photographs of this visit: it meant a lot to her father and so to her too.

Indeed, George VI carried his notes with him throughout the war; a poignant thing, because when the conflict actually arrived his greatest role was to support the bigger and even more sensitive personality of his prime minister. Thrown into Churchill's giant shadow, he never complained. George VI was privy to the deepest secrets of wartime, including the Enigma intercepts and prior knowledge of the invention and then the use of the atomic bomb. He and the arch-royalist Churchill became close friends, despite occasional spats. He worked hard, ruthlessly cut back the costs of the court and supported his extraordinary prime minister in every way. He famously refused to leave London during the Blitz – though the royal family spent their nights at Windsor, where the current Queen was largely sheltered from the privations of wartime. Buckingham Palace was bombed nine times.

He thought up the idea of the George Cross and George Medal to honour civilian heroes, building in a smaller way on his father's creation of the OBE, and visited British forces in North Africa, Italy and – most dramatically – heavily bombed Malta. He argued with Churchill over the latter's enthusiasm for going to France after D-Day, pointing out that as King he was unable to go and he was therefore being put in an unfair position. Churchill grumpily stayed at home a little longer. By the end of the war the King had become a genuine symbol of British doggedness: shy, devout, even in his awkwardness 'one of us' in an age when so many countries had monsters for their heads of state.

After the war was over, George supported Indian independence and demonstrated his hostility to South African racism during a visit there. Just as Queen Victoria had been horrified by US slavery, and had delighted in the close attention of her Indian servants, so George VI gave every indication of being genuinely colour-blind – though of course his empire as a whole was certainly not.

The King, however, was no radical and found it hard to swallow Churchill's 1945 election defeat. He was privately dubious about Attlee's socialist administration. Just as his father had had to cope with the first arrival of a Labour government in 1924, so the son had to swallow his instincts and deal with unfamiliar men holding alarming views. He coped but did not enjoy it. In many ways George VI remained a highly conservative pre-war traditionalist, meticulous (and fussy) about dress, honours and court precedence, obsessively keen on shooting – a thinner, clean-shaven version of his father. The future Labour leader Hugh Gaitskell said he was 'a fairly reactionary person'. In great pain, needing an operation on his leg to restore the blood supply choked by arteriosclerosis, he was told he should be operated on in hospital and refused on the odd grounds of court protocol: 'I have never heard of a King going to a hospital before.' But he worked intensely hard and bit his rebellious tongue, and kept the constitutional monarchy in good repair. And all this was observed and noted by his elder daughter, the serious-minded girl he knew would be queen, and whom he introduced early into the work and rituals that would entail. She talks about his influence even now. When she unveiled a memorial to him in the Mall in 1955 she praised his wartime steadfastness, his 'friendliness and simplicity', his 'warm and friendly sympathies', his 'unassuming humanity' and pointed out that he had sacrificed himself during bouts of serious illness: 'his courage in overcoming it endeared him to everybody'. These are precisely the qualities George V had hoped the monarchy would become associated with after the torment of the Great War.

So, the House of Windsor has seen an unusually direct transmission of ideas and behaviour from its origin in 1917 through grandfather, father and daughter. It can be summed up as modernization by conservative people with a strong sense of duty and purpose. Elizabeth II follows her grandfather and father as Britain's new model monarchs. They have been called the welfare monarchy, or the democracy monarchy, or even the suburban monarchy.

Suburban, the Queen is not. She may spoon her breakfast cereal out of a Tupperware container but her court retains the velvety sheen and scale of Victoria's. When she became Queen people talked rather pompously of a 'new Elizabethan age' and asked whether the Britain of the mid-twentieth century could surprise the world like the English of the age of Drake, Shakespeare and Bacon. The Queen put them right. In her Christmas broadcast of 1953 she said she did not 'feel at all like my great Tudor forebear, who was blessed with neither husband nor children, who ruled as a despot and was never able to leave her native shores'. Yet she went on to compare modern Britain, rich in courage and enterprise, with the poor, small but 'great in spirit' England of the earlier Elizabeth. The Tudors, of course, also reinvented themselves as a dynasty. In that, the Queen and the Windsors are more Tudor than mock-Tudor.

Glamorous Dickie

There are two other major characters without whom we cannot understand the Queen's reign. One is, obviously, her mother, the young girl successfully wooed in the world of the 'Bright Young Things' who would live on into the current century, a presence at the Queen's shoulder through most of her reign. The other is a less obvious influence, and a more ambiguous one, whose impact was at its height in the mid-twentieth century. Alongside the future Edward VIII on those post-1918 tours had been a besotted admirer who was also part of the family. Like the Prince, this man had been held in his grandmother Queen Victoria's arms as a baby and given, as one of his names, 'Albert' in memory of her husband. He is remembered now simply as 'Mountbatten', the Prince's cousin and one of the most exotic, too-big-to-be-true characters in twentieth-century British history.

As already noted, when Mountbatten was just fifteen his German-born but patriotically British father, Prince Louis Battenberg, had been forced to resign as First Sea Lord. He and his son were members of a relatively junior branch of the interwoven tree of European royal dynasties. But only relatively junior; the Battenbergs had holidayed with the Romanovs in Russia and felt entitled to meddle in the affairs of kings from Sweden to Greece. Louis Mountbatten, as he became, was a British naval officer in the Great War, who rose through the naval ranks between the wars, became very close to the future British king, and then topped that by marrying one of the richest women in Britain.

He got his great career break during the Second World War despite a series of early embarrassments as a serving captain. His destroyer, HMS *Kelly*, hit mines and once another ship, and was badly hit by bombers after Mountbatten had sent night-time signals which were picked up by the enemy. Yet Mountbatten's sense of theatre, and his ability to make stirring speeches, meant that after he had nursed the wounded ship back home, he became a national hero and the subject of a wartime propaganda film by Noël Coward, *In Which We Serve*. His real ship was later bombed and sunk off Crete, where Mountbatten's flotilla of destroyers was trying to hold off the German invasion. He was very lucky to survive; 136 members of his crew did not. Though the *Kelly* was facing impossible odds and none of this was his fault, his biographers and naval historians have generally concluded that he was a dashing but not particularly good commander of ships. But thanks to Winston Churchill, who had recognized a dynamic and publicity-conscious personality rather like his own, and with a little help from Coward, Mountbatten was soon raised far above his rank to become Chief of Combined Operations. Later he rose even further, to become Supreme Allied Commander for South East Asia. There he would successfully lead the fight to retake Burma and Malaya from the Japanese.

Wars accelerate everything, including promotions, but to go from being the captain of a destroyer mocked for depth-charging a shoal of fish to becoming one of the grand masters of strategy in a global conflict was quite extraordinary. Mountbatten's charisma and the surging self-confidence that communicated itself in ever wider circles mattered particularly in the difficult conditions of the early 1940s. He had always milked his connections and shamelessly lobbied for every job he wanted, right back to his appointment accompanying the Prince of Wales on his foreign jaunts. After the abdication, he had quickly switched allegiance to the new King George VI (Queen Elizabeth was dryly amused) and never forgot to remind all around him about his close royal ties. Long ago Churchill had acquiesced in his father's humiliating removal from the Admiralty; now Churchill was his fervent supporter. Mountbatten, it seemed, had everything. He had the flair for self-promotion that a tired Britain responded to, just like Churchill's favoured soldier, Field Marshal Bernard Montgomery. He had good looks, personal courage, charm and the self-possession of a very wealthy man. And he was part of the royal establishment at a time when that still mattered very much. No wonder so many well-placed people hated him with such cold and sparkling intensity.

Eventually the anti-Mountbatten camp came to include Churchill too. After the war, and Churchill's defeat in the 1945 general election, the new Labour prime minister Clement Attlee asked Mountbatten to become the last Viceroy of India and finish the independence negotiations with India and Pakistan. He did so, working to a very tight timetable and with energetic ruthlessness. He and his lively wife Edwina enjoyed the grand style of the final days of the Indian Empire. Their vice-regal house put Buckingham Palace to shame; their daughter compared it to the greatest palaces of the Russian Tsar, which 'Dickie' also knew. Beyond the busy but civilized withdrawal of the senior echelons of the Raj, a ragged dissolution began across the subcontinent. Mountbatten worked hard for a total of 125 days to end Britain's Indian Empire, taking brutal decisions fast, a man doing a job to a timetable set in London. Nobody had fought for the Empire harder or had loved it more than Churchill, who now regarded his former protégé as a traitor.

The partition resulted in terrible bloodshed, the worst slaughter and migration in the history of the subcontinent. This was not Mountbatten's fault. He and Edwina did their best to organize help. Yet at some level Britain no longer seemed to care about the agonies of its former colonized people. Mountbatten returned to the navy and continued to prosper until becoming Admiral of the Fleet and Chief of the

Defence Staff. He also became, in 1955, First Sea Lord – the job his father had been forced from forty-one years before. That great promotion was with the reluctant agreement of the elderly prime minister, Winston Churchill. Revenge rarely comes sweeter. 'Thrill to sit under Papa's picture,' wrote Mountbatten in his diary on his first day as he moved back to his father's old office.

Mountbatten was a huge influence on the Windsors during the earlier part of the Queen's reign – if not so directly on her, then on her husband and her son. First and most obviously, he acted as a kind of semi-guardian to Prince Philip from early 1930 onwards. In its most melodramatic version the story has Mountbatten shaping Philip in his own image, intriguing to marry him off to Princess Elizabeth and then exulting in a family triumph when she became Queen. This is greatly over-cooked. It is true that Mountbatten urged Philip to follow a naval career. It is also true that Mountbatten was as keen a dynastic matchmaker as any old lady in a Polish shtetl. At one point he tried to interest Prince Charles in one of his grand-daughters. In Prince Philip's case, he worked hard and success-fully to achieve his naturalization as a British citizen rather than a Greek one. It seemed a difficult business, finally achieved in February 1947, when Philip also took his mother's anglicized name, Mountbatten, rather than what would have been his paternal family name, the Danish one of Schleswig-Holstein-Sonderburg-Glucksburg. This made it much easier for him to marry. Finally, it is true that after the marriage, Mountbatten campaigned long, hard and unsuccessfully for the replacement of 'Windsor' as the dynastic name, with Mountbatten-Windsor. In this, he had the support of Philip, who, as we shall see, bitterly objected to not being able to pass his name on to his children.

But the Duke of Edinburgh has repeatedly made it clear that he thinks Mountbatten overstated his involvement in his upbringing, complaining that his own father and mother were being written out of the picture, and that he had spent more time staying with his grandmother and other relatives. One gets the impression that he resented 'Uncle Dickie' overplaying his hand. It was he, not his uncle, who decided he should marry the future Queen. Philip wrote a terse letter to Mountbatten at the time they were wooing, effectively, if humorously, warning him off: 'I am not being rude, but it is apparent that you like being General Manager of this little show, and I am rather afraid she might not take to the idea quite as docilely as I do . . .'[26] Much later, Mountbatten would develop a closer relationship with Philip's first son, Prince Charles. By then, he had long been a special intimate of the inner royal family, included in holidays and private visits, his self-serving and oft-repeated stories listened to with tolerant amusement, and his vast range of connections admired. Yet for all the affection and warmth there was something held back, at least by the older Royals.

For Uncle Dickie also provided an unsettling link with Uncle David. After their expedition to India, when Mountbatten married his heiress Edwina Ashley at a glittering society wedding, the future Edward VIII was his best man. The Mountbattens were key members of the Prince's 'set' and remained close friends during his brief reign. Though he disapproved of the abdication, fighting vigorously as a member of the 'King's party' alongside Churchill, Mountbatten kept in close touch with the exiled former monarch, offered to be his best man when he married Mrs Simpson and later passed messages between him and the court. He was on hand to rescue the pair from France in 1940 as the Germans closed in.

He was the middle man in negotiations about titles and money after the war, and he did his best to repair relations. Unsuccessfully: Queen Elizabeth the Queen Mother did not forgive the Duke of Windsor for his dereliction of duty.

Mountbatten had a greater sense of duty and was much more energetic than Edward, and always deplored the abdication. But he and Edwina had the same relaxed attitude to infidelity, and like the former king, Mountbatten was thought a bit 'too much'. He certainly lived in high style and had an almost endearing streak of vanity. He and Montgomery once counted each other's medals and when Mountbatten found he had one decoration fewer, he got himself awarded two more. He was inclined to woo the media rather than shunning them. For the Windsor dynasty, who had come to believe that success was about being comparatively quiet and subdued, it may have seemed a dangerously flamboyant style which had been tested and found wanting back in the 1930s. After the Duke of Windsor died Mountbatten claimed, perhaps more kindly than accurately, that he had been 'my best friend all my life'.[27]

The Queen Mother had spread a strong antipathy to that best friend throughout her family, and it is possible that a certain suspicion of Mountbatten passed to her daughter. It would not be surprising if there was a certain ambiguity about him in the Duke's mind too. So Mountbatten's strong influence on Prince Charles is a little more complicated than it might first seem. He was, as Charles said of himself while laying the wreath at Mountbatten's funeral, an 'honorary grandson' who had been emotionally supported by the older man for many years. This, however, is a story that must wait. If George V, her grandfather, Uncle David, Mountbatten and, of course, her father, George VI, were all shaping influences on the Queen, so too – of course – was her mother.

Queen Elizabeth

Queen Elizabeth as she was properly known, or the Queen Mother, as she was mostly known for the second half of her life, ended up as much loved granny figure. 'Mummy' to the Queen, to millions of her subjects she was an idealized doughty old duck, with a twinkle in her eye and a decent-sized drink near at hand. She seemed to have been always there. For almost everyone alive by the year 2000 that was literally true. Born in 1900, she lived for slightly more than the twentieth century. She was alive during the reigns of six monarchs: Queen Victoria, Edward VII, her father-in-law George V, Edward VIII, her husband George VI and her daughter Elizabeth II. To Britons old enough to remember, she was above all a living link to the Second World War and the Blitz in particular. Her comment after Buckingham Palace was bombed, that at last she could 'now look the East End in the face', was the most famous thing she ever said.

She seemed to some to overshadow her daughter when the two were present together. The Queen's family say she depended heavily on her mother as a sounding-board and source of fun. She was a flirt with men and well into her nineties enjoyed the company of a male with a raffish twinkle in his eye. She liked stories about 'naughty' friends and relatives and recommended the stories of Maupassant about love and romance. She possessed natural charisma, shrewd intelligence and could be very funny. The ballet choreographer Sir Frederick Ashton was a favourite dancing partner of the Queen Mother's at Sandringham when balls were held there. She would gesture to him when she wanted to dance. Once, as he went over to take her hand, the Queen herself interposed and suggested he dance with her. You cannot refuse your monarch. As they twirled round, passing the Queen Mother's table, she hissed at Ashton: 'Social climber!'

A good joke; and a characteristic one. For half her life she was a widow, but in general a merry one, whose role in the inner sanctum of 'the Firm' was enormously important. Strongly opinionated and occasionally steely to the point of cruelty, she was more interesting than her later public image of a little old lady who liked horses and gin-and-tonics and big pink hats. For one thing her drink of choice was gin and Dubonnet, a dreadful concoction, a taste for which she passed to her daughter. With those she felt relaxed around, she liked an argument and liked to win it, just as she liked to win at 'Racing Demon' – enough, it has to be said, to indulge in some outrageous cheating. Her husband's official biographer said of her that Queen Elizabeth had 'a small drop of arsenic at the centre of that marshmallow'.[28] She was famously vague about money and totted up large overdrafts. Yet her charisma, which in her day certainly rivalled that of Diana in hers, and her tough sense of Christian duty (the two were not alike in every way) kept her out of trouble.

Her strongly conservative views stayed mostly private and she became adept at blocking dangerous questions, or simply ignoring 'unwise' subjects, strategies passed down to her daughter. Nor was her conservatism simply partisan Tory beliefs. Queen Elizabeth was, for instance, passionately hostile to the Social Democratic Party, formed in the 1980s – but not because it was left of centre. She disliked the SDP because it had broken away from, and damaged, 'the good old Labour Party'. For her, loyalty was all. If Lord Stamfordham was the commoner who, with George V, created the House of Windsor, Queen Elizabeth was the aristocratic commoner who gave it much of its style and many of its codes.

'Commoner' might seem an odd word to use of the youngest daughter of the Earl of Strathmore, whose castle at Glamis in Angus could have been a setting for Disneyworld. Yet Lady Elizabeth Angela Marguerite Bowes Lyon, a vivacious, zest-filled and apparently sexy little dumpling of a girl, eventually became the first non-Royal to benefit from George V's rewriting of the family rules in 1917. She may have been brought up in a privileged family, with its fair share of bloodthirsty history, cads and romantic martyrs, and in a home with many ancient royal connections, but when she finally joined the royal family in 1923 she was looked on as an outsider and felt intimidated herself. The lack of precedent meant there was a rather pompous official debate about how exactly she would be described as the Duke of York's wife, and whether she would be a Royal Highness (she would). She herself replied to one of her oldest friends who had written asking how to address her: 'I really don't know! It might be <u>anything</u> – you might try "All Hail Duchess", that is an Alice in Wonderland sort of Duchess, or just "Greetings" or "What Ho, Duchess" or "Say, Dutch" – in fact you can please yourself . . .'[29]

Elizabeth had spent most of her girlhood in her family's southern house, St Paul's Walden Bury in Hertfordshire, with no fewer than nine older brothers and sisters. The girl called 'Buffy' by her family lived the golden Edwardian idyll as it still existed for a few, surrounded by servants and immaculate lawns, completely isolated from the Britain of Suffragette protests, trade union strikes and bitter political argument. It was a childhood of woodland rambles and hideouts, horses and

shooting parties, candlelit balls, in-jokes and family sing-alongs.
Elizabeth attended school only sporadically and most of her
education came from governesses, in particular a young
German woman who wrote in amazement about the grandness
and extravagance of life at Glamis Castle just before the First
World War. This lost world would leave some mark on
'Buffy's' daughter, because it put a very secure and self-certain
woman at the heart of the Windsor dynasty. She would pass
on much more than a love of horses and a fierce belief in
family loyalty to the current Queen.

The war brought out the old spirit of noblesse oblige as
Glamis and St Paul's Walden Bury were used for convalescent
soldiers, Lady Strathmore presiding over her hospitals. The
teenage Elizabeth knitted endlessly, packaged presents for
troops at the Front and stuffed sleeping bags. At Glamis, she
grew used to mingling with injured, plain-speaking working-
class men, an experience that would later help with her
'common touch'. During the war one brother, in the Black
Watch, was killed; another was taken prisoner (another had
already died after a cricket injury a few years earlier). Alongside
the privilege there was loss, grief and much dependence on
Christian prayer and church attendance, a quality inherited in
due course by her daughter.

Scottish-British patriotism and a passionate dislike of Germans were rooted in Elizabeth's character long before the
rise of Hitler. So, it has to be said, was her gusto for life –
food, music, dancing, parties, uncorked as soon as the war
ended. She was better educated than her own daughter, but
conspicuously failed at an open exam, writing afterwards,
'DAMN THE EXAM!! . . . What was the use of toiling down
to that – er – place Hackney? None, I tell you none. It makes
me boil with rage to think of that vile stuff, tapioca, eating for

– nothing? Oh hell . . . Yes, I am very disappointed . . .'[30] Given
the later criticism of her for failing to give Princess Elizabeth a
better and wider education, the tapioca may have a lot to
answer for. When she kept refusing Bertie, apart from being
uncertain about him, Elizabeth may have been properly nervous about the implications of becoming a 'Royal'. This was
an intensely formal, frock-coated and traditionalist court, presided over by a somewhat forbidding monarch. In a highly
revealing letter to Bertie, she wrote of Frogmore, the house by
Windsor Castle where Victoria's mausoleum was built: 'Having
never seen Frogmore, I imagine it as a large white Tomb full
of frogs! I can't think why, but that is the impression it gives
me – isn't it silly?'[31] She liked jazz and nightclubs, and ran into
trouble with George V when she and Bertie stayed out until
3 a.m. at a nightclub, the Follies, at London's Metropole Hotel.

William Shawcross, Elizabeth's official biographer, wrote
that upon her marriage she was entering 'a sort of golden
incarceration. The young Duchess could no longer go shopping
alone; she could not travel on trains alone, or on buses at all.
She was no longer able to see her friends as spontaneously as
she loved to do . . . All in all, the Duchess was isolated and
restricted in a way she had never been before.'[32] Her situation
was, in short, strikingly similar to that of another young
aristocratic woman who entered the family in 1981. Like Diana,
she proved an early hit with the public. Like Diana, she made
a particular success of an early tour of Australia, overshadowing
– as Diana did – her husband. Her smile was endlessly
discussed. Like her daughter, today's Queen, she would grit
her teeth and head off on extended royal tours leaving her own
children behind. If the Queen Mother and Princess Diana fell
out perhaps it was because of echoes in their stories, as well as
their differences of character and temperament. But did they?

It is most unlikely that we will ever know what they really felt about one another. As we shall see, Queen Elizabeth's daughter Princess Margaret burned the evidence in an inferno almost as tantalizing for the historian as the immolation of Lord Byron's diaries in his publisher's grate. Did the older Queen pass on tips and advice about the rare trick of becoming royal?

By the time the present Queen was born, her mother had already shown herself to be far wilier and shrewder than Diana would be. Elizabeth won over her growling father-in-law with apologetic letters, tact and charm. Formidable Queen Mary, pleased with her effect on her son, thawed too. And Elizabeth was quick to do her new duty as a cadet Windsor, picking up patronage duty, visiting duty, opening-things duty as if born to it. Above all though, despite those repeated refusals and perhaps against expectations, and certainly unlike Diana, she was sustained by a very happy marriage. Her influence on her daughter was perhaps less than her husband's.

She did not pass on her flirtatiousness or enthusiasm for racy gossip. The current Queen is more careful of money and more reserved than her mother was, and takes life more seriously. Yet when she died at the ripe age of 101 the Queen lost an extraordinarily close lifelong companion as well as a mother. Queen Elizabeth perhaps did her daughter her best service by passing on a passion for horse-racing, a world within a world where the Queen has been able to lighten up and forget human bloodlines for the even chancier business of equine ones.

Part Two

LILIBET

By now the reader might be feeling that in a book about the Queen we have spent long enough on her older relatives. But without knowing about them, it is quite impossible to understand her. Everyone is the product of family; but in the Royals' case the fusion of the personal and public makes the family history particularly significant. Almost everything about the Queen's public behaviour, from the time she spends with official boxes of paperwork and her attitude to public engagements and church services, to her annual pilgrimages from Windsor to Sandringham and Balmoral, or her solemnity in public and her suspicion of journalists, thrums and whirrs with the conscious DNA of Windsor traditions. The two last Georges, their Queens, and lesser royals of the twentieth century loom large today in the palaces. They hang in paintings, stare back from photographs and leave traces everywhere, in the furnishings and knick-knacks they once chose.

Of course Queen Victoria also casts a special spell in the rooms and palaces she created. She was the builder, in physical terms and in creating atmosphere. Her famous sense of morality, not overwhelmingly evident in British monarchy before, somehow suffuses the institution still, like background static. Without this history the Queen would not be the Queen. Without it Britain would be a slightly different place. The Hanoverians and Windsors have distinctive faces but a wide range of temperaments, from dutiful to reckless, careful to carefree, pious to naughty. The Queen is clearly on the dutiful, careful and pious end of the register. Even in very early photos, she stares back with a calm, unruffled and distinctly Windsor self-assurance.

So where do we start? At the birth of the first daughter, in the middle of a national crisis, to the second son of the King in a private house in central London? At a writing desk in Sagana Lodge in Kenya twenty-five years later, where a composed young woman is catching up on holiday letters, when her husband walks in to tell her that her father has died of a heart attack? Or at one of the dramatic moments in her long life after that, such as the apparent assassination attempt when she was riding her horse in the Mall? Different biographers have gone for different moments; but the true story of a human life begins with birth and the earliest years: this life is no different. The Queen was born into a world of quiet, calm, order and privilege. But outside the walls of 17 Bruton Street, Mayfair, where she was delivered by Caesarean section at 2.40 a.m. on 21 April 1926, Britain was a riven nation.

Days later, on 3 May, a General Strike would begin, which many thought would be the start of a socialist or communist revolution of the kind that had swept away some of the baby's relatives in Europe nine years before. As it happened, Britain would be spared political upheaval. The conservative, patriotic temperament of the middle classes would be shored up by its monarchy; and Elizabeth, whose birth was greeted by a modest group of well-wishers outside, would become its greatest twentieth-century monarch. One of the shrewdest historians of the period, David Cannadine, says she was a child of two worlds: 'She is a child of aristocracy, her mother of course was an aristocrat, not a Royal, and she was a child of empire – her father and her grandfather were emperors of India, and that was part of the apparently eternal order of things in 1926.'[1]

Bruton Street today is a small street of expensive art galleries, restaurants and car showrooms between Berkeley Square, where once the nightingales sang, and New Bond Street, where the fashion victims stalk. The Strathmores' house has been knocked down. In 1926, the Queen's parents were staying there after rejecting life in a pretty but unmodernized stuccoed country house in Richmond Park, which had been offered to them by the King – and which is now the Royal Ballet School, featured in the plimsolls-to-fame tale *Billy Elliot*. They had wanted somewhere more central, more convenient and cosier.

Four physicians of the utmost fame attended the Duchess and after a difficult labour, Buckingham Palace was told of the birth of a daughter early the following morning. During those tumultuous days leading to the General Strike the Duke of York was anxiously attending Commons debates. The King had made his feelings of private sympathy for the miners clear to one coal-owner: 'Try living on their wages before you judge them' he had replied to Lord Durham's outburst against 'damned revolutionaries'. (The interests of monarchy are not identical to the interests of big money; monarchy needs stability even more than money does.)

George V's government felt it was facing social breakdown and anarchy and was mobilizing the middle and upper classes to do their bit against the trade unions' militant eruption. The home secretary Sir William Joynson-Hicks, a peppery man, was obliged to break off preparations for the political crisis to be present at the princess's birth. This was a silly old tradition, said to date back to the suspicion that James II's wife smuggled in a male baby after a fake pregnancy, part of a Catholic plot which provoked the invasion of Britain by the Dutch in 1688. It probably had more to do with the old habit of courtiers crowding round the Royals at important moments, even into the birthing rooms. Either way, even in 1926 it felt a bit odd. Having a sense of tradition also means knowing which traditions to quietly drop.

In all this, one might have expected the Queen's birth to be little discussed. Though she was third in line to the throne, her uncle and his brother were both still comparatively young men. If her mother produced a son later on he would, under British laws of succession, have immediately leap-frogged Elizabeth. So it did not seem particularly likely that this golden-haired infant would one day reign. It is worth remembering that had George VI, her father, lived to a decent age, he could still have been on the throne well into the 1970s. Yet the birth of the Duke of York's daughter did capture the attention of newspapers, perhaps scrabbling around in dark days for some good, light news, and did attract an immediate small crowd in the street, which stayed for weeks. One newspaper speculated about her becoming a future Queen Elizabeth; but the overall tone was simply one of welcome for another young member of what was, by modern standards, still a small royal family, rather short on children.

Elizabeth was christened in Buckingham Palace with water from the River Jordan and cried during the service. She was soon put under the wing of Clara Cooper, or 'Alah' Knight, the brisk, lanky daughter of a Hertfordshire farmer who had looked after her mother from one month old. That summer the baby was taken to Glamis Castle, her mother's family's home, then back to London. But by January 1927, when she was nine months old, her parents left her for a 30,000-mile, six-month sea voyage to Australia and New Zealand. Her mother was upset to leave the baby; but the Empire called. Elizabeth would stay behind with her nurse and grandparents. Before she could have been conscious of it, the competing demands of royal work and family life were tugging in opposite directions. Is this proof of the brutal assessment of one royal librarian, who said that 'the House of Hanover, like ducks, produce bad parents; they trample on their young . . .'² Not really.

In the 1920s the upper classes saw far less of their children than would be considered normal now. Nurses, nannies and boarding schools left parents freer to pursue their adult lives. Today, we might think it heartless. Then it was ordinary. Beyond that, however, the weight of Crown and Empire rested on the Windsors with a gravity outsiders cannot properly understand. For seventy years, five monarchs – Victoria, Edward VII, George V, Edward VIII and George VI – carried the 'I' of Imperator, or Emperor, after the 'R' of kingship, and RI meant a global role. These people felt they themselves were a part of world history and had the job of carrying the story through to the next generation. If there were doubts about the longer-term loyalty of Australia and New Zealand to the Empire, then it was absolutely the job of the family to do their best to mend things. The yearning of a mother for a baby was a lesser matter. Hard choices; tougher people.

In fact, Elizabeth had a warmer upbringing than many of the children of the great aristocratic dynasties of inter-war Britain. Hers was a close, physically affectionate family. We know a lot about that upbringing because of the indiscretion of the Princess's governess, Marion Crawford, who lived with the family for sixteen years, from 1933 to 1949, and who then wrote a book, *The Little Princesses*, in 1950 about her experiences. Crawford, a Scottish teacher who had wanted to work with deprived children, had been recommended to the Yorks by titled relatives and became by all accounts a dedicated and energetic tutor to the girls. Since her book was published more than sixty years ago, former royal servants have gone public with much ruder and wilder accounts of life at Buckingham Palace. Crawford's book contains not a single damning fact or serious embarrassment of any kind. Elizabeth emerges as very serious and orderly but sweet-natured, kind and loving. Yet when 'Crawfie's' book was published, the retired governess was brutally cut off from all contact with the royal family. After a short and ignominious career as a magazine journalist she went into effective exile, having long delayed her marriage – not a happy one, in the end. When she died, no member of the royal family came to her funeral. Her name is never mentioned.

This is a story worth dwelling on. It is a strange one. 'Crawfie', after all – the nickname was given to her by Elizabeth herself – was someone who knew the Queen intimately and for a long time, during her formative years. Perhaps it was the fact that 'Crawfie' felt almost like family that made her behaviour seem so hurtful. Her crime was by today's standards a comparatively venial one: her affection, even adoration, for her charges shines through her writing. So why the intense anger, the guillotine blade of silence? The answer is that she was the first. Before her no intimate of the Windsors had 'blabbed'. Royal life is not private in the way most of us understand privacy. Even when not on public view the royal family is almost constantly surrounded by valets, maids, butlers, police protection officers, drivers and the like. Royal family members barely draw an unobserved breath. They know there is an insatiable interest in the smallest aspects of their lives and the briefest comment they make. Few of us could a bear a life under constant surveillance and commentary – imagine being

Nobody dreamt she would be Queen:
the baby Elizabeth with the Duke
and Duchess of York.

She preferred horses, even then.

Learning the ropes
in a family firm:
Princess Elizabeth
in 1932 after a
church service
near Balmoral,
with her formidable
grandmother,
Queen Mary, and
the man she called
'Grandpa England',
George V.

A future king, already
looking out of place?
The Prince of Wales, later
Edward VIII (*left*), and the
young Louis Mountbatten,
in a canvas swimming pool
on HMS *Renown* during
an imperial trip, 1920.

Too 'modern' for monarchy:
'Uncle David' with his niece,
Princess Elizabeth, in 1933.

'We four': a happy and private family before the storm, 1936.

Thrilled, nevertheless: Princess Elizabeth, royal note-taker, after her father's Coronation as George VI.

An exuberant Prince Philip of Greece prepares to entertain the young princesses during George VI's visit to Dartmouth Royal Naval College, 1939.

Early training for public performances: Princesses Elizabeth and Margaret in a private pantomime of *Aladdin* at Windsor, 1943.

Her most important teacher: Princess Elizabeth with her father, 1946.

Above left There were many rumoured suitors: Princess Elizabeth dancing with the son of the Marquess of Abergavenny at her first public ball in 1946.

Above A rare escape from Austerity Britain: playing tag with midshipmen aboard HMS *Vanguard* en route to South Africa for the post-war royal visit, 1947.

The secret is out. Princess Elizabeth and Prince Philip of Greece together at the wedding of Patricia Mountbatten and Lord Brabourne, 1946.

Watch your tongue, Daddy: the infant Princess Anne with Prince Philip, Princess Elizabeth and Prince Charles in 1951.

Above The final farewell. King George VI waves goodbye to his daughter at London airport, 31 January 1952.

Right Queen Elizabeth II, in black, arrives in what is now her kingdom seven days later.

Children in the East End get news of a knees-up.

The most solemn moment: 2 June 1953.

watched while eating breakfast, brushing your hair, dressing, exercising, finishing a last night-time drink. So the discreet silence of those around them is not merely convenient. It is basic to living a tolerable life, to having some at least semi-private space. Inside Buckingham Palace, even senior aides take great care to avoid bumping into the Queen or Duke by accident; this is to give them a little space of their own.

So, there is a shield wall around the senior Royals. Inside it, utter loyalty is expected. Crawford did not simply tell a few bland stories about the colour of wallpapers, or sweet things little Princess Margaret said. She yanked open the curtain on a sensitive part of Princess Elizabeth's life, her childhood and adolescent years, when the Queen's personality was forming. Having done that, Crawford continued writing about her, from presumed knowledge, in the press. Imagine how Elizabeth must have felt, eyeing up old and trusted staff in front of whom she needed to be occasionally off guard and relaxed, and wondering always – will your book be the next one? Back in the 1950s Elizabeth had no way of knowing how intrusively her family's lives would be prodded, not least by renegade members of the family itself. Marion Crawford may have been silly, even greedy, but she was not wicked nor, by her lights, disloyal. With royalty there are harsher rules. Cross a line and you are exiled.

And yet, having said all this, anyone truly interested in the Queen has had their imagination fed for years on the anecdotes and descriptions Crawford gave. The historian A. N. Wilson has gone as far as to say that because she lived so long with the princesses, and because childhood is the most interesting part of life, 'Crawfie will remain the most important Royal historian of the twentieth century and her book will deserve to be read when all the constitutional experts and all the spies at

Royal keyholes of the present generation have been forgotten.'[3] By royal standards, if not by Crawfie's, it makes sense to call this disloyalty.

So what does this unconventional historian tell us? That the Queen had a very happy, very secure childhood, underpinned by her mother's gusto, her father's attentiveness and her sister's companionship. There is enough detail of bath-time romps, dressing up, horseplay and laughter to be wholly convincing. George VI, both as Duke of York and King, was a physically active parent, keen on riding lessons and games with his daughters. It has been well said that he had a sense of fun, rather than a sense of humour; but for small children, the former is much more important. He liked cards and charades and mimicry and play-acting, and so did his daughters. The Duchess had written a note for him in case of her death, reminding him 'not to ridicule your children or laugh at them. When they say funny things it is usually quite innocent . . . always try & talk very quietly to children . . . Remember how your father, by shouting at you, & making you feel uncomfortable, lost all your real affection. None of his sons are his friends . . .'[4]

Whether or not George needed this excellent advice, his daughters were his friends. They lived for much of the time in a rather oddly extended Victorian house called Royal Lodge, now lived in by Prince Andrew, the Duke of York. It stands in the grounds of Windsor Great Park and had been rebuilt in the 1840s but was in poor shape and was renovated and extended by George. It is surrounded by huge trees and a chapel and beautiful gardens, and, once there, one could be a hundred miles from London. It also contains the miniature thatched and plastered Welsh cottage, a gift to Princess Elizabeth from 'the people of Wales' in 1932. It is much larger than a doll's house, with fully fitted rooms, including a 1930s bathroom and kitchen. Recently renovated by the Queen's granddaughter Princess Beatrice, it is very much the place where she and Princess Margaret played as girls, and the Queen still likes to visit it.

Later, after the family had left their last private house, a tall building facing Green Park across Piccadilly, which was bombed during the war and has now disappeared, the King would begin to educate Elizabeth in her constitutional role, ensuring that she read newspapers, understood public affairs and had a good grounding in politics. But from her early years, the tight 'we four' of the family gave her a sense of security and belonging she has never lost. If this was an abnormal family in its wealth, role and history, it was also a version of the 'Janet and John' foursome-family emerging in the suburbs of 1930s Britain.

Yet Crawford also shows that the princesses were almost entirely cut off from ordinary life. They had no friends outside a tight circle of relatives and a few high-born families. If the world was gawping through railings at the young girls playing Red Indians in a private London park, the princesses were staring back from upstairs windows at the traffic and crowds outside. Crawford's account emphasizes an isolation, which the deliveries of *Punch* magazines and visits of solemn-faced politicians hardly mitigated. There were attempts to take the girls into the real world of London, a trip on the Underground and to a YWCA, museum visits, a ride on a bus and excursions to swimming baths. Yet as soon as the princesses were spotted, unless people had been cleared away in advance, the fast-forming crowds and shouting made it difficult to continue. Soon a campaign by the IRA created 'security issues', which would dog Elizabeth all her life, another reason to build high that wall. When she moved to Buckingham Palace, a Girl Guide group was formed to help the princesses enjoy some relationships with girls their own age. It was a successful experiment but not a radical one: the other Guides and Brownies were all the daughters of relatives, noble families and courtiers. The Queen's curiosity about the lives of her subjects is real.

The likely future course of her life unrolled ahead of her by the time she was just ten. But her emotionally secure start allowed her to march down that claret-coloured carpet uncomplainingly. The Queen's character in her eighties is strikingly similar to the character described when she was a toddler and child. There was angst, rebellion, psychological damage and transformation in her family's story. There has been almost none of it in her formative years. Around her, uncles, sisters, sons and in-laws have misbehaved, raged against fate, or simply made bad personal choices. With only one significant exception, her marriage to Prince Philip, she has done nothing against the grain of what was expected. She has uttered not a single shocking phrase in public. There are no reliable recorded incidents of her losing her temper, using bad language or refusing to carry out a duty expected of her. People close to her speak of her wry wit, her talent for mimicry and her very shrewd intelligence, helped by an extraordinary memory for people and events. Outside a tiny circle, none of this is seen. She has a lovely, lightbulb-on smile. But, as if to save electricity, it quickly snaps off. (It is more often merely that she is concentrating.) Her most often used and most effective tactic is silence. Politicians say she is a mistress of the icy silence, the 'you may go now' silence, the 'I disagree' silence and the plain 'you make the running' silence. Otherwise, she understates by instinct.

Or, rather, by upbringing: the Queen grew up in a Lost World of Understatement, where people knew their place and protocol so well that these things were unspoken. Many have rebelled against that world; others find in it a strange freedom. In the inter-war years, details of title, degree, dress and address still mattered very much. She was born when the hierarchies of aristocracy, honour or chivalry were taken seriously by the middle classes, looking upwards – professional and business people who were themselves graded like the lines of sediment on a cliff face. It was a time when newspaper-reading working-class people could generally tell the difference between an earl and a duke and when 'respectable' was an accolade that mattered.

As scores of novels and plays remind us, this was changing. Beyond the Palace gates and the Bruton Street doors the great handbook of 'Society' had begun to lose its pages and then fall apart, after the 'Great War'. The aristocratic families had lost disproportionate numbers of the sons who were meant to inherit, and to keep the bloodlines going. Democratic politics, which was only fully established in Britain in the Queen's lifetime – women got the vote on equal terms to men only when she was two – would push meritocratic ideas ahead. No longer was birth, destiny. Money replaced breeding. This cultural revolution would eventually take the British to a point where the only person in the country who seemed to know her place in the old way sat at its lonely apex – the Queen herself.

The dominant event in her young life was of course the moment her father became king, after which she was next in line (the Heiress Presumptive, not the Heir Apparent, because being female she was only 'presumed' to succeed). Though the Yorks' home at 145 Piccadilly had been a place of strain and nervous tension as the drama unfolded outside, the princesses had been protected from much of what was happening. It seems that it was Crawford who told them. Her account is worth quoting: 'When I broke the news to Margaret and Lilibet that they were going to live in Buckingham Palace they looked at me in horror. "What!" Lilibet said. "You mean for ever?"' On the day of the proclamation, when Bertie left 'looking very grave' and dressed as an Admiral of the Fleet, 'I had to explain to them that when Papa came home to lunch at one o'clock he would be King of England and they would have to curtsey to him. The royal children from their earliest years had always curtseyed to their grandparents. "And now you mean we must do it to Papa and Mummie?" Lilibet asked. "Margaret too?" "Margaret also," I told her, "and try not to topple over."' When the King returned they curtseyed: 'I think perhaps nothing that had occurred had brought the change in his condition to him as clearly as this did. He stood for a moment touched and taken aback. Then he stooped and kissed them both warmly.'

The move to Buckingham Palace was more of a shock. Her mother described it as the worst move of her life, and Crawford found it uncomfortable in the extreme, painting a picture of a gloomy dilapidated grandeur, with awkwardly placed electrical fittings, endless corridors and chilly rooms infested with mice. It was not the courtiers or footmen which impressed Crawford but the sinister-sounding figure of the Palace Vermin Man who patrolled with various weapons including the 'sticky trap' – a piece of cardboard with a lump of aniseed in the middle, surrounded by a sea of treacle. Eventually the new royal family made Buckingham Palace, that grand hotel and staff head-quarters of British monarchy, rather more comfortable, but Marion Crawford remembered her first night there 'with a shudder . . . The wind moaned in the chimneys like a thousand ghosts, I was homesick as I had not been for a long time . . .'

Another child might have been traumatized not just by the move from a familiar house into a walled institution, but at the huge change in her likely future fate. One account claims that Elizabeth prayed furiously hard for a brother to be born. Perhaps. It smacks of a novel. Princess Margaret said later that she had asked Elizabeth whether it all meant she herself would one day be Queen: 'She replied, "Yes, I suppose it does." '⁵ But she did not mention the matter again and seems to have been, in her tidy, quiet way, relatively calm about it all. After the great event of her father's Coronation on 12 May 1937 she wrote her own account of it for her parents. It is the product of a cheerful, literal and eleven-year-old sensibility, finding the end of the service 'rather boring as it was all prayers', enthusiastic about the 'sandwiches, stuffed rolls, orangeade and lemonade' that followed, and exhausted by the day's end. But Elizabeth was clearly excited rather than intimidated by her initiation into the family business: 'I thought it all <u>very, very</u> wonderful and I expect the Abbey did, too. The arches and beams at the top were covered with a sort of haze of wonder as Papa was crowned, at least I thought so.' These are not the words of a girl horrified at the prospect of one day being Queen herself. In 1937, with a father still young, that day would have seemed unimaginably distant. But from now on, the Princess was treated with even greater enthusiasm and interest by the press, and learned – not least from her grandmother Mary – the solemn public demeanour expected of royalty.

Demeanour aside, how much was she learning? She never went to school. It has been often said that the Queen is therefore badly educated, lacking the formal curriculum and structure of a normal classroom. Crawford included examples of the timetable she had drawn up, and Queen Mary's advice on extra lessons; she also complained about the habit of the

Duchess, later Queen Elizabeth, of interfering and taking her daughters away from study for more enjoyable and frivolous times. Neither Crawford nor Queen Mary were much impressed by Queen Elizabeth's response to a request for more books. They arrived, but they were all by P. G. Wodehouse. Yet Elizabeth had a good French governess and learned fluent French early on. She did not face a long school day, and there was emphasis on dancing, drawing and riding alongside the French, maths and history; but overall it was a perfectly respectable curriculum.

By the time Elizabeth was thirteen, she was being taught some history by the Royal Archivist and was sent to Eton for lessons in constitutional history by the school's eccentric Vice-Provost Henry Marten, notorious for chewing his hankies and eating lumps of sugar kept in his pockets. Her sister Margaret always regretted not being similarly tutored. Meanwhile the King began to show Elizabeth state papers, and gently talk her through the duties she would one day have to take on. So it is not true to say the Queen was badly educated. She was just differently educated. She was, and is, very fast at absorbing information and always had remarkable powers of concentration. From early on, she became shrewd at sizing up people, and good at recalling names and faces. Going to school might have helped her understand non-royal life but the lack of a boarding-school education certainly did not cripple her intellectually.

A Sailor Prince

The one event in Elizabeth's life in the run-up to the Second World War that 'everyone knows' is that, aged thirteen, she clapped eyes on Prince Philip of Greece, a boisterous eighteen-year-old cadet at the Royal Naval College at Dartmouth. It happened in July 1939. She was there with her parents on a two-day visit from the Royal Yacht, the *Victoria and Albert*. Prince Philip was deputed to look after the girls – by himself, apparently, because of an outbreak of mumps among the other cadets. He played games with them, jumped over tennis nets, wolfed down platefuls of food and generally romped, ending by rowing his boat after the departing Royal Yacht until the King had to bellow at him to go back. There is a telling photograph, the first to show the two of them in the same frame. Elizabeth is looking intently at whatever is being paraded, solemn and rather alone. In the back of the picture, Philip is guffawing at some joke.

Censorious Crawfie thought Philip had showed off rather too much, but Elizabeth was delighted and she never took her eyes off him. Friends say she never has since. She began a correspondence with the Prince, which continued through the coming war, as he served with the navy in the Mediterranean and Far East. She put his photograph up in her bedroom. When she was chided for giving succour to gossips, she swapped it for one of Philip in a big, bushy beard, which she hoped disguised him, a not entirely effective stratagem. So for her it seems to have been love at first sight. It wasn't quite, because the two had met before, at a royal wedding, and at the 1937 Coronation; but unmemorable encounters between children barely count. True love, the classic *coup de foudre*, is rare enough to make the Queen a lucky woman.

To start with, it did not seem that way to everyone at the Palace. Philip was relatively poor and came from a scattered family, rescued by the Royal Navy after Greek republicans turned on his father, Prince Andrew of Greece, an army officer, in the wake of a disastrous war against Kemal Ataturk's resurgent nationalist Turks. But Philip was no stranger to the British Royals. His mother had been born at Windsor Castle and he was related to Princess Elizabeth through multiple cousin connections, reaching back to Queen Victoria and Prince Albert, who were great-great-grandparents of them both. His family was Danish, if anything, but really one of those royal hyphenated ones, purveyors of monarchs and princess wives to half of monarchical Europe.

The Greek connection had happened because after the country became independent of the Ottoman Empire in 1830 the 'protecting powers' of Britain, France and Russia insisted Greece be headed by an imported monarch. This was meant to limit the chance of civil war. The first choice proved no good. Then in 1862 a teenage prince from Copenhagen, Philip's grandfather, was selected as King George I. Though he proved popular and assiduous, assassination, a poisonous monkey-bite and various political revolts made Greek kingship a chancy business. The family, with strong German roots, tried to sit on the fence during the First World War. Philip's father, Andrew, was a dedicated soldier who had done his best in the war against Turkey which followed the botched Versailles peace. He had become one of the scapegoats for a humiliating national failure of 1921, promptly followed by a coup, another unhappy Greek tradition.

Prince Andrew might well have been executed by firing squad. Others similarly accused were. However, the Queen's trusty 'Grandpa England', George V, intervened, perhaps feeling guilty about his non-intervention after the fall of Tsar Nicholas. A British agent fixed things so that, in return for accepting exile, Andrew and his family would be allowed to escape. This they duly did from Corfu, where the bulk of the family had been living, by British destroyer. The infant Prince Philip slept in an orange-box as he went into exile with his parents and four older sisters. The family made their way to Rome, London and eventually to Paris, where they settled at a family-owned home, surrounded by other Greek exiles and the prince's brothers. During the 1920s they enjoyed a relatively settled and comfortable family life there, but eventually Prince Philip's parents separated. His mother, Princess Alice, became mentally ill, possibly with bipolar disorder, and certainly suffering from a form of religious mania, and was treated by Freudians, forcibly removed from her family and ending up in a Swiss clinic. She was therefore effectively separated from her son for much of his childhood, including the crucial years between the ages of ten and fifteen. She later became a nun in the Greek Orthodox Church and an intensely spiritual and almost saintly individual who nursed the injured and took great risks to save Jews in Athens during the war.

Philip is seen as a rough, no-nonsense man, but has reserves of spiritual interest which may be connected to the example of his unusual and little-known mother. She spent the last part of her life in London living with the rest of the royal family, much loved and admired. His father, meanwhile, wrote a book of war memoirs to defend his reputation and settled down in Cannes with a mistress whose claim to being an aristocrat was perhaps not soundly based. He never returned to his wife, even after her recovery. This being the Riviera in its grandest and most artistic flowering, it cannot have been a bad kind of exile. He too, however, had cut himself off from the son whose company he had once enjoyed. Questioned later in life about this, Philip shrugged it off as something he just had to get on with, but if he has been a defensive and somewhat suspicious adult, it is not 'psychobabble' to point to this disrupted childhood.

Prince Philip found some sense of stability in schools and from his mother's relatives in Britain, starting with his grandmother Victoria – herself a granddaughter of Queen Victoria. As important, however, were his mother's brothers, the Battenbergs, now known as the Milford Havens and the Mountbattens after the 1917 revolution of the names. George, Marquess of Milford Haven, was a particular help. Married to Nada, a wildly exotic Russian, he offered the young Philip a genuine haven during school holidays. After starting his education at an experimental American school in Paris, aged nine he went to the prep school Cheam, and after that to a boarding school at Salem in Germany, owned by relatives – unfortunately, just as the Nazis were coming to power. He was a multilingual, cosmopolitan boy, fluent in Greek and French as well as English, and with some German. His royal relatives were scattered all over Europe and he seemed always on the move, from schloss to palace, estate to hotel. But it was the close German connections which caused the most heartache later on.

All Philip's sisters married German princes who stuck with their country in the Nazi years, though only two of the brothers-in-law were still alive by 1945. His sister Sophie married Christoph Hesse, who joined the Nazi party and the SS, serving during the war in the Luftwaffe. His sister Cecile married Don Hesse, another prince, who also joined the Nazis. His sister Theodora married the Margrave of Baden, less keen on the Nazis but serving Germany through the war. His oldest sister Margarita married Friedel Hohenlohe-Langenburg, who joined the Nazi party too, and offered to introduce its leaders to British royalty.[6.] These sibling connections explain the later over-emphatic tone of British newspaper coverage explaining Philip's 'essential Englishness' when he became betrothed to Elizabeth – the result of a campaign of shameless spinning and

elbow-grabbing of editors by Mountbatten. The German connection divided him from most of his close family throughout
the Second World War and ensured that the groom's side of
the aisle was sparse when he married.

Philip's time at the German school in Salem was relatively
brief. He watched the steady advance of Nazi ideology in the
classrooms and appears to have found it all mildly risible.
Salem's visionary founder, Kurt Hahn, had already fled Germany, but would become a huge influence on Philip when
he too left Germany for Britain again. Hahn was one of the
great teaching visionaries of early twentieth-century Europe. A
brilliant Jewish intellectual who had been private secretary to
Imperial Germany's last Chancellor, Hahn believed Western
society had been badly corrupted, most recently by the cruelty
and militarism of the First World War. The next generation
must be better educated in morals and civic duty, he concluded,
and had devised the school accordingly. Though initially admiring of Hitler, Hahn became quickly disillusioned. He was briefly
imprisoned and eventually had to escape to Britain via Switzer-
land (the Labour prime minister Ramsay MacDonald intervened
on his behalf). In Scotland, Hahn set up another school, Gordonstoun, in the north-east of Scotland, urged on by influential
and rich admirers. Prince Philip was one of the earliest pupils.

Thus one exile moulded another. Hahn thought teenagers
had an inner sense of right and wrong, but had to be helped to
find it, which could best be done by testing them mentally but
also through physical exertion and adventures. Gordonstoun's
mix of cold baths, early runs, relentless outdoor activity and
social work was not so different from that of other progressive
boarding schools at the time, but it was undeniably tough.
Hahn wrote, 'Education must enable young people to effect
what they have recognized to be right, despite hardships,

despite dangers, despite inner skepticism, despite boredom, and despite mockery from the world . . .' and also, 'It is the sin of the soul to force young people into opinions – indoctrination is of the devil – but it is culpable neglect not to impel young people into experiences.'

Hahn would go on to found other schools, as well as the Outward Bound movement. But his influence is most clearly felt in modern Britain through the Duke of Edinburgh's Award Scheme, which reflects Hahn's belief in the importance of adventure and the toughening effect of a little adversity. (Hahn was the opposite of the educational experimenters who thought that children would grow to be kinder by being coddled.) He was no kind of locum parent but Hahn seems to have been a big influence in the way the young prince turned out – the Duke of Edinburgh's lack of self-pity, his belief in practicality, his defiantly rough edges, his well-hidden spiritual side and his interest in nature can be traced back not just to the buffeting of his unusual family life but to the Gordonstoun ethic.

As he left school, Hahn gave Philip a thoughtful final report, noting his recklessness, sense of service and intelligence. He said he was 'often naughty, never nasty'. Philip's debt to Hahn has been passed on in areas such as the plight of inner-city youth and the environment (interests in turn passed on to Charles). The Hahn-influenced Outward Bound rules, for instance, say, 'A direct and respectful relationship with the natural world refreshes the human spirit and teaches the important ideas of recurring cycles and cause and effect. Students learn to become stewards of the earth and of future generations.' How many royal speeches of the past half-century have echoed that? Quite a lot.

Prince Philip himself was tested very toughly: in 1937 another terrible family disaster struck when his sister Cecile and her husband the Grand Duke of Hesse were killed in an air crash. The pair had been flying with their two young sons to a wedding in London when the plane went down over Belgium, killing everyone on board, including the princess's stillborn fourth child. A lone surviving daughter, who had not been on the flight, died two years later of meningitis. Not long after that, George Milford Haven, who had been so kind to the young prince, died of cancer. Already with a tough protective shell, the double blows must nevertheless have hit the adolescent boy very hard.

After Gordonstoun, Philip joined the Royal Navy, going through the same training at Dartmouth that his uncle Mountbatten and Georges V and VI had experienced. He has said that he would have preferred being a fighter pilot in the RAF and there was some family pressure to join the Greek navy, but the British navy was an obvious choice. A recent biography has pointed out that, had Philip followed his heart, there must have been a high chance that he would have been killed in the Battle of Britain. But this was a choice of nationality as much as of fighting service. Philip remained a prince of Greece at a time when, however briefly, its royal family seemed to be coming back into favour. He could, in different circumstances, have hoped to be a king in Athens. The family pull in London, and perhaps the lure of a much bigger and more exciting power, was greater. If there had been any doubt as to the true nationality of this Danish-Greek-German boy who had had a French-American, English and Scottish education, then it was ended by the war, which saw him fight hard for Britain against the forces in which his sisters' husbands served.

For he had what people used to call 'a good war'. Prince Philip was first posted to the Indian Ocean, perhaps to keep him, as a Greek citizen, out of direct action. It was only after the summer of 1940 when Greece entered the conflict that he saw real fighting in the Mediterranean on the battleship HMS *Valiant*. At the Battle of Cape Matapan, using his searchlight to pick out Italian cruisers, which were duly sunk, Philip was mentioned in despatches. He was posted to a destroyer, becoming the youngest first lieutenant in the Royal Navy and serving in the North Sea. In July 1943 his ship HMS *Wallace* was involved in the invasion of Sicily and was saved from a night-time bomber attack by a trick Philip dreamed up, leaving a burning fake 'ship' as a decoy. Later, he served in the Far East as the Pacific war against Japan entered its final stages and witnessed the Japanese surrender. He was clearly a brave and talented sailor, but told his biographer Gyles Brandreth that he did not believe he would have progressed to the top of the service had he remained in it as a full-time career: 'Given the way of the British press, I wouldn't have got very far. Every promotion would have been seen as me being treated as a special case.'[7]

By the time the war ended, when Philip was seriously considering proposing to Princess Elizabeth, his character had been sufficiently well catalogued for him to be recognizably the same man he is today, aged ninety. Some things have changed, of course: he was flirtatious and physically boisterous, with a huge enthusiasm for practical jokes and sending up older people. That has gone. But as a naval officer he was considered both ingenious and energetic – and also peppery and abrasive. He was prepared to challenge anyone's opinion, and an extrovert, very different from his serious and shy future wife. He could be startlingly rude. Yet he was also guarded, sensitive and thoughtful and would give his children the close parenting he himself never had. Thus the sinewy paradox who has spent sixty years walking in the Queen's shadow, but also at her side.

Windsor in Wartime

The war years were not, the Queen has said privately, a time
of great privation or danger for her. While the King and Queen
kept returning to Buckingham Palace and lived there through
the worst of the Blitz, the princesses themselves lived at
Windsor Castle, their whereabouts a national secret. This was
sensible. The royal family was a prime German target and if
the King was killed Berlin had good reason to hope his exiled
brother might be persuaded to return as a puppet monarch.
On 13 September 1940, George VI and Queen Elizabeth came
close to death when a German bomb hit the Palace. Had the
window in the room where they were standing been closed,
instead of open, they would have been terribly injured by
flying glass; one of the workmen nearby was killed. Showing
true phlegm, a policemen observed to the Queen that it had
been 'a magnificent piece of bombing, if I may say so, Ma'am'.
(There was a post-war rumour that the attack had been
directed by one of Prince Philip's brothers-in-law, but according
to Philip Eade's biography of Philip there seems no evidence
for it.)

   The Queen wrote to her mother-in-law the following day,
after visiting the East End, that 'I really felt as if I was walking
in a dead city'.[8] Her natural ebullience soon reasserted itself,
emerging clearly at the end of a letter to a cousin: 'I am still
just as frightened of bombs & guns going off, as I was at the
beginning. I turn bright red, and my heart hammers – in fact
I'm a beastly coward, but I do believe that a lot of people are,
so I don't mind! . . . Tinkety tonk old fruit, & down with the
Nazis'.[9] The Queen took up revolver practice in case it should
be necessary to make a final stand against German paratroopers

while the King carried a rifle and revolver with him, and practised with them in the grounds of Buckingham Palace.

For the princesses, life was less interesting. Windsor Castle became the future Queen's home, as she thinks of it still, but during the war it was a partly packed up and sandbagged home, protected by troops and anti-aircraft guns. Its thousand-plus rooms, staff of hundreds and ancient walls, now reinforced with steel and concrete and barbed wire, provided a refuge steeped in gloomy history. Crawford commented that it was a fortress, not a home. The princesses could follow the war on the radio, and socialize, a little, with officers stationed at Windsor, but it cut them off even further from normal life. They were rationed, and had to rush down to an air-raid shelter in the dungeon – Elizabeth protesting initially that she had to dress properly first – but saw little of the reality of the war. The death of the King's youngest brother the Duke of Kent in an aircraft crash in 1942 was the kind of blow to this family that others all over Britain were having to deal with.

One of the Queen's earlier biographers, Robert Lacey, reflected that the war confirmed her already formidable sense of duty: 'The atmosphere of 1939 did not encourage whimsicality in anybody. So Princess Elizabeth developed from a serious child into a serious girl with no discernable break in continuity, and any tendency to eccentricity or rebellion was stifled . . .'[10] Surrounded by grim national news, literally surrounded by the castle's stony royal history, Elizabeth had no chance to experience the freer, wilder adolescence that, for instance, her mother had enjoyed in the 1920s. Her solemnity and her sense of duty were not created during the war; but those years reinforced and sandbagged that side of her character.

It was not, of course, all grim. The Windsor enthusiasm

for games and dressing up expressed itself in annual Christmas pantomimes, in which both princess dressed and acted (anyone curious about the Queen's youthful legs can turn to the picture of her costumed as Aladdin). It was this performance that had Prince Philip, invited to stay at Windsor during his leave, roaring with laughter, and perhaps began to fire his serious interest in Elizabeth. The Queen said later that she thought the pantomimes were her father's way of beginning to prepare the girls for a life of performance, their first time up on a stage: although Margaret enjoyed them hugely, she did not. (Prince Charles, however, did greatly enjoy his early years in school plays, something the Queen found a little perplexing.)

The Girl Guiding continued; there were dances and picnics and childhood games. Philip appeared from time to time, blown in on a sea-salted wind. Much time was spent with her younger sister Margaret, born four years after Elizabeth, completing the 'we four' quartet of the family. For most of their childhood the girls dressed alike; but they were not alike. There were tales of girlish fights, with Margaret prone to bite her sister, who responded with sometimes cutting remarks about Margaret's weight and clumsiness.[11] Soon enough it was clear to her that if her sister was to be Queen, she was left in a lifelong shadow. She was said to have complained: 'I am nothing.' Elizabeth was reported as retorting, 'Margaret always wants what I want.' Later anecdotes have Elizabeth firmly if fondly rebuking Margaret for not paying enough attention to being polite in public and being 'good'.

Temperament is a mysterious ingredient, composed of one's placing in the family, as well as genes. Margaret, still only fifteen by the time the war ended, was her father's cheeky pet – funny, clever, musical and allowed liberties, while Elizabeth was being trained for the throne. No doubt Margaret acted up to her place in the family order, but her talents for biting wit, mimicry and music suggest a woman who would have flourished better in other circumstances. In the last two years of the war, Buckingham Palace employed an RAF war hero called Peter Townsend as the King's equerry. Margaret would eventually turn to him.

Elizabeth had obstinately petitioned her father to allow her to do war work more substantial than the odd radio broadcast or ceremonial position and she finally got her way when she joined the Auxiliary Territorial Service. In the ATS, she learned to service trucks, drive cars, take apart engines, and perform some of the drilling she would spend her adult life observing from podiums. It was a very rare chance for her to mix with others of her age, though she was never quite allowed to forget her position, being whisked away after training sessions and rarely enjoying frank conversations with the others. She tried to make friends and hoped to do more; but Hitler fell first. In practical terms her contribution to the war effort was showmanship: to have a pretty young princess in military uniform, wielding a spanner, made fine propaganda.

When VE day finally came, Elizabeth and Margaret were allowed by their father to mingle with the crowds outside Buckingham Palace, marching arm in arm in a small party up Piccadilly, into the Ritz and then on to Hyde Park, singing songs and cheering, before standing outside the Palace with the rest and calling for the King and Queen to appear. With their caps pulled down, and in the crowded streets, the girls were barely recognized, though a Dutch serviceman noticed them and thoughtfully made no fuss. One of those in the group, the Queen's great racing friend Lord Porchester, then in the Household Cavalry, recalled: 'Everyone was very jolly, linking arms in the streets and singing, "Run, Rabbit, Run",

"Hang out the Washing on the Siegfried Line", "Roll Out the Barrel", that sort of thing all night . . .' It is poignant that this almost unique escape into a fragment of street life remains an important memory for the Queen.

The following day, she and the rest of the royal family drove into the East End and then south London to visit the worst-hit of recent V2 rocket attack sites. The Londoners she came across then were the people of a different capital, a different country from the London and Britain of today. They were still overwhelmingly white, extraordinarily shabby and poorly washed compared with modern Londoners, many in uniform and the rest in wartime coupon-bought clothing; a tea-drinking, cigarette-smoking, wireless-addicted people who were turning against the class-bound Britain of before the war. There was another wild party when Japan surrendered on August 14 and the Princess wrote in her diary: 'Out in crowd, Whitehall, Mall, St J [James] St, Piccadilly, Park Lane, Constitution Hill, ran through Ritz. Walked miles, drank in Dorchester, saw parents twice, miles away, so many people.'[12]

As monarchy-addicted as ever, the people would shortly kick out the great wartime leader Winston Churchill and usher in a Labour government. George VI, despite his irascible suspicion of socialists, would come to terms with an adminis-tration of patriotic, anti-communist reformers and the years of socialism and the championing of equality. His daughter would have to find ways of reigning effectively in the country they remade – part-nationalized Britain of the NHS, new towns and powerful trade unions.

The old grand London the Princess and her friends had partied through, with its aristocratic palaces, hotels and clubs, continued for a while as a citadel of tradition in a changing world. The imperial pomp of the Victorian monarchy was still just visible through the wartime grime. Soon officials in bowlers, striped trousers and rolled umbrellas were again walking to tea in the clubs of St James's. The Household Cavalry and Guards would be back in their scarlet and their gleaming breastplates, while from the palaces behind them, colonial governors with pith helmets and feathers were being despatched by the Court of St James. And in the aftermath of war, when London seemed a blackened and in places toothless old girl, attempts were soon made to revive the 'Season' and High Society of the 1930s.

This was not so easy. London Society, with the court at its apex, had relied on battle-fleets of wealthy aristocratic and landed families, whose sons and daughters would be married off after a round of parties and entertainments. But Britain was broke. Death duties had been increased to 75 per cent on estates of over £1 million and income tax was at historically high levels. Titled London landowners sold off swathes of their property in the capital; around the country, from Scotland to Devon, land was auctioned at rock-bottom prices. Of London's great private houses, where before the war so many social-season parties were held, hardly one was left intact. Even if they had not been bombed, they were soon knocked down for offices or converted into museums. As for the country homes, 400 were demolished in the decade after the war; in 1955, says the historian David Cannadine, they were going at the rate of one every five days.

The social world her parents had known vanished before Princess Elizabeth's eyes. Post-war gossips assumed that Princesses Elizabeth and Margaret too might be won by one of the heirs with map-names. The scions of Westmorland, Rutland and Blandford were suggested as potential suitors. The girls certainly enjoyed the company of Guards officers at post-war weekend parties at Sandringham and Windsor. Yet the Windsors were now a social apex without a mountain of wealth and glamour to support them. The old 'Season' did return, Queen Charlotte's Birthday Ball for debutantes, one of the key matrimonial markets of earlier decades, restarting in March 1946. By May 1948 the grandest of the 'Season' events was also back, when George VI in admiral's uniform mingled with 2,500 guests for the first 'presentation' of debutantes since the war. Though Princess Elizabeth was there, attired in dove-grey silk, she was perhaps sceptical, as she would later abandon the tradition. And soon, with the solitary exception (until 1960) of Londonderry House, all the private palaces had gone. The Royals had Clarence House, Marlborough House and Buckingham Palace, but they were left in lonely splendour.[13]

For the Windsors themselves, life was brighter. The royal calendar, which dated only to the early years of the century, revived in its comforting predictability, a round of Sandringham Christmases, Balmoral summers and Windsor weekends. Horse-racing, like football and rugby, was soon as popular as ever. The Ascot Gold Cup, which had been held at Newmarket during the war, returned to home turf immediately, in 1945. The Grand National, which had been cancelled in 1940, was back again in 1946. The Henley Regatta, cancelled during the war, returned as a shortened one-day 'peace regatta' in 1945. Yet the message of wartime service was a solemn one. Royal garden parties were back; but the first were held for some of the thousands of prisoners of war recently returned from Germany. Rounds of hospital, military and civic openings, parades and speeches were also soon being scheduled with a vengeance.

Princess Elizabeth was being trained in public engagements which were mostly stodgily routine. When she was knocked against a tree by her horse while riding at Windsor in September 1945, the Palace immediately reassured the press that she would be able to inspect the Grenadier Guards, attend a Girl Guides event and hand out diplomas in domestic science in Glasgow. She was sent to open extensions to schools for the deaf and disability centres in the West Country, a children's hospital in east London, to the National Eisteddfod at Mountain Ash in Wales, where she was proclaimed a bard – one of the Queen's less likely titles. Her speeches did not sound spontaneous. But she did her bit. In the country she sometimes escaped, efficiently despatching stags during stalks in the Highlands, and displaying her family's skill with guns, horses and excitable dogs.

Love and Marriage

All the while, Elizabeth had kept her secret, though not from those nearest to her. On 9 July 1946 there was the first 'proper' Buckingham Palace garden party since the war, which *The Times*'s reporter thought a glorious occasion: 'The spacious lawns of the Palace grounds are still brilliantly green from earlier rains and beneath yesterday's bright skies were the ideal natural carpet . . . There was, as at Ascot, relaxation of pre-war rules of dress . . .' The prime minister, Clem Attlee, was among 7,000 guests, ranging from foreign Royals to farmers. So too was one Prince Philip Mountbatten, back from service in the Far East a few months earlier. His name began to crop up in other newspaper reports of weddings and parties where Princess Elizabeth could also be found. By the end of the year the Greek prince had successfully applied for British citizenship and readers of *The Times* were being reassured: 'Non-naval readers of the report that Prince Philip of Greece had applied for naturalization may not recognize under that title the grandson of one very distinguished British admiral and the nephew of another ... But for the abnormal conditions arising from a state of war, he would ordinarily have become a British subject on passing out of Dartmouth in 1939 and formally entering the Navy.' It was a subtle piece of nose-tapping. This was no ordinary morsel of naval gossip.

For by then Prince Philip had asked Princess Elizabeth to marry him and she had told her father. The King, worried that she was too young, insisted on a condition. The young couple would have to wait. Imperial business must come first. The royal family were pledged to visit South Africa. This would be an important and lengthy visit, part of the Princess's training for the life to come. It would also, of course, give her the time and space to ask herself whether she was sure about marrying, a full four months to reflect before jumping. After eighteen months of close mutual admiration, Prince Philip's proposal had come at Balmoral. His later, studiously vague account was that 'one thing led to another. I suppose I began to think about it seriously, oh, let me think now, when I got back in '46 and went to Balmoral. It was then that we, that it became, you know, that we began to think about it seriously ...'[14] His 'you know' no doubt reflects an embarrassment about public soul-baring rather than anything else: like the Queen, he comes from a less mushy generation. She accepted at once, and began to work on her father. It had been a much less complicated wooing than that of George and Elizabeth following the previous war.

But it did not go down well with everyone. The courtiers' case against the Philip connection has been endlessly told – his German relatives, his bumptiousness, his lack of deference, all

of it tut-tutted about by Queen Elizabeth's family, the Bowes
Lyons and the Palace old guard, later described by Princess
Margaret as 'the men with moustaches'. A mixture of snobbery
with a whiff of racism echoed through the cold, grand corridors. But it seems that George VI himself took quickly to the
young prince – who, it is said, saw the King wearing his kilt
and with a grin promptly curtseyed. His caution was more
about his daughter's youth and inexperience: she had met her
fiancé, after all, when she was only thirteen. In the meantime
there had been serious alternatives put forward. A brace of
dukes' sons and the offspring of an earl had been mentioned.
They were all beside the point. Princess Elizabeth manifestly
believed in duty but she had a mind and a will of her own. So
the couple were engaged, but privately. Any public announcement would wait until the return from South Africa, when she
would have turned twenty-one.

The main purpose of the trip was to try to bind South
Africa more tightly back into the Commonwealth. The royal
party, aboard the last of the great British battleships, HMS
Vanguard, left behind a Britain huddling through a grim,
austerity winter, among the worst of the century, as they
steamed towards sunlight and plenty. The King felt badly
enough about it to cable Attlee and offer to come back; the
prime minister said no, because the mission was important. In
1947, though the real, India-centred Empire was dying, many
British people still thought of themselves as an imperial race
and looked to 'English' sister-nations overseas as a global
family. Empire Day was still celebrated; Australia, South Africa,
Kenya and New Zealand beckoned as places for ambitious
Britons to settle in and the idea of a globe-spanning British
trade system was thought sensible. Few politicians expected
independence to come soon to the African or Middle Eastern

possessions, and the British army maintained massive bases in the Mediterranean.

South Africa, so rich, so large, so strategically placed, was a weak link. Its rulers divided between the Dutch-speaking Boers and the English settlers, the country had stuck with Britain during the war. Jan Smuts had become the only non-British field marshal at Churchill's side and a hugely popular figure in Britain; but the anti-British Afrikaners were by now reasserting themselves. Among those on the rise were pro-Nazi racists who would later help create the apartheid system to lock the black African 75 per cent majority out of power. Wooing South Africa – cheering the pro-British faction, calming the Afrikaner one and making gestures towards the black majority – was a tricky, perhaps impossible task. Afrikaner newspapers were often hostile and the King found the strain of endless speeches hard; on one occasion he had to be cajoled into speaking by his daughter. But the welcome and celebrations in Cape Town were exuberant and on the surface, at least, the trip seemed to be a huge success. The royal party were followed by huge crowds. For Elizabeth and Margaret, their first time abroad was very special, a cascade of sensations. Elizabeth learned the absolute importance of time-keeping, prodding her mother forward when she dawdled, and managed to keep looking interested during long days of official engagements. The King's private secretary thought she had done extremely well, and was cheered about the monarchy's future. Yet in the longer term the trip was clearly a failure. Afrikaner nationalism rose to absolute power, while the more liberal English were cut out. King George detested the overt signs of racial separation, noted the rising hostility to Smuts, and described the officious Afrikaner police as 'Gestapo'.

Yet the trip will be remembered most for Princess Elizabeth's radio broadcast on her twenty-first birthday, making what she called a simple dedication: 'I declare before you that my whole life, whether it be long or short, shall be devoted to your service and the service of our great Imperial Commonwealth to which we all belong. But I shall not have the strength to carry out this resolution unless you join in it with me . . .' Though the speech had been written by Lascelles, the Princess had contributed her own thoughts and ideas and it made a noise right round the English-speaking world. Listening to it now there is something eerie, atavistic and mysterious about its phrases and cadences, as if a young woman was offering herself as some kind of living human sacrifice. It aroused real emotion among listeners, a call to arms from a Greater Britain. There was, however, soon to be no Imperial Commonwealth left: with India's independence six months later, the Empire disappeared. King George VI had been a king-emperor. His daughter would not be Queen-Empress. With India gone, South Africa seemed a significant part of the new Commonwealth's importance, but thirteen years later, after bitter rows and a formal declaration by the Commonwealth in 1960 of its multiracial status, South Africa would leave on its lonely voyage as an apartheid state.

The Princess, after enjoying riding on African beaches, the closeness of the family and the unaccustomed sunlight, returned to Britain as determined as ever to wed. The announcement came on 10 July 1947. Unlike some of the courtiers, the public seem to have welcomed the news enthusiastically, despite a hostile opinion poll eighteen months earlier. The Prince – as he was popularly known, even though naturalization meant that his title was now meaningless, and a simple Lt Mountbatten would have been more accurate – became for the first time a public figure. His MG sports car was identified, pointed out and photographed. His picture appeared everywhere. He was given a security detail and valet, even though he barely had the wardrobe to be brushed.

At a party to celebrate the announcement, other Royals noted that Prince Philip was still in his shabby naval uniform. His prospects were now golden but meanwhile he was poor. He travelled third class on trains. He was in an entirely different position from the still-rich aristocratic Old Etonians the court circles would have preferred. What he brought instead was a restless, enquiring energy and great physical glamour. His future title, Duke of Edinburgh, was settled with the help of friendly journalists. He would become HRH. The King sketched designs for his coat of arms. Both he and his bride were awarded the Order of the Garter. Thus was a partial outsider prepared for royal authority.

What kind of wedding would it be? This was the darkest moment of the austerity years. In 1947 Britain faced a grave financial crisis, a run on the pound, low productivity, feeble exports and recurrent strikes. That year, rations of meat, bacon, ham and fats fell below wartime levels, to their lowest ever; clothes rations were cut; petrol was in short supply; foreign currency could be purchased only for essential travel. How would people react to a luxurious wedding? Not surprisingly, both court and government trod warily at first. Prince Philip wanted an unostentatious ceremony. His future father-in-law was in gloomy mood about the very survival of the monarchy, with so many grand houses shutting up and the imposition of communist regimes in Eastern Europe. (Spasms of gloom and even panic about the future of the monarchy have been a feature of the Windsor mentality.)

Hugh Dalton, the chancellor, was detested by the Palace,

partly because his father had been tutor to King George, and the son was viewed as a class traitor for turning socialist. Now Dalton was preparing a wringing, grinding budget with more tax increases. Many Labour MPs, and no doubt many Labour supporters in the country, did not want an extravagant festival of a wedding. Following the announcement that Princess Elizabeth would be allocated a hundred clothing coupons for her wedding, with bridesmaids getting twenty-three coupons each and pages ten coupons, the Labour MP Mabel Ridealgh complained: 'It is the general impression among the workers that it would not be proper to spend large sums of money on this wedding when we are asking the workers themselves to economize even in the necessities of life.'[15] But Mabel had made a misjudgement. Already, towards the end of 1947 and despite a torrent of reforming social legislation, people were becoming weary of the shortages and red tape Labour was coming to represent. As preparations for the wedding gathered speed, it began to be clear that outside the eager platoons of the socialists, there was little enthusiasm for a puritanical, frugal event. The country wanted colour and it wanted fun. And that, after all, is the job of the monarchy.

Before the wedding went ahead, the King and his government wrestled about how much money Princess Elizabeth and Prince Philip would get. George VI had run a tight and frugal court during the war, saving a substantial sum (around £200,000). But was this money really his, or the Treasury's? He wanted a generous settlement for the soon-to-be-weds. Dalton and left-leaning Labour MPs wanted a far smaller settlement, symbol of a more 'simple, austere and democratic' monarchy. Some MPs wanted no money paid over at all, believing King George should pay for his daughter out of his own funds. The row went on, mostly behind closed doors. The government threatened the embarrassment of a committee of MPs enquiring into royal wealth.

The King stood his ground. Eventually Dalton was forced to resign anyway, having leaked his own Budget to a lobby journalist. His successor, Stafford Cripps, despite being another upper-class socialist with a reputation for flinty Puritanism, agreed a more generous compromise. (Like Dalton, Cripps had been no favourite at court: after one wartime lunch, when he instructed Princess Elizabeth not to forget her clothing coupons, she had thought him 'a dry old stick'.[16]) When the Cripps compromise was put to the Commons, Attlee's main argument was geopolitical. A ceremonial monarchy with simple people at its heart was, he argued, a good democratic alternative to fascist or communist symbolism. The job was a real one. It must be funded. So the King passed over half his savings and the couple would get about two-thirds of what he had hoped for. Even this deal only squeaked through Parliament: 165 Labour MPs voted for a lower payment still. There was some evidence afterwards that resentment about the annuities for the Prince and Princess spread beyond the parliamentary Labour party. How popular was the monarchy really? No one was certain.

In 1947, unlike 2011, it was not taken as read that a royal wedding, even one involving the heir to the throne, had to be a grandly public national ceremony. Historically, most royal weddings had been private affairs, with private parties and some waving from balconies or landaus. This time, the choice of Westminster Abbey followed the precedent set only by George VI and Queen Elizabeth and happened after talks involving the prime minister, Attlee. His verdict in favour of the Abbey drew a line under the financial haggling and made the wedding certain to be the major national event most of the

country wanted. The numbers of guests who could be accommodated in the vast and ancient space, and the traditional
processional route to it from Buckingham Palace, meant that
a grand spectacular was unavoidable. Elaborate preparations
were made for wireless coverage. Early on it was agreed that
film cameras were to be allowed in to make a cinema presentation, later to be shown around the world. Wire, painted
wood and electrically lit street decorations were built and
erected. Presents began to flood in from around the world,
ranging from grand confections of precious stones from Indian
princes to what Queen Mary thought was Mahatma Gandhi's
loincloth, which she considered very distasteful. (It was, in fact,
simply a piece of linen he had woven himself.) There were tins
of condensed milk and fruit from American and Australian
well-wishers who worried that the British were still starving.
These would later be distributed to some of the Britons who
were not quite starving, but were hungry and bored with
rationing. From ordinary Britons themselves there were nylons
and cigarette cases, humble knitted jerseys and pictures. The
presents were laid out in long lines at St James's Palace, flash
and ordinary alike, to be viewed by anyone who bought a
ticket.

What was the point of royalty if a royal wedding failed to
provide a gleam in darkling times? Princess Elizabeth took a
close interest in everything, but in her dress above all. It was
designed by Norman Hartnell, the man who so influenced
Queen Elizabeth's image during her early years. His parents
had owned a pub called the Crown and Sceptre in Streatham,
south London. A sub-conscious influence? At any rate, Hartnell
left Cambridge without a degree to become a designer to the
rich and fashionable in Jazz Age or 'flapper' London, producing
clothes for court parties and film stars alike. He moved to

Bruton Street in Mayfair, just along from where the Queen herself had been born, and was soon winning royal commissions, including from her mother. Hartnell became Britain's leading promoter of romantic and extravagant clothing, using a famous French seamstress for his showers of sequins and reintroducing the crinoline. Among his clients were Gertrude Lawrence, Marlene Dietrich and Elizabeth Taylor; among the rivals who admired him were Coco Chanel and Christian Dior.

The dress he created for the 1947 wedding was an extraordinary confection of ivory silk and tulle, corn-ears in crystal, embroidered stars and orange blossom. It required, among other things, 10,000 seed pearls. Almost inevitably there was a minor row about extravagance and patriotism: was the silk from Chinese worms? (Yes, but nationalist worms, not communist worms, retorted Hartnell.) A dozen huge and very rich cakes were ordered. The presents, the food and the dress were symbols not just of a wedding, or the returning glamour of royalty, but of all those things the British wanted for themselves but could not yet have. No one had the coupons for a Hartnell special. Nobody else could legally acquire the sugar, marzipan and candied fruit for the cakes, or do more than imagine the cornucopia of good things pouring in from abroad. But this seemed to produce anticipation, not jealousy. The wedding was like a giant shop window, a million noses pressed against it, and 'coming soon', or 'coming one day' written overhead. It was an early premonition, at the darkest economic hour, of the rosy consumerist dawn.

A darker future lay ahead for the once-grand family of European royalty who had also been invited. A dusty, rather moth-eaten horde of struggling-on and former monarchs and consorts converged on London with their old jewels and pre-war clothes, reminding everyone that the Windsors were rare, and lucky, survivors. Some were already exiles. Others were soon to be tipped from their thrones. The royal wedding was a reunion of the old clans, but it had to exclude many. The German relatives did not get invitations, for a start; not even Prince Philip's three surviving sisters. Germans in general were very unpopular and some of the in-laws had served the Nazis. British survival and victory had been won at a horrible human and economic cost, but London was the capital of a successful constitutional monarchy; few other countries could now say the same. Patriotism and monarchism joined arms. The message, the ceremony, was shown on screens across devastated Europe and in America too.

Up and down Britain, as Princess Elizabeth pledged traditionally to honour and obey her husband, millions of her future subjects held a 'good for us' party. She was being seen as a national symbol of youth, rebirth, and hope. Of course, nobody at the time could have expected that only five years later the Princess would become a Queen, and that her wedding would be outshone by the grander ritual of a Coronation. In the winter of 1947, it seemed that here were a couple with a long time ahead of them to enjoy a certain amount of privacy and freedom, and one another.

Prince Philip started with a real sacrifice: he gave up smoking to please his new wife. And he quickly discovered how radically their lives would now change. On honeymoon, initially at Mountbatten's home, Broadlands, they were spied on by snoopers hanging in the trees and pursuing them to church. The King wrote to Princess Elizabeth during the honeymoon to say that as he had handed her over to the Archbishop of Canterbury and married life, 'I felt that I had lost something very precious . . . I can, I know, always count on you, & now Philip, to help us in our work. Your leaving us has left a great blank in our lives but do remember that your old home is still yours . . .' This proved to be lucky. The young couple had been assigned Clarence House, just a few hundred yards east of Buckingham Palace. Later the home of their son, the Prince of Wales, in 1947 it was a mess, almost unliveable-in. While the couple waited for building works to be finished, they found themselves first at Kensington Palace and then back with the in-laws at Buckingham Palace. But they did not return to royal routine in every respect. Prince Philip was able to walk to work at the Admiralty across St James's Park, unthink-able nowadays. At night, apparently, he disdained pyjamas. As has been mentioned, it was a cold winter. Three months later, the Princess was pregnant.

It was during this period, from the late 1940s onwards, that Prince Philip's association with a cheerfully louche group of men, artists and actors, photographers and aristocrats, began to cause muttering. Baron Nahum, a photographer and friend, had what he called his 'Thursday Club' above an oyster bar in Soho where loud and sometimes drunken male parties would take place. Prince Philip has, as it happens, always been a very moderate drinker but this set allowed him to relax properly in jovial, undeferential company. This took him to the edge of a gamey, and indeed seamy, set which later included the defence minister Jack Profumo, forced to resign from the Commons for lying, and the man at the centre of the Profumo scandal, Stephen Ward. There were a few rumours about romances with actresses and society women but after a lifetime's worth of nosing and probing, not a shred of hard evidence has ever emerged, and it is a subject which irritates the Duke greatly. Because he was already under fire from courtier snobs who accused him of not being a proper gentleman (they meant a landed bore), the gossip was dangerous as well as being hurtful.

The birth of Prince Charles was greeted with cheering crowds outside Buckingham Palace and sonorous columns in the newspapers. *The Times* produced an editorial which shows just how far the mood of the press towards royalty has changed during his lifetime. This was, the paper said, 'a national and imperial event' and brought an heir to the throne with direct Danish blood, the first time that had happened since 1042. Interestingly, the writer thought that one day Charles might inaugurate a dynasty called Mountbatten. As for the Princess, she had 'fully established herself as the visible representative of the whole of the younger generation, the generation upon which rests the heaviest burden of the Empire's recovery'. This time round, it was no longer necessary to have a cabinet minister on hand for the birth; by 1948 the tradition had become too embarrassing. Other traditions, though, were maintained: the boy was named HRH Prince Charles Philip Arthur George, covering most of the royal bases. Thanks to his maternal grandmother's blood, he was the most Scottish heir to the throne since the ill-fated Charles I.

The couple of years that followed were perhaps the happiest of the Queen's life. She was fulfilling her duties, as the papers had noted, but they were nothing like as onerous as they would become. There was a successful visit to Paris, and in London a theatrical and aristocratic set gathered around the couple now generally known as 'the Edinburghs'. They finally moved into their own home. Prince Philip was soon appointed second in command of a destroyer in the Mediterranean fleet, HMS *Chequers*. The Princess followed later in 1949 and in Malta was able to live a near normal life as a naval wife, going shopping, to the hairdresser, making friends, eating at local hotels and restaurants. Even at this stage, the infant Charles was often left in London with his grandparents, something that seemed far less unusual than it would today. Abroad, the Queen began to cine-film her husband, watched him playing polo, and swam and danced. In August 1950 she gave birth to a second child, Anne. Prince Philip rose to command his first ship, the frigate HMS *Magpie*. The couple could look forward, it seemed, to a long period during which practical work and domesticity would dominate their lives; as Robert Lacey put it to the author: 'Inheriting the throne was something for the 1960s or even the 1970s.'

Yet almost immediately there were warning signs. The King was ill. It was cancer, presumably caused by his decades of heavy smoking. Londoners who saw him passing in the streets talked about his grey, shrunken face. A series of operations began. Though personally optimistic about his prospects, George VI needed Princess Elizabeth more and more to carry out engagements he could not manage. She had to be in Britain. Prince Philip could hardly command a Mediterranean ship from there, and so he dolefully gave up his much loved job and returned. He may have expected or hoped to return to full-time naval service. He would never do so. His wife took on more responsibility, greeting foreign dignitaries and riding in the King's place for Trooping the Colour. She presided at the Privy Council just before Parliament was dissolved for the 1951 election, which ended the Labour years and returned Winston Churchill to power. To many it already seemed that the young couple were eclipsing the monarch, rather as later Prince William and his new bride seemed to eclipse Prince Charles.

While that election campaign was being fought, Philip and Elizabeth went on a long tour to Canada, mainly by train, and visited President Truman in Washington, where they were fêted. Truman, star-struck, commented, 'When I was a little boy, I read about a fairy princess, and there she is.' Throughout the trip the Princess's new private secretary, Martin Charteris, had papers for the Accession Council under his bed, just in the case the King died.[17] Over the winter of 1951–2, however, the King seemed to have made a remarkable recovery. He went to Prince Charles's third birthday party, started shooting again and visited the theatre. There was a national day of thanksgiving for the King's recovery, celebrated in churches throughout Britain. The King was pleased to have Churchill back as prime minister – he was never keen on Labour. He could not, however, manage the next long-planned royal tour, which was to East Africa, Australia and New Zealand. The glamorous young ones would go instead. On 31 January 1952 George waved them off at the modestly sized and freezing London Airport. His life of meetings was about to end; hers, to begin.

People were not prepared for the death of George VI, at home or around the world. He was known to be unwell, but his routine seemed to have carried on well enough after a lung operation. The day before he died he had been out for a few hours' sunshine at Sandringham, banging away at hares as usual, before going quietly to bed where a footman brought him his night-time cocoa. When at 11.15 a.m. on the following wet, sleeting morning, 6 February 1952, special black-bordered special editions of the newspapers suddenly appeared on the streets of London announcing his death, just half an hour after the official announcement from the Palace, sombre and silent crowds spontaneously appeared on street corners, the Mall and at Westminster. Churchill, weeping in bed, thought it 'the worst news'. People came together, then, in public, rather than around television sets. Crowds gathered in newly republican India too, and in Australia and Canada. Even in the United

States the reaction was one of shock. One of the globally known figures of the wartime years, the figurehead of a nation still considered one of the world's leaders, had suddenly vanished. People died younger then, particularly those worn out by stress. But he was only fifty-six.

His daughter learned the news from her husband on their Kenyan holiday. They had been staying at the Treetops rest-house, on a platform in a giant fig tree watching wildlife. On the way there the royal party had come dangerously close to a large cow elephant protecting two calves. She had not scented them. They had guns. Prompted by Prince Philip they had gingerly, quietly, carried on to their vantage point. Perhaps in retrospect the danger to the not-yet Queen has been romantically embellished. But later in her reign, 'security' would have kept them far away. Instead, they sat in the tree and watched the elephants play. A local hunter with a heavy-calibre gun was there too, and not only for elephants: the first rumblings of violent rebellion against British colonial rule were being heard all around. Warm, colourful and far away Kenya might be. Paradise, it was not. Princess Elizabeth had been taking cine film of the wildlife, including an old rhino, while her staff at Mombasa were preparing for the next stage of the visit, to New Zealand.

The news that the King had died came first to a senior courtier, Lieutenant-General Frederick Browning. He passed it to Martin Charteris, via a journalist. Charteris confirmed it and then told Prince Philip's aide, Mike Parker, who told the Prince. Parker was later quoted as saying that Prince Philip 'looked as if the whole world had dropped on him' – as, in a sense, it had. His wife had gone out to order some horses to be prepared for riding. He told her. She began almost immediately to write the letters and messages apologizing for cancelling the rest of the trip, and making new arrangements. From the stoic generation, she showed no immediate distress. Lady Pamela Mountbatten, her cousin, went in to console her: 'In her usual extraordinary way ... she was thinking about what everybody else was having to do. Typically, she said, "Oh, thank you. But I am so sorry it means we have to go back to England and it's upsetting everybody's plans." '18

Interlude
The Queen in the World

Sixty years on, her staying power has given the Queen a personal knowledge of global leaders unmatched by any other person alive. She has had, as house-guests, such near-mythic figures as Emperor Haile Selassie, General de Gaulle, Lech Walesa and Nelson Mandela; controversial twentieth-century monarchs such as the Shah of Iran, Emperor Hirohito of Japan and King Faisal of Saudi Arabia; tyrants such as Ceauçescu of Romania and Mugabe of Zimbabwe; key first-generation African leaders such as Tanzania's Julius Nyerere, Kenneth Kaunda of Zambia, Mobutu Sese Seku of Zaire and Daniel arap Moi of Kenya; and central figures in Russian history such as Marshal Bulganin, Nikita Khrushchev (who took tea with her and found her to his surprise 'completely unpretentious') and Vladimir Putin. A short book could be written just about her relations with US presidents from Truman and Eisenhower, through to Kennedy, Nixon and Reagan, to the Obamas today.

'Reader No. 1' has seen every significant secret Foreign Office cable or telegram, and much of the MI6 advice, about international crises and problems from the 1950s onwards. As head of state of fifteen nations other than the United Kingdom, she has taken her overseas queenships very seriously. As Head of the Commonwealth, she has had a ringside, inside seat for the epic stories of the Indian subcontinent, African decolonization and the transformation of Asia. If she ever picked up her pen for something longer than a sweeping regal signature . . .

The assumption must be, however, that she would not. The Queen does keep a diary, but sadly not in the Pepys or Crossman or Alan Clark way. Most of her intercourse with world leaders has been at the level of the polite and uncontroversial exchange of expressions of goodwill. Her job is to meet, to listen but not to interrogate. She is Britain's Department of Warmth, the Secretary of State for Friendship. The records of her long and frequent visits to other countries contain endless pictures of singing groups of children, cheering crowds, banquets and march-pasts. A gorgeous cavalcade of dresses, often by Norman Hartnell or Hardy Amies, and hats, dresses or bags, shows the care taken to reflect local sensibilities. The presents received, paintings, silver- and goldware, jewellery, strange carved crocodiles and thrones and the rest, would fill a warehouse.

It is a curious business, this endless exchanging of gifts. Around the world, the corridors and studies of presidents, prime ministerial offices, and anterooms of official headquarters are stuffed with glass cases containing ceremonial swords, strangely ugly ceramics or models made of silver. They are grand clutter which always need dusting. Hardly any provide pleasure. There are exceptions: Nelson Mandela gave Prince Philip a hand-painted chess set of African figures which would make anyone smile. Some are particularly ugly and pointless: who would want a gilt model oil-rig on a stand in a glass box from Saskatchewan? But this is to miss the point. Gift-giving goes back to the earliest recorded human civilizations. It is a ritual to confirm lack of hostility, lack of war. Today the exchange of gifts is oil to smooth negotiations, balm for disappointing answers or grease to elicit better ones.

The Queen's travelling has been close to the centre of her own idea of what she is for. She has never seen herself as just, or even perhaps mainly, the British Queen. Though most of the trips have been tiring but not difficult, with predictable and reliable welcomes awaiting her, some have been tricky. She has been booed by French-Canadian nationalists and emerged from a church service in Dresden, bombed to pieces by the RAF during the war, to confront a sea of stony-silent and not entirely friendly faces. She has waited in the sweltering heat of the desert, while a panicking King of Morocco tore up the preparations for lunch and offered her only cognac. She has overridden the fears of ministers to visit potentially dangerous places in Africa and Asia. She has dealt calmly with inebriated Russians.

Head of the Commonwealth is a role she owes to the founders of modern India above all. After the Second World War, the Americans were campaigning against the British Empire as the prime example of clapped-out imperialism, getting in the way of their world-dominating commercial ambition. Even inside the British 'family of nations' there were serious strains. Burma became the first country to leave since the loss of the American colonies. On Easter Monday 1949 the Irish Republic went too. South Africa was already engaged in a debate about seceding. During the war the Australians had toyed with forming their own defensive alliance with the US. The formation of India and Pakistan as independent nations robbed George VI of his title 'Rex-Imperator'. What kind of international arrangement might winning-side but financially exhausted Britain make with her former colonies? What would the role of the Crown be?

Meetings in London produced various ideas, including a standing 'Commonwealth Conference' of which the King would be not King, but president. His private secretary, Sir Alan Lascelles, was derisive, telling King George that kingship was 'an ideal for which men are prepared to work, to fight, and to die; but nobody is going to die for a Conference'.[1] Under Nehru, however, India seemed keen to stay inside some kind of Commonwealth. So did the Islamic Republic of Pakistan. How could republics be accommodated to a monarch-led institution? With the Labour prime minister Clement Attlee taking the lead, negotiations led to a classic British compromise. India was not prepared to recognize the King as head of state, or have any truck with British royalty in patronage, oaths, honours or policy. But the Republic of India would recognize the King as Head of the Commonwealth. Eight countries – Britain, Canada, Australia, New Zealand, South Africa, India, Pakistan and Ceylon – duly attended a conference in London in April 1949 and proclaimed after it that the King would be retained 'as the symbol of the free association of independent member nations' which would be united 'as free and equal members of the Commonwealth of Nations, freely cooperating in the pursuit of peace, liberty and progress'.

This declaration, which embodied an idea the now-departed Irish republicans had argued for years before, would become the founding document of the modern Commonwealth. It meant that, as the Empire was wound up, newly independent states could reject the British monarch as head of state and choose republicanism, yet stay inside the old grouping. This was the idea that made the expansion of the Commonwealth possible while, of course, limiting its practical power. Of the fifty-four members today, only sixteen retain the Queen as head of state. They are mostly in the Caribbean or are small Pacific island nations, though Canada, Australia and New Zealand remain major examples. The existence of the Commonwealth is one of the features that separates the British monarchy from those of Scandinavia or Spain and makes it more than a tiny geographical remnant. No wonder that the Queen's first major act after her Coronation was to embark on a gigantic six-month tour of her wider authority.

The trip of 1953–4 was both the ultimate introduction to the life she would lead and an unrepeatable time of triumph for the Queen and the Duke. Britain's real power might be hollowed out and she might be heavily indebted but her post-war prestige was at its peak. She was the newest member of the atomic club, her fighting services had won great victories and across the former Empire there was optimism. South Africa was a problem, but Australia and New Zealand were seen almost as British versions of California, sunlit lands where graft was rewarded and a new world could be built far away from the class distinctions of Britain. In turn Australians and Kiwis had a seemingly unreserved enthusiasm for the British connection untinged by rising nationalism. The death of George VI had given Britain an unexpectedly young and beautiful head of state who was already a well-established international star (she had first featured on the front of *Time* magazine aged three). And this was just ahead of the real television age. If you wanted to see the Queen for yourself, you would have to go and stand and wait. The combination of national prestige and personal novelty would never come in quite the same way again.

It was a mammoth trip. The Queen flew across the Atlantic to visit Bermuda and Jamaica and then went aboard a hired commercial liner, the *Gothic*, because the Royal Yacht was not yet ready. Prince Charles and Princess Anne were left behind, as the Queen and Princess Margaret had been when their father made his pre-war overseas tours. On the *Gothic* the royal party passed through the Panama Canal into the Pacific, visiting Fiji and Tonga and arriving in New Zealand for Christmas. The Queen was the first reigning monarch to visit New Zealand and the welcome was rapturous; it was described by one writer as 'a national delirium'. From there she went to Australia, which was the most triumphant but also most exhausting section of the tour.

As in New Zealand, the Queen of Australia was the first reigning monarch to visit. She spent two months travelling 2,500 miles by train, 10,000 miles flying, and 900 miles by car; she made more than a hundred speeches and listened to twice as many. She heard her national anthem played an estimated 162 times.[2] It has also been estimated that three-quarters of the entire adult population of Australia turned out to see her. The result was a personal triumph which tested her resilience, her ability to keep a fixed smile in place for hours and her patience – she protested privately about long speeches from local politicians and must have finally realized just what a lifelong programme of listening would be like. The travelling was exhausting, there was little privacy and the Queen did not have much time off, endlessly changing clothes for public display and re-doing her make-up surrounded by curious ladies. Yet it was worth it: when she returned to Australia in 2011 for what is likely to be her last visit there, there would be plenty of people who remembered that 1954 tour as a one-off moment in their post-war history – who had stood at roadsides or in squares or beside schools, and waited and cheered and waved.

The Queen and the Duke then went on to Ceylon (now Sri Lanka), the Cocos Islands, Uganda and Aden before arriving in the Mediterranean, where they at last went aboard the spanking new *Britannia* and sailed home again, to be greeted by ships and crowds when they finally sailed up the Thames,

173 days after they had left. It had been a crash course in stamina and organization for the new Queen which must have reassured her greatly about the monarchy's continuing hold over people's imaginations. It provided a template for many other tours to come – the meticulously planned wardrobe, sending subtle compliments to different audiences, the grind of long, hot car journeys at slow speeds, the tweaking of similar speeches for local conditions. Yet in 1954 the press was far easier to handle than it would later become; royal news was still news about what the Royals said and did during public engagements. Patriotic feeling was at its most fervent. There were none of the diplomatic dilemmas or local political protests which came later; so, apart from the physical strain, this had been easy. In the long run, did it change anything? Without it, surely, the Queen would not have been quite as popular in her further-flung dominions as she stayed. Doing her bit for the monarchy, she strengthened emotional and sentimental links in a way which could not have been done without her physical presence. And that has stayed true throughout her reign. Even in the age of television and the internet, queens have to be seen if they wish to matter. Woody Allen once said that 80 per cent of success is showing up; for monarchy the percentage is perhaps even higher.

Abu Dhabi, 25 November 2010

Back home in Britain, great swirls of snow are blanketing the north and east of the country. Here, on a sweltering patch of grass and sand, with old Arab dhows bobbing offshore, hundreds of Britons in cream suits, sunglasses and hats are waiting for the Queen. Lines of Arabs in traditional dress are there too, waving sticks in a traditional greeting while girls in shocking pink and lemon dresses vigorously swirl their hair. Incongruous is one word for it. Out of a gold-coloured Range-Rover come the Queen and the Duke of Edinburgh, greeted by Sheikh Khalifa bin Zayed al-Nahyan, the ruler of Abu Dhabi. Off they go to view a modernist pavilion, unveil a rather dull-looking plaque and then walk in a circle past the grinning, waving crowds. Bouquets are thrust and accepted. A sophisticated expat teenager screams: 'She looked at me! She's loooovely . . .' The Queen is nodding, smiling, looking interested, making small talk and keeping to time.

She had touched down late at night and been whisked straight off to the gigantic Sheikh Zayed mosque, to pay her respects at the tomb of the late ruler of the United Arab Emirates and watch children recite the Quran. That had been quite a scene too: the Queen was in stocking soles and wearing a strange headdress that made her look like a Russian boyar's wife – or a beekeeper, thought some of the watching photographers – as she walked across the world's largest hand-woven carpet and under the world's largest chandelier, so big that when it's cleaned they have to lower a man inside it. After her outdoor walkabout she will change into a grand evening gown and decorations for a state luncheon to meet all the sheikhs of this confederation of emirates. Sheikh Khalifa will give her (and her husband and son) the Order of Zayed, the United Arab Emirates' highest civil decoration. In return she will make him a Knight Grand Cross of the Most Honourable Order of the Bath. There is an investiture for the vice-chairman of Emirates Airline and a doctor specializing in diabetes. The Duke of Edinburgh will watch a fly-past of jets. The Queen will meet children and business delegations.

Then they will be off again, this time to the neighbouring state of Oman, whose Sultan Qaboos deposed his father in

1970 and has become the longest-serving ruler in the region. Some of us travelling in the Queen's wake are by now beginning to pinch ourselves. Sultan Qaboos, we are told, studied A levels in England, went to Sandhurst, trained at Suffolk County Council and is a passionate fan of classical music, particularly organ music. He has the world's only bagpipe-playing camel-mounted soldiers, some of whom can also parachute and play the bagpipes simultaneously. He is a notable religious liberal and has been almost Prince Charles-like in his keenness to preserve his country's old buildings, mainly Portuguese and medieval forts. He seems to be – though nobody quite says so – gay. His country is the same size as Britain with a population of only around 3.5 million. Again, the Queen and the Duke are flung into a round of parades, banqueting, receptions and a horse display to celebrate the fortieth year of the Sultan's reign, moved to accommodate the Queen's schedule. In a land of shark's-tooth peaks, broiling sand and turquoise-topped minarets, the original source of frankincense, we seem to be in a world somewhere between Narnia and Brigadoon. What is it all for? What is this about?

These are the eighty-seventh and eighty-eighth overseas state visits the Queen has undergone in her reign. They have taken her from fjords and frozen northern palaces to tiny islands and the world's busiest, dustiest capitals. They have been made to dictators and elected presidents, old tyrants and courageous reformers, communists and nationalists. They have happened by royal yacht, aircraft and train. Very different, they have each involved similar rituals, some of them so archaic they go back to the embassies and diplomacies of old Egypt and ancient China: the gifts, the elaborate feasts and the speeches fluffed up with tactful evasions and courteous euphemism. In the old days the monarchies of Europe could spend years preparing for royal visits. These days they have been thrashed out – two a year, normally – by the royal visits committee of the Foreign Office, Buckingham Palace, overseas embassies and host governments. The Queen travels with a couple of ladies-in-waiting, her personal staff and whatever ministers and others are needed. There will be military men and diplomats there, a few security people and a raggle or taggle of journalistic camp-followers, generally confined to battered late-night buses and airport lounges as they try to keep up. The Queen has no more choice about where she goes than they do. If 'her' government says she should go to Bulgaria or Tanzania, that's where she heads. Because, underneath the gilded icing of 24-gun salutes, exchanged Grand Crosses, dancing displays and elaborately exchanged compliments, this is a cold-hearted, contemporary and wholly serious business.

Take that original scene, with Arab dhows and stick-waving welcome party. What was actually happening was the unveiling of the British architect Norman Foster's winning design for a new national museum for the UAE. It features five fin-like triangles of glass and will be built on an island off Abu Dhabi, an ambitious plan to make this corner of the Gulf a world artistic centre. There will be a Performing Arts Centre by Zaha Hadid too. Thanks to Lord Foster and the British Museum, whose director Neil Macgregor is also present, Britain has a slice of this huge, oil-funded investment. That vast, glittering mosque the Queen visited had brought work to the British consulting engineers Halcrow Group and Hill International, the lighting company Speirs and Major and the British artist Kevin Dean. The agreement in Abu Dhabi, the world's seventh-largest oil producer, committed both governments to a further massive rise in bilateral trade to £12 billion by 2015. The oil companies BP and Shell have been in the UAE since it started, but these days, design and construction are becoming as important. Prince Andrew, the Duke of York, who attracted press criticism while Britain's business ambassador, and later withdrew from the role, told me that though the UAE was Britain's largest market in the Middle East, 'the rest of the world has woken up to its potential . . . we have to find ways of increasing our penetration of the market . . .' He is right. More than 4,000 British businesses are working in the UAE, and around 100,000 Britons live there. On the other side of the coin, investments from the UAE include the London Gateway project, a port and 'logistics park' in Essex, whose footfall is twice the size of the City of London and which, if it hits its target of 36,000 new jobs, will make it the largest job-creation project in the UK, during tough economic times. Everything from London hotels to football clubs, including Manchester City, is owned from here.

The Gulf oil states, from Qatar, which will provide much of Britain's imported gas for the next generation, through to Bahrain and Dubai, have become an economic battleground where European countries can no longer take anything for granted. Britain's oil and gas bonanza in the North Sea is now over and will not be quickly replaced by wind farms or new nuclear plants. Britain now depends on imports and rightly fears too great a dependence on Russia. Its very future as an advanced economy is in play. The cultural links matter, as they always have done: part of the political message of the new museums and galleries, which will display works by Manet, Cézanne and Ingres, is that they display Western values and aesthetics in the middle of the Arab world. Here, as almost everywhere, the new rising powers – and above all China – are challenging hard for influence and investment. And influence matters as much as the money. The UAE and Oman have strong defence links with Britain – lots of Sandhurst-trained officers, kit and shared intelligence. (Dubai's Crown Prince won the Sword of Honour at Sandhurst.) Both countries look across the water at Iran and south at Yemen, where al-Qaeda is again organizing. Without them, fighting in Afghanistan and Iraq would have been almost impossible. Without their help, the struggle against Islamist terrorism becomes much, much tougher. The Gulf is rich – a source of oil, gas and money – but is also surrounded by danger and political instability. The Queen knows very well this is not Narnia. It is one of the switchboxes of modern capitalism.

So can it really matter that an eighty-four-year-old lady with her eighty-nine-year-old husband arrives by aircraft and does a lot of walking, nodding, smiling and talking? In this day and age? Well, it seems to. The UAE and Oman are monarchies themselves, and in Oman's case an absolute monarchy. In this modern version of the 'great game', nations must play the cards they have; and Britain can play the Queen. Few of her rivals have a long-serving, internationally famous monarch in whose company sheikhs seem comfortable, talking horseflesh and architecture. In the case of the UAE, the Queen knew its founder, Sheikh Zayed, who died in November 2009. Her visit to him in 1979 is still remembered locally, not least because each schoolchild's history book has a picture of it. Three decades on, her arrival had been preceded by the visit of the Indian president. Given how many Indians work in the Gulf, and how closely the UAE follows Indian affairs, this might have been reckoned a more important meeting. The Queen's visit was a vastly bigger event, with large crowds and signs across Abu Dhabi, and much more local media coverage. In Oman, Sultan Qaboos regards her with almost filial affection. He moved the celebration of his national day so that it could match her timetable. Here, British influence is still seen almost everywhere. Bordered by both Yemen and Saudi Arabia, the moderate and relatively plural (though religiously conservative) version of Islam practised in his country is immensely valuable. Qaboos has been in close touch with Prince Charles too, and keeps a home in England.

Consider all the contracts, long-term deals, expressions of friendship, media coverage and personal links restored or established in a visit of just a few days' duration. Then remember that, with a couple of such expeditions every year (at least) and the same again of inward-directed state visits, such as the one from President Zuma of South Africa, this is only part of the endless monarchical diplomacy. Remember the similar visits to Malaysia, the Baltic states and the Balkan ones, to the United States and United Nations, to India, Turkey, South Korea. Add it up and ask again if it matters. We see the Queen in action overseas doing her trademark walkabouts, or standing straight and silent while soldiers march past her, or sitting with other heads of state. These are such familiar images that most of us barely register them. Really, though, she is operating much more like a door-opener, or perhaps a human assault vessel. She goes first, ushered straight to the centres of power wherever she is, and behind her, in an eager V-formation, come the ministers, civil servants, the military and the salesmen. Of course, it is not always the same. There are plenty of countries less interested in British royal visits, or where less is at stake. But every visit has its agenda. The parades and the dinners look impressive enough. But the story behind the story they want us to see is the story that counts.

David Cameron summed it up after the visit of the Emir of Qatar, another Gulf leader who had invested an extra £2 billion in Britain shortly before his State Visit of 2011: 'The Qataris don't have to invest in Britain. They have a huge wealth based on more natural gas than Saudi Arabia. They are an extremely wealthy country.' Britain had plenty of advantages, but the monarchy was one of them: 'It's an institution people admire and she is an individual people admire. And that's good for Britain.'

Part Three

THE QUEEN AT WORK

The British constitution, like almost all constitutions, is played out as an endless mutter of meetings. So much 'chatter', so carefully recorded – Parliament, cabinet, cabinet committees; and then the endless meetings inside government offices. Outside Westminster are courts, tribunals, quangos, city halls, local government, police committees. One way or another, an outside observer might think that the British, when not in bed or watching television, are mostly in meetings.

There is one weekly meeting that is not recorded, reported, filmed, minuted or even discussed. It is the old meeting, described by an old word – the 'audience' between the Queen and her prime minister. Neither the Queen nor any premier has discussed with outsiders what is talked about, except in the most blandly general terms. She has audiences, too, with the most senior military men, and with retiring cabinet ministers and chancellors. These audiences are the last dark little box in the middle of Britain's maze of meetings. What are they for? Have they, in any way, changed the lives of the British?

Walter Bagehot, the nineteenth-century journalist who audaciously tried to explain the British constitution (and, *mirabile dictu*, largely succeeded), said the Queen had the right to be consulted; to advise; and to warn. He was talking about Queen Victoria but reading Bagehot was part of Queen Elizabeth's own training for her job and his little list is so generally accepted that we may assume she agrees with it. Even in relatively recent times British monarchs have used all three rights vigorously.

The Queen's father expected to be consulted about the detail of wartime operations, insisting Churchill kept him fully informed even during the most frantic and stressful periods of fighting (something Churchill never complained about). George VI is also widely credited with warning Clem Attlee, the post-war Labour prime minister, to appoint Ernest Bevin foreign secretary, rather than Hugh Dalton, a man detested by the Windsors. If so, it was a good nudge, since Bevin became one of the greatest foreign secretaries Britain has ever had. But it was the Queen's grandfather, George V, who was the last truly interventionist monarch. His advice, complaints and warnings were familiar to successive prime ministers from Asquith to Baldwin, and covered everything from the future of the aristocracy, creeping ministerial socialism, the response to the General Strike and the rise of the dictators. George V, founder of the dynasty, was a bridge between the assertive monarchism of his grandmother and the very cautious approach of his granddaughter. He was an obedient constitutional monarch but not a silent or uncomplaining one.

The Queen's role is harder to gauge. Though her first prime minister was Churchill, she grew up during the most vigorous dose of socialism ever administered to the British, and with an acute awareness of the need to tread carefully. She has repeatedly been challenged and tested over royal finances and has always been aware of a vocal minority of republicans at home and abroad. Her disposition has been quieter and more cautious. We are not even sure what she really thought of her prime ministers. The least discreet of them, Harold Macmillan and Tony Blair, have been pretty discreet. There have been rumours of favouritism, that she liked Harold Wilson best of all and detested Margaret Thatcher. But this is mere gossip and in the case of Lady Thatcher at least, wrong. Sadly for writers, the Queen has been the soul of discretion.

Even so, the story of her relationships with the eleven men and one woman who have served as her prime minister is central to the meaning of her reign, and can be told in surprising detail through public documents, diaries, recollections and the observations of those around them. Some general points can be made about those audiences. First, by general agreement of civil servants and politicians who have worked with her, the Queen has an extraordinary memory and is very sharp. She enjoys political gossip, remembers detailed precedents and, as she has grown older, has acted more and more as a kind of human library upon which younger premiers can draw. She is 'the fount of honours' but it may be more important that she is a 'fount of memories'. Though we do not know what was said at her audiences, except in a very few and marginal cases, it is known – for instance – that Wilson's got longer and longer as he struggled to hold his Labour governments together, while Blair's were comparatively short.

Piecing together hints and using obvious logic, we can also assume that the most interesting part of the Queen's audiences is when prime ministers talk to her about the problems they are having with their own colleagues. The historian David Cannadine argues that 'separating out the functions, as it were – a chairman of the board and chief executive – is actually rather a good idea, and that's what we have in this country; whereas in America you have a President who is both chairman of the board and chief executive; and that is actually quite a lot harder'.[1] Prime ministers have plenty of people with whom to discuss the awfulness and treachery of the Opposition. They have Number Ten staff, other ministers, even journalists. There are far fewer people with whom they can candidly discuss problems inside their own governments.

Wilson became most enthused about his royal audiences as he felt most besieged by ministers from left- and right-wing factions of the Labour Party. Ted Heath was simply a lonelier man. Margaret Thatcher had her troubles with 'wets': the Queen had a royal-box view of those cabinet battles, and reassured Mrs Thatcher in 1986, after Michael Heseltine walked out from her government over the Westland affair, that there had been worse moments. John Major struggled with Euro-sceptic 'bastards' and in 1995 would have had to discuss with the Queen in some detail his unusual decision to step down as Tory leader, while remaining prime minister, in order to provoke a fight. At a leaving dinner, Tony Blair wryly remarked that the Queen was the only person with whom he could expatiate on the fine personal qualities of his colleagues.

The highest elected office is a lonely place. An experienced, shrewd and above all reliably discreet confidante is one of the advantages of constitutional monarchy, when it works, a bless-ing that other parliamentary systems rarely offer. The audi-ences are not primarily for the Queen's benefit, however much she might enjoy hearing at first hand what is happening. It is her job to support and get along with her prime ministers. Some, like Alec Douglas-Home, a Scottish landowner, or David Cameron, who went to school with one of her children, Prince Edward, may be more obvious social pairings than others, such as the Presbyterian minister's son Gordon Brown or the grocer's daughter from Grantham. But the challenge of learning about and developing relationships with people from less familiar backgrounds is interesting too.

Lord Butler, who was cabinet secretary during the Thatcher and Major periods, says he thinks that first of all, 'all prime ministers have felt that they could talk to her in absolute confidence. That it wouldn't go any further. They also felt, I think, that she gave them sympathy because she was a figure in the public eye and had been for so long, and so they could talk about some of the agonies that you get from that ... I think a session of therapy is a rather good phrase.' Sir Gus O'Donnell, his latest successor, says something similar: 'She's seen it all before – the ups and downs, the wars, the recessions, the recoveries, the good times, the bad times – and she's seen the way different governments respond to these events ... and she gives sound advice, I'm sure.' He had once asked John Major exactly what she said and was quite properly slapped down: 'I don't know what she says but all I can say is, the impact looks rather good from the outside.' Everyone who works with the Queen, and who has been interviewed for this book, says she has been a good judge of character. Human judgements about the character of a premier – liking, admiration, puzzlement – have mattered more than class.

The new Queen was still making her way back to England from Kenya when, on 6 February 1952, Winston Churchill's cabinet was meeting in the House of Commons. Ancient precedents and modern conditions collided. The last time a monarch had been proclaimed while abroad was in 1714, when the German George of Hanover succeeded Queen Anne. A different age, but not an entirely alien one: Anne's reign had seen two-party politics properly emerge and the Union of Scotland and England. She had not really had a prime minister, though Churchill's brilliant ancestor and general the Duke of Marlborough had been a prime mover at court. Then, as in the 1950s, questions of the titles, status and political reach of the Queen were much debated: Anne was the first sovereign of a United Kingdom of Britain, but was also separately Queen of Ireland and, with arcane arrogance and a fine disregard for the facts on the ground, called herself Queen of France too.

The new Queen, at twenty-five, was in a very different position, but her politicians agonized about titles. The cabinet thought phrases such as 'the Crown Imperial' could 'cause difficulties'[2] in the post-war world, and substituted 'Head of the Commonwealth' into the recital of titles. Among the countries of which she was now head of state, Pakistan and Ceylon were not Christian, still less Protestant, so 'Defender of the Faith' seemed wrong for all her realms. That would have to be fudged. She was no longer Queen of 'Ireland': it would have to be Northern Ireland. And so on. Ministers argued hard and passionately, citing historical precedents with vigour. From the very first moments of her reign, the Queen's politicians were entangled with difficult and emotive questions of protocol.

All of this may seem arcane; but Britain was a country soaked in monarchical history. In 1952 the war had been over for only seven years. It loomed large. Contemporary British films included *The Wooden Horse*, about an escape from Stalag Luft III, *They Were Not Divided*, about the Guards Armoured Division, *The Cruel Sea*, about the Battle of the Atlantic, and *Angels One Five*, about the Battle of Britain. Audiences who came to watch them stood to attention for the national anthem. Regimental reunions and British Legion clubhouses were busily attended. The monarch's picture hung everywhere, from town halls to pubs. National Service had almost a decade still to run. Historical consciousness was stronger; from the films about Captain Hornblower, Queen Victoria or the Scarlet Pimpernel to the patriotic histories of H. E. Marshall's *Our*

Island Story (serious) and Sellar and Yeatman's *1066 And All That* (less so). British children were still taught the traditional kings-and-queens-and-famous-battles version of history; British comics imagined the British invading space wearing moustaches and RAF-style caps and theatre audiences accepted the censorship of plays by the Queen's Lord Chamberlain.

Monarchy was sewn through almost every aspect of public life, from the words used by hanging judges to the deferential caution of the BBC and newspapers to every mention of the former King and now the Queen. Monarchy was for most people the holy of holies, a national religion. No British monarch more recent than Queen Victoria was permitted to be impersonated by actors in films or plays. The fierce Commander Richard Colville, a former naval officer who regarded the media with contempt and was the Buckingham Palace Press Secretary, ordered that the Queen could not even be filmed without his express permission. Broadcasters cringed before him. Newspaper editors, muttering about 'the abominable no-man' nevertheless ensured that only the most anodyne of references to royalty appeared.

As a moving spirit in the world, the British Empire had gone but its body remained sprawled across the earth. The loss of British India and its partition into two independent states had been a shock to many in the United Kingdom, and those who understood the figures knew Britain could not afford imperial pretensions; but the great pull-out from other parts of the world had not yet begun. Empire Day, 24 May, was still celebrated with marches and pageants. Much of sub-Saharan Africa was British. So were Cyprus, Malta, Aden, the Gulf States, Somaliland, the West Indies and Hong Kong. British troops sweltered in a vast camp in Egypt; British companies treated Persia as virtually their own property. There was an

intense bond with what was known as the White Commonwealth. The term 'British race' was used without embarrassment or raised eyebrows. (Except for highbrows.) Though the
Empire Windrush had arrived with 500 West Indian workers
four years beforehand, in 1952 mass immigration had not yet
begun to alter the shape of the country, which still looked
white, merely tinged with exotic incomers at its edges. Just
two years earlier the British Empire Games had been held in
New Zealand; the next games would be called 'Empire and
Commonwealth'.

The Royal Navy, though it was already being scuttled and
broken up in shallow seas and at shipyards, was still seen as
the great steel fist of British power. Many thought a renewed
age of British glory, based on new technology and old standards, was just around the corner. There were plenty of older
people who could remember Queen Victoria's reign, and who
had not yet realized the immensity of the new power of the
United States. So it was hardly surprising that questions about
the new Queen's titles were debated so seriously by the old
men of her first cabinet. Lower down the tree, others were
making lesser verbal adjustments – for senior barristers, King's
Counsel, to become QCs; for the words of the national anthem
to change; for new stamps, banknotes and coins to be printed
and minted; and for freshly cast pillar boxes and new photo-
graphic portraits.

Harold Macmillan reflected that ministers were preparing
for the Accession Council, one of the last remnants of the
Anglo-Saxon Witan, 'this strange and ancient body'. The following day Churchill broke into his familiar prose-poetry in a
broadcast: 'I, whose youth passed in the august, unchallenged,
and tranquil glare of the Victorian Era, may well feel a thrill in
invoking once more the prayer and anthem, "God Save the

Queen".' These were men who had lived through two world wars as members of the ruling class and who knew full well that Britain's place in the world was falling but who were flushed with optimism about the prospects for a different, better one under a fresh, new Queen.

Churchill had come across her as a girl and had found time during the grim days in April 1941, when the British army in Greece was desperately evacuating before the German advance, to send her roses for her fifteenth birthday. Now old, ill and barely able to cope with the demands of being prime minister, he still cast a pungent word-spell over the country. The Queen puts him in a different category from any of his successors and recently recalled being gently rebuked by him. When she and Prince Philip returned from their gruelling post-Coronation six-month tour of the Commonwealth in May 1954, Sir Winston was invited to join them for the last part of the voyage on the still-new Royal Yacht *Britannia* from Yarmouth up the Thames. There were cheering crowds and a 41-gun salute from the Tower of London; but the Queen remembers the grim weather and saying to Churchill as they went up the Pool of London, 'Look at this awful dirty river.' Churchill turned on her with a growl: 'This is the silver thread that goes through British history – never forget it.'[3]

No later prime minister would have dared to correct her like that. She complained at times that he failed to listen to her properly – rather as Queen Victoria complained that her great prime minister Gladstone addressed her as if she was a public meeting. As it happened, on that day on the Thames, Churchill was bluffing a bit. According to his doctor, he was chilled to the marrow, had a cold and 'had never been up the river before'. When he had first come aboard, 'I did not at once recognize a masculine figure in khaki trousers. It was the

Queen, who had taken off her coat.'[4] Princess Elizabeth revered Churchill but, by the time she came to the throne, the Conservative grandees were already talking about how to ease him out of Downing Street.

Shortly before George VI had died – so the Queen Mother told Anthony Eden – the King had made up his mind to have a talk with Churchill about retiring. His death meant it never happened.[5] Churchill, though deeply saddened by the King's demise, had seized on the opportunity the new reign offered as another excellent reason for staying put. He would be there for the Coronation, naturally. There was, surely, no tearing hurry about that? Churchill's fruity blend of romanticism and self-interest made it perfectly obvious to him that the new Queen would need his grand-paternal, guiding hand for some time to come.

The Coronation: What It Meant

Back in 1953, all was optimism and widening horizons. The Queen's Coronation that June was a national carnival but also a religious celebration and a yearned-for moment of patriotic rebirth. A year of planning went into it, from the invitations and seating plan at Westminster Abbey to who would make the sandwiches at fêtes in villages and housing estates. In the main avenues of central London through which the procession would pass, arches were raised with lights, bunting and crowns. But ceremonial arches appeared in most British cities, and in small towns and villages too. In factories at Birmingham and York (and there were factories there, in those days) flags, bicyclists' pennants, savings boxes, chocolates, biscuits, badges and tea-caddies were manufactured. In Stoke and the Potteries mugs, plates, teapots were fired, painted and packed, the first such painted and coloured ware since before the war. Decorative plants with red, white and blue flowers were nurtured by market gardeners. Newspaper editors planned lavish special editions. The best-known writers were signed up by magazines well in advance.

The Coronation Headquarters, centre of the official planning, opened in Berkeley Square in London, a stone's throw from the Queen's birthplace, in October 1952. Prince Philip, already straining for a more substantial public role, was given the job of chairing the preparations. Far away, the people of St Keverne on the Lizard in Cornwall began a difficult negotiation with the Ministry of Food. They had roasted a whole ox for the accession of the last monarch and they were jolly well going to do the same for Elizabeth. This was fighting talk: rationing of meat would last more than another year and to start with, the ministry was outraged.

Peter Hennessy, now Lord Hennessy, has been one of the premier constitutional and social historians of the reign, and for him as a small boy, the Coronation was a pivotal moment. He remembers like million of others the Coronation mugs at school, a Dinky Toy version of the Golden Coach and going to watch the great event on his family friend's television in Barnet. But it was about more than the Coronation as a national celebration; Britain had captured the airspeed record and conquered Mount Everest and had the first jet airliner (the Comet);

> And you had stories of empire which nobody would dare write or read in that way these days, and here [Britain] was, an ancient settled nation, naturally good at ceremony, comes through the heroic 1940s, standing

alone, and yet at the same time we would produce the most advanced bits of kit in the world; and it was one of those rare moments of optimism. And the Queen looked terrific. She was beautiful, and she had this dashing consort . . . and it was going to get better.

For Hennessy it was 'the zenith . . . a better yesterday'. He would benefit from the 1944 Education Act and he felt Britain was on a virtuous upwards cycle of improvement. For him the Coronation was 'a tonic . . . Wonderful. Life has never been the same since.'[6]

Hennessy has a rare and exuberant ability to put these feelings into words but his memories are shared by so many others. The Queen has been Queen of a nation in decline, and many would say her greatest achievement has been to soften and humanize that inevitable process. At the time of her Coronation, though, it seemed she might have a very different reign to enjoy.

Meanwhile, a moon-faced man with a reassuringly familiar voice, deep and rich as after-dinner chocolate, began to assemble a great pile of Coronation facts and figures. The Queen was happily married but it was almost as if she had another suitor. He would soon appear on the Thames in a damp Dutch barge he had bought and which would be moored opposite Westminster to allow its proud owner easy access to the ceremony. Richard Dimbleby was not exactly wooing the Queen, adore her though he did; but his employer, the British Broadcasting Corporation, was certainly wooing the monarchy. This would be the first proper television Coronation, though in 1937 three cameras had been allowed far from the Abbey, at Hyde Park Corner. For the BBC, which was engaged in a losing battle to fend off commercial television, the Coronation was a perfect opportunity to show what it, a cadet member of the establishment family, could do. Like the monarchy the BBC had done well out of the war. Like George VI, the BBC in its Lord Reith era had been instinctively anti-Churchill but, like the King, it had become a supporter and buttress of the war leader. As the House of Windsor, so had the BBC helped tie Britons and imperial subjects together through the darkest years.

As a result, in the early 1950s the BBC had a position hard to imagine today. It was not quite like the Church of England. Its first director general, as a Scottish Presbyterian, would have regarded that as a bit flashy. But thanks in part to Reith, a passionate monarchist, the BBC was solidly part of the establishment – powerful, authoritative, clean-shaven and suavely self-certain. Its director general, Lieutenant General Sir Ian Jacob, had been an assistant to the war cabinet but its patriotism was more complicated than that of the court, because it had incorporated the voices of radicals, such as George Orwell and J. B. Priestley. Yet it was a part of the establishment, which by the time of the Coronation felt it had special rights, and it had vaulting cultural and moral ambitions. Its wireless services, ranging from the popular Light Programme through the meatier Home Service, to the highbrow Third Programme, were meant, in the words of Jacobs's predecessor, to lead the listener 'from good to better, by curiosity, liking and a growth of understanding'.

The first reaction of the Palace old guard, and of the cabinet, was that television remained a vulgar medium, which should not be allowed inside the Abbey – this despite the fact that it had been used to broadcast the funeral of the King in February 1952, helping spark the first wave of mass television purchases. That October, the Palace announced a veto, a decision taken on the advice of the Archbishop of Canterbury and the Duke of Norfolk, and backed up by Churchill and the cabinet. The BBC refused to take no for an answer and began a quiet lobbying campaign, focused first on the Duke and Archbishop. When the message finally reached Churchill that – as it happened – the Queen herself was in favour of televising her Coronation, he told the diarist Colville that it was, after all, she who was to be crowned, not the cabinet. 'She alone must decide.' It would turn out to be a good decision, not least because it made the Coronation the first one ever to be genuinely witnessed by the people; even in Saxon times that had been more a hope than a practical reality.

Now the BBC went into action, planning the biggest outside broadcast ever, including ninety-five sound commentary positions (mostly for overseas audiences) and an unheard-of twenty-one television cameras, five of them inside the Abbey. The newspapers began an informal beauty contest about who would be given the ultimate job of reporting on the Coronation itself from a glass-sided box high above the altar. One popular choice was John Snagge, then probably the best known voice on the wireless – for it was still, just, the age of wireless. Richard Dimbleby, however, was the favourite in newspaper polls, and with his bosses. He had been a brave and unorthodox radio reporter during the war, accompanying RAF bombing raids and witnessing the liberation of Belsen. But he had royal form too. In 1939 he had been the first BBC reporter specially assigned, and accepted, to cover a royal tour, when George VI and Queen Elizabeth had visited Canada. During it, Dimbleby had played the piano for the King and had a long late-night discussion with him about Hitler, democracy and world affairs. Dimbleby's script for his broadcast describing

George VI's lying in state is a perfect model of evocative, romantic news prose and he was a passionate monarchist.

He thought the House of Windsor 'means justice, respect for the rights of the individual, and freedom' and adored the new Queen: 'She has a great sense of humour that lies just below the surface . . . Photographs rarely do her justice; she is smaller, slimmer, and altogether more lively than they make her. She has a flashing smile . . . and a clear, incisive voice.'[7] This was the man the BBC decided should be, for millions, the voice explaining the images never seen by a mass audience before. He would go on to report on a succession of royal marriages, Queen's speeches and state occasions. These included more funerals: old Queen Mary, the Queen's grandmother, had died at the age of eighty-five just ten weeks before the Coronation. Sad timing, but it barely caused a pause in the frantic preparations. Obsessive about proper preparation, Dimbleby spent six months preparing his notes on every aspect of the service. When he left his chilly boat on the morning of the great day, he clambered into the commentary box at 5.30 a.m. and stayed there for seventeen hours. He must have rationed the tea.

The Coronation was probably the most important moment in the Queen's life and certainly the most important official moment. As the day drew nearer, she practised the complicated ceremony in the Buckingham Palace ballroom, using sheets to mimic her 60-foot train and wearing the heavy crown to familiarize her neck with its weight. Dray horses were borrowed for the carriages, the original beasts having gone during the war. Dukes drilled. Bishops rehearsed. A short walk from the Palace was the royal apothecary, Savory & Moore of New Bond Street, where the holy oil was compounded by its head dispenser from a formula which went back to Stuart times and possibly further back still. It is supposed to involve ambergris, musk, orange, jasmine and rose water. Peers ordered their ceremonial garb and were told that, by special dispensation in these tough economic conditions, rabbit fur would be considered an acceptable alternative to ermine. Thinking ahead to the long day before them, they were also told they could hide sandwiches in their coronets. Churchill later claimed that he vetoed the charging of the 3,000 Abbey guests sixteen shillings each for sandwiches and had ensured alcoholic drinks would be available to crowds waiting in the Royal Parks.

There was a guarded welcome for the announcement that the Coronation would be used for a general amnesty of remaining wartime deserters still at large. Though there were theoretically 13,000 of them, many were thought to be Irish and outside the reach of the law and some had certainly died. The *Spectator* reflected approvingly that 'several thousand skeletons can now come out of several thousand closets'.[8] When that Coronation amnesty was proposed – some men had been on the run for eight years and often had not been back to see their wives or families – it was noted that 'the Queen was very keen on this', even though the armed forces were hostile. London began to disappear under scaffolding and resounded to the banging of hammers as porches, arches and seating were prepared. The papers contained quite a lot of sniffy complaints about the vulgarity of some of the street decorations but much of the speculation focused, of course, on the weather.

At the BBC, lessons were being learned from the broadcasting of the King's funeral, when it was felt that there had been too many boring studio items and not enough 'from the London streets'.[9] Meticulous arrangements were made to keep the Commonwealth up to speed. Canada was then the only other Commonwealth country to have regular television broadcasts and RAF Canberra bombers were to fly the film over, stopping only for a quick refuelling break in Greenland in Operation Pony Express. In the US, the rival NBC and CBS companies planned their own race to air. The interests of French speakers were taken more seriously than perhaps they would be today; one of the five commentators inside the Abbey was French and the Coronation would prove a major hit across the continent. Monarchs, cavalry detachments, horses, presidents, ministers and journalists arrived from around the world. Every rentable room in London was let, entire hotels booked up, road closures planned, shopfronts bedecked with red, white and blue, coronets and profiled pictures of the young Queen. The wise looked at the weather forecasts and worried.

Coronation Day itself, Tuesday, 2 June 1953, did indeed start cold and wet, not just in London, but across most of the United Kingdom. Some 30,000 people are estimated to have slept out overnight on the paving stones and verges of the processional route, with another 20,000 trying but failing to find a good spot to watch from. Writers who went among them remembered the war and the Blitz of a decade before and were impressed by the communal spirit and unquenchable cheerfulness. The journalist Philip Hope-Wallace, who overheard a parent tell a fractious child, waiting for twenty-eight hours, 'Sit still, or I'll crown *you*', was impressed by the endurance: 'The crowds schooled to sit out the Luftwaffe's visits on hard cold stone were not going to be put off by a drop of rain. Nor by the fantastic coldness.'[10] Many had wrapped themselves in newspapers, which had become sodden overnight. They then had the dilemma of whether to use special Coronation editions of the fresh morning papers as keepsakes or insulation.

Not many ended up unread, one hopes, because their front pages announced the astonishing news that with perfect patriotic timing, the New Zealander Edmund Hillary and his guide, Sherpa Tenzing, part of a British-led expedition, had become the first climbers to make it to the top of Everest. Tea was being sold, and jokes made about brandy being more wanted. Overnight there had been some sing-songs and impromptu dancing, but not much because of the rain. The people who waited so long and would have a long walk home afterwards through streets first closed to traffic, then becoming hopelessly congested, were rewarded by one of the most glittering displays of old-fashioned pageantry in Britain's post-war history. It was a long clatter of cavalry horses' hoofs and chinking uniforms, a carnival of exotic costumes, foreign potentates and military marching. There were familiar faces: Churchill, who delighted in uniforms, was done up in his Admiral's gear as Warden of the Cinque Ports. Below a cocked hat and blue-and-gold tunic which would have suited some South American liberator of the previous century, he beamed and waved. There were unfamiliar faces too. Tonga's jovial Queen Salote Tupou III – the 'tallest queen of the smallest monarchy' who lived largely on roast suckling pig and travelled in an open carriage despite the rain, was a particular star.

Waiting inside the Abbey, they shivered in their finery. The Countess of Huntingdon told the readers of the *New Statesman* that her prime memory of the day would be the 'element of pity and sympathy' felt for the Queen, 'for between the inhuman magnificence of the Crown and the glittering of the vestment-like golden robe, the Queen's face was very young, very human, very tense'. But beyond that it was, 'Oh, the cold!' The peeresses had been confined in what became in effect a wind tunnel: 'Our teeth chattered, we quaked inwardly with cold, we wrapped ourselves in our trains and watched our arms turn blue.'[11] Richard Dimbleby was in the relative comfort and warmth of his commentary box, surrounded by his mass of typed and handwritten notes. Later, after it was all over, he would express his amazement at the poor behaviour of some of the peerage, who he felt had behaved like litter louts: 'Tiers and tiers of stalls in which the peers had been sitting were covered with sandwich wrapping, sandwiches, morning newspapers, fruit peel, sweets and even a few empty bottles.'[12] Well, they had been very cold.

Outside London, the rest of the country celebrated and coped with the rain. On the Moray Firth, too far north for television reception, the warship HMS *Welcome* and local fishing fleet skippers collaborated in an impromptu naval review through a force-eight gale. Further north still, in Stornoway in the Hebrides, a spry ninety-two-year-old minister celebrated an open-air service and told his parishioners about his memories of an equally wet parade in Edinburgh for Queen Victoria. In Belfast, and across loyalist Northern Ireland, decorative arches were erected. The Welsh hills had beacons, first smoking and then blazing. Villages across Britain planted Coronation trees, held running races, fancy-dress parades, football matches, teas for everyone in the hall, and beer-fuelled Coronation suppers in pubs. In Dorset, there were tug-of-war contests between neighbouring hillside villages and in St Keverne in Cornwall they triumphantly roasted their ox, providing a glut of hot sandwiches.[13] In London, 350 foreign guests who could not be fitted into the Palace for the formal lunch were treated to a first outing of the day's most famous culinary invention, 'poulet Reine Elizabeth' or Coronation Chicken as it was quickly renamed. A dish of poached fowl in a sauce including curried onions, red wine, apricot purée and mayonnaise, it was created by Rosemary Hume of the London Cookery School and its degraded versions are slathered into lunchtime sandwiches throughout Britain to this day. Made properly, it can be quite pleasant.

Further afield, public holidays had been declared across the Commonwealth, with yet more fêtes, parades and parties. South Africa had grand military parades and schoolchildren around the world had been given the day off. For people outside Britain, and indeed across much of the country itself, the only way to follow the day's events was by radio. In South Africa, 69 per cent of the English-speaking population was estimated to have listened in. Later, when television films had been flown in, Germans, French, Italians and many more would queue to watch the ceremony. In the United States, 85 million watched the rival NBC or CBS programmes. For most people in Britain too, this was the television Coronation. The collective memory is of people huddled round a small, rented set in someone else's house or in the pub. The statistics back it up. Surveys suggested that 53 per cent of the adult population, some 19 million people, watched the BBC's *Coronation Special* and of those the biggest proportion, 10.4 million, watched in friends' houses while 7.8 million had rented or bought a set to view in their own home. A further 1.5 million watched in public places, such as cinemas, town halls and pubs.

Afterwards a remarkable 98 per cent of those polled declared themselves 'completely satisfied' with the coverage, a proportion the BBC has not always achieved since. At the start of the 1950s most British people had never seen a television set. TV was not available in northern and central England or much of Scotland. Within five years of the Coronation, TV ownership had risen sixfold and the country's entertainment habits were being overturned. Historians often credit the change simply to the Coronation. This is self-evident nonsense. While it is true that the BBC's coverage of the Coronation propelled huge numbers of people to hire television sets, many of whom then bought them, nothing short of a totalitarian invasion or the plague could have halted the spread of the new medium. Still, it would be as important a symbolic moment in the growing of age of television as the General Strike of 1926 had been in the acknowledgement of radio's power.

On the day itself the coverage focused on the details of the Queen's silken dress, her serious demeanour and the intricate choreography of the ancient ceremony, which goes back to at least 973 when King Edgar was crowned at Bath, as recorded in the Anglo-Saxon Chronicle. The presentation by the Archbishop of 'Queen Elizabeth your undoubted Queen' and the answering aristocratic cries of 'Vivat!' were perhaps the most dramatic moments. For the Queen nothing mattered more than the religious and spiritual heart of the ceremony, still vivid in her mind as an observer from 1937. Devout, she would not have dissented from Archbishop of Canterbury Geoffrey Fisher's words in sermons before the Coronation, that she was 'God-called' to exert a spiritual power, leading her subjects by her personal example.

The words he used about her giving herself as a sacrifice echo those she had broadcast from South Africa on her twenty-first birthday. The Coronation was a ceremony intended to awe and even to intimidate; and not only those watching, but its subject also. At its heart was not the procession, or even the firm thrusting of the heavy seven-pound crown onto her head, but the private moment when under a canopy Fisher anointed her with holy oil: 'as Solomon was anointed King by Zadok the Priest and Nathan the Prophet, so be thou anointed, blessed and consecrated Queen over the Peoples, whom the Lord thy God hath given thee . . .' This ancient tradition of anointing goes right back to biblical times, though by 1953 no other monarch in the world experienced it.

For Fisher, the service was meant to demonstrate too that the Queen would exemplify domestic duty and fidelity and a united family home. (He had perhaps not studied the alleged origins of the ceremony, for King Edgar the Peaceable had been a notoriously libertine ruler, peaceful neither on the battlefield nor in the bed-chamber.) His argument rang out resonantly through 1950s Britain. Family was at the heart of the monarchical project: the royal family, then the British family, itself composed of traditional families, clustering round that family; then a further family of nations around that. Watching the Queen in the Abbey were young Prince Charles in a silk suit: the three-year-old Princess Anne, rather cross, had been judged too young to come and left at Buckingham Palace. Prince Philip, in full naval rig, would be the first to pledge his allegiance to her, kissing her on the left cheek and promising to become 'your liege-man of life and limb and of earthly worship; and faith and truth I will bear unto you, to live and die, against all manner of folks' – a sonorous promise he has stuck to. Later the 'family' metaphor for royalty, which seemed so obvious and strong that day, would be brutally challenged. But whoever's fault all this was, it was not hers. The Queen would do her lifelong best to live up to the Archbishop's uncompromising words.

In the immediate aftermath of the Coronation, a time of parades, services of thanksgiving, a full-scale naval review at Spithead (there was even a Soviet ship) and Trooping the

Colour, writers competed to find profound meaning in the ceremony.[14] The editorial in a highbrow magazine of the day, *Time and Tide*, on 13 June exemplified the mood. The popular historian C. V. Wedgwood declared that no Queen or sovereign 'was ever crowned more fully in the presence of the people', which was factually accurate. The magazine's editorial assertion that 'Britain has regained in the past few days that spiritual and moral ascendancy in the world which was hers in 1940' was certainly not. In the same magazine Robert L. Green, writing 'As an American', reassured readers that for Britain, 'the years of dullness and cold caused by war and recovery were forgotten'. There was much in the same vein, and few sour notes anywhere to the right of the Communist Party.

The diarist in the *New Statesman* thought the Coronation would have increased the number of people who felt 'the whole thing is out of date, antiquated stuff . . . Working-class Britain was simply forgotten.' Its formidable editor, Kingsley Martin, did not agree. He thought Labour's traditional hostility to the monarchy had been silenced by the correct constitutional behaviour of George V and George VI and that the Queen was safely outside politics: 'The first rule for all monarchs who wish to preserve their crowns in a democracy is that they should unreservedly accept the advice of the Prime Ministers and never under any circumstances become involved in party politics.' The Queen is not an avid reader of the *New Statesman* but she followed the Editor Martin doctrine as closely as the Archbishop Fisher one. Martin went on to make one of the most thoughtful assessments of the value of monarchy to a democracy, which deserves to be quoted more often: 'Constitutional monarchy is a subtle device which enables us, anthropologically speaking, both to adore and kill our Kings; by dividing supreme authority into two, we can lavish adulation upon the Crown and kick out the government when we choose.'[15] And so, since 1953, we have.

The Old Elephants and the Young Queen

The monarch's most important political job is to appoint a new prime minister if the incumbent should resign or die while in office. This was particularly uncomfortable during the early years of the Queen's reign because of the Conservative habit of not electing a new leader but allowing one to 'emerge'. In June 1953 Churchill, still frustrating his colleagues by his unwillingness to retire, suffered what seemed a devastating stroke. He was quietly hustled out of Downing Street to Chartwell, his home in Kent, to recuperate, though with little hope for a full recovery. During that summer an establishment news blackout, agreed by press tycoons strolling on the Chartwell lawn, meant that most British people had no idea that their prime minister was incapacitated. The Queen knew more than her subjects, though she wrote him a handwritten letter to say she hoped his stroke was 'not too serious and that you will be quite recovered in a very short time'. It was serious; but, by an extraordinary act of will, Churchill did recover enough to carry on, monitoring his ability to feel his own stubble, to tie his bow tie, and so on, until he was able to accept an invitation from the Queen to go to the St Leger at Doncaster races and to Balmoral. At both places, large crowds gathered to cheer – whether more for the Queen or for Churchill it was hard to tell. He was able to speak to the Tory conference in Margate that October and did not finally stand down as prime minister until April 1955.

For understandable reasons, including pride and worry

about his successor, Churchill was in danger of entangling the new Queen in a political crisis. During the quiet, slow summer of his illness, in August 1953, Macmillan had realized Churchill would use the excuse of the post-Coronation tour to delay again. Though the Queen could dissolve Parliament by telegram, if there was a deadlock in the Conservative Party about his successor she would not be able to intervene, Macmillan noted, 'in one of those rare crises where the Crown still has a role to play'.[16] Senior Tories were alarmed enough to debate whether four of five of them should go to the Queen in a group and ask her to put pressure on Churchill. Lord Moran, Churchill's devoted doctor, thought 'there is only one person . . . who can get him to do this and it is the Queen'. Lascelles was consulted but reckoned it would not work: 'If she said her part, he would say charmingly, "It's very good of you, Ma'am, to think of it" – and then he would very politely brush it aside . . . The King might have done it . . . but he is gone.'[17]

The Queen would have been put in a horrible position had she been asked, in effect, to terminate the career of the country's greatest war leader. He was the most senior of what we might call her elephant-premiers – the grand old men with wartime experience, who felt a fatherly relationship towards the young Queen, though without always treating her well. Churchill, Eden and Macmillan come into this category (Alec Douglas-Home had a different relationship) and the real break did not come for another decade, with Harold Wilson in 1964. It would have been better for the country had Churchill retired a couple of years earlier. He was no longer up to it and Eden would have been more seasoned in office. But it was unreasonable to have expected the Queen to fix this so early in her reign. Mind you, one can never be sure how she would have reacted if asked. Later, when someone remarked to her how marvellous it must have been to have Sir Winston as her first prime minister, she replied: 'Not at all. I found him most obstinate.'

In any event, she put no pressure on Churchill. His audiences with her, for which he dressed up in morning coat and top hat, grew longer and longer. He said they mostly talked about racing and polo and expressed anger at anything touching the Queen's status. A *Daily Mirror* headline in November 1953 asking 'Why Not Open the Palace to the People?' aroused his particular fury. The previous February Lord Moran had recorded an interesting conversation during which he complained to Churchill about the possible abolition of the upper chamber and got little sympathy from the prime minister: 'The House of Lords means nothing to him. The history of England, its romance and changing fortunes, is for Winston embodied in the Royal House. He looked at a new photograph of the Queen. She was in white, with long white gloves, smiling and radiant. "Lovely," he murmured, "She's a pet. I fear they may ask her to do too much. She's doing so well." '[18] Churchill was entranced and doubly pleased to be made a Knight of the Garter by her in June 1954.

This enchantment with the Queen did not extend to her husband. It may well have been worsened by an old man's jealous crush, but Churchill was already hostile to Prince Philip's family. He blamed Lord Mountbatten personally for the loss of British India, a ludicrous charge, reminding us that Churchill's sense of history had largish blind spots. He thought Mountbatten was in general rather to the left in politics, which was not a ludicrous charge. According to his doctor, Churchill said he did not like or trust Prince Philip, and just hoped he would do the country no harm. This mistrust crystallized in

Churchill strongly opposing Philip on the sensitive question of the family name.

The problem went back to the terms of George V's creation of the Windsor dynasty. In 1917 he had simply not thought through the possibility of the Crown passing to another Queen and her children and, therefore, the fate of the new Windsor surname. Before the start of the Queen's reign, legal advice had been that, as with any family, the children would take their father's surname. Prince Philip was not particularly hung up on the name Mountbatten, itself a modern invention, and suggested Edinburgh, or even Edinburgh-Windsor, as possibilities. But he wanted to be recognized for himself. At a dinner party in his home Broadlands on the eve of George VI's funeral, Lord Mountbatten then stirred things up. He boasted that 'the House of Mountbatten' now reigned. This was heard by that ardent royal traditionalist, Prince August of Hanover, who passed it back to George V's widow, Queen Mary. She was outraged and protested to the prime minister. Churchill immediately took her side.

After the cabinet meeting of 6 March 1952, which discussed the issue, Harold Macmillan noted that, 'poor Churchill, who wants to adopt a paternal and fatherly attitude to the Queen, was clearly much distressed himself, and a little alarmed for the future'.[19] Macmillan thought Queen Mary was behind it all, favouring Windsor 'and all the emphasis on the truly British and native character of the Royal Family. It is also clear that the Duke has the normal attitude of many men towards a mother-in-law of strong character, accentuated by the peculiar circumstances of his position ... It is more than likely that he has been told that we are suspicious of him on political grounds.' They were. Underneath the apparently banal question of the royal name were deeper currents. Tory ministers feared that Philip and his uncle Mountbatten hoped to mount a gentle constitutional coup, influencing the Queen towards some kind of joint – and more leftish – monarchy. There was no evidence for that, but Philip was certainly seen after the war as more open to Labour than the traditional royals. By 3 April Churchill was reporting back that the Queen had accepted that her children would be Windsor. Her private secretary Lascelles described standing over her like one of the barons at Runnymede. Nastily, Macmillan wrote in his diary that although 'this has been a painful episode ... it is a very good thing that the influence of the Consort and his family should have had an early rebuff'.

It was unfortunate that the cabal of men in charge paid so little heed to Prince Philip's feelings and the hurt seems to have rankled for a long time. The Queen is said to have been hurt too, and it caused trouble because Philip's very identity in his new family was being questioned. He famously complained that he felt 'like a bloody amoeba'. The Queen may have felt she had no option but to side with her father's memory and her ministers' views against her husband, but it was a badly handled episode. She later tried to make it up to him, provoking another cabinet debate in February 1955 as to whether he could be called 'Prince of the Commonwealth' – but Canada and South Africa were not keen. Scottish members of the cabinet likewise vetoed Churchill's notion of 'Prince of England'. Macmillan noted that the Queen 'still hankers after some distinctive title for the Duke of Edinburgh' but it was reckoned that simply calling him 'the Prince' was 'too Machiavelli'.

There the matter rested, not happily. The Queen continued to treat Churchill with deference. When he finally left office, she and the Duke of Edinburgh joined him for a farewell dinner party at Number Ten, an honour not repeated until

Wilson left office in 1976. Later, as reports came in of his failing health, she was initiating the idea that when he died he should lie in state in Westminster Hall. He would be the unique commoner, in death as in life.

It was a rough time for Prince Philip generally. The Queen had wanted him to take over from her as Colonel of the Grenadier Guards, a role she had had since her teenage years and one she particularly valued. A particularly savage lieutenant colonel led a revolt against having 'some bloody Greek' and Prince Philip quietly retreated, hurt, and became Colonel of the Welsh Guards instead. When his son grew to the age when as Prince of Wales that job was appropriate for him, it was suggested that Philip go to the Grenadiers after all. A lesser man might have told them where to stick their bearskins. Prince Philip accepted, becoming a very engaged and committed figurehead for the Grenadiers, and remains so today. Though, as we shall see, the family name continued to cause arguments, perhaps the final say about Prince Philip's status did not come until 2011 when, aged ninety, he was made Lord High Admiral, a title the Queen herself had carried till then.

The cabinet continued to spend what seems an inordinate amount of time discussing minor royal questions. Pursuing a property claim, Prince Ernst of Hanover, who had been on the German side in the war, tried to claim British citizenship through an Act of 1705. For obscure reasons the cabinet was told this would have had the effect of stripping the Mountbattens of their legal status. Macmillan recorded that as to Mountbatten himself this didn't matter, since 'Admirals of the Fleet, it seems, are bastards anyway', while his brother Lord Milford Haven might lose his seat in the Lords, 'but he was a bad lot, so nobody seemed to mind'.[20] This gives something of the acrid establishment atmosphere of the time. One of the oddities from the Prince Ernst case was that it became clear that, by the same 1705 Act, Prince Philip had been legally British all along and Mountbatten's campaign to naturalize him had been entirely unnecessary.

Prince Philip, meanwhile, ignored his defeat and began the most vigorously successful years of his life as consort, a time when he was regularly voted the most popular member of the royal family and seemed quite likely to turn his role into a much bigger one. He threw himself into promoting the cause of efficiency in business or scientific managerialism. He was president of the British Association for the Advancement of Science; and in a series of speeches through the 1950s and into the 1960s, he poked the stodginess of British industry in the eye, mocked the dead hand of trade union conservatism and demanded more vigour. In 1961 Prince Philip famously asked why British industry was in decline and suggested it was a national defeat 'comparable to any lost military campaign . . . Gentlemen, I think it is about time we pulled our fingers out.'

It was an analysis widely shared by worried economic observers. Nearly a decade before, one of the founders of the Institute for Economic Affairs, Oliver Smedley, had warned that Britain could not survive 'in an intensely competitive world if our energies, enterprise and adaptability continue to be fettered by the outmoded trappings and controls of the centrally planned economy'.[21] Popular criticism of inefficient trade union practices and restrictive cartels had been a rising issue through the decade, hitting the cinema screens from the Ealing comedy of 1951, *The Man in the White Suit*, to the 1959 Boulting brothers' *I'm All Right Jack* starring Peter Sellers, who in his Goon days had been a favourite of the Windsors. In the press, in thoughtful magazines and among free-market academics, the need for a brisker, more aggressive attitude to wealth making was heard again and again: these years of consensual 'Butskellism' and declinism always had their dissidents.

Prince Philip's speeches led to a popular conviction that he was a vigorous stirrer-upper and modern man, and he was. His unhappiness over the loss of the Mountbatten surname did not make him pause in testing the old verities of the Palace, and relishing outsiders' challenges about the point and purpose of monarchy. It is safe to speculate that these matters did not trouble his wife, more instinctively conservative (with a small c) than him, and with a much clearer public position. What Prince Philip lacked was a mechanism, a powerful lever or organization of his own which could have given his energy some kind of wider grip. He was condemned by the job he had taken on to be forever a commentator, a speech-maker (and he is a good one), occasionally a chairman – but never an executive. It is a dilemma his oldest son wrestled with too.

There is a sense of 'battle joined' in his speeches of the later 1950s and 1960s. It was not obvious that Britain was going to continue her industrial slither downwards. The giant Unilever was successfully importing American industrial and commercial techniques; ICI was spending more on research and development by the end of the 1950s than all British universities together; ruthless tycoons like Hugh Fraser and Jack Cotton were cutting a swathe through commercial property and retail; both the steel and car industries had formed major alliances on the 'bigger is better' principle, and the first motorway was about to open. The City was stuffy, but on the move towards reasserting an international role that would soon result in the Eurobond market. From Alec Issigonis's radical Mini of 1959 to Christopher Cockerell's hovercraft, which the former radar developer had invented in 1956, Britain had not lost her inventiveness. Prince Philip became a representative voice for rising concern and anger about the poor industrial and scientific performance of Britain generally, something apparently forgotten in the later brouhaha about his tactless 'slitty eyes' remark and similar. Even Harold Wilson's Labour Party seized the fashionable enthusiasm for efficiency and better management as a major theme. Prince Philip, in his first two decades as consort, was relevant, pungent and popular.

Not all critics of fustiness, however, nor all modernizers, were welcome. Two figures, one the relatively obscure John Grigg, later Lord Altrincham, and the other the wrinkled celebrity Malcolm Muggeridge, both took pot shots at the monarchy during this period. In an obscure journal picked up by the mainstream press, Grigg attacked the Queen's speech-making abilities, complaining that she sounded like 'a priggish schoolgirl, captain of the hockey team . . .' and her way of speaking was 'a pain in the neck'. Muggeridge attacked the royal 'soap opera' in an American magazine in 1957, just ahead of the Queen and Duke's visit, complaining about the dreary and conservative aristocrats surrounding them. His thrust was more against the knee-jerk and sugary monarchism of the British media than the royal family itself; but it was published under a headline questioning the need for a Queen; the self-same media quickly whipped up the story. What is odd, looking back, is not what the men said. They may have been rude, robustly articulating a minority view, but it was a free country. What was really remarkable was the fury of public reaction. Grigg and Muggeridge were threatened, abused, screamed at, pilloried and assaulted. To criticize the Queen was still beyond the pale.

Yet the country was on the turn. Old habits of deference and respect were fraying – a social change which was accelerated, at least, by the disastrous premiership of the Queen's second prime minister. Personally Eden, who had fought gallantly in the First World War, as well as acting as Churchill's anti-appeasement lieutenant and wartime foreign secretary, was well known to the royal family. He had first met the Queen as the seven-year-old Princess Elizabeth in 1934, when he was appointed Lord Privy Seal. George V was at his most choleric; furious at anti-monarchist comments by the socialist Stafford Cripps, who had claimed his attack on 'Buckingham Palace influence' was not meant to refer to the King himself. The King confided in Eden, as a good royalist: 'What does he mean by saying, Buckingham Palace is not me? Who else is there, I should like to know? Does he mean the footmen? D'you see the fellow says there is going to be a general election in August? Who is he to decide that? Damned cheek, I call it.'[22] Later, in 1947, during the worst of the austerity years, Eden had been a vocal supporter of the monarchy in the Commons against those calling for a slimmed-down Scandinavian style.

By 1955 he had become another of the elephant-premiers, though a younger, more dashing tusker than Winston, his succession so widely agreed that there was little danger of the Queen being drawn into this handover. He had been at the top of government throughout the war and was hugely admired in the country. Though his would be one of the shortest and worst premierships in modern British history, drawing the Queen into the most potentially dangerous politics of her entire reign, as he entered Downing Street there was no reason for Elizabeth not to view him with respect and affection. In private Churchill and other Tories had worried about his frail health. Had the Queen taken widespread soundings in the Conservative Party she might have found a surprisingly strong groundswell of support for another candidate, Rab Butler.

This is not the place for another reprise of the Suez affair, one of the most trawled-over episodes in post-war British history. The key facts were that the Suez Canal, through which much of Europe's oil and other commodities arrived, had been nationalized by Egypt's new leader Colonel Nasser after the fall of a pro-British puppet king. The British government connived with the French and Israelis to provide an excuse to evade international law and invade Egypt. Eden's ruse, which had been cooked up at a cloak-and-dagger meeting in a villa on the outskirts of Paris between French, British and Israeli ministers, was an Israeli attack. This would allow Britain and France to intervene to 'separate the combatants'.

Crucially, the United States was kept out of the loop and would prove a ferocious and deadly critic of the British. Eden saw Nasser as a lesser, Arab version of Hitler, a demagogue who must be confronted. In Egypt and across the Arab world Nasser was seen as a visionary and liberator; but in Britain, at least to begin with, Eden's case was overwhelmingly accepted. He was the anti-appeaser, after all, a voice much of the country instinctively trusted. Yet soon hard questions were being asked: Was this not an act of outdated imperialism? Should things not be left to the world's new policeman, the United Nations? Was the government telling the whole truth? Was this not, in fact, a British act of aggression? These questions began to bubble from liberal newspapers and the Labour benches in the Commons, to foment mass demonstrations in the streets. Britain was divided.

Even at the time, many suspected Eden's account. To maintain the ruse, he had to lie to Parliament and conceal the truth even from some of his own ministers. The reason this was potentially so dangerous for the Queen is that she presumably saw, and carefully read, the private papers from Number

Ten, the Foreign Office and the secret services. Did they reveal what was happening? Maybe, maybe not. Senior members of MI6, many cabinet ministers and most of Whitehall had been carefully kept out of the loop. It is possible, as most historians think, that Eden with the help of his officials concealed the truth from the Queen in his audiences with her, and there were two in the crucial month. This would have been outrageous for a properly functioning constitutional monarchy, if humanly understandable to save himself embarrassment and to protect the Queen. Alternatively she was one of the select few to know the dangerous truth and was silently drawn into his lie. Which was it?

The Queen's own private office was split about Suez. Her private secretary Michael Adeane, a traditional conservative in the mould of his grandfather Lord Stamfordham, was pro-Eden and pro-Suez. But the two assistant private secretaries, Martin Charteris and Edward Ford, who had both served in the Middle East during the Second World War, were anti. Over the years there have been persistent rumours that the Queen and Prince Philip were also hostile to the invasion. These surfaced in their clearest form in a book by the historian Robert Lacey for the Queen's Silver Jubilee in 1977. Lacey, a *Sunday Times* writer, had excellent access, eased by Lord Mountbatten, who wanted such a book to be published, and who in deepest privacy gave Lacey a lot of help. Lacey wrote that: 'Elizabeth II appeared to friends and relatives genuinely surprised by what had been carried out in her name in October and November 1956.' Either she 'went along with the strategic deception of the rest of the world – including the United States [and of course Parliament] – or else she was taken in by it, like everyone else'. When the manuscript began to circulate, and Eden discovered that Lacey had concluded the Queen did not know the full truth about Suez, he was furious, fully understanding the gravity of the accusation that he had deceived his monarch.

Eden concluded Lacey must have been told this by Mountbatten or by Prince Philip and insisted to Lacey that the Queen 'understood what we were doing very well'.[23] Ill with cancer, the former prime minister was staying at Eton and decided to confront Mountbatten, a man he now described as 'gaga' and 'a congenital liar'. Mountbatten, who had come over from Windsor, said in his diary that, 'I didn't attempt to deny it . . . It was the author himself who had put the question and I thought I had answered it sufficiently tactfully not to produce the particular statement that had appeared.'[24] Lacey came under heavy pressure from Eden and his former foreign secretary, Selwyn Lloyd, to change the story. He did not. It can now be said that Mountbatten was indeed Lacey's source and had told him clearly that the Queen did not know about the deception involving Britain, France and Israel on which the Suez attack had depended. The question then is, did Mountbatten really know this? Had the Queen told him? Or the Duke?

A significant factor not known at the time was that Mountbatten actually tried to resign as First Sea Lord and was ordered by the politician in charge of the Admiralty, Lord Hailsham, to stay at his post. That was news that would surely have been known by the Queen at the time and gives strong credence to the belief that she knew about Eden's plot, or at least that something very strange was going on. At all events, when Eden, stricken by illness, went to Sandringham in January 1957 to tell the Queen that he was resigning, she expressed deep personal sadness and offered him an earldom. She wrote to him almost immediately afterwards:

My Dear Anthony,

You know already how deeply I felt your resignation last week, and how much I sympathize in the tragic turn of fate which laid you low at the moment our country is beginning to see the possibility of a brightening in the international sky . . . much has been said and written in the past week about your record in the House of Commons and as a Statesman; I am only anxious that you should realise that that record, which has indeed been won in tempestuous times, is highly valued and will never be forgotten by your Sovereign.

He replied in emotional terms:

It is the bare truth to say that I looked forward to my weekly audience, knowing that I should receive from Your Majesty a wise and impartial reaction to events, which was quite simply the voice of our land. Years ago Baldwin told me that the post of Prime Minister was the most lonely in the world . . . that I have not found it so is due to Your Majesty's unfailing sympathy and understanding.

These are not the words of a Queen outraged about being kept in the dark, or a statesman embarrassed about keeping her there. The two had had longer than average audiences while Eden was prime minister and after he had gone – most unusually – the Queen accepted the Edens' private hospitality. In 1994 Charteris, himself on the anti-Suez side, added more to the jigsaw in a recorded interview with Peter Hennessy. He said the Queen was deeply concerned about Suez, about 'the fundamental dishonesty of it all, the collusion of France and Israel . . . and also she was very concerned about the effect of this action ... on Commonwealth opinion and United States opinion'. That Charteris describes the 'collusion of' France and Israel, as opposed to 'with', is interesting. Mountbatten, Eden and her own private office would all have wanted to protect her, as well as understanding that she had an ultimate constitutional right to know what her government was doing.

My belief is that the Queen knew the essential story but that Eden had deliberately held back the most embarrassing part of his plan from her, precisely in order that she should not be contaminated if it went wrong, as it certainly did, and that, saying nothing directly, she appreciated this. In any event the Suez crisis showed how easily a monarch could be drawn into disastrous plans hatched by a prime minister. It implies that then, at least, the audiences were more about the Queen listening and sympathizing than about her actively questioning or warning. If so, that would fit with her cautious character. It is possible to imagine her grandfather or indeed her son insisting on more information and thus becoming more closely entangled, for good or bad, with such a plot.

The Queen's political education by her early prime ministers was next tested by the succession to Eden. Naturally the Queen would appoint the Tory she was advised the party would most rally behind, and thus the politician with the best chance of parliamentary success; but in 1957 the question was not entirely easy to answer. Who could say whom the party really wanted? The newspapers, including those well connected to Conservative circles, assumed the prize would go to R. A. Butler. Eden himself preferred Butler and, according to his own private papers, signified 'my own debt to Mr Butler'. But Harold Macmillan was also considered to be a sound candidate. Nor was it just a case of appointing any leading Conservative and assuming that the government would continue. Suez had left deep wounds in Parliament and the country. The Tory Party was divided, embarrassed and angry about how things had turned out, with many blaming – variously – the Americans, the media, Eden himself or anti-Suez voices, which had included Butler's. This time, Buckingham Palace could not simply stand aside and wait.

Two men became critical. One was Sir Michael Adeane, the Queen's private secretary. The other was Robert Gascoyne-Cecil, the fifth Marquess of Salisbury, Leader of the Lords, a friend of the royal family's, grandson of Queen Victoria's last premier, and himself a long-serving Conservative minister who had resigned over appeasement in 1938 and later served under Churchill. The Cecils are one of the ancient political dynasties of England. No grandee was grander than he. Though the Queen did not formally ask Eden for his advice, she did ask him how the view of the Conservative Party should be canvassed. Eden suggested using Salisbury. Adeane, a long-serving courtier and grandson of Stamfordham, who had been working at the Palace since 1936, was also old-school in his instincts. He was wry, recessive and loyal. Before serving George VI he had been aide-de-camp to Lord Tweedsmuir, the former novelist John Buchan, in Canada (and his son later became private secretary to Prince Charles). Now Adeane called Salisbury, who had just been shooting with the royal family for three days at Sandringham, and asked him to take soundings. Salisbury then roped in Lord Kilmuir, the Lord Chancellor. Between them they decided the neatest solution would simply be to ask members of the cabinet one by one which man, Butler or Macmillan, they favoured. This poll would then be supplemented by advice about the mood of the Tory backbenchers, delivered by the then chief whip, a young man called Ted Heath, and the party grassroots, through its chairman, Oliver Poole. Neither Heath nor Poole did any polling of their own. Was this quite kosher? Apparently so: Kilmuir told Salisbury that the Queen could take any advice she liked 'and that she did not have to wait – indeed, ought not to wait – for the result of a Party meeting and election'.[25]

This led to one of the most famous and repeatedly described vignettes in Britain's post-war parliamentary history, with the cabinet members being led in, one by one, to see Salisbury in an anteroom at the Privy Council Office to be asked, in his lisping voice, which it was to be, 'Wab or Hawold?' With only two or perhaps three exceptions, they voted for Harold Macmillan. He was also the favoured candidate of Heath, speaking for the backbenches, and of Poole, speaking for the party members. Meanwhile the Queen had asked Eden whether she should also consult Churchill. Despite his fondness for Butler, when the Grand Old Man arrived at Buckingham Palace with Salisbury, a Union flag rug draped over his knees, he too plumped for Macmillan. The whole process had been remarkably fast. On Tuesday 8 January 1957, Eden had been down at Sandringham to tell the Queen he was going. By lunchtime two days later Macmillan had been to Buckingham Palace and was prime minister.

Almost everyone who has studied the party breakdown has concluded that, despite the surprise of the newspapers and Eden's own preference, Macmillan was the obvious choice. Butler had been an appeaser and in the mid-1950s that still mattered. More important, he was seen as indecisive, excessively wily and not entirely loyal over Suez. There were thought to be more Tories, both in Parliament and the country, dead against Butler than there were against Macmillan – who would indeed quickly bind the bleeding wounds and stage an impressive Conservative comeback. Salisbury came from a noble lineage and was great friends with the royal family; but he was hardly holding one of the primary offices of state and was no longer an elected politician. It was a rum and old-fashioned way of switching prime ministers and it would sow seeds of doubt in many people's minds about how Britain was run.

Democracy and Big Mac

Some fifteen months earlier a dishevelled and rather brilliant journalist on the *Spectator* called Henry Fairlie had written a column about the well-connected traitors Burgess and Maclean in which he coined the term 'the establishment' to describe the social exercise of power in England. What had happened over the Tory succession suggested that a magic circle of grandees was indeed still shuffling society's cards and pulling Westminster's strings. It was a compelling idea, but by then already out of date and only partially true. Debs were still presented at court. At Ascot and royal garden parties, the top hats, tails and uniforms were as ubiquitous as ever. As the 1950s waned a startling number of the cabinet were inter-related Old Etonians. Macmillan and aristocratic friends went shooting at Balmoral and Sandringham and the prime minister was mildly surprised at a flurry of media hostility when the Queen proposed to go tiger-shooting on a visit to India. In the City, bowler hats and rolled umbrellas remained 'the thing' and Whitehall followed a near-military system of ranking and caste. The only long-haired people at the BBC were female typists. Yet the establishment's instincts and solidarity were coming apart – not that they had been quite that strong anyway. Even apparently tight social circles and families fell out, as they have always done. Salisbury himself had been among the old-school aristocrats who were most suspicious of Prince Philip.

Now he intervened in another highly sensitive Windsor dilemma. The trouble had begun on the day of the Coronation when journalists, already in the know, had noticed a gently intimate stroking by Princess Margaret of Group Captain Peter Townsend's lapel. Discretion still held, just about, in the British press; but in New York the story about a possible further marriage, this time of the Queen's sister, was swiftly published. It was followed, twelve days after the Coronation, by a British Sunday paper, the raucous *People*. This hypocritically told the story only to denounce it as obviously untrue, since 'it is quite unthinkable that a royal princess, third in line of succession to the throne, should even contemplate marriage with a man who has been through the divorce courts'. Mischievous though it was, the newspaper had put its inky finger on a real problem. Divorce was a serious social and moral stigma. Under the archaic Royal Marriages Act, until the summer of 1955, when she would be twenty-five, Princess Margaret needed her sister's permission to get married: a full two years away. The Queen, observing constitutional propriety, would in turn need the assent of her government. What would she do? What would it do?

Townsend, a decorated RAF war hero who had arrived at Buckingham Palace as equerry to the King in 1944, had had an unhappy wartime marriage, which had recently ended in divorce. He had been spotted by the young Margaret during the South African trip of 1947 and, though he was nearly sixteen years older than the Princess, they had fallen in love soon afterwards. He had declared his love at the beginning of Coronation year and informed the Queen's private secretary, still at this point 'Tommy' Lascelles. A horrified Lascelles barked at Townsend that he was either bad or mad. Churchill agreed, and Townsend was rather brutally sent off to an RAF desk job in Belgium to get him out of the way of the vivacious and determined princess. There he bided his time, assuming that once the deadline passed and Margaret was twenty-five he would be free to marry her. Then in October 1955, Salisbury, a leading High Anglican, told his cabinet colleagues that he could not accept that the Queen's sister could ever marry a divorced man – despite the fact that Townsend had been the innocent party in his divorce. Since the cabinet had to approve the marriage and would have been riven had Salisbury made a public issue of this, and resigned, the peer had effectively destroyed Princess Margaret's hopes.

Old ways or new? Love or religion? The press was now divided, with the more popular papers, and those on the left, backing the Princess's right to marry. Eden had broken the news to her that, if she went ahead, she would lose her position in the line of succession and her expanded Civil List allowance. She would have to live abroad. The story, having been ignited by a popular newspaper, was now concluded by the highbrow *Times*, which argued in its editorial for 24 October that the Queen was society's 'universal representative in whom her people see their better selves ideally reflected; and since part of their ideal is family life, the Queen's family has its own part in the reflection'. The proposed marriage would make it inevitable 'that this reflection becomes distorted'. Princess Margaret finally bowed to the pressure and announced that she had decided not to marry Townsend, 'mindful of the Church's teaching that Christian marriage is indissoluble, and conscious of my duty to the Commonwealth . . .' It seems to have been a devastating blow to her. She told friends later that she particularly blamed Lascelles and Churchill for what she had been put through and never completely recovered her balance. Of course, no one can ever know how a marriage that did not happen might have worked out, but this was a warthog-like assertion of the rule book which seems cruel and faintly silly.

What did the Queen do? Earlier biographers who knew those involved believe she stood aside from her sister's dilemma, refusing to discuss it and deliberately avoiding taking a position. From a modern perspective this might seem odd. After all, Townsend knew the Queen and Prince Philip. They seem to have liked him, and wished both him and Princess Margaret well. Should she not have been assertive in her sister's cause? The answer is surely that she decided to think as Queen first and sister second. Only two years before, in her Coronation Oath, she had promised the church and the world that she would uphold the highest values of Christian family life. She meant it. She could not ignore her bishops or ministers. She was pulled by natural affection. But she was also tugged by duty, and time and again in her life it has been duty whose pull proved strongest. Thankfully the Townsend episode would not be repeated. Attitudes were changing and divorce slowly became more socially acceptable. But this was an ominous early signal of the problems ahead for the 'ideal family' version of modern monarchy. Real families are untidy. Emotions cannot always be conveniently bottled up. Press prurience rarely helps.

For the press was sick of the old habits of discretion, firmed up by wartime patriotism as well as censorship, and now coming loose. The Margaret affair was an early clang of the warning bell. Prince Philip's decision to tour a swathe of the Commonwealth without his wife in *Britannia* for six months during the winter of 1956–7 prompted newspaper speculation about the state of the Queen's marriage, leading to an official statement from the Palace: 'It is quite untrue that there is any rift between the Queen and the Duke of Edinburgh.' Well-meant but ham-fisted, the statement only inflamed the story. In this period too, Prince Philip became infuriated by the press coverage, complaining bitterly to friends about it and sounding increasingly cynical about journalism. An outward-going, optimistic man, keen to explain himself, would begin to turn into a more suspicious one who went about expecting to be misunderstood. This was a bad loss for the British monarchy but there was probably no help for it. The press was not going to defer or self-censor for long. Papers were fighting cut-throat battles for a large and lucrative market, increasingly worried about television swiping their profits, and in no mood to hold back on good stories.

In any event, it was unwise to build the institution on the implied promise that Royals would never again misbehave or love unwisely. The 'family monarchy' of George V and George VI, following the uxorious Victoria, was not the whole story of kings and queens in Britain or anywhere else; historians have always plundered royalty for its scandals. So should the Queen, perhaps, have used her popularity during this period to reconsider family values and personal morality as the central building block of modern monarchy? Easy to say. But what would she have put in its place? And how could she have advanced some new idea? This was a time, after all, when she was a happy and contented mother and wife herself, deferring happily to Prince Philip in domestic matters. After the Townsend episode there seemed to be no family problems ahead. These were years of innocence.

Not in politics, however: there are no innocent years there. As a fierce imperialist, Salisbury would fall out with Macmillan over decolonization and emerge as the first president of the right-wing Monday Club. Indeed, by that Easter Salisbury had resigned over Cyprus, believing Macmillan had not been tough enough with the rebel leader, Archbishop Makarios, and leading Macmillan to reflect that throughout history 'the Cecils, when any friend or colleague has been in real trouble, have stabbed him in the back'. When the Macmillans went to Balmoral for their first August visit, perhaps tactlessly, Salisbury was among the party. It did not, seemingly, go smoothly, with Macmillan tending to lecture the Queen and being unimpressed by Prince Philip: 'He is *against* us being a nuclear power. I don't altogether like the tone of his talk. It is too like that of a clever undergraduate, who has just discovered Socialism.' This was an absurd judgement on Macmillan's part: the grand premier had clearly had his tweeds ruffled by Prince Philip, who though studiously non-party, always sounded more like a radical of the free market, pro-business right, than of the left.

Macmillan went on to become a pivotal prime minister in the Queen's reign, in that, after the ups and downs of the Churchill and Eden administrations, she had time to develop a longer and somewhat more equal relationship with him. He was in a sense her first 'normal' prime minister. As foreign secretary in 1955 he had been impressed, and somewhat chastened, to discover how hard she worked to understand political issues, in this case over Iraq: 'I did my best to explain the position to her, without boring her. She showed (as her father used to) an uncanny knowledge of details and personalities. She must read the telegrams very carefully.' There were signs that he bored her from time to time – once, when gloomily mentioning his possible resignation, he was rather hurt at her 'lack of consternation' – but in general, whatever her private feelings, the relationship seemed to blossom. He sent her long despatches and often referred to her close reading of papers and sympathetic understanding of his problems. Adeane encouraged him to stay for a drink after his weekly audience, and Macmillan did his best to please her in small ways, trying, as we have seen, to help in the vexed question of Prince Philip's title and the family surname.

Abroad, 'the winds of change' swept through much of Britain's African territory although the country still aspired to global reach with her newly purchased nuclear weaponry and initially stood proudly aloof from the experimental European Economic Community. From 1959 as Secretary for the Colonies, Iain Macleod was charged with what was, in effect, a fire sale of the remaining parts of the British Empire. On this issue the Queen now began to assert herself directly, showing a new steeliness during a row in 1961 over whether or not she should go ahead with a visit to Ghana. In 1957 Ghana had been the first black Commonwealth country to win independence, under Kwame Nkrumah, closely followed by Nigeria. The visit had already been delayed, because of the Queen's third pregnancy, greatly to Nkrumah's personal distress. By now, however, he had established a personal, anti-democratic and indeed dictatorial rule in what had become a republic. This led to deep questions about the purpose of the Commonwealth. Ought it to be an organization of democratic nations under the Queen, or was it a family which continued to embrace its members, more or less however they behaved? Apartheid South Africa, disliking Macmillan's decolonization policy, declared itself a republic and left the Commonwealth in 1961, but some of the same issues, of human rights and democracy, applied to black nations too. Many British politicians, putting democracy before the brotherhood of the Commonwealth, wanted the Queen to cancel. Macmillan worried that if the matter came up in the Commons he might be defeated.

The Queen was determined to go. According to Macmillan she told him she 'means to be a Queen and not a puppet' and, if ordered not to do what she thought was her duty, 'did not know how she could carry on'. The biographer Lady Longford records the Queen arguing that cancelling might push Ghana towards the Soviet Union: 'How silly should I look, if I was scared to visit Ghana and then Khrushchev went and had a good reception?'[26] In the run-up to her visit Nkrumah had organized a round-up of dissidents, after which a terrorist bomb went off in the capital Accra, blowing both legs off his statue, so apart from the political dilemma there was a clear risk to the Queen's safety. She did go, made a speech stating that the Commonwealth family could include a wide amount of disagreement, danced with Nkrumah and was hailed locally as 'the greatest socialist monarch in the world'. At the banquet many of the seats were unfilled, having been prepared for opposition leaders now in jail.

Though the Queen had demonstrated her cool unconcern for her own safety – a trait repeated later – and gritty determination that the Commonwealth should come first, she had not resolved the central dilemma. Or rather she had done so in a way that has often seemed very unsatisfactory since. 'Family' was to be treated with kid gloves, at the national as at the personal level. The Commonwealth, an organization of high ideals, pragmatically accepted some brutal and undemocratic regimes rather than lose members. The excuse that it was better to stay close and try to influence them is what parents say about off-the-rails teenagers. But what is tough love, and what is merely fluffy appeasement? Macmillan's withdrawal from empire, essential as it was, would involve the

Queen in more morally difficult choices as she worked hard to create a real role as head of a fractious Commonwealth – some of whose members were now looking more to communist Moscow than to monarchical London.

Macmillan's great trick was to keep a good front, while paddling desperately below the water as he tried to adapt to radically different circumstances. This impersonator of an unflappable toff must in private have brought his Queen much bad and dramatic news, even without 'the winds of change'. There were the embarrassing deals that needed to be done with the United States to maintain a British nuclear capacity that worked; the loss of South Africa from the Commonwealth; the terrifying stand-offs between the US and the USSR; the startling decline of British manufacturing and recurrent problems with trade balances and inflation; the consequent plea for membership of the Common Market and President de Gaulle's humiliating 'non'; the sexual and spying scandals at home. For the Queen, all this must have added up to one of the hardest periods of adaptation of her reign. That frothy post-Coronation enthusiasm for a new Elizabethan Age was crashing like spume against a comfortless, rocky shore.

To safely sustain the monarchy the Queen would have to change it. She was greatly helped by Prince Philip, who, after the outside attacks on the stuffiness of the monarchy by Lord Altrincham and Malcolm Muggeridge, seems to have been emboldened in his reformist ideas. He was enthusiastic about opening up the Palace for lunch and supper parties, which allowed the Queen to meet a wider range of people. Characteristic guest lists from 1957 included the pianist Myra Hess, the Labour MP (and future prime minister) Jim Callaghan, the runner Chris Brasher, the Ealing film-producer Michael Balcon, the editor of *The Economist*, Donald Tyerman, the poet John Betjeman and the actress Joyce Grenfell. If these were modest steps towards a more informed and informal style, they seemed radical to those used to her father's court. Then the Queen, on her own initiative, finally abolished the aristocratic flummery of the Season. The presentation of debutantes at Buckingham Palace, waiting on gilt chairs in their white silk dresses until summoned by the Lord Chamberlain to curtsey to the Queen, sitting on her throne below a red canopy, had continued until 1958. In that year, 1,400 girls were paraded over three days until the Queen ended the practice. What made the presentations a target for reform, rather than some of the other old customs of monarchy? Partly, it was that the bloodstock market aspect of it was embarrassingly class-conscious. Partly, it had become a subject for jokes: in the tart words of the Queen's tart sister, 'every tart in London was getting in'.

A more significant reform for most people was the Queen's reluctant agreement to appear regularly once a year on television. Prince Philip backed a long-time ambition of the BBC by persuading his wife to give her traditional Christmas Day broadcast in vision rather than by radio. It was a gamble. The radio microphone had been an instrument of torture for her father, while the Queen felt uncomfortable talking to a camera. She lacks the glib actorly touch that an autocue requires. Yet the gamble paid off, with nearly half the entire population watching the message by the early 1960s. The Christmas messages became an important way for the Queen to communicate directly and although most of what she said was unsurprising, gently optimistic and routine, she worked hard with Prince Philip on the tone, and often made headlines. Even when she did not, millions found the address becoming a ritual part of a British Christmas, even standing to attention in front of their television sets to watch it.

These were only modest reforms at a time when the country was changing very fast. Was the Queen let down by her advisers at the time? In criticizing the tweedy and unimaginative atmosphere of the old court, Altrincham and Muggeridge had had a point. It would be unreasonable to expect the Palace to be ahead of the times, but it had fallen a long way behind the changing atmosphere of the country, and, despite Prince Philip, would stay well behind. The key courtiers were by now old and very cautious, too distanced from the Queen's generation, never mind younger ones. Her instinct usually was to wait for advice and consider it, rather than to initiate change herself. Nor were the politicians of the time any help. The Queen was moving into a country where the ghosts of George V and George VI were no longer sufficient guides. Nor were the cabinet ministers. Macmillan needed her as part of his controversial balancing act and enjoyed playing the elderly uncle; but she would need to move beyond him, too.

His eventual departure was even messier than Eden's, though at least quicker than Churchill's. By the summer of 1963 Macmillan's government was struggling under the embarrassing blow of the Profumo spying, lying and sex scandal. Macmillan was facing a growing rebellion inside the party he had led with guile and brutality. In October, unable to urinate and in growing pain, he was diagnosed with a benign tumour of the prostate and informed that an operation was essential. He took the gloomiest medical view possible of his condition and determined that because of the risk that he might have cancer, and because of the length of time he would need to recuperate from the operation, he must immediately resign. This time round, however, there was a real choice of successors.

They included, yet again, Rab Butler, but also the popular Lord Hailsham; three new stars, Reggie Maudling, Edward Heath and Iain Macleod; and a man who seemed the outsider, Lord Home. Since Macmillan's illness coincided with the Conservatives' annual conference at Blackpool, some kind of contest in front of the party faithful was inevitable. Macmillan wanted to stop Butler, who was probably the favourite choice of the cabinet. Lying in the King Edward VII Hospital for Sick Officers, he called Home to his bedside to persuade him he might have to stand and then used him as his messenger to the Tory conference, carrying news of his resignation. In Blackpool, meanwhile, Hailsham made something of an ass of himself with what Conservative grandees thought vulgar self-promotion. Home, with the status of Macmillan's man, began to mobilize support. This left the problem of stopping Butler. And at this point Macmillan's manoeuvring drew in the Queen.

'Soundings' were taken of the party (now generally regarded as fixed) which showed a surprising surge on all sides for Lord Home. He too had been at one time tarred as a member of the appeasement camp but by now was known as a likeable moderate, and gentle aristrocrat. Macmillan, through Adeane, arranged that the Queen should visit him at his bedside – passing in front of television cameras and the world's press – so that he could tender his resignation in person and offer her advice about his successor. That advice, read to her from his bed, was that she should summon Home to Buckingham Palace and ask him whether he could form a government. This was a clear and obvious 'bounce' which gave Home a royal stamp of approval before full or systematic advice had been taken from the party. When they heard what was happening, some of the most talented Tory ministers, including Enoch Powell and Iain Macleod, were inclined to rebel on Butler's behalf and refuse to serve under Home. But Butler, seeing the prize snatched from his hands for a second time, flinched and, perhaps too loyally, declined to join the protests. Macmillan had fixed the succession, rather more successfully than Eden had. The Queen of course had only taken her prime minister's advice. But had she allowed herself to be used? We must remember that this was a still a young woman, trained to receive the advice of older men – men her father's age. According to Ben Pimlott, a later biographer, 'When she got the advice to call Alec she thought, "Thank God." She loved Alec – he was an old friend. They talked about dogs and shooting together. They were both Scottish landowners, the same sort of people, like old school friends.'[27]

Alec Douglas-Home, who now had to renounce his title and stand as an MP for the Commons, had thought he would be the unity candidate but found there were many puzzled and angry colleagues he had to persuade – and some he could not. By the 1960s it was no longer obvious that a straightforward, benign but clearly aristocratic Scottish laird, who loved his salmon fishing and grouse moors, was an electoral asset. Douglas-Home was indeed a close friend of the royal family – particularly of the Queen Mother's family, the Bowes Lyons. Courtiers too would have seen him as 'one of us'. The Queen herself was not at the time blamed directly for her part, but there was fury in much of the Tory Party, and more widely in the country, about the fix; and the choice of Douglas-Home in 1963 may well have made possible Harold Wilson's squeak-home election victory the following year.

The most cogent attack came by Iain Macleod in the *Spectator*, when he attacked Macmillan for presiding over an

Old Etonian 'Magic Circle' which had plotted to deny Butler the premiership, and the episode came to symbolize all that was wrong and fusty about British political life. Macmillan, wilier than the Queen, had used her ruthlessly as cover to achieve his ends. Douglas-Home had been summoned under the unquestionable authority of the Queen's Prerogative, endlessly invoked by Macmillan before and afterwards in his explanation of these events. Any possibility of Butler refusing to accept what was going on was dashed by her involvement. In truth, of course, the Queen had had nothing personally to do with the succession. Neither she, nor Adeane, nor anyone at Buckingham Palace, had taken personal soundings or had personal debates about the possible candidates. They too were presented with a fait accompli masquerading as obsequious advice. Here was the final example of a still relatively young Queen being used by her politicians rather than protected by them. The storm was violent if short and nothing quite like this ever happened again. Parties would in future choose their leaders by more conventional means. Politicians would display more genuine care for her reputation. And the Queen would grow wilier.

Interlude

Britannia and the Waves

It is 16 April 1953. Sir Winston Churchill is still in Downing Street, Stalin has recently died, the first James Bond novel has been published, Crick and Watson have announced the double helix structure of DNA, Hillary and Tenzing are heading towards the summit of Everest ... and the Queen is at John Brown's Shipyard on the Clyde in a downpour. She is armed with a bottle of something unpleasant-sounding called 'empire wine' to name a new ship, *Britannia*. The vessel will be the eighty-third Royal Yacht, going back in an unbroken line to the reign of Charles II, a family tree of wooden Dutch-style boats, gorgeously decorated miniature warships, paddle steamers and steel-clad steam ships. This new one looks nothing like most people's idea of a yacht. It is more like a child's drawing of a ship, with simple lines, a single big funnel, and three masts. As the rain falls, the Queen tells 30,000 Scottish shipyard workers, their families and their bosses how much the building of the ship had meant to her father: 'He felt most strongly, as I do, that a yacht was a necessity and not a luxury for the head of our great British Commonwealth, between whose countries the sea is no barrier but the natural and indestructible highway.' Whack goes the wine, hooray go the crowds and the national anthem wafts up into the mirk.

So from the very first *Britannia*'s fate and the Commonwealth's were said to be closely interlinked. As Prince Philip later pointed out, she was the first Royal Yacht to be genuinely ocean-going. The need for a new vessel to replace the last of three *Victoria and Alberts* had been discussed before the war and was revived by George VI in 1951. By then Britain was under two shadows, the shadow of post-war austerity and the new shadow of the Cold War. So the original pre-1939 plans were trimmed – the King himself asked for a smaller ship – and the new Royal Yacht was designed so that it could be converted into a floating hospital in any future war. At nearly 6,000 tons, with two steam turbine engines providing 12,000 horsepower, she was relatively underpowered. Despite post-war shortages, the construction was rushed forward partly because it was hoped that the sick King might be helped by sea voyages, such as his post-war visit on a battleship to South Africa. He died long before *Britannia* was ready.

For anyone interested in the Queen's personal taste *Britannia*, now moored at Leith docks in Edinburgh and open to the public, is well worth a visit. In her palaces and castles the Queen inherited the furnishings. These she chose, with the Duke's enthusiastic assistance. What they preferred will be familiar to millions of middle-class people of the 1950s, a clean-lined, light, unfussy Scandinavian style of decoration with comfortable, simple chairs and beds. It is a response to the heavier, more ornate styles of the previous generations. There is no dark red, no gilding, no heavy oak or strong patterns, but instead cream, light grey, simple lamps and light wood desks. The Queen's working desk is small and businesslike. The Duke's bedroom has the male simplicity of a naval officer's taste. By the time the yacht had ended her long service, she was also filled with gifts and oddities picked up on the way, from whalebones lifted from a beach by Prince Philip to presentation swords from Arabia, spears from the South Seas and carved sticks from everywhere. But the effect is of comfort and calm, not of monarchical splendour. There are flashes of grandness, including a special bay for the royal Bentley, which would be unloaded by crane, and the almost Venetian elegance of the Royal Barge; but this feels more like a large Home Counties detached house loaded onto a ship than a floating palace. It has little of the gold-leafed and marbled swank of the vast gin-palace cruisers the super-rich stable at St Tropez or Cannes or in the Caribbean. One politician who travelled aboard her felt 'there was a homeliness about *Britannia* which fits in with the Queen's personality. It's not a grand place. It's not a place for thinking grand thoughts.'

The Royal Yacht would be critical to the story of the new Queen's reign. Most of it, anyway. For we fast-forward to 11 December 1997. Not Glasgow, this time, but Portsmouth. Cold, clear weather. Tony Blair is Labour prime minister and after a decision taken by the former Conservative government *Britannia* is being decommissioned. A dozen members of the royal family are there, and the Queen is the last of them to leave the ship she has called home for forty-four years. *Britannia* still looks good, with her deep blue hull, flags fluttering and brass gleaming. The Royal Marines Band plays 'A Life on the Ocean Wave'. The Queen seems to be in tears. The ship has taken her and other members of her family on 968 official voyages across the globe. A staggering range of presidents, prime ministers and other notables have been entertained on board. She has travelled a total of 1,087,623 nautical miles, calling at over 600 ports in 135 countries. On *Britannia* the Queen has scampered around barefoot, gossiped endlessly late at night after visits, mimicking foreign guests, and held family-like dinners for bickering Commonwealth leaders. For those with her the last hour of the day aboard ship was often particularly fascinating. 'She would kick her shoes off, have a whisky, and it was "Did you see? Did you see? that chap was looking a bit wobbly."'

Britannia was indeed an ocean-going refuge. The Queen has said that while Buckingham Palace is for work, Windsor Castle for weekends and some state visits, Balmoral and Sandringham for holidays – albeit interrupted with a lot of work and entertaining – the Royal Yacht was where she could fully relax. One royal servant recalls her saying it was her only true break of the year: 'I walk on at the end of a long summer season, I am absolutely exhausted and you won't see me for a couple of days . . . and at the end of a fortnight I can get off at Aberdeen with a spring in my heels, ready for another year.'

The atmosphere on board reflected this. The crew were naval recruits who had volunteered to become Yachtsmen, and who learned a new routine, including the importance of moving around in plimsolls while the royal family were aboard, so as not to disturb them, and how to keep their eyes off the Queen as they worked. In turn, she knew almost all of them by their first names and took a keen interest in their welfare and families. She would become alarmed if any took unnecessary risks. As to who was accepted, one officer says, 'There were only two questions: have you got a prison record; and have you got a sense of humour? And if they laughed at the first, there wasn't any need for the second.' In this close atmosphere, the Queen would go ashore on remote islands for long private walks. If she turned round during the first minute or two, it meant she would like company and someone would join her for a privileged, frank gossip; otherwise she went on alone.

Her children have honeymooned on board, and she and her husband have used the yacht to range through some of the most remote areas on the planet, visiting tiny island members of the Commonwealth otherwise inaccessible for state visits. 'Wherever you went,' says one senior officer, 'everybody came out to look at her and the national dailies were full of it, and the TV news too. There was just an extraordinary aura she carried.' The state visits would typically start at 8 a.m., because of the importance of getting the ship neatly at rest before the morning winds. The Royals would disembark at 10 o'clock, for a round of official visits, lunches, teas, dances, speeches and openings, returning to the yacht at 5 p.m. to prepare for a formal dinner two hours later. Fifty-eight guests would be seated, the Queen presiding at an oval table with two long tables named Victoria and Albert below her. Then at 9 p.m. another 250 people would arrive, each one greeted individually, for the reception, which would continue until the Marines Band beat the retreat at 10.30 p.m. At five to eleven, the president or local leader would go ashore and at 11 p.m. the vice-admiral commanding would signal down the old voice-pipe for the engines to take her slow ahead. This routine could be used to visit a remarkable number of countries in a short time: once, for instance, Prince Philip managed eight state visits in the Caribbean in eleven days.

The official side of the Royal Yacht's work produced plenty of memorable cameos. Nobody present has forgotten the banquet the Queen threw aboard her for President Yeltsin of Russia at St Petersburg. The wine served at such dinners is generally excellent, if poured into dispiritingly small glasses. Yeltsin was notably insistent on plenty of refills and began to harangue the Queen about the problem of whether or not he should stand for re-election. Normally, she is meticulous about avoiding political comment, but finally she turned and looked hard at him: 'Mr President, from what you have been saying, you will certainly stand again.' He roared with delighted laughter.

By tradition there are no speeches at such banquets, but soon afterwards diners spun round in shock at what appeared to be a grenade going off, with a huge bang and a splinter of glass. It was Yeltsin's fist slamming onto the table before he rose to his feet to deliver a long speech in Russian. The Queen was eloquently expressionless. After the last guests had staggered into the night, *Britannia* made her way for two miles downriver past sunken submarines and cargo ships. There was no proper illumination, except for what had been described by the Russians as a 'firework display', in which the explosions were provided by out-of-date howitzer shells. It was a notably tricky exit to the open sea, not helped by the fact that the chain-smoking Russian pilot was unsure whether 'port' or 'starboard' meant left or right.

On the other side of the political divide, the Queen hosted a banquet on *Britannia* for all the living US presidents. Ronald Reagan caused surprise by saying loudly as he arrived that he had an announcement to make. He now had Aids. He then tapped each large ear – 'one for each'. Other *Britannia* evenings included ribald and rivalrous conclaves of Commonwealth leaders for the heads of government meeting off Cyprus, and riotously successful visits to the Caribbean. On one of these, Prince Philip was solemnly shaking hands and making polite enquiries of hundreds of guests coming aboard from Antigua. One was a giant local man, looming over the Duke, accompanied by his short but sturdy wife. 'What do you do on the island?' asked the Duke. The man eyed him coldly: 'Cocaine.' Prince Philip, though rarely lost for words, was taken aback and questioned loudly how it could have happened that a drug dealer had been invited on board. The wife overheard him:

'No, no, Dook. Not cocaine. Cookin'. We got a restaurant.'
These are the small incidents that, according to one close
observer of the Duke, make his official life bearable. 'The
immense tedium of much of his work means that he gropes
at anything that can be made into a joke, or a story.' Like the
Queen, he has seen most of it before.

Sans *Britannia*, many smaller members of the Commonwealth may never see another major royal visit again. None
of that will have had much impact on the hard-faced money
men of the Treasury, particularly in difficult times. *Britannia*,
with her crew of 260 sailors, 178 of them permanent, and
her twenty-six bandsmen, eventually became a mild embarrassment to the navy. In 1953 when she was launched, the Royal
Navy was the world's third-largest surface fleet; by the time
she was decommissioned, it had around thirty ships. She stood
out more, and was going to cost more to keep going. Yet her
cost–benefit ratio was easy to work out, even if you put all
the Commonwealth and other political roles completely to one
side. From 1990 onwards *Britannia* was used more and more
aggressively to promote British trade. In the following five
years she was doing around sixty such missions a year. Overseas CEOs and company presidents, from the Middle East to
the US, would be invited on board for presentations by groups
of British companies, often in electronics, engineering and
finance.

'We'd go twenty miles off the coast, so their mobile phones
wouldn't work, and we'd got them,' recalls an officer. Though
companies such as BAe and Racal had good reason to know
the effectiveness of the work, it is hard to put a clear cash
value on them. But one careful estimate found that in a three-
year period tax collected for the Treasury, after deals done
by British companies aboard *Britannia*, was running at around

£700 million a year. Given that the yacht was costing the government around £100 million a year, it would seem a good deal. Not everyone agreed, even in the Royal Household. One official says that although the ship was a wonderful refuge, 'my personal view was that it had to go, and you can get the same benefits from hiring a ship for a week or two. It was a very expensive operation, with red boxes being helicoptered out every day from London, containing quite routine stuff; and the Marine Band and so forth.' The same source adds, however, that the Queen's need for occasional privacy was poignantly clear even aboard: 'Until you're there, you don't realize the lack of her human rights in being in that job: even on *Britannia* there was a certain amount of nervousness that another boat was going to come alongside.' In the end, filled with photographs of the royal children and childhood memories, 'it was like anybody else's holiday cottage ... except that it was a ship'.

During the outbreak of the Falklands war in April 1982, Vice-Admiral Sir Paul Greening, then commanding *Britannia*, argued strongly that she should go to the conflict as a casualty evacuation ship. He was overruled, partly because of the unusual type of fuel oil she burned and partly in case she was too tempting an Argentine target: the liner *Uganda* went instead. This undermined part of the historic case for the Royal Yacht, and a decade later the vultures were hovering. She was too old to be fully modernized and strengthened. One senior former courtier says that by the 1990s she was 'on her last legs, full of asbestos, with old turbines; it was like trying to run a [Rolls-Royce] Silver Ghost in today's world. It was lovely, it was beautiful but it was basically over.' The navy offered John Major's government a deal: they would pay for the half of the yacht's costs, the £5 million needed for the crew's pay, if the two most relevant departments, the Foreign Office and the Board of Trade, shouldered the rest. The ministers concerned, Douglas Hurd and Michael Heseltine, declined.

Heseltine came aboard at Helsinki just after the Yeltsin visit in October 1994 and by one account asked Rear-Admiral Sir Robert Woodard, commander of *Britannia*, how long it would take the two of them to walk to their rendezvous with the Queen. One and a half minutes, he replied. Then, said Heseltine, you have one and a half minutes to justify the Royal Yacht. Woodard said there was no point, since the cabinet had obviously already decided to get rid of her, but he could not resist adding that she was a goose laying golden eggs, and, if you had such a creature, it did seem stupid to argue about who was paying to feed it. 'That's rather clever,' said Heseltine; but he did not save *Britannia*. Douglas Hurd, later Lord Hurd, said later that he blamed himself mainly for not getting the 'New Labour' politicians on board *Britannia* while in opposition, well before the 1997 general election, as a result of which Tony Blair's government had no substantive debate about replacing her.

Blair himself sounds defensive about the decision, but also regretful: 'Don't forget this happened just when we came in, and it was a time when we were keeping to some very tough financial measures.' To preserve *Britannia* would have taken 'a significant sum of money . . . It would have been a very hard sell at the time.' It would have 'seemed like a luxury expense.' But, adds Blair, had the decision come towards the end of his ten years, 'maybe I'd have taken a different view of it . . . it must have been a very difficult thing for them (the royal family) personally.' In the Queen's Diamond Jubilee year, a group of wealthy business people, backed by some cabinet members, are proposing a new yacht as a 'thank you' for the

Queen, privately funded, and built on new 'green' principles. But this would still require public money for its maintenance and, at the time of writing, no final decision has been taken. Will enough private money be available, and from suitable sources?

Back in the late 1990s there were lengthy and detailed discussions in Whitehall and Buckingham Palace about a replacement, which would have been a 'national yacht' able to combine business promotion with royal tours – 'a perfectly sensible piece of kit we could have produced', according to one of those involved – but not enough support was expressed by private sector sponsors. 'The Queen and Prince Philip's hearts weren't really in it for a replacement,' says an official who was there at the time. They loved the old ship, but did not have the appetite for a fight with ministers for a new one. Prince Philip has said bluntly the decision was wrong: she was 'sound as a bell' and with new engines could have gone on for half a century.[1] But he bowed to the politics. So, goodbye, *Britannia*. The goose still looks good, but it is all clever taxidermy. She is a gleaming, motionless museum, tethered at Edinburgh's port, Leith, and almost as popular with foreigners as when she was alive.

Part Four

OFF WITH HER HEAD!

The Queen in the Sixties

For the Queen, Harold Wilson was not quite an unknown quantity when he arrived in Downing Street in 1964. In 1948, while visiting Russia for trade talks, he had refused the offer to stay on to dine with Stalin by explaining he was due at Buckingham Palace to meet Princess Elizabeth and her husband.[1] When he became prime minister the Queen had already encountered him as Opposition leader. The word was that he was a keen monarchist, despite the strands of republicanism evident in Labour in the mid-1960s. Richard Crossman, the Labour minister and diarist, noted acidly that Wilson was 'devoted to the Queen and is very proud that she likes his visits to her'.[2] But Wilson made a small point early on by refusing to go to kiss hands wearing a tail-coat, but only a regular black jacket (oddly combined with formal striped trousers).

Later this would be described as a 'modernizing' gesture but on all the real issues, from the Queen's interests as Head of the Commonwealth to the royal finances, Wilson would back her strongly. His Tuesday audiences became steadily more important to him – or so his staff felt – in both his 1964–70 and 1974–6 governments. They crept up in length from twenty minutes, to half an hour, to an hour and, at least once, to two hours, with the Queen offering him drinks afterwards. His staff described him as being 'euphoric' after audiences and thought she had changed his views on some subjects. They worried that he was too besotted.[3] He later said he enjoyed the audiences because they were the only times when he could have a serious conversation, which would not leak, with somebody who wasn't after his job. By now her technique was being described as 'Socratic': she would not venture opinions herself but by careful and persistent questioning, could get a prime minister to reflect again on the issues of the week. When he resigned, the Queen gave Wilson a photograph of them in the rain together, which he kept by him for the rest of his life.

If this sounds insufferably cosy, then what was talked about during those audiences cannot have been. Like Macmillan and Douglas-Home before him, Wilson was dealing in a world perched on the edge of nuclear annihilation. Some of the grimmest messages a monarch has had to read were the secret protocols for Britain's slide towards nuclear war with the Soviet Union, which were presented to her during Wilson's first full year in office, 1965. The grisly game-playing had gone on long before, but it was only during Wilson's first administration that it became clear that Buckingham Palace possessed no copy of GWB, or the War Book. The historian Peter Hennessy, who uncovered the story, wrote: 'The Queen did not fully know either the drill that, should the stage of a nuclear exchange be reached, would leave her kingdom largely a smoking and irradiated ruin or the plans for carrying on her government in its aftermath.'[4]

Whitehall planners had decided that she did not need the detailed picture. She was sent a summary of the stages to war. These included, for example, 'Military Vigilance' or 'Orange' for an expected enemy attack within one or more hours, and 'State Scarlet' for 'an enemy attack within a few minutes'.

Shakespearean code words followed for the preparations to mobilize the armed forces and the removal of key members of the government to a village-sized nuclear bunker outside Bath (which, it later turned out, the Russians had known about for ages and would have quickly obliterated). As to the Queen herself, just as with her father ahead of a likely Nazi invasion, there had been discussions about evacuating the royal family to Canada. In the case of Soviet threat, no final decision had been taken but early on in any crisis she was to board *Britannia*. The plan seems to have been for the Royal Yacht to be sent to a Scottish sea loch, where she would be partly protected from Soviet missile attacks.

On board, the Queen would be joined by the home secretary, who in 1965 was Roy Jenkins. He had to be there because since Prince Philip and the Queen's private secretary are both members of her Privy Council, she would then have enough of a quorum to appoint a new prime minister after the previous one had been killed. Peter Hennessy says the Royal Yacht's wartime purpose as a hospital ship was always a cover story: 'It was her floating nuclear bunker . . . it would lurk in the sea lochs on the north-west coast of Scotland; the mountains would shield it from the Soviet radar and at night it would go quietly from one sea loch to another. It wouldn't be static, as I understand it.' Ashore, her kingdom would be broken down into a dozen mini-kingdoms but from the ship she could create new governments, 'so the British constitution was taken care of, even unto Armageddon, and that's what the Royal Yacht was for . . . with that little group of Privy Councillors, ready to do the business, when her kingdom is a smoking and irradiated ruin; dreadful thought'.[5] The Queen knew about all this: released official files show that Churchill briefed her in 1954 about the decision to go from atomic bombs to the far more powerful hydrogen bomb; she was a close reader of secret intelligence throughout the Cold War, the so-called 'Red Book, copy number one'. The world of the 1960s, remembered now as the decade of social revolt, looser morals and 'liberation', was for those at the top of the power structure a much more serious and frightening place.

It was also the decade when the royal family seemed to give up trying to change with the times, sticking firmly with the hats, tweed jackets, polished brogues and cut-glass accents of the immediate post-war era. The Queen had observed the spirit of the age. In 1962 she had gone to see *Beyond the Fringe* satirize Macmillan and had been much amused. But at this point, she was also withdrawing more into family life, with the birth of Prince Andrew in 1960 and Prince Edward in 1964. Both boys spent more time with her than had their older siblings. By then perhaps it was becoming apparent that the tougher upbringing of the heir to the throne, who had been sent to his father's school, Gordonstoun, had not been an unqualified success.

Prince Philip was an active and hard-working parent. His children recall his reliable reading of bedtime stories, his enthusiasm for chasing and running games and his steady presence. He was genuinely the head of the family, away from the public gaze, and largely too the person who ran the complex royal estates. Yet nobody could say his relationship with his oldest son had been smooth. He had wanted Charles to be a man's man, in his own image; but the two were very different. By now perhaps he had realized that his son's temperament was simply not suited to the rough and tumble of Gordonstoun, an extroverts' and sporty institution: he had enjoyed himself more in the remote setting of an Australian outback school, Timbertop, in 1966. Later Prince Charles would go to Cambridge and get a degree in history, a first for any member of the royal family. Even there, his image was as a rather nervous 'square' young man, instinctively out of sympathy with the rebellious and exhibitionist times.

Every generation reaches a moment when the changes of style and attitude among younger people become bewildering. It was during Wilson's premiership, with student protests and a collapse of the old deference, that the Queen began to seem slightly bewildered. 'The Sixties' has become a phrase rather than a decade, and it was in fact in 1972 that the Queen herself came across bottle-swigging, fist-clenching republican student protestors, during a visit to Stirling University. But by the later 1960s the monarchy was confronted by left-wing dissent unlike anything George VI had faced. Wilson's royalist instincts were important in the Queen's reign, because he stood atop a party which had real strains of republicanism in it.

Labour was influenced by communist-dominated trade unions, which were, at least in theory, republican. Its left-wing factions, though not nearly as extreme as the Trotskyists who infiltrated the party later on, contained strong anti-monarchists. Cromwell, the Levellers, Tom Paine and the Victorian radical Charles Bradlaugh, who had refused to take the Oath of Allegiance when elected an MP in 1880, were among the heroes of Tribune Group socialists. All this was diluted by the mainstream, pro-monarchy beliefs of the vast majority of Labour voters and MPs, and Labour at no point posed a serious threat to the institution. Still, it is perfectly possible to imagine an alternative leader to Wilson who would have been less sympathetic to the Queen and whose government might have clipped and reduced the monarchy, starting a trend. As it was, Labour republicanism expressed itself only in irritated asides in politicians' diaries and the smallest of symbolic protests. Of these, the case of Anthony Wedgwood Benn, as he then was, and the Queen's head, was the most memorable and telling.

Well ahead of the 1964 election, Benn had been planning to change the design of British postage stamps as part of a cultural campaign against the older order. He told the Oxford Labour club in May 1963 that a new Labour government should introduce 'mood changing measures . . . like no dinner jackets for Labour Ministers at Buckingham Palace, mini-cars for official business and postage stamps without the Queen's head on them'. Benn added in his diary, that 'this last suggestion was the most popular thing in the speech. Republicanism is on the increase.'[6] Benn's soft republicanism at this stage included plans to abolish the honours system, removing from the Crown all traditional lists and substituting a system under which people would be 'thanked' by the House of Commons, after which they might be invited to a reception in Parliament and given green ribbons to wear, with the title 'PC' (standing of course for 'Parliamentary Citation' not 'politically correct'). He planned 'certain grades of gratitude: "high commendation", "special thanks", and so on down to "general thanks"', thus mirroring the OBEs, MBEs and knighthoods. Thus republicanism was creeping ahead stealthily, closely connected to left-wing resentment at the class-bound, Lords-influenced tradition of the British state. Hereditary power was a big issue more generally for Benn since he was in the middle of renouncing his hereditary peerage. His nine-year-old son Hilary, later himself a Labour cabinet minister, whipped up a small storm by telling American broadcasters Britain should have an elected president, not a Queen.

When Benn arrived to take the oath of admission to the Privy Council after Labour's victory, he found it 'terribly degrading' and made a point of chatting during the rehearsals:

Her first, rather overwhelming, prime minister: the Queen and Sir Winston Churchill, 1953.

A triumphant, if exhausting, tour: the Queen was the first reigning monarch to visit Australia, 1954.

Her first US President: the Queen and Prince Philip with President Eisenhower in Washington.

The Empire is dead,
long live the Commonwealth.
The Queen in the streets of
Karachi, Pakistan, 1961.

Not quite a royal carriage: the
Queen travels on the London
Underground's just-opened
Victoria Line, 1969.

The cars would
get bigger: Prince
Charles drives Prince
Edward in a go-kart,
photographed by
the Queen, who is a
keen taker of snaps.

Reinventing
tradition.
Prince Charles's
1969 investiture
as Prince of Wales,
at Caernarvon
Castle.

A 1970s family: the Queen and the Duke of Edinburgh celebrate their silver wedding anniversary.

One of her best advisers: Sir Martin Charteris, the Queen's private secretary, pores over paperwork with her aboard *Britannia* in 1972.

Where she was most relaxed: the Queen at dinner on the Royal Yacht.

Labour's leading monarchist: Harold Wilson and the Queen in Downing Street for his farewell dinner in 1976 – an honour not given to all prime ministers.

The glamour of royalty does not excite everyone: the Labour defence secretary Fred Mulley at an RAF review during the 1977 Silver Jubilee.

But royalty does bring out British eccentricity: a congratulatory postcard too big even for the Buckingham Palace mantelpieces is delivered in 1977.

The Silver Jubilee was a much-needed tonic during a bleak period for Britain.

Always keeping her balance: the Queen comforts her horse Burmese, after blank shots were fired at her during the 1981 Trooping the Colour. At the time, she must have thought she had narrowly escaped assassination.

'We then went up to the Queen one after another, kneeling and picking up her hand and kissing it, and then bowing. I made the most miniature bow ever seen . . . I left the Palace boiling with indignation and feeling that this was an attempt to impose tribal magic and personal loyalty on people whose real duty was only to their electors.'[7] As postmaster general, Benn then set to work to get the Queen's head off commemorative stamps. He wanted more modern, better-drawn pictures of today's world, and felt the original portrait of the Queen, by the artist Dorothy Wilding, was too fussy. He was tampering with a purpose, fiddling – with an agenda.

Unlike the stamps of almost every other nation in the world, those of the UK nowhere mention the country's name. The Queen's head is enough. Working with the famous designer and artist David Gentleman, Benn eventually got permission to put the issue to her directly, which he did on 10 March 1965. His diary account is a drawing-room comedy of misunderstanding and circumlocution. Benn had shrewdly picked his battlefield, commemorative stamps for the Battle of Britain, about as patriotic and unquestionable a project as it would be possible to imagine. If the Palace accepted that the Queen's portrait would spoil the excellent drawings prepared for these stamps, Benn thought, he would have opened up a gap through which he could push through his wider plan. Queenless stamps might then lead to many other Queenless initiatives. Dust down those scarlet banners!

Benn put his Battle of Britain argument to the Queen in person, arriving with a box of designs. She alternately smiled, frowned, seemed embarrassed, denied she had any personal feelings about her head being on all stamps, and later allowed Benn to spread out a range of Gentleman's designs on the floor. For forty minutes or so, Benn seems to have done almost all the talking, and left the Palace believing the Queen agreed with him, or at least would not confront him. He was now 'convinced that if you went to the Queen to get her consent to abolish the honours list altogether she would nod and say she'd never been keen on it herself and felt sure the time had come to put an end to it. Of course when you do that you have to be terribly charming and nice . . .'⁸ Many people have left the Queen's presence, before and since, having mistaken her cautious politeness for agreement. In this case, any smiles or nods were tactical. The Queen had not agreed. As Benn beavered away to commission and publicize headless stamps to be shown to the Queen, her private office went quietly to work on Harold Wilson and the civil service. Benn's own civil servants more or less ignored his plans. In July the Queen's private secretary, Sir Michael Adeane, told Benn she was 'not too happy' about a set of six Battle of Britain stamps with her head missing from five and Benn made a small tactical retreat, 'in view of the bad press I'm getting and the delicate political situation'. The loyalist press celebrated a Buckingham Palace victory.

Benn, however, was not finished. The delicate verbal fencing went on. Benn congratulated himself on charming Palace officials and mused, 'I'm sure the Palace is a lot more frightened of me than they have reason to be.' He developed a better relationship with Adeane but eventually realized that Wilson was never going to back him because 'he finds the Queen a very useful tool . . . in the long run his attitude simply strengthens the reactionary elements in our society'. Number Ten ordered Benn to stop commissioning headless stamps. He tried a final line of attack, proposing to write to the Queen and get her verdict on the record. Either she would be shown to be rejecting, personally, the advice of one of her ministers, himself as postmaster general, or the subterfuges of her private office would be exposed. Benn's own private secretary was aghast and told him that this was going too far and would bring the Queen into public controversy. By this point, Benn did not have the support of his prime minister, of the Stamp Advisory Committee, or his own civil servants and had to back down. The Queen's head stayed. Benn wrote that he was putting his 'palace vendetta . . . on ice'.

For the Royal Mail, the main outcome was the commissioning of a new portrait of the Queen by the artist Arnold Machin. A conscientious objector who had been imprisoned during the war, Machin was from the Potteries town of Stoke-on-Trent, where he had trained in ceramic sculpture. In 1964 he had produced the semi-sculpted silhouette of the Queen that would be used on the new decimal coins first circulated in the mid-1960s and now he did something similar for stamps. His portrait was clear and small enough to sit at the edge of commemorative stamps, as well as filling the regular ones, allowing a much wider range of designs. Originally Machin wanted the Queen's image to be cut off at the neck. She, perhaps understandably sensitive, did not wish to be cut off at the neck. A rather fuller dress neckline was used, and a modest design classic appeared – the same portrait still seen on every British stamp nearly half a century later. When Benn left as postmaster general, the Queen said she was sure he would miss his stamps. Benn thanked her for being supportive: 'She gave me a rather puzzled smile and I bowed and went out backwards.' Much later, by which time Benn had become the snow-headed grandpa of British socialism, the Queen was urged to invite him to the Palace to reminisce. She paused: 'No. He doesn't like us.'

The stamps saga may be trivial, but it was not meaningless

and it remains telling. A clever politician trying to take on the fuddy-duddy Palace found it subtle and just as political in its response. The Queen clearly had a strong objection to Benn's proposal and one can see why. Once her image begins to be removed from stamps, then it could equally well go from coins and public buildings; and the iconography of monarchy starts to blow away. This was not a small matter for her. The problem returned in 2010 when it became clear that the coalition government's plans for privatizing the Royal Mail had not included formal guarantees about the Queen's head. Symbols matter. Benn understood that, which was why he persisted so hard. As his contemporary diaries make clear he did have a republican agenda, if not a full-throttle one. Like his son and wife, he admired American republican democracy and had seen stamps as a probing line of attack that might have led to other things, beginning with the honours system.

Yet in person, mindful of her constitutional role, the Queen showed no sign of having a view – indeed, denied that she had one. She refused to be backed into a corner or held publicly accountable for any decision. Instead the well-oiled, rarely noticed cogs of the British state revolved on her behalf – the private secretaries at Buckingham Palace, Number Ten and in Benn's own office, connected in turn to the Stamp Advisory Committee and lowlier civil servants in the Postmaster General's Office, blocked Benn so effectively that he ended up confessing that he was knocking his head against a brick wall. Trying to be charming, and using all his skills of media handling and irrefutable-sounding logic, Benn was simply outplayed. Meanwhile other Labour ministers with republican instincts kept their comments for their diaries and displayed only the tiniest signs of rebellion, such as small bows and curtseys, or small delays for meetings. The Queen notices a lot, so she surely noticed these minor discourtesies.

Of all the cabinet ministers privately offended by the duties required by the Palace, none was more outspoken in his diary, published after his death a decade later to much tut-tutting, than Richard Crossman, the irreverent intellectual. He wrote down more about the Queen than any other public diarist of that era. His own journey was from near-apoplexy about the flummery of court ritual (noticeably more formal in 1964 than it is today) to growing admiration for the Queen and her deft use of silences and confidences. On the way, he was a shrewd observer of the uneasy relationship between the Queen and her first socialist ministers. He began in October 1964 expressing outrage about the ritual of kissing hands to become members of the Privy Council: 'I don't suppose anything more dull, pretentious, or plain silly has ever been invented. There we were, sixteen grown men. For over an hour we were taught how to stand up, how to kneel on one knee on a cushion, how to raise the right hand with the Bible in it, how to advance three paces towards the Queen, how to take the hand and kiss it . . .'

When eventually the ceremony (now gone) happened for real, Crossman found 'this little woman with the beautiful waist' who had to go through 'this rigmarole' for forty minutes: 'We were uneasy, she was uneasy.'[9] At that stage Crossman was housing minister, but from August 1966 until 1968 he was leader of the Commons and Lord President of the Council. In this latter role he was the prime link between Parliament and the Queen, expected to attend all Privy Council meetings and present a large number of decisions for royal approval.

Crossman had a long and deep interest in the British constitution but found these duties onerous and irrelevant.

On 20 September 1966 he travelled to Balmoral, noting
that the Grampian mountains were not as beautiful as the
Scottish west coast, and finding the building 'a typical Scottish
baronial house, looking as though it had been built yesterday,
with a nice conventional rose garden and by the little church,
a golf course, which nobody plays on except the staff'. His
ill-temper and mild contempt were not diluted by the formal
meeting with the Queen during which 'I read aloud the 50 or
60 titles of the Orders in Council, pausing after every half
dozen for the Queen to say, "agreed".' It was, he felt, two and
a half minutes 'of the purest mumbo-jumbo' which had
required four ministers, 'all busy men, to take a night and day
off to travel to Scotland'. Once the official business was over,
however, Crossman's irritation evaporated and his diarist's
observation took over:

> I noticed this time even more than last how shy she can
> be ... If one waits for her to begin the conversation,
> nothing happens. One has to start the talk and then
> suddenly the conversation falters because both are feeling,
> 'Oh dear, are we boring each other?' She has a lovely
> laugh. She laughs with her whole face and she cannot just
> assume a mere smile because she's really a very spon-
> taneous person ... she finds it difficult to suppress her
> emotion. When she is deeply moved and tries to control
> it, she looks like an angry thunder-cloud. So, very often
> when she has been deeply touched by the plaudits of the
> crowd she merely looks terribly bad-tempered.[10]

Sir Godfrey Agnew, the long-serving clerk of the Privy
Council, told him a story about an earlier meeting which had

gone badly wrong because the four ministers, coached by the then cabinet secretary Sir Edward Bridges, had been kneeling on the wrong side of the room; when they crawled round they knocked a book off a table, which the Queen picked up, looking 'blackly furious'. Later, Bridges had gone back to apologize, and the Queen told him, 'You know, I nearly laughed.' He had realized that 'when she looked terribly angry it was mainly because she was trying to stop herself laughing'. It is a truth about the Queen that perhaps too few journalists and photographers have understood.

Later on the Queen became genuinely cross with Crossman when he missed a Privy Council at Balmoral because of the Labour conference: 'I made a little explanation and a half-apology about the misunderstandings between the Party and the Court . . . She didn't relent, she just listened and I thought that was that.'[11] The Balmoral incidents rankled, and he was soon complaining again about the absurdity of having to travel north, at a dinner with Jeremy Thorpe and the writer Kenneth Rose. One proposed Privy Council date had been judged unacceptable by the Palace because the Queen was out for lunch that day and so could not entertain her ministers: Crossman had replied that he would eat instead in the servants' hall. 'Not very agreeable for the servants, perhaps,' said Rose, dryly. Crossman's encounters with the Queen continued at Sandringham, which he characteristically dismissed as 'an extremely dull, Edwardian baronial house' where there was more 'mumbo-jumbo'. It was here that Benn's successor, Ted Short, presented the Queen with more acceptable postage stamp designs than Benn's 'awful ones' and the Queen, apparently 'said she would be pleased, and she was' – rather giving the lie to the notion that she did not mind.

By now Crossman felt that he himself was getting on better

with her, because 'every time you see her, she tends to like you better simply because she's got more used to you'. He had once asked Agnew whether she preferred the Tories to Labour 'because they were our social superiors and he said, "I don't think so. The Queen doesn't make fine distinctions between politicians of different parties. They all roughly belong to the same social category in her view." I think that's true.' Again, it is an observation that has been repeated by later civil servants and politicians. It does not, of course, mean that she regards the social category as a particularly exciting or elevated one.

The following year, in February 1967, Crossman again came across a harder edge of the Queen. A fairly obscure Labour backbencher, Emrys Hughes, who represented famously radical South Ayrshire, had introduced a bill into the Commons the self-explanatory title of which was 'The Abolition of Titles Bill'. As a private member's bill without government backing, it had zero chance of success. Crossman, as leader of the Commons, like the home secretary Roy Jenkins, regarded Hughes as 'a jester' and thought any attempt to stop his bill being debated would look foolish. The Queen clearly disagreed. She was worried about this apparent assault on her prerogative. Her private secretary Sir Michael Adeane approached Wilson, who in turn contacted the Lord Chancellor and chief whip to quash the bill. Crossman recorded: 'Ha, ha, there it is. I shall have to arrange it. This is a good example of the Queen and the PM hobnobbing together, the kind of stuffiness I don't take seriously.'[12] Crossman and Jenkins later did stand up to Wilson and insisted no action should be taken to stop Hughes's bill which, when it was finally debated on a Friday in March, attracted just three or four other MPs into the chamber. It was the dampest of damp squibs, emitting no spark or sputter. Crossman visited the Palace, where 'The

Queen said that she'd looked through all the papers on Saturday and found nothing there.' Crossman corrected her: there had been reports in the *Guardian* and *The Times*, which had both called it a flop. He could not resist gloating that he and Roy Jenkins had been right to take no action: 'It was a mistake to say this, since she didn't reply.'

Like the story of Benn and the stamps, the Hughes incident is interesting because it throws a rare light on the Queen acting behind the scenes to protect her role; being excessively nervous about a political flea bite; and putting down an uppity minister by merely staying silent. This latter technique is famous among those who have said something inappropriate, or with which she disagrees, or have merely out of nervousness burbled on too long in front of her. 'She never argues, she just looks at the person very blankly. The corners of her mouth don't turn down. It's not a hostile look. It's just a complete blank – and it's devastating,' says one who has watched it happen. Crossman got on better with the Queen as time passed, or thought he did, though he never stopped slightly pushing things. On a later Balmoral visit, when the Queen was late for the Privy Council by twelve minutes, she explained that at the furthest part of her ride, her horse had got a stone in his shoe – 'one carries one of those pen-knives, doesn't one, as an instrument for taking out stones, but today was the one day I didn't have it'.[13] (The horse had been given to the Queen by the Soviet Communist minister Bulganin: she found 'those Russian horses are very obstinate'.) That evening, perhaps inspired by the Soviet theme, Crossman asked the Queen if she had followed the unfolding saga of the traitor Kim Philby and was briskly put in his place: she did not read about such matters, and clearly would not dream of talking about them.

Later on, Crossman had another falling-out with the Palace

over his detestation of grand public events: this time, he was trying to get out of attending the State Opening of Parliament in October 1967, pleading a 'diplomatic illness'. The Duke of Norfolk, in charge of the ceremony, appealed to Harold Wilson, whose office replied that Crossman 'suffers from a phobia about public occasions of this sort which make him unable to attend'. The Duke was not put off, but wrote to Crossman saying he was alarmed and disturbed and that only the Queen could allow him not to go. Wilson was by now 'flustered' and so Crossman went by night to see Adeane, who said he could have cleared it with the Queen, and could still do so. He then added: 'Of course, the Queen has as strong a feeling of dislike of public ceremonies as you do. I don't disguise from you the fact that it will certainly occur to her to ask herself why you should be excused when she has to go, since you're both officials.'[14] Crossman, of course, went, though the experience inflamed his republicanism and he thought it 'like the *Prisoner of Zenda* but not nearly as smart or well done as it would be in Hollywood . . . far more comic, more untidy, more homely, less grand'. The Queen's speech, for which he was responsible himself, was 'appalling'. It may be doubted whether the Queen really dislikes ceremonial occasions – it would make her life a long torture and there is plenty of counter-evidence of the great interest and attention to detail she displays. Yet Crossman, grand man that he was, was instantly disarmed by Adeane's implied comparison of two simple state workhorses trudging together in harness.

But would anything actually change? Crossman was self-knowing enough to understand that real republicans inside the Labour government were a small minority of middle-class intellectuals while 'working-class socialists . . . are by and large staunchly monarchist. The nearer the Queen they get the more the working-class members of the Cabinet love her and she loves them.'[15] There is a wider truth here, which can be thought of as Cheltenham Gold Cup syndrome. At that famous race meeting, and indeed most race meetings, there is a social compact between working-class punters, including of course Irish ones, and the remnants of the aristocracy, all drinking similar amounts though of different beverages, and most of them dressed with cheerful exuberance. The middle classes, particularly those portions of the middle classes which are industrious, sober and serious, are absent. CGCS applies to monarchism in politics too, with rare and interesting exceptions, one of which we shall meet shortly.

In the 1960s, radical republicanism was growing stronger on the fringes of politics but was nowhere near the centre of power. There were however issues which could create an impermanent coalition of newspapers, backbench MPs and many voters; and they included the Queen's finances.

Towards the end of this first Wilson government, in 1969, the royal finances had been catapulted into the headlines by none other than Prince Philip, who used an American television interview on 9 November to complain that 'the Firm' would 'go into the red' the following year because the Civil List allowance was inadequate. He told the broadcaster NBC that the royal family might have to move into smaller premises and give up playing polo. As the predictable media storm blew in, Wilson proposed that the whole matter be investigated by a parliamentary select committee, but only after the 1970 election. Though this takes us into the time of Heath's government, it is right to discuss it now, not least because the star role in defending the Queen was played by none other than that recently rejected royal servant, Harold Wilson. The Select

Committee on the Civil List, to give it its full title, was one of the most important investigations into the monarchy of the Queen's reign. Its membership included Tory grandees such as Norman St John-Stevas but also Wilson, the former home secretary Roy Jenkins, and the working-class Labour republican Willie Hamilton. Crossman, no longer in the Commons but editing the then-influential *New Statesman*, kept up a barrage from outside. The new Tory chancellor, Tony Barber, chaired the select committee.

The big problem was inflation, which had roared ahead since the money agreed for the Queen's public role had been settled at the time of her accession in 1952. The wage bills in particular had far outstripped her budgets. It was an age of militancy and the Civil Service Union proudly told the committee that it had managed to get average wages for Royal Household staff up by 200 per cent since 1953, against 126 per cent for the country as a whole. Even with that, said the union, there were recruitment problems since 'the long and irregular hours are often regarded as outweighing the "glamour" of the background of the job'. It meant 'foreigners' were now being recruited into the kitchens and housemaids' department which, suggested the union, might pose problems of security. The monarchy was indeed dipping deeply into its reserve funds, which were about to run out. Something had to be done. But it was impossible to separate this entirely from the great mystery of the Queen's private wealth.

In tough times, could she not be making more of a personal contribution, given her palaces, artworks, investments and estates? We will look in more detail at this later on, because in 1970 the truth was mostly hidden from view. 'Rich lists' had been popular in American journalism for years and were now appearing in British papers. The Queen regularly appeared close to the top. This was easy to achieve by guessing the capital value of the royal family's historic accumulation of buildings, land and goods – but how much was genuine personal wealth was harder to work out. She might live in gorgeously decorated rooms but they belonged to the institution of the monarchy, not to her. She could not sell the furniture, buildings or paintings and spend the proceeds on something else. Her personal tastes were modest. All her life she has preferred simple food to fancy and the odd Dubonnet and gin to fine wine. She travelled for duty, not fun, and, apart from horses, had few indulgences outside the ritual of the royal year. Her wardrobe was statecraft, not pleasure. So what of the wealth was hers? How much ought to be taxed? These appeared as new and interesting questions, and the committee proved a tough investigator. A figure of £100 million, fabulous in those days, was widely touted. Lord Mountbatten realized what damage an exaggerated view of the Queen's wealth could do her, and urged Prince Philip to help sweep away some of the traditional secrecy. Eventually Jock Colville, the former courtier who was now a senior member of Coutts, the royal bankers, suggested £12 million was more accurate.

The committee was not entirely impressed. A draft report, which it rejected, even described the Palace request for a review as 'the most insensitive and brazen pay claim made in the last two hundred years', while one of its Labour members, Douglas Houghton, suggested that the Royal Household should simply become a government department, answerable directly to Parliament. This would have removed the direct connection between Palace staff and the Queen, and would have been completely unacceptable to her, said Lord Cobbold, then the Lord Chamberlain: 'It is almost an item of principle that the Queen regards these people as her own servants and they regard themselves as her servants.' Other ideas included removing Prince Philip's separate household and radically cutting back those members of the royal family getting state money. Princess Margaret, it was suggested, should be content with free accommodation, while the Duke of Gloucester, being 'very remote from the throne', should have his payments abolished.

The Court Party fought back. The payments to Royals were not simply fees for public duties. They were an acknowledgement that, because of their birth, these were mostly people who could not simply go out and earn their living in the ordinary way. (The consequence of 'Royals for hire' became clear much later on, and was not pretty.) In essence, the committee's argument was between radicals who wanted the monarchy brought firmly under the thumb of the Commons, on a year-by-year basis – mild Cromwellians – and the monarchists who thought a strong measure of independence was essential for the Queen. Not surprisingly, the monarchists won. The radicals were in the minority, and did not include Wilson: the inclusion of Houghton and Willie Hamilton, the monarchy's most unrelenting foe at the time, now looks like a classic piece of establishment window-dressing.

The committee did its best to itemize the Queen's work, from the ceremonial duties, the reading of state papers and the endless visiting, to her private meetings with ministers and ambassadors and her work managing the palaces. She of course did not answer questions herself. That job was taken by Adeane, who emphasized in long and detailed evidence how hard she worked, including unprecedented numbers of foreign visits, and how much of a strain being constantly on display really was. With Wilson playing a leading role in defending and protecting her role, the committee eventually recommended not cutting back, but more than doubling the Queen's state income, from £475,000 a year, to £980,000. These were difficult times for the British economy, and many Labour and Liberal MPs thought the proposals far too generous. In the end, most Labour MPs abstained and in the Tory-dominated Commons of the early 1970s the settlement passed easily, with a majority of 121 votes. Yet 47 MPs voted against, and there were eloquent speeches in favour of the Queen paying tax on her private income, and a cutting-back of the size of the monarchy. Princess Margaret in particular came in for some sharp criticism for her lack of involvement in official duties.

Overall, it was a pyrrhic victory for the Queen's forces. First, the legislation created a system of parliamentary review of the Civil List. Admittedly, this was only envisaged as happening every decade. But it meant the Queen would in effect have to explain and justify royal housekeeping to the Commons for the rest of her reign. Second, the row over tax and her unknown private wealth would not go away. It had been a subject barely mentioned during the previous two decades. Now it was referred to again and again in the press and by critical MPs. Not until 2010, forty years on, did the Palace win back this ground and re-establish some financial independence.

Willie Hamilton became the public face of anti-monarchism in the 1970s and 1980s. Unlike Crossman, he was no middle-class intellectual. Hamilton was the child of a Durham miner who had grown up 'in spitting distance of the pit' and in appalling poverty, a life of cockroaches, insanitary outdoor toilets, grime and growing anger. Born at exactly the moment in 1917 when George V was creating the House of Windsor, Hamilton vividly remembered that, aged ten, he had been lined up outside the school gates to wave at 'some royal personage' who was to go past in a car. It was cold. The wait was long. The car flashed past. 'That day, a little revolutionary was born.'[16] After wartime army service and a job as a school-teacher, Hamilton fought communists in Fife and became a Labour MP in 1950.

In some ways, he was a dangerous enemy. He was dogged, hard-working, uncorrupt and entirely fearless. After his experience on the select committee, he went on to write a controversial and bestselling book, *My Queen and I*, which lambasted the institution, the Queen herself and her family. He saw the monarchy as the ermine coat covering a rotten system. He focused particularly on the cost, the tax question, the large number of 'minor royals' and the absence of any real political role for the Queen. Yet Hamilton was in other ways the Queen's ideal foe. He was a vinegary and vituperative man who took delight in the number of chips on each of his shoulders, and he did not shrink from personal attacks on the monarch, describing the Queen as a clockwork doll. A flavour of the Hamilton style comes from a Commons debate at the time when he mocked those who liked the Queen Mother for her pleasant smile – 'My God, if my wife got that pay, she would never stop laughing' – and said of Princess Margaret, 'Why, oh why, are we giving this expensive kept woman [£35,000] for doing what she does?'[17] This made him easy for the newspapers to caricature, and for some of his colleagues to dismiss. Unfashionably dressed, pinched-looking and rarely understated, he was soon among the most unpopular politicians in the lounge bars and Conservative clubs of Middle Britain.

The Rogue Royalists of Africa

Wilson's reluctance to engage with Labour republicanism was temperamental, but he also had more urgent issues to confront for which he needed the Queen's help. None was more dangerous for the Commonwealth or more embarrassing to London than the defiance of the white minority rulers of Rhodesia. With just one sixteenth of the total population, they had been aggressively fending off any move towards black majority rule and were close to breaking with the rest of the Commonwealth. The authority of the Queen was a central part of the dispute because, paradoxically, hardly anyone was more naturally royalist to their bones than a treason-plotting white of Rhodesia. The Rhodesian story is tangled and became truly tragic after Robert Mugabe took over as ruler of the country and turned Africa's breadbasket into an economic wilderness of thuggery, theft and malnutrition. The Rhodesia/Zimbabwe story throws up hard questions about Britain's role in Africa, the decolonization project, and the Queen's own position as Head of the Commonwealth.

In the 1890s, a huge area north of South Africa had been invaded and colonized by British settlers. What is now Zimbabwe and was then called Southern Rhodesia was the richest and most British-dominated part of the northwards push. It became a self-governing colony. To its north was a protectorate, Northern Rhodesia, with far fewer whites but large mineral deposits. Alongside this was a smaller protectorate, Nyasaland, with sparse, mainly Scottish settlement. In 1953 London brokered a deal to join these three into a single Central African Federation, a 'federal realm of the British Crown'. For ten years this unlikely union, with the Queen's head on its coinage and postage stamps, and its flag incorporating the Union Jack, survived. It stitched together the self-consciously white-colonial south with territories likely to become black-ruled much more quickly. Arguments about the future of colonial Africa crackled through Whitehall – not about the eventual end of white rule, regarded as inevitable, but about the timescale and conditions. London's overriding policy was that no former dominion or colony could be granted independence without majority rule. For the CAF the hope had been to find some middle way between the apartheid and white-supremacist South Africa and emerging Marxist black independent states. But the independence movements of what became Malawi and Zambia forced the pace. When they triumphed, the whites of Southern Rhodesia opted to go it alone, and reject any early steps towards majority rule.

They were led by Ian Smith, a pugnacious farmer. During the war he had been an RAF Hurricane and Spitfire pilot and, after being shot down over Italy, had helped Italian partisans fight the Germans. Rugby- and cricket-playing, blond and intensely patriotic, he thought of himself as a 'Britisher' and was about as passionate a monarchist as any Home Counties Conservative could imagine. He was a most unlikely rebel and much of Tory Britain, including many newspapers, was cheering for him. Smith was essentially asking for Wilson to accept his word that one day, eventually, Rhodesia would move to majority rule – but only after a long period of education and the final defeat of any communist guerrillas and rebels. Wilson and his advisers did not believe Smith and thought his plan was to continue white minority rule for ever. Trust quickly broke down on each side, and some of the behaviour on the British side was petulant, or plain petty.

When Sir Winston Churchill died in 1965, Smith was

invited to the state funeral but somehow his invitation for lunch with the rest of the leaders and the Queen went missing. Smith was eating with the South African ambassador when, as he recalled, 'a gentleman in a splendid uniform came up to our table. He informed me that he was the Queen's equerry, and as the Queen had noticed that I was not present at the lunch, she had asked him to make enquiries ... The Queen was concerned, the equerry said, and had sent him post-haste to the hotel to express apologies and ask me to accompany him.' Smith left for Buckingham Palace where the Queen left her group and immediately went over to express her sorrow that his invitation had not arrived. Prince Philip joined her: 'I was touched by the genuine interest they showed in Rhodesia, and also by how well informed they were. I was impressed too by the amount of time they devoted to talking with me, and by their sincere hope that our problem would be solved amicably.'[18]

It was not. Smith's break with Britain, his Unilateral Declaration of Independence, ended with the flourish, 'God Save the Queen'. He sent word of UDI to Wilson to arrive at exactly 11 a.m. London time on 11 November 1965, the moment of wartime remembrance, as a barbed reminder of Rhodesia's role in two world wars. Elizabeth II was proclaimed 'Queen of Rhodesia', a title she never acknowledged. In the early years of UDI, at least, many of the trappings of monarchy remained. Rhodesian soldiers and airmen kept the uniforms and traditions of the British. The 'Royal Rhodesian Air Force', with RAF-like roundels on its aircraft, continued until 1970, and the country's flag incorporated the Union flag until 1969. The Queen's portrait stayed in government buildings. She was on Rhodesian banknotes and coins, and indeed on the un-Bennish postage stamps of the country rebelling against her.

The rebels seemed more monarchist than the old country itself. When the RAF was sent to Zambia, ostensibly to protect its power supplies against a possible Rhodesian attack, RAF officers were soon fraternizing in Rhodesian messes. When, in 1966, Wilson invited Smith aboard the cruiser HMS *Tiger* for further talks, the ship's petty officers invited the rebel Rhodesian leader for drinks, toasted him, and promised the ship's company were entirely on his side. The notion that Britain could have declared war on Rhodesians, many of whom had fought for her during 1939–45, was fantastic. By such slight indications as her insistence that he join a lunch, the Queen suggested that she was at least unhappy about Wilson's attitude to Smith. With his sporting record, down-to-earth interests and service background, he seemed just the kind of man who in other circumstances would be a welcome guest at a Windsor dine-and-sleep; it is hard to imagine Prince Philip preferring the company of a Nkomo or Mugabe.

But Smith had become a pest. The conflict between traditional 'kith and kin' patriotism and the Queen's legal position was expressed most starkly in the figure of Sir Humphrey Gibbs, the governor of Southern Rhodesia. Though a farmer and friend of Ian Smith's, his loyalty to the Queen meant that he refused to accept UDI and formally dismissed Smith and his cabinet. Flying the flag from government house in Salisbury (later Harare), Gibbs hung on surrounded and isolated, refusing to accept the legality of Rhodesia until, in 1969, a referendum finally declared the country a republic. The Queen made her views clear by making him a GCVO – a Knight Grand Cross of the Royal Victorian Order. This is her personal order, much more personal than the KCMG (Order of St Michael and St George) which Gibbs would have expected (and also got) because of his Commonwealth role. Sometimes it is only through such subtle distinctions that the Queen can show her true feelings.

Wilson was well aware that military and personal loyalty to the Queen had been one of the few cards he could play with Smith. At one point he flew to Balmoral to suggest to the Queen that Mountbatten might be used as a go-between. That never happened, but Wilson's psychological thinking was not daft. The Rhodesian whites found rebellion against their monarch almost – though not quite – as painful as contemplating black rule. They wanted to keep as much of the form of their British origins and loyalties as possible. Yet for the Queen to acquiesce in any way would have outraged the black-majority members of the Commonwealth and, in all probability, have split or even ended the institution. When push came to shove, the scale and inclusiveness of the Commonwealth mattered more than the painful rebellion of people who had stood by Britain and considered themselves to be British.

For their part, Smith and many Rhodesians felt bewildered and betrayed by their monarch, who seemed to be siding with Marxist despots and left-leaning United Nations politicians against their own. As they lost most of their remaining supporters, even ingenious sanctions-busting actions and a ferocious 'bush war' against black nationalists failed to hold back the tide of change. But the game was not finally up for some time, until Margaret Thatcher came to power. So it was another British prime minister who oversaw negotiations that led to the creation of Zimbabwe in 1979. The horror of what followed, for blacks as well as whites, sheds an unsettling light on the simple 1960s faith in progress and democracy. The story also shows, of course, that when it comes to protecting its position as linchpin of a worldwide Commonwealth, the 'family firm' is hard-headed and unsentimental.

Sometimes, too much so. The grim history of Britain's entanglement with the bloody regime of Idi Amin in Uganda shows how dangerous sentimental Commonwealth attachments can be. Amin ousted the Ugandan leader, Dr Milton Obote, in 1971, when the latter was at the Commonwealth conference in Singapore. The official British reaction was approval, since Obote had been a threatening and 'unhelpful' figure. When the then prime minister Edward Heath was told about it by his private secretary he said he was 'not wholly displeased': the Foreign Office knew little about Amin but a Ministry of Defence official had remembered him from his days in the King's African Rifles and had found him 'the best sergeant he ever had'.[19] Other officials described him simply as 'a splendid type'. Amin flattered British susceptibilities. He had fought against the Mau Mau in Kenya, had risen through the native, British-officered KAR, and was an accomplished rugby player. Better still, he made an early request to come to London and meet the Queen. Heath duly arranged this, a visit that took place on 12 July 1971. At Downing Street they were impressed by his smart and military appearance, though when Amin left, the foreign secretary Alec Douglas-Home suggested the new leader might be mad: Amin had told him Uganda was about to be invaded by the Chinese navy and wanted military support.

Amin went on to supervise a murderous tyranny that is estimated to have killed 100,000 Ugandans and included the expulsion of Uganda's Asian population, around 30,000 of whom came to Britain. Revulsion spread as stories of his cannibalism and torture squads emerged; but he remained the leader of a Commonwealth country, able to play on his British connections in an increasingly deranged mix of menace and humour. Uninvited to the 1973 Commonwealth meeting in

Ottawa, he wrote to the Queen's private secretary demanding she send a Boeing 747 to Kampala to ferry him and his party to Canada, and arrange a band of Scottish pipers to greet him. The Queen's staff consulted Heath, who decided it would be too extravagant, and declined. Amin shrugged and went on murdering political foes and friends – churchmen, bank and business leaders, playwrights, journalists and many more – whose bodies were dumped in crocodile-infested rivers. He awarded himself the Victoria Cross, declared himself King of Scotland and apparently wrote to the Queen in 1975: 'I would like you to arrange for me to visit Scotland, Ireland and Wales to meet the heads of revolutionary movements fighting against your imperialist oppression.' He also sent her a Telex inviting her to come to Kampala if she wanted to meet a real man.

This produced much tittering in the British press, but Amin was the very worst of bad jokes. His taunting and inversion of what the Commonwealth was meant to stand for, and the reluctance of that organization to antagonize its black members, damaged both it and the Queen. His antics implied that the successor to the British Empire had no clothes. It has plenty, but the sad story of the African rebellions points to its lack of muscle. Countries are suspended – Pakistan after a military coup, for instance – and leave, as Fiji and Zimbabwe did. But there are few real sanctions. It is a club. Though today, with fifty-four members, it comprises around a third of the world's population, the vast majority of that figure, around 94 per cent, is in Asia and Africa; India by herself accounts for more than half. So the Commonwealth straddles some of the world's richest and the world's poorest countries. On trade talks, attitudes to regional politics and much else, they are often at loggerheads. The Commonwealth boasts some proud examples of successful democracy among the 'old

Commonwealth' countries, including India and Britain herself. But it also includes, and always has included, corrupt and despotic regimes, despite the high and principled language of its founding documents and successive secretaries general. It gives Britain extra heft at other international bodies when the Commonwealth is speaking as one voice but – sadly and wrongly, perhaps – most Britons barely notice its existence.

Enter the Film-makers . . .

It was perhaps no surprise that, buffeted by inquisitive MPs over the money and with the Commonwealth no longer easy to handle, the Queen and her advisers began to take risks in the late 1960s in trying to project a fresher image. Since the Coronation the fortunes of the Windsors and the influence of television had become intertwined in ways neither the Queen nor the BBC could have predicted. On the one hand, television had meant that for the first time the Queen could be entertained privately and nightly in much the same way as her subjects. She has never been big on Wagner operas or Pinter plays. She likes the same middle-brow comedies, soap operas and sporting coverage as do most of her fellow Britons. For better or worse, television has democratized taste and given the Queen a window on her country earlier monarchs did not have. On the other hand, the television cameras have intruded and caused the Queen difficulties in policing her privacy. These are not always the obvious problems of access or eavesdropping.

For, fundamentally, television flattens. In person, most British people would feel some sense of awe in the Queen's actual presence. Distanced by the TV lens, they feel none. We want to see more and more, close-ups and private moments. We have the illusion of intimacy. We want to know more. Monarchy must respond to changing public tastes but monarchy depends on an aura of mystery and personal distance, Bagehot's 'magic'. How is it possible to reconcile familiarity and magic? Through her reign, the Queen has struggled to answer that question.

The earliest years had been no problem. Richard Dimbleby's encyclopedic knowledge of royal and constitutional history, and the fixed cameras needed for state occasions, meant that a genre of slow-marching, hushed reporting established itself. The Palace had simply refused to allow cameras anywhere near private family moments; even filming the outside of palaces was frowned upon. The BBC hierarchy rarely pushed requests for more access. Broadcasters dressed formally and waited with shiny shoes for formal announcements.

This changed quite soon. Prince Philip had had experience of TV in making scientific programmes and then in 1966 he had been a key figure in giving the go-ahead for *Royal Palaces of Britain*, a documentary by Kenneth Clark (who later made the series *Civilisation*) about six royal palaces. That had been the first time most people had seen inside the walls and gardens of Windsor Castle, Buckingham Palace, the Palace of Holyroodhouse, Kensington Palace, St James's Palace and Hampton Court – the paintings, the décor, the flowers, the grand ballrooms. It was a safe subject, in safe hands, safely produced as a joint venture by the BBC and its upstart commercial rival ITV. Broadcast by both channels on Christmas Day 1966, it was a success. If the Coronation cameras had shed daylight on the ancient ritual, Clark had pulled back the curtain on the country's once mysterious royal residences.

But the most startling royal attempt to change with the times came two years later, when the Queen decided to allow television cameras to follow her and her close family for a television documentary film. *Royal Family* went a giant step further than *Royal Palaces* had and allowed the cameras to pore over the Queen, the Duke and their children. It followed some of the ritual and pomp of the royal year and tried to explain the Queen's job. But its punch was in answering, at least partly, the question, 'But what are they *like*?' It allowed anyone with a television a view of the Windsors apparently so intimate that only a handful of courtiers and family friends had been there before. As in 1966, Prince Philip was crucial to the project, chairing an advisory committee to oversee the experiment.

For seventy-five days during 1969 a film crew of eight, again working jointly for the BBC and ITV, were allowed remarkable access to the family. The film's producer was the head of BBC documentaries, Richard Cawston, a tall and debonair former army signals officer whose career at the Corporation had made him a master of camerawork, sound, the cutting room and the dubbing theatre. Cawston knew he could hardly ask the Queen for a second take, so everything would be at least partly spontaneous 'cinéma-vérité'. The camera team became so familiar that the family did indeed almost start to forget they were there.

The Queen, according to Cawston, became quite an expert about problems of lighting and sound recording. Forty-three hours of film were edited to produce the 105-minute final programme. Most viewers today would be struck by the upper-class 1950s accents and old-fashioned clothing, but the informal shots of a family barbecue at Balmoral, the Queen driving her car, walking with dogs and chatting with the young children, are still fresh and interesting. The Queen smiles and sometimes laughs as she goes about the serious business of reigning. Prince Andrew and Prince Edward, who had barely been seen by the public, seem normal, cheerful boys. The shrewd script by Antony Jay, later of *Yes, Minister* fame, was respectful but lightened with gentle jokes. Of the royal Rolls-Royces he noted, 'no cars in the world can have been driven so far, so slowly'. Jay says now he thought the film had emerged 'because in the 1960s there couldn't have been a decade that was more anti-monarchy . . . It was about classlessness. It was about equality. It was about being popular. And all the things that the royal family represented, like order and respectability, were jokes.' In the press, even the conservative press, he felt, there was 'a feeling that, you know, the royal family – well, their time's gone. Nothing to do with us. What are they? Oh, they're just an irrelevance.'

Lord Brabourne, the film producer married to Mountbatten's daughter, had come up with the idea, says Jay. He thought, 'if only people could see what the royal family is like, they'd feel much, much better disposed towards them. And he put up this idea for a film, a BBC film, just showing them. Not a defence of the monarchy, but just an explanation, a portrait of it.' Jay says he was much impressed that the Royals, though well used to cameras, were much more worried about what the microphones might pick up, not on their own account but that they might hurt other people: 'That they might say things that would upset people, particularly, you know, the high ranking people, dignitaries from other countries and all the rest of it, who might be upset by what they said. So they were much more worried about the sound than they were about the pictures.'[20] They need not have worried. Cawston, in Jay's reckoning, was a great diplomat as well as a great film-maker. Though the BBC had a 'very strong republican element' at producer level higher up, the film was considered a great coup and so there was a strong element of BBC self-censorship in not wanting to offend, 'a sort of deferential sense of respect and obligation towards the monarchy and there was no doubt who was the boss in the operation'.

When it was shown in the summer of 1969, *Royal Family* became easily the most watched documentary in the history of British television, with 23 million people tuning in to see the first showing, in black and white, on the BBC and another 15 million watching it when it was shown on ITV in colour.[21] An estimated 68 per cent of British adults watched the film. The reaction was everything the Duke of Edinburgh would have hoped for. Even the *New Statesman*'s republican-leaning television critic John Holmstrom found that the Queen, 'who doesn't always look very appealing or animated on newsreels, emerges as a warm, engaging and even girlish person, capable of little giggles of motherly pleasure . . .' He concluded that Cawston and Jay should be given knighthoods: 'They'll certainly have added a decade or two to the life of the British monarchy.'[22] In the *Spectator* they welcomed the film and mocked the idea that by letting in the cameras the monarchy had devalued itself: 'If the sight of the Queen making salad is thought to dissolve the magic of monarchy, what about this sort of comment: "His late Majesty, though at times a jovial, and, for a King, an honest man, was a weak, ignorant, common-place sort of person . . . his feebleness of purpose and littleness of mind, his ignorance and his prejudice . . ."' before revealing that the remarks came from their own obituary of William IV.

The Queen and the Prince seemed pleased by the huge audience figures and the general reaction. Perhaps at the Duke's suggestion, the Queen gave her appearance fee and share of the profits, £60,000, to the British Academy of Film and Television Arts, which helped it move to its current headquarters in Piccadilly. Neither Cawston nor Jay was honoured at the time, though Jay was knighted later on. He also wrote the film *Elizabeth R* and was made a Commander of the Royal Victorian Order. He was interested enough in the Queen's role to later consider making a sequel to his *Yes, Minister* called *Yes, Ma'am*. Yet in retrospect, there were faint indications that letting in the cameras was a tricky business. Stuart Hood, the *Spectator*'s television critic, felt that it had been 'the apotheosis of home movies' whose purpose must have been 'to promote the idea that one family is very like another. It may even presage a move to a Scandinavian type monarchy.'[23] If the first proposition was tenable, the second was certainly not the message intended. After the year of its release, the Queen did not permit the original uncut documentary to be shown again.

Those who suggested that *Royal Family* was intended as a riposte to inquisitive politicians, or even to bizarre rumours about the supposed ill-health of the Queen and younger princes, were told this was all nonsense. The film had been meant as a prelude to the investiture of Prince Charles as Prince of Wales a few days later on 1 July.

Prince Charles had by now undergone much of the training his father had wanted for him – head boy at Gordonstoun, further toughening up in an Australian outback school, RAF jet training and university – he was then at Cambridge, studying history. The next step would be the navy, but before that he was to be introduced to his public role. The investiture was, in its way, as ambitious an attempt to re-project a modernized monarchy as Cawston's film. This time, however, the choreographer was not the Duke of Edinburgh or a BBC producer, but one of the younger and newer Royals by marriage, Princess Margaret's husband, Anthony Armstrong-Jones, who had become Lord Snowdon after their wedding in 1960. The child of a barrister and a mother from a notably arty family, divorced early, Armstrong-Jones had become a successful society and royal photographer. Thanks to another upwardly mobile Welshman, David Lloyd George, the ancient practice of 'investing' Princes of Wales had been moved to the spectacular setting of Caernarvon Castle and turned into a patriotic spectacle as long ago as 1911. The romantic and artistic Lord Snowdon, appointed by the Queen Constable of Caernarvon, decided it was the perfect opportunity to design a contemporary royal pageant, theatrical and television-friendly.

The castle would be refurbished. Giant stages would be erected. The largest perspex structure ever made would be created, all to show off the young prince. Snowdon began a struggle with the more traditionalist Earl Marshal, the Duke of Norfolk. A wickedly perceptive article in the *New Statesman* saw this as a fight between old monarchism and the new ways, between 'the greatest expert in ceremonial nonsense outside the Vatican' and Snowdon's 'Mary Quant' world-view: 'One could search the universe in vain for two men who have less in common . . . the Duke knows the exact degree of precedence between, say, an Irish countess and the eldest son of an English baronet; he can spot an incorrectly dressed Herald Extraordinary at a hundred yards flat; but he has neither the desire nor the talent for designing canopies and pennants, has no knowledge of textiles and the uses to which they can be put; he is not trendy and has no wish to be.'[24]

By 1969 it was at last the Sixties in the full meaning of the phrase, and so Lord Snowdon won. The investiture was indeed a carnival of colour and modern design, meant to show Wales as being both romantically ancient and also, with its Severn Bridge and nuclear power stations, determinedly modern. On the day an astonishing 250,000 people thronged the streets of the small town and the television coverage, with a young, oddly vulnerable-looking Prince Charles repeating his vows of fealty to his mother in English and newly studied Welsh, was spectacular. Philip Howard, writing in *The Times* caught the mood of rapturous excitement: 'There were proud peacock processions, frequent fanfares of silver, snarling trumpets, coveys of red dragons ... hymns, harps and heraldry, choirs carolling, brass bands booming, dodders of druids and bards ... lions rampant, regimental goats ... It was the greatest television spectacular in history, a carnival to entice tourists to Wales for years.'

So it was. And yet it was not quite the unvarnished success for the monarchy Lord Snowdon had hoped for. This was a time when Welsh nationalism was on the march, and in a more militant mood than ever before. An 'explosive device', later found to be a dummy, was discovered under a railway bridge on the royal route. Two naval minesweepers patrolled the entrance to Caernarvon harbour and a team of frogmen was waiting on board the Royal Yacht to search for under-water bombs. There was a gelignite explosion at Abergele, where two men were killed, apparently by their own bomb. In Cardiff Post Office six sorters had a narrow escape when a parcel bomb exploded, the fourth bombing in the city in three months. Telegraph wires running along the railway track to Caernarvon were cut and later a soldier was killed when a military police van caught fire and exploded. Among the crowds there was scattered booing and a few eggs were thrown. None of this amounted to anything like the serious unrest emerging in Northern Ireland. Nor would the 'Free Wales Army' amount to a serious threat when some of its adherents later faced trial. But the mood had changed from the unrestrained enthusiasm the Queen had enjoyed when she announced during a visit to Cardiff in 1958 that Prince Charles would become Prince of Wales, or during her 1963 visit to Caernarvon. Welsh national pride was no longer automatically loyal to the British idea. The Scots had shown flickers of nationalism when students stole back the Stone of Destiny, used during Coronations, from Westminster Abbey on Christmas Day 1950. Scottish nationalists later attacked letter-boxes with 'ERII' on them, since she was the first Queen Elizabeth in Scotland. Now Welsh nationalists were causing trouble too. Monarchism relies on common symbols, reliably beckoning common responses. It seemed that different parts of the United Kingdom were beginning to lean in different directions, while the centre seemed less sure of itself, for all its pageantry and colour.

The Swingeing Seventies

Though the 1970s was a difficult decade for the British state (not necessarily for the British people, who enjoyed foreign holidays, better health and a greater variety of food than ever before) these were in general good years for the Windsors. The Cawston film, the settlement of the financial argument, the emergence of Prince Charles as a public figure and of Princess Anne as a horsewoman good enough to compete at the Olympics, added up to a family success story. Prince Charles was in his action-man phase, a trained RAF jet pilot and then naval officer who seemed to be relaxing more into his public role, and had already taken on important royal visits to Japan, South America and the US. He was learning to make speeches: intermittent speculation in the media about girlfriends was still genial, even friendly, in tone. Under the surface, the story was not so happy. As a man carving his own place in the dynasty, Charles had become increasingly cut off from his parents. He had been unable to form a very close relationship with his father, and while in awe of his mother, found her mostly physically or mentally focused on her job. One of the questions raised time and again by people who know the royal family is the dilemma of 'what went wrong' and the extent to which the Queen can be blamed for her oldest son's unhappiness.

It is interesting, and true, that we seem to find it easier to empathize with ancient historical times than our own recent past. Nothing is as far away as the world of our grandparents. The Queen had been brought up in a largely male world, dominated by ritual and duty. She had close and loving parents but from a very young age her responsibilities had been drummed into her. The speech she gave in South Africa on her twenty-first birthday was the speech of a true believer – in monarchy, nationhood, God and destiny – which left little room for an ordinary relaxed family life. She became queen of a nation and a wider Commonwealth that were quick to criticize absences and jealous of their right to see and hear the monarch. Time-management rules her every moment. The diary is her most unrelenting master. And Charles was her first child. The aristocracy had developed habits of bringing up sons who went to Eton, Harrow or a handful of other posh schools and mingled at dances and hunts, going on to live lives surrounded by friends they had made early. But the royal family are not aristocracy. They are apart. Furthermore, the Queen had had no brothers or close childhood male friends.

She had never attended a school herself. So it should hardly be a surprise that she sub-contracted much of the job of looking after Charles to Prince Philip.

He, as we have seen, had had a disrupted childhood himself during which boarding school had been a delight and an inspiration. So in turn it was no surprise that he hoped Charles would thrive, as he had thrived, at Gordonstoun and then in the navy. None of this makes Charles's unhappy early life happier. But it ought to ram home the glibness of psychologists (and poets) who rush to blame the parents for every problem faced by children in later life. Parents are people too. They have their own lives, and their own problems, and a retrospective orgy of blaming every previous generation for the troubles of the next leads nowhere but to emotional quagmire. In the end, individual temperament matters more than anything else. Another son – indeed Prince Andrew, perhaps – could have lived Charles's early life and enjoyed every moment. So blame is inappropriate. Charles was simply very different. Genetic shuffling ensures these mismatches happen all the time.

Thinking of himself as a future monarch, however, Charles was becoming increasingly independent-minded. Though there were two charitable trusts raising money for good causes and connected to the Silver Jubilee of 1977, he was becoming interested in the idea of his own Prince's Trust, which would disburse grants to individuals, as well as organizations, in order to give deprived teenagers a fresh start in life. Though there were aspects of him that contrasted with his parents' values (his fascination with Eastern spirituality, say) there was also much that he had learned from them, and from the very same institutions he had flinched from. He believed in physical challenges, self-discipline, order and authority. He was no kind of hippy. He recoiled from the joshing, alpha-male atmosphere of the navy but he was a traditionalist when it came to the military, to ceremonial and protocol. He loved the humour of the Goons, routinely referred to as 'anarchic' – but he was quick to rebuke secretaries for spelling errors or to blast equerries for minor failures. So, as he began to take a more active and prominent public role, the Prince was already a complex figure.

There were parts of him strikingly like his father. Prince Philip's interest in science is not shared by his son, but they both painted. They were both passionate about the natural world – the Duke of Edinburgh through his lifelong association with the World Wildlife Fund and worries about overpopulation, and his son through his equally strong concern for the world's wild spaces and rainforests. They had been at the same school, and served in the same navy, and were both close to Lord Mountbatten, and shot and stalked; and both read poetry, and took a close interest in things military; both wanted do to something practical for young people. Is there such a gap in philosophy between the Duke of Edinburgh's Award Scheme and the Prince's Trust?

Prince Philip had endured half a lifetime of being bored at ceremonials, of being maliciously misquoted (though sometimes accurately quoted, which could be bad enough) and of having to bite his tongue. His son was by now experiencing the same tribulations. The difference was that Prince Charles was complaining, quite loudly, though at this stage only to friends and to staff. Despite this, during these years the royal family was at its most united. The Queen began to sound more relaxed. Her role as 'head of our morality' fitted well with a new motherliness and she had a very strong team around her.

The key non-family position around her is that of private secretary. One of those who has followed the court all his working life describes it as 'the only appointment in the Royal Household that really matters a damn'. Adeane, Lord Stamfordham's son, and a personal link to the court of George VI, finally retired from the job in 1972. The obvious man to replace him had been Martin Charteris, who had been the Queen's private secretary when she was Princess Elizabeth and had been with her in Kenya when she heard her father had died. But the Lord Chamberlain, Lord Cobbold, had introduced a rival, Philip Moore, a pilot who had been shot down during the war and risen through the civil service. In 1966 he became the Queen's assistant secretary. He was somewhat stiff and over-talkative, according to one who knew and partly admired him, who says, 'She got frightfully impatient with him at Balmoral. She wanted to rip through the papers and select the most important ones; Moore would plod slowly through everything.' Charteris realized that there was a plan to give the job to Moore and did what was, in the circumstances, rather a brave thing. He went to the Queen and confronted her. Who did she want as her next private secretary? 'You, of course,' replied the Queen. Charteris then in effect told her to get on with it. Moore did succeed, later on, in 1977, but the appointment of Charteris gave the Queen one of the wittiest and shrewdest senior advisers she has ever had, during a harder time ahead.

There was, for a start, a further toughening of attitude in the British press. Ann Leslie, one of the great reporters of her time, covered her first royal tour for the *Daily Express* in 1968, when the expected style of reporting was simply to note the colour and style of the Queen's clothes and make some anodyne remarks. From the first, she says, the press were not made welcome: 'Mao Tse Tung in China used to classify his enemies in various gradations and journalists were the ninth stinking category of enemies, and in a way the Court feels that about us, and I don't blame them, really.'[25] But the press were getting stroppier. Leslie says the journalists and photographers found that 1968 tour, which was to the Caribbean, 'stunningly boring and tiring' because of the transport problems of always trying to get ahead of the Royal Yacht. In Dominica, Prince Philip was opening a hospital, and, when the matron told him about the terrible mosquitoes, he replied along the lines of, 'Well, you have mosquitoes, we have the press.' The reporters and photographers revolted. Leslie remembers: 'We ordered him to apologize ... We pointed out to his horrified press secretary that actually he needed us more than we needed him ... and if he didn't behave and stop insulting us we would snap our notebooks shut, put our cameras down on the ground – or we'll start photographing close-ups of tropical flowers.' The Duke succumbed and came over to apologize, after which, says Leslie, 'he was rather unnervingly charming to us. We're not used to that.' Leslie was working for a keenly royal newspaper, the *Daily Express*, and went on to write for another, the *Daily Mail*, and describes her readers as 'definitely the "knit your own Royal" and "Royal biscuit-tin" types; to begin with, there was no danger that the irritation of reporters would spill into hostile news stories.' But, she adds, 'then along comes Murdoch, who is of course a republican'.

Harry Arnold, one of the reporters who caused many teeth to be ground at the Palace, says he believes the Queen's reign saw a revolution in attitudes. Asked what had caused it, his reply echoes Ann Leslie: 'In two words – Rupert Murdoch.' Arnold was there on the day the Australian tycoon bought the *Sun* in 1969 and he became the paper's first royal correspondent seven years later; he says that it was clear from early on that Murdoch, who had developed classic Australian republican views, wanted the Royals to be treated as just another story and given no special favours. It was more, says Arnold, about selling papers than republicanism and arguably the Royals have done more for Fleet Street than Fleet Street has done for them. For a long time this shift would not directly affect the Queen, who was generally regarded as so popular as to be untouchable. More often, it was focused on her husband, her sister and then her children. Arnold recalls, with some glee, a gaffe the Duke made during the first royal visit to China where he told some students they would be 'slitty-eyed' if they stayed too long there; the fact that the Queen seemed angry with him the next day was regarded as a further coup.[26] What happened in the British popular press was simply that Murdoch's less reverential, cheekier, chancier attitude to the Royals, along with his page-three girls, shorter stories and terrible punning headlines, proved a winning formula; and one by one his critics became his imitators.

At this time the worst problem the Royals faced was that they seemed increasingly out of touch with the times. It was impossible to associate the Queen and her immediate family with the new mood and trendy culture of the Sixties and Seventies. They sought solace in Scottish glens and mountains, with guns and rods. They dressed formally and traditionally. They were more comfortable with dogs, horses and military types than with rock music, film stars or designers. The Queen Mother retained a lively, if unadventurous, interest in the arts but the same could not be said for her daughter, who had giggled at Wagner, quite enjoyed farces and drew the line at serious literature. The monarchy was loved and in some sense represented a broad swathe of middle-class and working-class traditional Britain – the churchgoing, prudent, self-disciplined and patriotic people who still formed a majority.

The royal family did not represent the new social forces, both heroes and villains, reshaping the country. Despite the odd OBE lobbed at a pop star, and sometimes lobbed back again, the monarchy during the Queen's middle years was out of touch with the times. Charles grew his hair a little longer. There were half-hearted attempts to suggest that Princess Anne was trendy in her mini-dress and beehive. But it was never convincing. The Queen, with her corgis and headscarf, was the antithesis of the age's signature tone, a brittle metropolitan trendiness tinged with revolutionary utopias and self-analysis. Most monarchists would say, 'and a good thing too', but there were dangers when Elizabeth's court seemed even older than its years. There was a culture war going on, and a generational conflict, and the House of Windsor was all on one side.

Not quite true: there was also Princess Margaret. She had struggled to recover from the shock of the destruction of her love affair with Peter Townsend. She had emerged as the funniest, most open and theatrical of the Windsors, though she shrewdly understood the role she was being forced into. She told the writer Gore Vidal, one of her many intellectual friends, that where there are two sisters, one being the Queen and the source of all honour and goodness, the other 'must be the focus of the most creative malice, the evil sister'.[27] To begin with, she was merely the wild one, the one who went dancing into the small hours in London nightclubs, who had a series of romances, who defied convention by smoking in public. If her sister and mother expected anything particular of her, it was that she might marry one of the wealthy heirs in whose company she was often seen, partying at Windsor or in London. She had royal duties of her own. She was colonel of a dozen regiments in Britain and other Commonwealth countries and was a keen patron of charities, particularly concerning children and the disadvantaged, playing something of the role that Diana would later on. But these did not amount to a life.

She lived with her mother in Clarence House. Because of the long saga of the Townsend love affair, by the time she was free again most of the obvious suitors were already married and she came to think she would always be single. This changed when she met Anthony Armstrong-Jones, the later creator of the Caernarvon investiture, but to begin with a young photographer with royal connections. They clicked quickly and managed to conduct a romance in semi-public without Fleet Street noticing, something that would have been unthinkable later on. But it was only when Margaret was told by Townsend in December 1959 that he was about to marry a Belgian woman that she accepted Armstrong-Jones. The following day she told him 'yes'. Before the wedding, he was moved from his bachelor pad in Pimlico Road to Buckingham Palace. The marriage took place in May 1960, the first big royal television event since the Coronation. Before the birth of their first child, Armstrong-Jones was raised to the peerage as Lord Snowdon.

They then began a life which, though by no means wicked, was certainly a startling contrast to the home life of our own dear Queen. Snowdon worked hard to do his bit as a royal worker, learning the duties of consort from Prince Philip. He even learned to shoot, a skill that was, and still is, expected of people who mix with the Windsors. But he and Margaret moved in a very different set. She stopped travelling in a stately Rolls-Royce and took to a Mini or rode pillion on Armstrong-Jones's motorbike. Their circle included Peter Sellers and his wife Britt Ekland, Greek shipping tycoons, the Aga Khan, the ballet dancer Rudolf Nureyev, rock stars like Mick Jagger, actors such as David Niven, trendy journalists, the hairdresser

Vidal Sassoon and the designer Mary Quant, alongside the more predictable rich aristocrats. They holidayed in Sardinia, Venice and the Caribbean. Princess Margaret became, as we saw, an easy target for Labour republicans who did not quite dare snipe at the Queen but found they could call her sister extravagant and lazy – and worse – and get away with it.

For better or worse, here was one part of the extended Windsor family that seemed connected to the more relaxed spirit of the times. Snowdon and Princess Margaret brought a sense of style and a fizz of fun. Unfortunately they were also of the age in not working very hard at their marriage. Both were soon having affairs, gleefully pursued by the paparazzi. At the centre of what seemed a glamorous and hedonistic world, there was coldness, sadness and mutual humiliation. Lord Snowdon and Princess Margaret began to spend more and more time apart, often leaving their two children in Britain – though both grew up to be thoroughly normal and well-balanced adults.

One place the photographers could rarely reach was the small Caribbean island of Mustique, where the couple had honeymooned. It was owned by one of Margaret's long-time friends, Lord Glenconner, Colin Tennant, whose family had been influential in the industrial revolution in Scotland, and who was fabulously rich after selling the family business. He had bought Mustique as a hideaway but then turned it into a very upmarket holiday resort, frequented by rock stars and the super-rich. He offered Princess Margaret some land to build a house there. It would become her favourite hideaway and a place British newspaper readers associated with exotic but mysterious naughtiness. Tennant played up to it all: on his fiftieth birthday party, attended by Princess Margaret (Princess of Misrule), he was crowned king of the island, while local youths paraded around wearing gold-painted coconut shells as codpieces. This was as obvious an 'anti-kingdom' to the decorum and seriousness of her sister's court as is possible to imagine. The Princess was surrounded by a little misrule court of flatterers and hangers-on, who adored her wit but whom she would often flatten with a swipe of Hanoverian hauteur. Snowdon pursued his own life, working ever harder, and seen with other women.

When she was forty-three, in 1973, Margaret was introduced by Glenconner at lunch in Edinburgh's Café Royal to a twenty-five-year-old Welsh charmer, whose life had been a muddle and a struggle up to then, called Roddy Llewellyn. Their affair would last eight years and scandalized many because of the gap in their ages and Llewellyn's poverty. This is the story that really opened the floodgates in the press. In 1976 the *News of the World* covered its front page with a story about Princess Margaret and a young Welshman. The dying marriage was killed by the affair and the couple divorced two years later. Arnold and his rivals spent their first years also in pursuit of the 'Who will Prince Charles marry?' mystery, and Arnold was the man who revealed Lady Diana Spencer to be the winning answer.

This second phase was dominated by the love affair between Diana and the public, with the press as panting middle-men; and it ended, of course, in disaster. Robert Lacey, the journalist and pioneering biographer of the Queen, puts it like this: 'I think the reign of Elizabeth II will be looked back on above all in terms not of the particular political crises but of the way in which the monarchy adapted to the media, was nearly brought crashing down by the media – I'm thinking of what happened at the time of Diana's death – and has since emerged into calmer waters.'[28] He argues, rightly, that one can see the entire history of the twentieth-century monarchy in terms of its struggle with the media, from George V's rebranding exercise in 1917, through the abdication crisis, George VI's struggle to master radio broadcasting and the emergence of a more critical, then impertinent press in the post-war period. (Now we have an octogenarian Queen whose office has adapted with vigour to the world of Facebook and Twitter; it would be a surprise if she began a blog, but it cannot be entirely discounted.)

Princess Margaret, like her father and grandfather, was a heavy smoker. She was also, like many of her generation, a heavy drinker. The combination, and an accident which left her with badly scalded feet, produced a dramatic deterioration of her health in later years. She was admitted to hospital with alcoholic hepatitis and had part of her left lung removed. She suffered strokes and lived in seclusion at Kensington Palace before dying aged seventy-one in 2002. The men in her life all remarried; even the apparently doomed Llewellyn became a successful television gardener and inherited the family baronetcy. Often the butt of cruel humour and dismissive abuse, Princess Margaret's life showed how hard it is to cope with the pressure of royalty without a strong work ethic and an abnormal amount of self-control. She was badly treated when it mattered most and struggled to find a way to live happily. Her sister's words about the importance of duty and marriage uttered so long ago seem poignant. The Queen has been a paragon of duty and determination; but in her marriage and the security of her role she has been lucky too.

One of her quiet successes has been that the more journalists observe her at work, the more they admire her phlegm and grit. Ann Leslie, a woman who rarely takes posh prisoners, says she gapes at the Queen's readiness to affect an interest in aero engines and foreign leaders when she would much rather be talking about horses or simply resting. On one sweltering day in Bangkok, she says, 'I was watching the jet engine parts makers and they were glowing because they got the impression somehow that, although she was very dignified, and she's not going to gush, because gush is not her default mode, that she really did care about them and their engine parts. And I thought, this woman is bloody brilliant.' That experience, multiplied, is the real explanation as to why the Queen has weathered the prejudices of newspaper proprietors and the storms of newspaper wars so successfully.

Friends and Foreigners

If 'the Sixties' were not, for many people, the reality of life in the actual 1960s then 'the Seventies' did not feel like the 1970s as actually experienced by those leading Britain. It is hard to imagine anyone less trendy, unbuttoned and at ease with himself than Edward Heath, who won his election victory in June 1970. The Queen was at the Ascot races and it was not until 7 p.m. that he was summoned to the Palace. Previous Tory prime ministers had been grander figures. Here was a man from the lower middle class, who had been elected by his party and who had no interest in grouse moors, horse-racing or indeed country life generally.

This was a different kind of Conservative. Immediately, he had a favour to ask: there was a party at Windsor that night for Lord Mountbatten and the Queen Mother, both seventy. Would she mind if he was late? 'She threw back her head and laughed, saying that all the family had been discussing whether or not I would still be able to come . . .'[29] But the relationship developed and, like later premiers, Heath found his weekly audiences, at 6.30 p.m. on Tuesdays, had the *omertà* of the therapist's office: 'It was always a relief to be able to discuss everything with someone, knowing full well that there was not the slightest danger of anything leaking.' He would talk about politics but also the personal affairs of fellow politicians and foreign leaders. Northern Ireland and his attempt to 'join Europe' were early topics. Afterwards, he would stay for a drink with her private secretary – Sir Michael Adeane, and then Martin Charteris.

Heath already knew the Queen and Duke of Edinburgh from informal lunches, though he was as socially awkward with royalty as with any other branch of the human family. In his memoirs, he recounts an early lunch when he was sitting next to Princess Margaret, who spent the first two courses talking to another guest. 'She then turned to me. I had always been taught not to initiate a conversation with a member of the royal family. So while awaiting her opening gambit I just looked back, and remained silent. So did she.' On the third go, he asked her whether she had been busy and got the acid reply, 'That is the sort of question Lord Mayors ask when I visit cities.'[30] It gives a clue to the difficulties the Queen must have had with Heath: 'She did not find him easy,' says one former civil servant, 'But who did? That was Ted.' Yet she worked hard at the relationship, paying her first formal visit to Chequers in October 1970 to see Heath and President Nixon, who was there for talks. At Balmoral, Heath was politely asked about his latest yacht-racing exploits and answered at considerable length.

But Heath was prepared to offer unwelcome advice if necessary. In 1971 the Commonwealth heads of government conference, a biennial event the Queen cares passionately about, was due to be held in Singapore. And the Canadian prime minister had established the expectation that the Queen would go to Commonwealth heads of government meetings even when they were not held in the UK. Meanwhile the Commonwealth was at war with itself because of the confrontation between Rhodesia and the 'front-line' black African states. Heath felt she should not go. The Queen put up a counter-argument, that if the conference had been in London, as until then it had been, she would have been present and the situation would have been just as explosive. The fact of it being in Singapore was not a reason for her failing to attend. Heath retorted that London simply had a different atmosphere. The grand buildings and the proximity of Buckingham Palace and Windsor would make it likelier that people would be on their best behaviour. In Singapore she would meet each one of the warring leaders at a time when it was almost impossible to arbitrate between them.

This was a key example of the limits of the Queen's ability to knock heads together at the top of the organization. She cannot go against a British prime minister who has dug his heels in. On 15 October 1970 he wrote advising her formally not to go and, however reluctantly, she agreed. Adeane, her private secretary, wrote back five days later conceding defeat: since her only interest was to help the Commonwealth and 'as it seems probable that her presence on this occasion might well lead to controversy and embarrassment, she agrees that it would be better to stay away'. In the event, it was a rough conference and Heath thought he had saved her from 'political and personal unpleasantness'. Later she got in some gentle verbal revenge. In 1992 Heath, long retired, was at Buckingham

Palace discussing the first Gulf war with the Queen and the US Secretary of State, James Baker. A real row bubbled up between the men, since Heath had been to see Saddam Hussein himself in a much criticized visit, when he warned him to get out of Kuwait. Heath told Baker he should have done the same. The Queen intervened and said Baker could not have gone to Baghdad. Why not, Heath asked the Queen. *He* had been able to. '"I know you could," said the Queen; "but you're expendable now."'

Heath's greatest political work during his three years in office had been Britain's entry into the European Community. This might be thought to have huge implications for the Crown, since Britain was joining a supranational organization many of whose members assumed they were on a motorway towards political union. The sovereignty of the sovereign, never mind the nation, was at least in question. Constitutional opponents of the project in Britain saw the entire structure of the 'Crown in Parliament' under attack, a historic surrender of a thousand years of proud independence. Yet there is not the slightest sign that the Queen or other Royals objected. Far from it. In speeches the Queen dutifully lauded her government's achievement, and she suggested in her 1972 Christmas broadcast that somehow the Commonwealth family of nations was now joining hands with another extended family. This was pious but, given the rivalries, implausible.

When Heath celebrated Britain's formal membership in January 1973, with a 'Fanfare for Europe' gala concert at Covent Garden, followed by a dinner at Lancaster House, the Queen and Prince Philip were guests of honour and Heath recorded that 'my heart was full of joy . . . at the recognition which Her Majesty the Queen had given to our country's great

achievement'.[31] By 'our country's', Heath of course meant
'my', and this may have simply been another example of a
Crown-bedazzled politician's self-delusion. Yet the Queen did
seem to be comfortable with British membership of the EEC,
despite the unease it caused to some members of the Commonwealth concerned about their agricultural trade and her own
role. Perhaps she reflected that the Dutch monarchy had
managed perfectly well in the new bloc.

When Heath's crisis-stricken government, exhausted by its
battles with the trade unions, finally gave way and he called the
first of the 1974 elections, the Queen was at the other end of
the world, enjoying a February tour of the South Seas. As the
election campaign raged at home, she travelled through Pacific
island territories, New Zealand and finally Australia, before
flying back to London for the close of polling. There she faced
a new dilemma, not this time a question of party leadership but
of parliamentary arithmetic. The voters had returned a hung
Parliament, in which Wilson's Labour Party, not Heath's Conservatives, had the largest single bloc of seats. As when Gordon
Brown faced a similar outcome in 2010, the Palace stuck by
the constitutional doctrine that the prime minister remained
prime minister until he or she had resigned. Just as Brown
hung on until it was clear that Labour could not form a work-
able coalition with the Liberal Democrats, so Heath spent
an agonizing weekend trying to stitch together a deal with
Jeremy Thorpe, the Liberal leader, before finally resigning on
the Monday. The Queen had the power in theory to invite
anyone else she liked to try to form a government, but it was
so overwhelmingly obvious that the right choice was to invite
Wilson back that there was no real decision to take. There were
several exchanges of messages between Buckingham Palace and

Number Ten but no sense of constitutional crisis, still less the dangers of the Macmillan or Eden successions.

For the Queen, the more serious mid-1970s political challenge came not in Britain but in Australia. The crisis played out there in 1975 boosted republicanism and demonstrates the dangers of the Queen's theoretically political role when others try to exploit it. Australia's prime minister was the intellectual and fiery Labor politician Gough Whitlam. His government had introduced numerous reforms but was in deep trouble, scandal-hit and struggling with an economic crisis. He had a majority in the lower house, but not the upper house, the elected Australian senate. His Liberal Party opponent, Malcolm Fraser, decided to use the senate to block Whitlam's budget bills, thus bringing government to a standstill and forcing a general election. The Queen became involved because her representative in Australia, the governor general Sir John Kerr, then intervened. He abruptly sacked Whitlam and appointed Fraser prime minister.

Whitlam wanted to appeal to the Queen directly but his dismissal was so fast he was unable to use this constitutional right – because he was no longer prime minister. Kerr, who Whitlam believed was acting in concert with Fraser to ditch a properly elected Labor government, was using the same 'reserve' powers of the monarchy that at least allow the Queen, in theory, to sack British prime ministers. The words that matter are 'in theory'. Kerr was not, it should be emphasized, a grandee governor general sent out from St James's with a plumed hat, fine command of ancient Greek and long family tree in the West Country. He was a tough Australian lawyer from a working-class Sydney family, who had risen through the law, specializing in trade-union cases. Kerr had spent the war in Australian intelligence and then wanted to be a Labor politician himself, though he later drifted to the right. He had been appointed by the Queen but had actually been chosen by none other than Whitlam.

The Queen was so little involved in his decision to sack her Australian prime minister that Kerr did not even tell her until he had done it. He wanted to protect her from controversy, he said later: a governor general was expendable but a Queen was not. Still, he had acted using her authority and in a way that infuriated many Australian socialists. Whitlam emerged from the parliament building to greet an angry crowd and began his speech, referring to the official proclamation calling an election: 'Well may we say "God Save the Queen" because nothing will save the Governor-General', and telling his supporters to 'maintain your rage and enthusiasm' for the election ahead. The Queen was asked to intervene, presumably by sacking her governor general and reinstating Whitlam, on the grounds that the sovereignty of her people had been infringed. That would have been an even more provocative reassertion of personal authority, and she declined to get involved.

What would have happened had Whitlam won the election, instead of – to his great surprise – losing it? He had been lukewarm about the monarchy from the start, earlier introducing a bill proclaiming that in Australia the Queen would not be known by her full British title, but only 'Queen of Australia'. There had long been a republican strain in Labor politics, fuelled by Irish anti-monarchism and the huge distance between Australia and the 'mother country'. Shared wartime memories still counted for a lot, but immigration from Europe and Asia was beginning to gently erode the Britishness of the nation. So it is perfectly possible that Whitlam's next Labor government might have cut the link in the 1970s. Even as it was, Australian republicanism became stronger.

Nothing dramatic has happened. The 1986 Australia Act formally severed any rights of the UK to interfere in Australian politics and five years later the Australian Republican Movement was formed. References to the Queen were removed from the Australian Oath of Allegiance. Australian barristers ceased to be Queen's Counsel. In 1991 a new Australian Labor prime minister, Paul Keating, who had served under Whitlam, called for the Australian flag to be redesigned, dropping the Union flag from its edge, and began moves to prepare for a republic. The Queen watched almost silently, though in Australia a pro-monarchy organization was formed. When she arrived for her 1992 visit she invited Keating aboard *Britannia* and before he could deliver a pre-prepared speech told him that she was the last person who would stand in the way of Australia becoming republican. Now, she said, I gather you have fifty-four nationalities in Australia today. There must be a time when I am completely redundant; you will let me know, won't you? Keating, according to those present, was both silenced and disarmed. Later on the same trip, he fell foul of the British media by committing the solecism of putting an arm round the Queen; but that was a more protective gesture than she might have expected.

The following year Keating set up a Republic Advisory Committee, which led to a Constitutional Convention to thrash out the fine detail of how a 'resident for president' might actually be chosen. After a change of government, the referendum was finally held in 1999 and the Australians, to general surprise, stuck with the Queen by a 55 per cent majority. Yet if one of the major realms of which she is sovereign is ever to reject her, or her heir, Australia is the likeliest candidate. Julia Gillard, the country's prime minister in 2011, is a republican (though hard-liners are suspicious that she is 'soft' on the subject) and so was her predecessor, Kevin Rudd. Both suggested that she should be the last monarch of their country – a poignant thought, given her visit to Australia just months before her Diamond Jubilee year for the Commonwealth heads of government meeting. Yet opinion polls are unclear and Prince William is one of the most popular royals in Australia since his mother. You never can tell.

Canada, which replaced a Union-dominated Red Ensign with a national maple-leaf flag in 1965, was going through a similar re-evaluation. It, however, had the large French-speaking and increasingly separatist minority in Quebec to complicate matters. During the 1960s and 1970s the rise of the Parti Québécois had given an angrier and more urgent edge to republicanism, though cementing the monarchy more strongly in English-dominated provinces of Canada. The Queen had an early, first-hand experience of the problem during her 1964 visit to Quebec when there had been protests, including long lines of people silently turning their backs to her. After she left, fights with the police and arrests led to the day being dubbed 'Truncheon Saturday'. There had also been reports of assassination plots against her. She was back in Quebec, however, for the opening of the 1967 Expo fair, and again in 1976 for the opening of the Montreal Olympics. She also had to deal with the impish, charismatic and unpredictable Pierre Trudeau, Canada's independent-minded premier during 1968–79 and 1980–84.

Trudeau is a fascinating case-study in early rebels who metamorphose into mildly conservative figures. He had been an anti-conscription protester during the Second World War, a

French-Catholic intellectual interested in Marxism, and a persistent enemy of Mackenzie King, Canada's pro-British wartime leader. As prime minister, he became known for stunts such as sliding down the banisters at Buckingham Palace, doing an impromptu dance behind the Queen and meeting John Lennon on his world peace tour. With his background, it was soon being asked whether he was also a republican. Yet in office Trudeau had to confront not only Quebec separatism but also extremist groups; he developed into a tough operator, determined to keep Canada united, if by now bilingual. He denied being republican and continued to invite the Queen to Canada. When Whitehall was uncertain about the wisdom of her going, British ministers were reminded that it was none of their business. She was Queen of Canada and Trudeau was her prime minister, just as much as Douglas-Home, Wilson or Heath. And when, during his 1980s term as prime minister, Trudeau decided that Canada's constitution should be 'patriated' – that is, properly written down and established for and in Canada, rather than as an appendage of British law – he said the Queen approved. In his memoirs, Trudeau said he had been impressed by her grace in public and the wisdom of her private conversations.

The 1982 patriation, which included a Canadian Bill of Rights and Liberties, did not lead to serious new questioning of the monarchy and is now a cornerstone of Canadian identity. It has been a classic example of the wisdom of the gentle, unprotesting retreat of British power, just as the Queen's handling of Trudeau helped ensure that a potential enemy of her authority ended up as a supporter of it. In his final despatch to London in 1984, the British high commissioner, a career diplomat called Lord Moran, who had been in the service since the 1940s, took a harsher view. Trudeau's great contribution had been to defeat Quebec separatism and terrorism but 'he has not been greatly respected or trusted in London. He has never entirely shaken off his past as a well-to-do hippie and draft dodger ... Many of my colleagues here admire him. I cannot say I do. He is an odd fish and his own worst enemy.' It was the kind of thing a retiring official can say; it was passed around with many snorts of amusement in London, but would get an icy glare at the Palace. It was in Trudeau's era that the notion of vesting Canadian sovereignty in the governor general, and so passing to a republic, began to be seriously discussed. There is now an active republican organization, Citizens for a Canadian Republic, which argues that when the Queen dies, the monarchical connection must go and a native-born Canadian become head of state. By 2010, when the Queen again visited Canada, though not Quebec, opinion polls showed a clear majority, 58 per cent, in favour of severing the country's ties with the monarchy after her death.

Back in the 1970s, Australian and Canadian lessons were debated in Britain, too. The thought of 'losing' such giant and final pieces of the old story caused much unease. Yet the ambiguities of the Queen's role could not be ignored. Was she purely symbolic or were there situations in which she not only could intervene in politics, to unblock a crisis, but ought to? How did one distinguish between her role as head of different states if their interests collided? There could be no precise parallel of the Australian crisis which had ousted Whitlam, since Britain did not have an elected second chamber. Yet there were questions about how she might act in Britain if the parties or Parliament were stuck. Suppose Harold Wilson, who returned as prime minister in 1974, had suddenly resigned. Should the Queen appoint a stop-gap herself to allow 'the Queen's business' to continue smoothly?

If so, was she not giving a potential candidate for the job an unwarranted leg-up? Or should she simply wait, passively premier-less, for the party to choose a new leader? There was much debate about this between the Palace and Downing Street. The formula devised by Martin Charteris was that the prime minister must stay in office, resigning only as party leader. The party would choose a new leader and at that point there would be a seamless switchover, leaving the Queen entirely out of it. This was exactly what happened when John Major resigned as party leader to confront his Tory critics: he remained prime minister while the contest went on and indeed assumed he would continue to be prime minister after he had flushed out his enemies. When Wilson shocked the political world by announcing his resignation in 1976, he did indeed stay in office while Labour conducted its election for a new leader, so that the Queen was not involved.

On that occasion Jim Callaghan beat the left's much loved intellectual Michael Foot to become leader, and, in short order, prime minister too. Wilson's announcement had spawned a score of pop-eyed theories involving blackmail, Russian spies, or South African ones, and corruption. His loyal press secretary Joe Haines is convinced that the revelation by his doctor to Wilson of the early onset of Alzheimer's disease was the true reason for his exit. If so, he must have indicated this to the Queen privately in September 1975 during his annual Balmoral visit. Apart from his wife Mary, the Queen was the first to know that he was determined to go the following March. On 6 December 1975 he told her at his audience that he would leave around 11 March, and later the same day said at dinner given by his lawyer Arnold Goodman that 'I mentioned that matter to the Queen' so nobody could then say he had been pushed into it at the last minute. He told Barbara Castle the same thing – 'she's got the record of it'. The conspiracy theorists had a field day anyway, of course; quite whether Wilson thought the Queen would write to *The Times* or call the *Today* programme to explain it all was never clear.

On 23 March 1976 she and Prince Philip went to a farewell dinner at Number Ten, a convivial evening that went on until nearly midnight. She had done the same for Winston Churchill, but for nobody since. It was a mark of considerable respect and affection. They had been through a lot together. Wilson was not a great prime minister. He had spent so much time dodging and tacking to keep Labour united that he was rarely able to grasp the great issues and change the direction of the country. But he had been in charge during a time of ferocious and unsettling social upheaval, of political unrest, middle-class paranoia and inter-generational strife; and he had kept the show on the road. As the quintessential 'Sixties' politician, he had remained a resolutely old-fashioned and un-hip figure – podgy, dressed for comfort not fashion, phlegmatic and traditionalist. He smoked pipes and cigars, not marijuana; he liked HP sauce, not curry sauce; he had been in the Scouts, not a pop band. So, though he was only the Queen's second prime minister to have been born in the twentieth century, and although he was the son of an industrial chemist from Huddersfield, Wilson would not have been as alien a figure to the Windsors as some have made out: there is generational solidarity, as well as the class one. 'He adored the Queen, he really did,' says one senior Whitehall figure who worked with him. The Wilson years had been marked by scandals and conspiracy theories but the Queen managed to keep well clear. She cannot have liked some of what he did. Asked to approve a seat in the House of Lords for Marcia Williams, Lady Falkender, Wilson's controversial secretary and gate-keeper, the Queen rolled an eye: 'Must I?' But she complied.

Royalists and Republicans

There were two major moments of royal stocktaking in the seventies, the Queen's silver wedding anniversary and her Silver Jubilee of 1977. Jubilees, culminating in the Diamond, have been among the most characteristic celebrations of the Windsor dynasty. It is worth pausing and reflecting on them. Where did the idea come from? When did they start? The first 'modern' Jubilee happened in 1809 when writers and politicians began to raise a hubbub for something to mark the fiftieth anniversary of George III's accession. Rather as in 1977, it came when the country was badly in need of cheering up. The Napoleonic wars were at their height, with the high taxes, reduced imports, wounded soldiers and physical isolation they had brought to Britain. In Spain and Portugal, the Peninsular war was grinding grimly on. George's reign had seen the great naval victory of Trafalgar four years before, but he was also associated with the loss of the American colonies and by this time was almost blind and suffering grievously from rheumatism.

The idea of celebrating his exceptionally long reign was seized upon as a national dance of defiance, a knees-up in the darkness. There were services of thanksgiving around the country, with ox-roastings and formidable amounts of beer being consumed. Special food was issued to soldiers and sailors. The King freed all debtors to the Crown. Many other debtors were released from prison, after being gorged on beef and plum-puddings. Deserters were pardoned. Prisoners of war were released and sent home, except for the French. George III celebrated with prayers and fireworks at Windsor, while in London huge crowds turned out for a thanksgiving service at St Paul's, afterwards thronging the illuminated streets, dressed in patriotic garter-blue sashes.

All this did a lot to boost the King's popularity. Within a year he had begun the sad descent into madness and dementia, which made necessary the Regency Act and the rule of his fat, rebellious son; but the notion of the jubilee had been established. The next long-reigning monarch was Victoria, whose Golden Jubilee of 1887 had an entirely different atmosphere. At the very zenith of empire, it was grander, more military and more imperial, celebrated in India, Australia, New Zealand, Canada and Africa as well as in Britain. It was the moment when the Queen left behind her years of seclusion as 'the widow of Windsor' and it did much for her popularity, too. The ceremonies in London included a gathering of the vastly extended royal family network of Europe, a parade of Indian troops behind the famous gold coach, in which the crownless Victoria sat and waved, and a service at Westminster Abbey. There was an Irish terrorist plot to blow up the Queen, government and assembled notables, which failed partly because of London's unreliable public transport system. Around Britain, there was enough collective memory to repeat the ox-roastings, feasts, beer-drinking, bonfires and dances of 1809.

Victoria was still reigning in 1897 when her Diamond Jubilee was celebrated in similar fashion, though with more looking back and the first tremors of suspicion that Britain's age of dominance might not last for ever. In the following century, the most significant such celebration had been the Silver Jubilee of George V in 1935. This happened once more at a time of national gloom and uncertainty – among the most fulsome messages of congratulations was one from Herr Hitler. The by now familiar pattern of beacons, fireworks, ox-roastings, parties and church services followed. When the King and Queen visited the slums of east London, the royal coach and horses were followed by enthusiastic roller-skaters and cyclists. There was a sea of flags and cheering faces: one sign in a particularly dilapidated area read simply, 'Lousy but Loyal'. It was after this that George reflected, 'I'd no idea they felt that way about me: I am beginning to think they must really like me for myself.' This was probably not false modesty. Before opinion polls and relatively isolated from public opinion, it took a big occasion to show the monarch the people, as well as vice versa.

So by the 1977 Silver Jubilee there was an established tradition to work from. We knew what jubilees were for. They were moments of stock-taking and reflection, both about the state of the monarchy and what had happened to the country. They were bad news for oxen and good news for brewers. They had become dates in the national life not unlike big birthdays or diamond weddings in family life. The historian David Cannadine makes a simple but powerful point about them:

> If you live in a republic – let's take the United States of America – and you think about the period of history that the country's chopped up into, it is four years for a president, eight years if you're lucky, and then it's a hundred years, for centenaries or centennials, and that's about it; whereas if you have a monarchy, especially if you have the present Queen, who has reigned for twenty-five years, then fifty years, then sixty years, what you get

is this sequence of jubilees which provides you with the
opportunity for structured retrospection . . . that otherwise
you don't have.[32]

What are jubilees? They are catch-your-breath, look-around
and what-does-it-all-mean years.

In 1977 the question was this: after the overblown romantic
optimism of the 'New Elizabethan Age', how had the post-war
country and the Queen done? The Windsors were unscathed
by scandal. Behind the scenes the work of Palace officials to
avoid controversy had been largely successful. Genteel lack of
relevance seemed the greater threat. In 1972 the Queen celebrated her twenty-fifth wedding anniversary by reminding her
listeners of the bishop who, when asked what he thought of
sin, replied that he was against it: so she was 'for' marriage. Her
'family monarchy' was intact. Divorce had become a national
addiction and the young behaved with much greater sexual
openness, even abandon. But, Princess Margaret apart, the
Windsors were straight-laced and together. Prince Charles was
seen most often in uniform at the bridge of naval vessels or
in helicopters, or on a polo pony. Princess Anne had married
Captain Mark Phillips the following year, at Westminster Abbey.
Phillips declined an earldom and their children, Peter and
Zara, would grow up outside the glare of publicity, though
the couple would later separate and divorce.

Princess Anne was already one of the unflashy stars of the
family. A superb horsewoman, she would take part in the 1976
Olympics as part of the British team, riding her mother's horse
Goodwill: she says today it is a rare, possibly unique case, of
the same person breeding both horse and rider. She had her
father's bluntness and plenty of guts. In March 1974 she had
been the victim of an attempted ransom kidnap on Pall Mall

on her way back from a charity film screening. The kidnapper shot and wounded three men, including her driver and protection officer, and told the Princess to get out of the car, to which she replied 'Not bloody likely' before bolting out of the other side and eventually being helped by members of the public. Though one of those random events that can threaten the lives of royalty, the incident was also of its time: the would-be kidnapper claimed he wanted to use the planned £3 million ransom to fund the National Health Service, a crude version of the 'Robin Hood' rhetoric becoming more popular as politics became more confrontational.

Ahead of the Silver Jubilee, if the royal family was in good shape, the country was not. With strikes and the three-day week haunting Heath's domestic premiership, then union militancy returning with added edge in the Wilson–Callaghan government, there had been debates about whether Britain was even governable. Day after day the press reported alarming economic news, dire threats about inflation and the continuing menace of a Soviet Union which now seemed more powerful and threatening than ever. Back in 1968 there had been a brief, abortive discussion between a press baron called Cecil King and Lord Mountbatten about some kind of coup against Wilson, which Mountbatten had brushed contemptuously aside. Even in the mid-1970s there were plenty in the upper reaches of the business and political world who thought that the unions and socialists might only be reined in under some kind of temporary junta. Hostility to joining Europe, fear of Soviet-sponsored communists infiltrating industry and despair about the cycle of terrorist violence spinning out of control in Northern Ireland produced an almost paranoid mood on the right.

As with her grandfather in 1935, the Queen's Silver Jubilee

provoked some MPs to call for – well, not *too much* celebration because of the tough economic times. The leftist and republican minority was more vocal than ever, though not, according to the polls, any larger. *The Times* writer Philip Howard asked how seriously Britain should take the case of the radicals, who felt that monarchy had become 'a soporific for a geriatric society, and comic relief to the death-rattle of a nation'. He concluded that despite all the current problems, 'There is a great advantage in having your official head of state above competition and so above party contention. Constitutional monarchy is, paradoxically, a democratic institution: by giving your official head of state no power, it makes her representative of all her subjects, particularly the weaker ones.'[33] By the beginning of the Silver Jubilee year it was not yet clear how widely that assessment was still shared. As ever with monarchy, there would be no clear line between the popularity of the private family and the usefulness of the institution.

On the other side of the political divide, there was a mutinous feeling. For the first time in the Queen's reign, living standards had actually fallen during the previous two years. Inside the Labour Party, Trotskyists and Marxist local authority bosses seemed to be gaining influence. In jubilee year, the communists would organize their own celebration, socialists would distribute 'Roll on the Red Republic' badges and students would hoist red flags over Ruskin College, Oxford, to commemorate the sixtieth anniversary of the Bolshevik revolution. All of which may have added to the gaiety of the national conversation but did not really amount to a hill of red beans. Photographs of the Queen were removed from some town halls. During the jubilee some others, such as Manchester, decided to 'waste' no money on celebrations or decorations and effectively boycotted the event. Summing up the change in mood the *New Statesman*, which at the time of the Coronation had produced such a reflective and nuanced argument for the monarchy, now ran an anti-jubilee special edition mocking the Queen as 'the doll in the golden coach'.

In different ways the views of both right and left were the reflections of elites. Assessing the mood of the majority of people who had no particularly strong political views is far harder. The best assessment, based on personal memories and conversations, might be summed up as simply a feeling of a loss of innocence. The optimistic uplift of the 1950s, essentially romantic and conservative; and naïve peace-and-love hopes of the 1960s counter-culture seemed equally discredited. There was more rudeness and more violence about. Union confrontations had become angrier. In Northern Ireland, the early idealism of the equal rights marchers had given way to a cycle of vicious killing, torture and banditry. Even in popular music, the lull, twang and sugar had been elbowed aside by the raucous insurgency of punk ('God Save the Queen/ The Fascist Re-giiime'). Where in this picture did the real Queen Elizabeth II and her family fit? All in all, it did not seem an ideal time for a party to celebrate hereditary monarchy. The government was dubious about, and initially hostile to, a big national tour. Would it go off all right? Would it not be a damp squib?

The jubilee year had begun with a long round of Commonwealth tours. In Britain, it only really got going in the early summer, with loyal addresses from the Houses of Parliament. Speaking to MPs, the Queen made a sharp-edged reference to the fact that she had been crowned Queen of the United Kingdom of Great Britain and Northern Ireland. Scottish nationalism was on the rise, fuelled by the discovery of North

Sea oil, and her words caused some offence. But as the domestic tours began, including most riskily to Northern Ireland, it became clear that people were very much in the mood for a party. As in 1809 or 1935, anxieties made the jubilee more welcome, not less. On 7 June around a million people gathered in central London to watch the Queen and her family go by coach to St Paul's for a thanksgiving ceremony. Harking back to George III, a chain of 101 beacons had been lit around the country – no mean feat, considering the awful weather. Overnight, as at the Coronation, people had been camping out in London. Innovations included a river tour of the Thames, larger-than-ever fireworks displays and the painting of London buses silver.

At her speech to a banquet in the capital's Guildhall, the Queen drew attention to the disappearance of the Empire that had still been visible at her grandfather's Silver Jubilee. During her reign, 'I have seen, from a unique position of advantage, the last great phase of the transformation of the Empire into Commonwealth and the transformation of the Crown from an emblem of dominion into a symbol of free and voluntary association. In all history this has no precedent.' It was an unusually frank assertion of her personal enthusiasm for the Commonwealth, but was there a message about the domestic meaning of monarchy? Here too the Crown no longer symbolized power, but democracy. It was a message that would have perplexed her ancestors. The Crown's strength was its weakness? Its meaning was that it did not mean too much?

These paradoxes were little discussed in the streets. For more than anything, 1977 would be remembered as the year of the street party. It was a tradition which smacked more of the austerity Britain of the original Coronation, though it was on balance good news for oxen. Streets were closed to traffic so that long snakes of linen-covered tables could be laid out and bunting and flags criss-crossed between top-floor windows. Piles of sandwiches, biscuits and cakes were arranged, record players brought out into the blustery open, neighbours uneasily reintroduced themselves and there was some embarrassing dad-dancing. Villages and housing estates organized beer tents, tug-of-wars and imitations of the dire television jolly-pranks series *It's a Knock-Out*. At London's biggest jubilee party, at Alexandra Palace, the impressive feat was achieved of drinking the place dry: up to 160,000 people were there and 180 barrels of beer were emptied. The capital also won a competition for best-decorated street party, the honour going to the terraced-brick neighbours of Protheroe Road in Fulham. But other areas, such as well-heeled and liberal Hampstead, seemed emptier of street celebrations. One journalist noticed that 'the wealthier the street, the less likely it is to have a party'.[34] Maybe so: but for millions, the collective effort involved in closing streets, introducing neighbours, organizing food and drinks and putting up decorations was a delightful, energizing and nostalgic surprise.

What, if anything, did any of this mean? The Queen was still young enough for it not to be a celebration of her reign's length and certainly not, given the temper of the times, its splendour. Perhaps 'virtuous nostalgia' is the best bet. The jubilee gave people a shot of the national family feeling that had existed in the immediate post-war years and which seemed to be falling away. There was a sense of 'we're still here, still hanging on'. Amidst the consumerism and political bickering, people could turn towards each other again, an 'imagined community' perhaps, but one with real warmth. The most visible additions to that community were the immigrants from

Asia and the Caribbean, who in 1977 made up around 3.3 per cent of the population, or 1.8 million people. It was noticeable that jubilee celebrations were as keenly supported, even more so, by the new Britons as by the old. Was this, then, a lowest-common-denominator 'good old us' jubilee? Yes, but it was perhaps needed at the time. Looking back now, it refreshed and reasserted the meaning of constitutional monarchy and helped produce a new generation of royalism, leading up to the wedding of Charles and Diana four years later, which would be the most exuberant royal display before the bad years began.

Meanwhile, Wilson's successor, James Callaghan, continued the tradition of Labour Party super-patriotism. A traditionalist with a naval background, he revelled in his part in the 1977 celebrations. He particularly enjoyed the Review of the Fleet, since his father had been a rigger on an earlier Royal Yacht, the *Victoria and Albert*, in the time of George V. Like Wilson, Callaghan brushed aside the attempts of Labour left-wingers to abolish the Civil List or make the Queen pay income tax. His cabinet had a long discussion about what gift they should send her for her jubilee, with the suggestions ranging from Tony Benn's of 'a vase carved in coal by a Polish miner' to Shirley Williams's of a saddle, before they finally decided that a silver coffee pot, purchased by the prime minister's wife, Audrey, would be safer. Callaghan's weekly audiences were said to be 'genial and relaxed' and the Queen offered him moral support over issues such as the continuing sore of Rhodesia. Callaghan, for his part, tried to interest the Prince of Wales in the world of politics, getting him to sit through a cabinet meeting and attend a session of Prime Minister's Questions. But he felt, probably rightly, that Prince Charles was not much interested in the formal side of constitutional politics, preferring his own causes: in Whitehall the experiment was judged a failure.[35]

The end of the 1970s saw several further blows to the royal family. The worst was the murder of Lord Louis Mountbatten by an IRA man, Thomas McMahon, when Mountbatten was on his small wooden fishing boat off the coast of County Sligo in the Irish Republic. He had a summer home there and had been long warned of the danger by the Irish police, for the area was also popular with IRA men on holiday. On 27 August 1979, while off on a lobster-potting and mackerel-fishing expedition with friends and family, his boat was blown to pieces by a remote-controlled bomb. He died shortly afterwards of his injuries. Also killed were two teenagers, one of them his grandson, the other a local boy, Paul Maxwell. His daughter's mother-in-law, Lady Brabourne, who was eighty-three, died the following day. Timothy Knatchbull, then fourteen, Mountbatten's grandson, had grown up as the inseparable twin of Nicky, who died: the two were so alike that at times even their parents struggled to tell them apart.

He remembers it as a glorious summer day in the middle of an idyllic holiday, part of a routine he had known since a toddler. Mountbatten was his hyperactive grandpa, still at seventy-nine always at the centre of games and projects, and looking forward to the catch of fish, crabs and perhaps lobsters. 'We had been going for a few minutes – beautiful, flat, calm sea, not a cloud in the sky.' Meaningless chat was going on when, 'There was this almighty bang, just a recollection really of a thud . . . and the next thing I remember is lying on the bottom of another boat.' He could hear worried Irish voices and felt intensely cold. In hospital in Sligo, his eighty-three-year-old granny died in the bed beside him. His mother lay opposite: 'Her face was unrecognizable, held together by 117 stitches twenty in each eyeball. My father lay in a nearby ward, his legs horribly smashed up with wounds from top to toe. Between the three survivors we had three working eyes, no working eardrums.' He came round from three days in intensive care to find his sister Joanna, who told him: 'When you arrived in the hospital you were unconscious. You woke up. Nicky never did.' At that moment, he says, he knew the unimaginable had happened, 'And I knew really in an instant that either I was going to survive or I would never get over it ... I looked at her, she looked at me, and as her eyes filled with tears I followed, and crumbled.'[36]

It was the worst terrorist attack the royal family has suffered. Ironically, according to government papers held at Dublin's national archive, Mountbatten had told the Irish ambassador as long before as 1972 that he was in favour of a united Ireland and would have been happy to help towards reunification. Of the murder, Gerry Adams, who was then vice-president of Sinn Fein, told *Time* magazine that the IRA had 'achieved its objective: people started paying attention to what was happening in Ireland'. Adams told the magazine's Erik Amfitheatrof that, 'The IRA gave clear reasons for the execution. I think it is unfortunate that anyone has to be killed but the furore created by Mountbatten's death showed up the hypocritical attitude of the media establishment ... What the IRA did to him is what Mountbatten had been doing all his life to other people; and with his war record I don't think he could have objected to dying in what was clearly a war situation.'

The blow was felt particularly heavily by Prince Charles, who in his journal described reacting with 'agony, disbelief, a kind of wretched numbness, closely followed by fierce and violent determination to see that something was done about the IRA'.[37] He reflected that he had lost someone who could tell him unpleasant things he did not want to hear, a man who 'combined grandfather, great-uncle, father, brother and friend'. Mountbatten had indeed been closer to the heir than almost anyone else, advising him on girlfriends, warning him against his tendency to self-pity and stiffening his sense of duty. The murder not only outraged the country generally but later on must have made it particularly hard for the Queen to swallow her feelings and accept that a future prime minister, Tony Blair, would develop a cordial relationship with Mr Adams as part of the Northern Ireland peace process.

Timothy Knatchbull's testimony is unusual in the Queen's story because he experienced at first hand the warm and mothering side of her the rest of the country hardly ever sees. With his mother still completely incapacitated in hospital, he and his sister Amanda were invited by the Queen to Balmoral to help them recover. After being delayed by a fog-bound aircraft, they arrived at the castle between 2 and 3 a.m. and the driver had warned them everyone would have gone to bed long before: they should sneak in and find their bedrooms.

> None of it. We arrived through the door and we make a quick left turn and I looked down this long imposing corridor and the sight that greets me is of the Queen, Prince Charles at her side, and she's sort of steaming up the corridor at us . . . it's difficult to describe but it had this sort of feeling of a mother duck gathering up her lost young. And just a total look of care and concern on her face – from Prince Charles as well. And it was a wonderful moment, total surprise. And they led us to the back of the house where they had soup and sandwiches – no one else

around ... just the two of them ... and they really wanted to go into their default setting of love and care, of asking about family, of plying us with soup and sandwiches and wrapping us up in a sort of motherliness coming from the Queen.

The pair tried to prevent her taking them to their rooms and starting to unpack their cases. 'She was in unstoppable mothering mode, leading Amanda and me down the corridor, pulling open the drawers, getting clothes out.' Only with some difficulty was she persuaded eventually to leave them and go to bed herself. In the time that followed, the same pattern persisted. The Queen sat the teenage boy next to her at meals, oversaw the dressing of his wounds and sent him to bed when he looked tired. 'She was brilliant. She was able to draw me out. If I felt a little lost she'd catch my eye and turn the conversation towards me. And within ten, twenty, thirty seconds she had me at the heart of the conversation again, throwing out ideas, chatting, laughing. This is the gift of truly remarkable motherhood and generosity.' It left him with 'a strange warm glow that's really never left me. And it's about the care, the loving tender care that the Queen [has] as a mum.'

Knatchbull's memories are a rare frank glimpse of the Queen as mother; she was not, of course, his mother, but she had been very close friends with Patricia Mountbatten since the two women were girls. She had attended Patricia's wedding as a bridesmaid; their children had arrived in a similar pattern. Later, Knatchbull watched the Queen greet Prince Edward, home from school, with the same exuberant warmth that he found at Balmoral. Others who have been family friends of the Queen also comment on her motherly instincts: one man had been stalking at Balmoral and was late off the hill, to find the Queen pulling her Land Rover to a halt and embracing him with relief. The Queen's own children have learned to be circumspect about intimate family time but say the picture is accurate. Princess Anne, for instance, says she learned early that her mother's absences from home were part of 'the service life' which was not unique to the Queen (she was probably thinking of the armed forces). She had learned that it was 'not a personal thing – she's not going away because she didn't like you or, you know, there's something wrong with the system; it's because there are priorities and you will get your time, and that's what happened'. Princess Anne adds that Knatchbull's experience was for her an expectation: 'As all mothers, she's put up with a lot and we're still on speaking terms so I think that's no mean feat!' She thinks 'it was pretty good mothering' achieved inside a strict timetable but one in which quality made up for quantity: 'The quality of the time that you get is something that you make yourself.' In an interview with the author she spoke with real feeling – a useful corrective to the fashionable view that that the Queen was somehow a distant or cool mother.

She certainly had other things on her mind in the late 1970s, however. These were years of constant IRA threat and attack. As Queen of the United Kingdom of Great Britain and Northern Ireland, she was acutely aware of the blood-soaked and unhappy condition of the final three words of her title. A vicious war was being fought between Irish republicans, hostile to everything the Queen symbolized, and 'loyalists' who loudly proclaimed their passionate devotion to the monarchical state while drawing its soldiers and police into death and danger every day. In Northern Ireland, as nowhere else, the symbols of the Queen's reign, from cap-badges to letterboxes, had become controversial. The prefix 'Royal' was a rallying point or provocation. Her visits to Northern Ireland had become steadily more difficult and briefer, as the security risk increased.

From now on, the physical threat to the Queen was even more firmly in everyone's minds. So when, on 13 June 1981, while the Queen was riding her beloved horse Burmese at the Trooping the Colour parade, a youth fired shots at her, the first fear was IRA assassination. The youth was mentally disturbed; the shots were blanks; the Queen showed icy courage and expert handling of her horse; royal life went on. Then, the following July, when another disturbed man, Michael Fagan, managed to climb over the railings at Buckingham Palace and make his way to the Queen's bedroom, again the immediate question was – 'What if the IRA . . . ?' Fagan arrived to meet his monarch at 7.18 a.m., having slashed one hand with a broken ashtray. Again she displayed impressive sang-froid, eventually managing to leave her bedroom and get help when he asked her for a cigarette. Similar things had happened in the past. The Queen's mother, for instance, had been confronted in her room in 1940 by a drunken deserter.[38] But now, it was more serious.

Just after the Fagan incident, two IRA bombs had brought death almost to the front door of Buckingham Palace. On 20 July members of the Household Cavalry on their way from their Knightsbridge barracks to change the guard were hit by a nail-bomb attack. Two soldiers died; seven horses were also killed. Another bomb went off under the bandstand at Regent's Park where the Royal Green Jackets were playing to tourists and relaxing office workers. The two attacks killed eleven people and injured fifty more. This was a world which challenged the Queen's private motto, 'I have to be seen to be believed'. Politicians were of course also at risk, and before long Downing Street would be hemmed in by security railings, and London would resound to the throb of police sirens as ministerial cars accelerated through traffic behind motorcycle escorts. The Queen has always been protected, by some of the most experienced officers in the country, and she heeded advice. But she never cancelled and never stopped showing herself during the worst of the danger. As for Lord Mountbatten, in the words of the writer Kenneth Rose, 'he was eulogized as a Renaissance man and buried like a medieval emperor'.

Interlude
Money

From the mid-1980s a quiet and still mostly unknown Palace revolution had been taking place, as reformers upended the old 'country house' atmosphere of the court, seized back control over much of the day-to-day running of the monarchy from the government, and radically increased its efficiency. As we have seen, the royal money question had flared up regularly during the Queen's reign, from the 1950s onwards. Again and again Whitehall initiatives to 'keep the Queen out of politics' had briefly calmed things down, while leaving a residuum of public doubt. Most people struggle to understand large figures, and the real cost of the monarchy is a confusing subject. So a few basics are in order. There are three sources of the Queen's money. There has been the Civil List. This is money paid by the Treasury to the monarchy for its upkeep. The money comes from the revenues of the Crown Estate – property owned by the monarchy – most of which has gone straight to government. There is a private estate which funds much of the queen's other spending, and there are her private investments. (The two together are known as the Privy Purse, which makes them sound like a huge velvet handbag.) All these revenues come gnarled with complicated history.

The Crown Estate comprises the lands owned by kings and queens since the Norman Conquest of 1066, and in some cases earlier than that. Through the Middle Ages, as the cost of running a more populous and complicated country slowly rose, the money from these lands was used by rulers to fund their personal government, and many estates were given to noble-men in return for their support, particularly when rebellion threatened or weak monarchs had to buy popularity. Through the centuries the scale of these once vast Crown lands shriv-elled. But they remain even today a large holding, worth around £6.6 billion and including everything from forests and farmland to some of the grandest streets in London. The Crown Estate has 450 farms, Scottish grassland, more than half Britain's foreshore, all the seabed out to the 12-mile limit, swathes of Regent Street and St James's in London's West End, the quarries which produce the soft white Portland stone so much of grand Britain is built from, and forests in the West Country.

Once the revenues were simply collected by the Crown, but in 1760 George III agreed to hand them over to his government, in return for a 'Civil List' payment from Parlia-ment for his expenses. It was always wrong to say simply that the taxpayer funded the monarchy; the Crown Estate mostly subsidized the state. From 2000 to 2010 it paid £1.9 billion into the Treasury. But this way round of doing things meant that MPs were able to regularly monitor and debate royal spend-ing, which, as we have seen, meant monitoring the monarchy itself. Prince Charles had long chafed at this and, as one of the higher-spending and more ambitious members of the family, wanted the Crown Estate revenues to revert to the royal family, giving them independence from politicians. This seemed the most unlikely of pipe-dreams.

For decades the Civil List had been a nagging problem for the Queen and her ministers. This was not because the public had turned against her in person but because inflation, combined with a more aggressive press, had turned the annual upratings into, in the words of one insider, 'an increasingly painful running sore'. Every year there were front-page stories about the Queen's 'pay rise' and the extravagance of the Windsors. Buckingham Palace got it from left and right. During the grim years of economic failure in the 1970s there was a rise in republican resentment about the Civil List. But during the Thatcherite 1980s, when the rest of Britain was being vigorously shaken about in the name of efficiency, many asked why this ancient system was not also being sorted out.

To make things worse, the whole issue was becoming confused with the second main source of royal income, the Queen's private wealth, and whether she should pay tax on that. Nobody else has such a hard-to-disentangle mix of wealth which is hers, wealth which isn't really but belongs to the Crown, and wealth which is somewhere in the middle. The wonderful paintings and jewels are the Queen's in the sense that she looks at them and wears them whenever she wants to. But she cannot sell them. They pass down, some for private use, some to be looked at in public spaces. Castles and palaces range from those never lived in by members of the royal family, to country houses, which are their private property. Putting to one side the jewellery, lands, palaces, art and other assets held personally, but in trust for the nation – assets she cannot deploy herself – the Queen's main source of independent income comes from the Duchy of Lancaster. Dating back to a grant of land made by Henry III in 1265, the Duchy now holds farmland across the north of England; very valuable buildings in London between the Strand and the Thames; an industrial estate in south London; offices and shops in Birmingham, Manchester, Harrogate, Stoke; foreshores and moorlands, the tiny Victorian railway station that features in Harry Potter films, a private airfield, and much else. It is much smaller than the Crown Estate. Its asset value was £323 million in 2009 and it currently pays the Privy Purse (the Queen's account) a little over £13 million a year. Out of this, she now funds the Royals except for herself and Prince Philip. (The Duchy of Cornwall, founded by Edward III in 1337, supports the Prince of Wales and his family: its income is slightly higher than Lancaster's, around £15 million a year. Like the Queen, the Prince cannot make profits by selling Duchy assets.)

The Queen also has private investments, which have been guesstimated to be worth billions. This is wildly out: in 1993 Lord Airlie, then Lord Chamberlain, said on her authority that the lowest figure publicly discussed, £100 million, 'is grossly overstated'. But the private Buckingham Palace opinion polls, conducted early each year for the Queen by the opinion pollsters Mori, had also shown rising public hostility to the Queen's exemption from income tax. Public polling showed the same thing. By 1991, a year before a spate of royal divorces and the publication of *Diana, Her True Story* by Andrew Morton, one found 79 per cent thought the Queen should be taxed on her income. Another poll the same year got a 42 per cent agreement to the proposition that the Royals were an expensive luxury the country could not afford.[1] It is not hard to see how dangerous the combination of these feelings and the contemporary royal family scandals might have been to the future of the monarchy, at least as a grand and relatively expensive national project. It was a genuinely difficult time for the Queen and the mission she had dedicated herself to since girlhood. That the money did not cause her serious damage is the achievement of two royal reformers above all, Lord Airlie and Sir Michael Peat.

David Ogilvy, the 13th Earl of Airlie, is a crucial figure in

the story of the monarchy towards the end of the twentieth
century. A tall, handsome man of the Queen's age, immaculately dressed and softly spoken, he is almost entirely unknown
to the wider public. This is how he likes it. Another senior
figure describes his importance as rivalling that of Prince Albert
for the Victorian monarchy. A Scottish landowner and Old
Etonian who served in the Scots Guards during the war, he
has estates in Angus not so far from Balmoral. He became a
family friend early on – the Queen was at his fifth birthday
party – and worked as a merchant banker after the war. Airlie's
career in banking ended when he left the chairmanship of
Schroders on 31 November 1984. He went to work at Buckingham Palace the following day. These were the high days of
Thatcher radicalism, and it is hardly surprising that a banker
found the Royal Household behind the times. The Royal
Household's spending was outstripping the Queen's income
and she was digging deeper and deeper into a dwindling
reserve: the problem needed urgent attention. 'We were simply
running out of money,' says a figure from the Palace at the
time.

Airlie suggested that the Queen call in outside consultants. Peat Marwick Mitchell, perhaps the best known of the
troubleshooters, were chosen to do 'a complete review, top
to bottom, with total latitude'. For an institution so used to
running on private, traditional lines, this was a big step for
the Palace. At the time almost every big corporation seemed
to be spending more and more on consultants; but for the
Queen to summon the bean-counters and efficiency experts
was something else. Naturally, the man chosen was not quite
an ordinary bean-counter. Running the team was Sir Michael
Peat, product of Eton and Oxford, whose great-grandfather had
founded the firm (now KPMG). Bald, lean, fiercely intelligent

and iconoclastic, he had royal connections too. Peats were the auditors of the Queen's private funds, the Privy Purse, and as a younger man Sir Michael had gone in with his father to do this. Like Airlie, he would switch from the world of finance to work full time at the Palace, later moving from the Queen's team to become Prince Charles's private secretary and thus part of the campaign for the reversion of the Crown Estate money. He and Airlie now unleashed something like a private Thatcherite revolution inside Buckingham Palace. If in 2012 the monarchy seems in good shape that is not all the Queen's achievement: the Queen's fixers are part of the tale.

With a team of four Peat began work during the summer of 1986. He had finished the job by the end of the year. His 1,380-page report contained around 188 detailed suggestions, from cutting footmen and administrators to cheaper ways of entertaining. 'Like a knife through butter' was how one Palace source described Peat's effect on the royal finances, cancelling bloated catering and transport contracts, bringing in modern management and better, brighter people, slashing overhead costs and taking back many of the functions then being run by the government. Portion control arrived for banquet catering; many petty corruptions were ended. What was described as 'the country house set' who had been running the Royal Household by and large disappeared.

They had been, said one observer, nice and charming people in their way, with their shoes polished to a blinding degree by valets. They were good company at excellent dinners and always ready to join the royal family for shooting and fishing at Balmoral or Sandringham. But they had allowed the state to take over more and more of the job of running the monarchy, resulting in a lack of independence, energy and enterprise at Buckingham Palace, a form of 'genteel ossification'. In the late 1970s the Labour prime minister Jim Callaghan had wanted to go further and fully nationalize the working of monarchy under a special Department for Royal Affairs. Now Airlie and Peat were determined to go in the opposite direction and cut the Royal Household free from direct Treasury control. To a degree that has never been fully understood, they privatized the Queen.

They started by negotiating a new deal with the Treasury about the painful Civil List problem for the previous two decades, and some years later, in 1990, Margaret Thatcher's government in its final months finally agreed a deal. Sir Andrew Turnbull, a Treasury civil servant seconded to Downing Street, who later became cabinet secretary, chaired a group with Airlie and Peat; the Treasury's Sir Hayden Phillips; and the Inland Revenue. One senior official, who had been involved in earlier rounds of negotiation, insists: 'The attitude of the Treasury was not that we wanted to make great savings in the Civil List because frankly it was chicken-feed. This was an establishment manoeuvre to protect the Queen. We wanted to have a Civil List review as rarely as possible.'

The Queen agreed to strip the minor Royals from the Civil List, and to pay for them herself. From now on, only she, Prince Philip and the Queen Mother would receive money directly from the Treasury. The rest would be funded from her private income, mainly the Duchy of Lancaster money. Some other Palace expenses, such as staff pensions and security costs, were prised out of the account and pushed into general government spending. The effect, however, was to give Airlie and Peat their chance to take over most royal management themselves: 'We wanted to be more masters of our own destiny.'

Annual deals had meant it was impossible to plan ahead.

Both sides, Whitehall and the Palace, decided that a ten-year deal would be the obvious answer. The major problem was inflation. Inflation had been rising sharply for four years and was running at around 9.5 per cent by 1990. The Treasury was very anxious about suggesting that it would not be under control again soon; but equally edgy about setting any future figure which the press would then discuss. Eventually Airlie suggested the deal should be based on the average of the previous decade, 7.5 per cent. The Treasury agreed. The annual money was then doubled but frozen. This would be too generous in the first few years but would then be eroded by inflation. 'She got £7.9 million a year, which we knew was more than she needed in year one, but by the end of year ten, having built in inflation at 7.5 per cent, would be about right,' says one of the civil servants involved. Turnbull and Sir Peter Middleton, the then Treasury boss, had cleared their lines politically by telling the Labour leader Neil Kinnock ahead of time. 'Well, you can't do fairer than that,' he had replied.

In fact, because inflation fell, the deal was to begin with more generous than intended. The Queen was able to build up a cash surplus of £35 million by 2000. Any surplus, it had been agreed, would be rolled over for the next decade. And indeed, after the ten fat years, came the ten lean. By the time David Cameron's coalition government looked again at the royal books in 2010, the Queen had received an unchanged annual payment not for ten years, but for twenty. Behind the scenes courtiers were quick to ask what other parts of the state had been able to live within a cash-frozen budget for two decades. But much more important was that for twenty years, years covering the worst crisis for the monarchy since the abdication, the Queen was spared the annual fulmination about her expenditure from the press and republican politicians. Had the reformers not been at work before, the year of disasters could have led to a downward spiral in the Queen's story – not the end of the British monarchy, but its radical diminishing. Palace nervousness about public opinion is often overdone – but neither can support for the institution be taken quite for granted.

At the same time as all this was going on Airlie and Peat took back control over most of what Whitehall had been administering. In 1989–90 Airlie managed to wrest back the day-to-day running of the major palaces from Whitehall, when the Department of Environment's Property Services Agency was abolished. The Lord Chamberlain now took responsibility for Buckingham Palace, St James's Palace, Clarence House and Windsor Castle. For the Royal Household, it was a big gamble: 'We had to collect a team almost overnight. We didn't have anybody – we may have had the odd plumber, but we had to start afresh. Behind the headlines about marriage breakdowns and royal soap-opera, it was a considerable achievement: the Royal Household, with the Queen as chairman, took back in-house the business of monarchy, from ministers and from Whitehall. "The Firm" was run once more like a private company. And at its apex was the monarch itself.

'The Queen's very businesslike. You send a memorandum and it's back the next day, or certainly within twenty-four hours. She's intuitive and has good judgement; and whenever I go to see her, I have to remember that she has more experience than anybody else and that she knows more than I do. At the end of the discussion, I always felt better. She is very calm, cool and collected about these things,' says one of those involved. 'More for less' was the slogan. The cost of running the Royal Household was slashed, while the staff numbers were radically increased. Peat multiplied the size of the royal machine but divided the cost, squeezing what he used to call 'the inefficiency reserve' – the dripping, bloated costs of mismanagement by government officialdom.

Meanwhile, Airlie had made big changes to the structure of the Queen's little state-within-the-state. The Lord Chamberlain became a chief executive, or mini-prime minister, overseeing a monthly committee of the five heads of the different departments. His role is hard to express (the Palace's official job description includes fourteen separate duties) but the job is meant to be part-time, a mix of strategic manager, adviser to the Queen, a bridge between her and the Prince of Wales, and with a brief 'to get the best out of all employees by helping to create a pleasant but professional atmosphere'. Of the qualities needed according to the official job description the most important may be simply 'to have the confidence of the Queen' and 'a wise and balanced approach'.

The job, which is not advertised on the *Guardian* public sector appointments website, tends to go to a male aristocrat near retirement age. Lord Chamberlains are vague about who exactly recommended them, but they will always have met the Queen before and will be interviewed by her. She told one, 'If I am going to do my job, I have to have very good people working for me; and it's got to be a nice atmosphere because if you work in that atmosphere, people want to do their best for you.' If this makes it sound genteel, then it is. But if it makes it sound gentle, then it often is not. Until 1968 the Lord Chamberlain, assisted by former naval officers of steely views, was responsible for censoring plays. More recently Lord Chamberlains have had to bring the Queen some of the worst news and most difficult decisions about her family, including plain speaking about her errant children, which has not been easy.

The Queen had asked Airlie to look at the other great

conundrum, whether she should pay income tax. He was close to a deal when the great fire at Windsor broke out and had planned to explain his proposals to her in the quiet of Sandringham the following January. Now that she had agreed to a fixed cash deal for the Civil List and to pay for the younger Royals from her own pocket, Airlie and Peat had to try to come up with a plan which would ensure that the Queen did not run out of cash through huge new tax bills. They had been at it with the Treasury team and Inland Revenue since February. 'Then came the [Windsor] fire – bang! And that weekend's press was very upsetting – "The Queen's so rich! Why can't she pay?"' The prime minister, John Major, said he would be making a statement on Monday in the Commons. The Queen, suffering from a bad cold, still coming to terms with the fire and with her 'annus horribilis' speech at London's Guildhall just ahead, had to go through her tax plans in a rush – like so many of her subjects. She was, apparently, highly pragmatic and simply told her officials to get on with it.

Airlie had insisted, to start with, that she should not pay inheritance tax for 'sovereign to sovereign bequests' so that the Crown Estate could pass essentially unaltered from reign to reign. The alternative, the Palace argued, was that the glamour and authority of the monarchy would shrink with each accession until it was a meagre sliver of an institution. The bad luck of a quick couple of successions would mean Balmoral going, and Sandringham too. Soon Britain would be left with 'a pauper monarchy' unable to demonstrate any independence from the government of the day at all – which, as we shall see, the new theorists of monarchy thought would be a disaster. The Treasury agreed, though even today the decision rankles. The Queen agreed to pay income tax and capital gains tax on her Duchy of Lancaster money and on her private investments.

Yet mandarins fretted that, in reality, the deal was still overly generous. Airlie and Peat's new deal would be followed by the announcement in April 1993 that parts of Buckingham Palace and the Windsor grounds would be opened to the public to help pay for the costs of the Windsor Castle repairs. The Royal Collection of paintings, drawings and other artworks, one of the world's great collections, was turned into a department of its own, properly managed, and for the first time, well displayed for the paying public and competently catalogued.

The cost of the monarchy is not a serious economic issue. It is a chemical indicator of popularity. The old ways of somewhat complacent senior courtiers, excessive numbers of footmen living pretty well, unchallenged grace-and-favour apartments and a general vagueness about priceless possessions such as the Royal Collection were not in themselves the problem. But as MPs discovered in the expenses scandal of 2009, what seem comparatively small issues can come close to destroying the reputation of entire institutions.

So what, in the final count, does the monarchy cost the British? In her 1959 book *How the Queen Reigns* the journalist Dorothy Laird (a relative of the author) calculated that the government grant to the Queen 'amounts to between twopence and twopence halfpenny per person in the United Kingdom each year. That is the cost of one cigarette.'[2] Laird adopted a narrow view of the cost of the monarchy. Cigarettes have also been taxed more heavily as time passed. But on a roughly similar basis, taking into account grants, the Civil List and annuities, what the government describes as its total support for the Queen as head of state (£32.8 million in 2011) and a packet of twenty cigarettes at £6.30, the sum now works out at the cost of two cigarettes. The Queen also now pays a large amount of money on her private wealth in tax, which she did not do in 1959. Looking at head-count, the lavishness of entertaining and Royal Household salaries relative to other London-based wages, the Queen today certainly does not operate more extravagantly than before; indeed, less so. The more important point about the cigarette comparison – today we might say less than half the cost of a cappuccino at a high street chain – is that it is very small. The 70p compares to a rough figure of £23,000 at the time of writing as each Briton's share of the national debt.

During 2010–11, the question of how the British monarchy is financed was radically revised and, once again, the Queen was closely involved. Before the 2010 election, her Treasurer and grandly titled Keeper of the Privy Purse, Sir Alan Reid, began talks with his fellow Scots, the Labour prime minister Gordon Brown and chancellor Alastair Darling. Instead of three separate payments from the government – the Civil List, grants for maintaining the palaces and the travel budget – he wanted a single system. Up to then, if the Palace spent less on travel, it could not transfer the cash to repair a leaky roof. It also had to negotiate with three separate government departments, one of which, the Culture and Sport department, was already obsessed with the Olympics. Palace officials felt they were being treated as part of its tourism remit. With an election looming the prime minister was no doubt trying to work out whether a new system of financing the Queen would win him, or lose him, votes. At any rate, Labour passed the decision on to the Tory-led coalition that won power.

The coalition moved fast. It was the prime minister David Cameron's office, and that of the chancellor George Osborne, which first came up with the idea of paying for the monarchy through a percentage of the Crown Estate revenues – 15 per cent – rather than a specific sum voted every ten years or so by MPs. This would help take the funding decision out of politics. But there were two obvious questions. First, would it simply lift the financing of the monarchy out of Parliament's eye line and hide it from public scrutiny? Second, if the Crown Estates were well run (and they included potentially big new revenues from, for instance, offshore windfarms) then might not the Crown become ever richer? To resolve these, Sir Alan and the Queen agreed that their spending would in future be scrutinized each year, not by a private company, KPMG, or the Treasury but by the Public Audit Office. This means a committee of MPs, the public accounts committee, would have the right to examine the books and the Palace officials. Second, to stop the Queen or her successor doing too well out of future profits, a system of reviews and caps on money in reserve has been set up. In future it will be easier to cut the percentage than raise it. Palace figures say the Queen was clear that any recipe for future profligacy would be unwise: 'she is very aware that she rules by consent'.

There was, however, a brisk debate between the politicians and the Palace about the transitional arrangements. These are tough and mean that in effect the Queen is taking a 19 per cent real-terms cut in her income during 2011–13, including her Diamond Jubilee year. The chancellor George Osborne had insisted that only Britain's overseas aid budget and the health service could be ring-fenced: the Queen had to share the belt-tightening. Again, she was directly involved herself in the decision. A couple of other financial decisions at the same time are of real significance for the monarchy's future. First, the deal struck by the Queen can be carried over when she dies into the next reign. Second, the arrangements for the money from the Duchy of Cornwall, the £17 million or so of income going to Prince Charles, have been reorganized. The current system dates back to Henry V, of Agincourt fame. The Cornwall money goes to the sovereign's eldest son and heir. So if an heir to the throne was female, she would not get it. The new system corrects that. It also means that if Prince Charles happens to die before his mother, this substantial sum will go to Prince William, the Duke of Cambridge, as heir, rather than to Prince Andrew, the Queen's eldest surviving son.

So there is a chance, at least, that the long and vexed question of paying for the British monarchy has been settled. Only a chance: any future monarchy perceived to be a spendthrift, particularly in hard times, would find politicians returning to the issue. The Queen seems unsentimental about money and has willingly made big changes – being taxed, ending the Civil List and taking more responsibility for spending. Her income from private investments is important to her – but mainly to finance her continuing fascinated involvement in horseracing.

Part Five

INTO THE MAELSTROM

A wide variety of experienced, shrewd politicians, civil servants and courtiers who observed the Queen's relationship with Margaret Thatcher at first hand, agree. It was (long pause, pained expression) 'difficult'. Here were two women of a similar age though of very dissimilar background, previously strangers, conjoined during the most tumultuous and confrontational years of post-war politics. Among the most radical of the Thatcherite thinkers were some whose contempt for the old, flabby institutions of a weary country reached even to the monarchy. They (naïvely) tended to see the United States as a model in politics and economics, a briskly invigorating meritocracy where wealth was made, not inherited. They disliked the Queen's tolerance of left-wing dictators in the Commonwealth and had no more patience for the easy life and unchallenged rituals of the court than they did for BBC executives or tenured academics.

Ardent young men from think tanks saw 'Margaret' as their real queen, the Boudicca modern Britain had summoned. Even older gurus of the right, such as Enoch Powell, warned that the Queen's overseas ambition was mere swollen pride. In the 1970s the Marxist left had derided the monarchy and she had been assaulted on punk T-shirts. The hostility of right-wing radicals in the 1980s was as serious. By then many on the left had begun to delude themselves that, deep down, the Queen was secretly on their side, so 'one nation' that she was really a leftie herself.

Margaret Thatcher herself gave no shrift to anti-Queenism, at least in public. In her memoirs, she said that 'stories of clashes between "two powerful women" were just too good not to make up' and praised the Queen for her conduct of the weekly audiences. These, said Lady Thatcher, were no mere formality: 'they are quietly businesslike and Her Majesty brings to bear a formidable grasp of current issues and breadth of experience'.[1] The Tory revolutionary was so punctilious and respectful of her monarch it was almost embarrassing. She curtseyed lower than the Queen thought necessary. 'It was the starchiest relationship. She was deferential, much too deferential. The Queen was not requiring so much,' said one long-time observer. 'The Queen had some most amusing and well-observed lines about Thatcher,' says a family friend.

Some senior Whitehall sources believed that there was an early 'stiffness' between the Queen and Mrs Thatcher. Several say that each of them found the choreography of having two women at the apex of British life slightly awkward, which was why they rarely appeared together. There were early and earnest discussions about which should go to which national events, including to pay their respects at disasters. Some officials recall meetings to make sure the prime minister was not wearing a similar outfit to the Queen. Others say no: the Queen 'does not notice what other people wear'. Margaret Thatcher's refusal to leave with the rest of 'the ladies' at the end of dinner caused some discussion before she came to Balmoral. Throughout her reign the Queen's relationship with prime ministers had been with men, either older than herself and to be respected, or younger and to be helped by almost maternal listening. Here was someone different.

There were ice-breakers, none more effective than Denis Thatcher, whose role as prime ministerial consort was not so different from Prince Philip's. He was equally adept at making himself scarce when 'the wife' had state business to attend to, while intervening to protect her at tricky social moments. Denis Thatcher got on well with the Queen Mother, enjoyed a drink as much as she did, and was punctilious about royal protocol. This went some way to making the annual Balmoral visits easier, though unlike other prime ministers, the always-impatient Margaret Thatcher used the trip north to Scotland to get through party business as well. She would visit Tory officials in Edinburgh, stay with Sir Hector Laing, the genial leading elder of Scottish Toryism, at his estate, and perhaps manage a meeting of North East Scottish Conservatives, before arriving at Balmoral. This time management was noted, with some wry amusement, by the Palace. Once she arrived, there was the problem of entertaining such an uncountrified and work-focused prime minister. Asked whether the prime minister would be joining the rest walking on the hill, the Queen dryly replied, 'I think you will find Mrs Thatcher only walks on the road.' And later when Denis Thatcher suggested to his wife it was time to retire for bed – the Queen has a strict 11.15 p.m. curfew – she apparently replied with a puzzled: 'Bed? What we would do up there?' Afterwards this caused some royal giggling.

After a first evening dinner at the main house, a black-tie one with local guests, the ritual second evening of each Balmoral visit features a barbecue organized mainly by Prince Philip. It takes place at a bothy or sometimes a summer house on the estate and begins with the Duke setting off in a Land Rover with a special trailer, ingeniously kitted out with cutlery, plates, glasses, drink and food. 'When you arrived there, Prince

Philip would be cursing away getting the barbecue going, and the Queen laid out the knives and forks and the equerries got the whisky going, and the seating plan was not at all hierarchical,' says one participant. Prince Philip would arrive with a beautifully cooked but very rare piece of beef, 'which didn't suit Margaret at all, she hated rare meat', and the Queen would ensure she was sitting next to a new, or relatively junior guest, to put them at ease. Another visitor recalls 'feeling as if I was in some kind of virtual reality' where the Queen and Prince Philip were 'playing at being normal people'. Once as the Queen handed round and gathered in plates, Margaret Thatcher, upset to see her monarch doing a menial job unaided, kept trying to leap up to help. Eventually the Queen hissed: 'Will somebody tell that woman to sit down?' The story seems emblematic of their relationship: a prime minister with a strong sense of authority and deference only trying to help, and a Queen who cannot help feeling irritated by her. A similar story is told about the annual diplomatic reception at Buckingham Palace, a mammoth two-hour affair, crowded and intensely hot. At one of them, Mrs Thatcher felt faint and had to sit down. The following year, it happened again. The Queen, physically tough and moving through the crowd 'like a liner', glanced over at her prime minister and said, 'Oh look! She's keeled over again.'

That, however, is not the whole story. As Mrs Thatcher's time in office went on, the Queen became more used to her and a mutual affection steadily grew. A senior Buckingham Palace official at the time recalls being struck by how vigorously they would talk together. Another says: 'The Queen always saw the point of Margaret Thatcher. She understood that she was necessary.' One long-time courtier remembers hosting a private lunch for the Queen and Lady Thatcher, after the latter's retirement, and finding that 'the Queen was much more fond of Margaret than I realized, though amused by her'. Later in the conversation, when the former prime minister began lecturing the table on how, if she were still in charge, she would be dealing with the unions, the Queen quietly said, 'Well, I think it's time to go.' Another former adviser says that the Queen greatly admired her as someone who had fought their way to the top: 'As someone who inherited her position, she is interested in meritocrats.'

The real question is whether the royal family in any way opposed the principles of the Thatcher revolution. This was always suspected, both by 'true believers' in the government and by some on the left. Prince Charles was inclined to be interested in urban poverty, was he not? Lord Charteris, the private secretary who perhaps knew the Queen best of all his tribe, told the historian Peter Hennessy in retirement: 'You might say that the Queen prefers a sort of consensus politics, rather than a polarized one, and I suspect this is true, although I can't really speak from knowledge here [Hennessy thought he was dissembling]. But if you are in the Queen's position, you are the titular, the symbolic head of the country, and the less squabbling that goes on in that country, obviously the more convenient and the more comfortable you feel.'[2]

A more jagged-edged version of this broke surface in July 1986 in a front-page story in the *Sunday Times*, owned by the Australian-American republican Rupert Murdoch, which cost the Queen's then press secretary, Michael Shea, his job. Shea had briefed the journalist Simon Freeman and had been so blithe about it that he had boasted to other Buckingham Palace officials there would be something 'pretty good' in the paper on Sunday morning. The paper's editor, Andrew Neil, had brought in its veteran political editor, Michael Jones, to work with Freeman and the result seemed sensational. The Queen thought Mrs Thatcher uncaring, confrontational and socially divisive; she had worried about the social fabric of the country during the miners' strike; was unhappy about Britain's use as a base for US aircraft bombing Libya the previous year; and did not agree with Mrs Thatcher over the vexed question of sanctions against apartheid South Africa (the Queen apparently siding with the pro-sanctions majority of Commonwealth members, not with Britain's prime minister). The Queen, said the newspaper, was on the warpath: she was 'an astute political infighter who is quite prepared to take on Downing Street when provoked'.

The newspaper insisted that its wide-ranging analysis of the Queen's pro-consensus and anti-Thatcherite views had been fully briefed by the Palace, which had been well aware that they would be publicized. It seemed almost suicidally daring and made the Queen sound nearer to Tony Benn than to Mrs Thatcher. When the story broke, Mrs Thatcher was in Edinburgh, staying with the Queen at the Palace of Holyroodhouse for the Commonwealth Games, which had been badly disrupted by the decision of many countries to stay away in protest at Mrs Thatcher's South African policy. The Queen placed Shea between the two of them over dinner. After he had said sorry to Mrs Thatcher, Shea later said that she patted his arm and told him: 'Don't worry a thing about it, dear. I know it's a lot of nonsense.' But was it? A nasty row broke out. Shea denied the story completely, saying that reports 'purporting to be the Queen's opinions of government policies were entirely without foundation'. Neil, for the *Sunday Times*, hit back, and came close to accusing the Queen's private secretary, Sir William Heseltine, of lying about the source of the story – something that still rankles in Palace circles to this day. Yet Shea had certainly briefed Freeman. He had not, he later told the historian Ben Pimlott, had a prior briefing with the Queen herself, nor heard her criticize the prime minister. And indeed if the Queen had talked bluntly about her feelings towards prime ministers, somebody, some time, would have overheard her and reported it. 'She would consider that completely unconstitutional, just out of court,' says one veteran. Officials who were in the Palace with him feel that Shea had a slight tendency to grandstand and had been led to go too far by the wily journalist. As is the way at the Palace, nothing was said and he was never publicly criticized; but he left the job shortly afterwards.

There is no doubt that the Queen's lifelong enthusiasm for the Commonwealth was at a different level from any feeling Mrs Thatcher might have had. Heath had not had much Commonwealth feeling, and this had been noted in the Palace. In his case, it was passionate pro-Europeanism that was responsible. Thatcher was not pro-European but she was even more hostile to socialists in the Third World. As we have seen, the Queen was prepared to meet and discuss life with left-wing dictators rather than risk their leaving the Commonwealth and has always believed in the long-term benefits of membership of this club. In 1986 Sir Sonny Ramphal, then head of the Commonwealth Secretariat and no mean street fighter himself, piled into the *Sunday Times* controversy on the side of the Queen. One close observer at the time agrees that the Queen was 'pro-consensus' and heard first hand about the difficulties of miners' families and other hard-pressed communities during the days of strikes and riot. She was by no means unsympathetic: 'The idea of saying that there "is no such thing as society" is anathema to the royal family. They could never agree to that. But the time had come for a tempestuous force like Mrs Thatcher and I think the royal family, and the Queen particularly, would give her every credit for that.'

Relations were good. Mrs Thatcher's redoubtable and controversial press secretary, Bernard Ingham, was regarded as a real friend by the Palace. Unlike later Labour prime ministers, Mrs Thatcher made a point of staying for a whisky or two after her weekly audiences – 'though with a certain impatience' – in order to ensure that Buckingham Palace felt in the loop. By the end of Mrs Thatcher's time in office, according to courtiers who observed them, the Queen had become 'a mix of fond and amused' of her prime minister and was genuinely sorry to see her go. Indeed, the Queen invited Mrs Thatcher to join the Order of Merit – a rare honour, and one in her personal gift.

During the Thatcher years the biggest single event for the royal family was undoubtedly the carnival-atmosphere wedding of the thirty-two-year-old Prince Charles and Lady Diana Spencer on 29 July 1981. It came, rather as the Queen's wedding had, during a tough year. In 1981 it was not post-war austerity but the high unemployment, continuing inflation and social divisions of the early Thatcher period that people needed to be distracted from. Diana Spencer was a twenty-year-old girl whose parents had divorced but whose family had multiple royal connections. Her older sister had been married three years earlier to the Queen's assistant private secretary, Robert Fellowes. Prince Charles had briefly dated another sister, Sarah. The Spencers had royal blood themselves, legitimately and illegitimately, running back to the Stuarts. They were familiar with the world of hunting, polo and country life the Windsors liked. Diana's father, Lord Spencer, had been an equerry to George VI and to the Queen in her earliest years on the throne.

Diana had no string of previous lovers who might have

brought embarrassment and caused problems with the Act of
Succession. She had seemed artless, genuinely enthusiastic
about Charles and, to most people's eyes, a perfect choice. He
had met her shortly after the murder of Lord Mountbatten
when she had told him how sad he had looked at the funeral,
and how lonely. She had touched him, and, while all relationships are mysterious to outsiders, the two had seemed to be
genuinely in love. Charles was serious about marriage being an
institution to last a lifetime and seemed to have no illusions
about what a tough choice he would be for her. Once she had
visited Balmoral and Sandringham and the story about a
possible match was out, Diana was hounded by photographers
and survived by dint of shy smiles and downcast eyes. The
Prince was urged by family and friends to make up his mind
and, with only a little hesitation, had proposed. Yet they met
fewer than two dozen times before they were married.

Later events made hindsight about this marriage one of the
few British growth industries left. Prince Charles was not only
a dozen years older but had much more traditional tastes than
most men of his age. He had a deep streak of pessimism and
had long been close to an early girlfriend, now married,
Camilla Parker Bowles. He was cultured, sensitive, spiritual
and driven by duty, even while he hated some of what that
involved. Between proposing to Diana and his marriage he had
been absent for many weeks on an extended royal tour to
Australia and America – just the kind of duty his mother had
been criticized for when she had left him behind as a child.
Diana was by contrast an enthusiast for the emotional pop
culture of the early 1980s. Her only experience of the outside
world was the comfy one of posh girls in west London,
satirized at the time as 'Sloane Rangers'. She could have no
idea of what life as a Windsor would really be like. At best,

this would always be an optimistic throw of the dice. Yet plenty of couples make a marriage work despite differences of age and interests.

The assumption that this was a lifelong commitment which would hugely strengthen the royal family was shared by the Queen and the Duke of Edinburgh, uncountable numbers of fervently monarchist subjects, almost all of the media and – of course – by the royal couple themselves. The only political heckles came from the left, who resented the possibility that Mrs Thatcher's government, then at its pre-Falklands War low, might gain a patriotic boost from the celebrations. Charles and Diana enjoyed their day as global celebrities (it is estimated that nearly three-quarters of a billion people around the world watched the wedding) and continued for some years as an apparently successful couple, producing the next heir with commendable promptness.

The Prince of Wales's story over the next few years became the story of his marriage. Behind that, though, there was another story, which had as much constitutional weight – the Prince of Wales's politics. In a conventional party-political sense he has no politics and gets understandably irritated when it is claimed otherwise. The Prince is certainly no socialist. He has tried hard all his life to avoid party-political tags or direct interventions in the main themes of political argument, such as the economy, Britain's membership of the EU, the Iraq war or the size of the armed forces. Yet he has strong views on other things, which are close to 'real' politics, and becoming closer. And on those subjects his views have been growing more strongly conservative (with a small 'c') as he has grown older. In the Thatcher years this brought him into conflict with Tory radicals, rather than socialists.

During the 1980s his habit of writing critical letters to

ministers began. He spent more and more time on his charitable work, above all the Prince's Trust, becoming involved with an outspoken architect called Rod Hackney, who drove the more radical end of the Prince's work. After a conversation on a train between the two of them was leaked and then confirmed to the newspaper by Hackney, Charles found himself in the middle of a serious row. He had, reported the *Manchester Evening News*, become worried that he would inherit the throne of a divided Britain, split between haves and have-nots. This sounded very like an attack on Britain's radical prime minister, and Mrs Thatcher's office was furious. Writing to Hackney after his apology, Charles said these were 'overtly political phrases of a kind I would never, ever use because I know exactly what the political reactions are likely to be ... it is essential that I operate in this field of community architecture, inner city housing, deprivation, etc. by steering my way very carefully through a political minefield'.[3]

The Prince may have been chastened but he was not deflected. He continued to push the cause of small business and regeneration, particularly in some of the more deprived black areas, and badgered Mrs Thatcher to meet minority community leaders, which she eventually did, though no major initiative followed. During these years, his office was growing in size, he had established his own country base at Highgrove in Gloucestershire, and he was beginning to take a closer interest in the running of the huge farming estates owned by the Duchy of Cornwall. More and more time was spent at the private meetings between Buckingham Palace staff and Downing Street discussing and divining the thinking of the Prince of Wales. The Queen, however, kept herself well away from the controversies of the high noon of Thatcherism. To this day we have no knowledge about whether she sympathized with 'the

Lady' or her critics in the European Union; and whether she had real qualms about the loss of British – that is, her – sovereignty to a Brussels-led super-state. She may have persuaded many leftish and liberal observers that, deep down, the monarch was no Thatcherite. The latex-puppet satirists of *Spitting Image* showed her with a Socialist Workers Party badge and a bust of Lenin, which was a good joke. The poor state of the Opposition led many to believe that, in some obscure way, the Crown was a buffer to the Crown's ministers, yet there was no hard evidence for this at all. The drama and sadness when Mrs Thatcher lost her job, in a giant public humiliation, evoked the Queen's strong sympathy.

The Storm Breaks

When a young diplomat called Robin Janvrin joined the Palace press office in the spring of 1987, after helping organize the Queen's 1983 visit to India, he could have expected a relatively easy time ahead. There were overseas problems inside the Commonwealth, but in Britain these seemed golden years for the royal family. The press was still entranced as well as obsessed by the spectacle of Charles and Diana. Princes William and Harry were toddlers and their mother no longer looked so gaunt or unhappy as she once had. The royal couple had performed brilliantly as a pair during a tour of the Arabian Gulf the previous autumn and would dazzle the media again during their visit to Australia the following January, for the country's two hundredth anniversary. Prince Andrew had married an old acquaintance of Diana's, Sarah Ferguson, who, with a polo connection to the Royals through her father, seemed eminently suitable. She was almost instantly written into the newspapers' Windsor soap opera as the cheerful, unstuffy royal recruit, known as 'Fergie', a 'pal' for Diana and a breath of fresh air. When he married in July 1986, Andrew became Duke of York, a title with special meaning for the Queen and Queen Mother since it had been George VI's, and his father's too. Some of those close to the family believe that Prince Andrew, despite his occasional scrapes, has always been the Queen's favourite. Watching the two of them together joking and gossiping, one can easily believe it.

This seemed a time of Windsor renewal and optimism. The mood of self-confidence was summed up by the decision to make a television show for 1987 under the direction of Prince Edward, the youngest of the Queen's children and an enthusiast about the world of broadcasting. *It's a Royal Knockout* would reveal the younger generation romping and cavorting with celebrities – Rowan Atkinson, Meat Loaf, Barbara Windsor – for charity. That was the idea. Senior courtiers, including the Queen's private secretary William Heseltine, objected but were overruled. The press declared that the resulting television show was awful. Princess Anne was particularly embarrassed and Prince Edward, confronted by derisive newspapermen, walked angrily out of the subsequent press conference. This ought to have been a warning sign of the dangers of playing a media game, of letting the floodlights in upon magic, without very careful preparation. It ought to have alarmed courtiers about changed generational attitudes more than it did. 'There was a general feeling that if it's for charity, it's OK. Frankly, we had got cocky,' says one of those involved.

Behind the scenes, as the world now knows, a very different story had been unfolding, which would embroil the House of Windsor in its worst time since the abdication crisis and turn these years at Buckingham Palace into a time when desperate fire-fighting almost overwhelmed reform. The Queen had been puzzled by Diana's moodiness and odd behaviour but she and Prince Philip had done their best to welcome her into the family. This was not working. Charles and Diana were deeply unhappy, going through the long misery of a marriage that was failing. Both were having affairs. Charles was deeply involved with his original love, Camilla Parker Bowles, using aristocratic retreats and discreet friends to fix their trysts. Diana had employed James Hewitt, a soldier, and later James Gilbey, a car salesman, as solace for her loneliness. Terrible rows between Prince and Princess went on, sometimes in the comparative privacy of Highgrove, the Prince of Wales's Gloucestershire retreat, sometimes in front of gossipy outsiders. There were rumours and echoes of the trouble but it remained sufficiently vague for the Queen and Duke to be able to ignore what was happening.

According to Jonathan Dimbleby, author of Charles's biography, neither of his parents raised the marital problems, or Diana's behaviour, with him. A book by the journalist Anthony Holden, which told some of the story in 1988, had been brushed aside. There was at the Palace a not unreasonable feeling that many marriages went through difficult times and that it would probably all blow over. 'I don't think one could overestimate the drama of the relationship between the Prince and Princess of Wales; everybody knew there were problems but no one believed that it was going to end as it did,' says one senior figure. Another adds that soon the Palace officials were 'shell-shocked' by the media fall-out and barely able to look ahead, never mind plan.

Everything finally spilled into the open during 1992. The year began in January with old but embarrassing pictures being published showing the Duchess of York on holiday with a

Texan friend, Steve Wyatt. They were not explicit but laid bare how distant her marriage to Prince Andrew, who was endlessly away on his naval duties, had become. Prince Andrew soon told his mother that his marriage was over. The worse story to come was prefigured with more press photos, this time of Diana alone and lonely during a visit to India, famously in front of the Taj Mahal, that monument to married love. She had a keen eye for an image and had effectively used the press photographers to send a public message about her inner feelings. In March came the formal announcement that the Yorks were to separate and the following month the announcement that Princess Anne, the most private and hard-working of the Queen's children, and her husband Mark Phillips were to divorce. All this was very bad. But the real disasters for the family began with the publication of Andrew Morton's book *Diana, Her True Story*. This started with a serialization in the *Sunday Times*, which created a media firestorm. The book changed everything. Because Diana had collaborated with the writer, not simply with photographers, she had smashed all the old codes of privacy.

Had the Prince and Princess of Wales experienced their marital troubles twenty years earlier, it is possible they would have been ignored by the media and been given time to try to sort them out in the deep quiet of their own home. By the 1980s that reticence was impossible to imagine, particularly given the readiness of the Princess to spill the beans. She had grown up in the new celebrity-driven media climate, in which public voyeurism and the exhibitionism of the famous were lolling on the same sofa, two kissing cousins. The deadly urge to be 'understood' was one she found irresistible. Later even Prince Charles, needled and jabbed all his life by a half-amused, half-censorious press, would decide he wanted his side of the story told. The tale of their marital crisis broke at a time when the press and public wanted a diversion. Britain was in the teeth of a recession, governed by a prime minister in trouble. Though John Major had confounded the pundits and won a clear mandate on a big national vote, by April 1992 he was working with a slim Commons majority and a divided party. It was all rather grey and depressing.

There are some periods in the Queen's story so momentous that they have to be given special treatment. 1992 is remembered by Palace officials as the worst time in the history of the modern monarchy; worse even than the ominous-seeming days after the death of Princess Diana in 1997. Twenty years on, it is possible to see more clearly what she wryly described at the time as her 'annus horribilis'. The sequence of family break-ups; an increasingly intrusive and unforgiving press; the bad luck of the Windsor Castle fire which fuelled public debate about the royal finances; and a government that was too weak and unpopular to offer much help to a Queen in difficulty – this was very bad luck. One or two of these events could have been managed easily enough but, like the famous 'perfect storm', each amplified the rest. And this multiple crisis seemed to have fallen upon the Queen, if not quite out of a clear blue sky, at least out of a typically English one of light clouds and sunny spells. In fact it was the culmination of problems reaching back through the previous two decades.

One was the self-written mission statement of the Windsor dynasty. Marriage had been at the cornerstone of the Queen's Christian mission since she addressed the Mothers' Union rally of young wives at Westminster in 1949. It is worth recalling her words at the time: 'We can have no doubt that divorce and separation are responsible for some of the darkest evils in our society today.' She followed them with a trenchant attack on materialism and selfishness. These days, it takes a stretch of the imagination to see that post-war, austerity-shadowed Britain as a place of self-indulgence or conspicuous greed, but emphasizing the sanctity of marriage probably seemed a safe enough message in 1949. As we saw earlier, it formed an important subtext to the Coronation four years later. In the early years of her marriage the Queen had been a 'fairy-tale princess' in her own right and, as she bore children, she continued to be portrayed as the ideal of young British mother-hood. Presenting the royal family as an emblem of personal moral rectitude had built on the close 'we four' unity of George VI's time. It made the royal family a social example as well as a constitutional mechanism – its political role has never been enough for true monarchism to thrive. In the early years of the Queen's reign, all this was easy to explain. Divorcees were kept well away from the royal enclosure at Ascot or royal garden parties. Even Princess Margaret had been barred from marrying her first love on straightforwardly traditionalist grounds.

Yet within a few years of that stern decision standards were visibly slipping and more than forty years later the Windsors had been as afflicted by changed attitudes to fidelity as many other British families. The Queen's wide-eyed, serious-looking children had grown into adults struggling with old human dilemmas about how to be happy. Sexual frankness, the pill, society scandals and relaxations of the divorce law were pushing Britain away from the Christian certainties of the Mothers' Union and towards a world in which a good sex life was being treated as virtually a human right. Once, the moneyed and aristocratic world had tended to view lovers and adultery as a price worth paying when appearances needed to be kept up. Something of those blasé male attitudes persisted among older Royals such as Lord Mountbatten, who is said to have helped Prince Charles with early trysts. Now, what had seemed to their parents wise discretion looked to a new generation mere hypocrisy. Let it all hang out. The post-1960s morality of authenticity, openness and 'being true to yourself' were pushing aside tact, restraint and discretion.

Alongside this had come that utterly changed mood in the press. Buckingham Palace people have tended to blame the 'Republican and vulgarian' Rupert Murdoch for this. Not quite so: it is true that his *Sun* and *Sunday Times* newspapers were the most aggressive tormentors of monarchy in this period, closely followed by his *News of the World* (R.I.P.), but mockery and intrusive reporting only sold newspapers because public taste had grown coarser, or at least less deferential. The *Sun*'s Kelvin Mackenzie might make menacing jokes about 'whacking the Germans' (by which he meant the Windsors) but other editors were also combining fawningly obsequious leader columns and savagely destructive news attacks. The Queen herself was almost always kept above the fray, occasionally lampooned for not paying taxes, gently mocked by cartoonists, but in general seen as beyond reach. Her children, however, had been demoted to the level of celebrities, meaning they took their place in the endless 'set 'em up, knock 'em down' game which also chewed up and spat out rock musicians, actresses and television stars. They have developed their own responses. One reads attentively through stories about himself, noting error after error – but then admits to turning the page and reading about someone else with cheerful credulity – 'No! they didn't?' Another says briskly: 'Just never read it. Life's too short.'

However persecuted members of the royal family feel, the British press had reverted to its oldest traditions, which are robustly scurrilous. The comparatively self-censoring and high-minded newspapers of the 1930s through to the late 1950s, which the Queen and Duke had grown up reading, were the product of an abnormally serious geopolitical time. Now once more politicians were being splattered with dirt, cackled at and abused – and so with anyone else who caught an editor's eye. Murdoch had only changed the economics, by breaking the print unions, and returning an invigorated press to its pungent origins. What followed in the twenty-first century was a Murdoch press – and other newspapers too – swollen by power and riding for a fall, which duly came with the phone-hacking scandal.

Meanwhile, as Andrew Morton's book came out, Murdoch ensured maximum publicity and maximum damage. Morton, an urbane former tabloid reporter, had written an account of serial attempted suicides by the Princess, including when she was pregnant with the heir to the throne, and of self-mutilation, wrist-slashing and bulimic vomiting. He portrayed a marriage dying because of Charles's infidelity, a collapse hastened by the coldness and mental cruelty of the Windsors. In that, it was a brutal, passionate, full-frontal (and unfair) attack on the Queen, the Duke of Edinburgh and the Prince of Wales, portraying them as dysfunctional to the point of inhumanity. Pacily written and detailed, its most sensational claims were filleted and repeated (they hardly needed to be hyped) by the *Sunday Times*. Millions of people, and many other journalists, simply did not believe them. They were 'too much'. They could not be true. But before the newspaper published, on 7 June 1992, its editor Andrew Neil had been convinced by Morton that not only was his book based on a series of reliable, and sworn, statements by friends of the Princess, but that she had directly authorized their passing on to the writer.

The final decision to publish had been agreed by Andrew

Knight, the News International boss in Britain, and by the company's founder, Rupert Murdoch, himself. It was seen at the time, and has been since, as a plot directed at the institution of the monarchy. Again, no. Murdoch may be no friend of the royal family nor indeed of other British institutions, but this was finally a decision for his editor. Andrew Neil published because this was a huge story, which would sell a lot of newspapers. He was an experienced man, who had been editor for nearly a decade and was fully aware of the storm he was sailing into.

To start with, the Prince decided not to hit back. He wanted to believe that his wife was not involved, or at least that she had been betrayed by blabbermouthed friends. As the storm howled, the Palace had no plan to respond with. There was nothing to say. Its first move was to downplay and in part deny what Morton was saying, encouraging Lord McGregor, the then chairman of the toothless Press Complaints Commission, to protest at the 'odious exhibition of journalists dabbling their fingers in the stuff of other people's souls in a manner that adds nothing to legitimate public interest in the heir to the throne'. Fine-sounding words. McGregor had uttered them after checking with the Queen's private secretary Sir Robert Fellowes, who was also the Princess's brother-in-law. Diana had not been the source for the book, had she? Diana assured Fellowes that she had not been involved. But she had deceived this upstanding and old-fashioned royal servant. She had passed the key material to Morton. Later, she barely tried to deny it. She staged a public meeting with a former flatmate who was one of Morton's key witnesses – like the Taj Mahal photograph by Arthur Edwards, this was a blatant hand-signal to the public about what was really going on. Then, when asked by the Queen's press secretary to sign a statement repudiating the book, she refused to do so. Fellowes, whom the Queen had known since he was a small boy, had been put in an impossible position. He apologized to McGregor and honourably offered to resign. Wisely, the Queen turned him down.

As other editors attacked Andrew Neil for irresponsibility, intrusion and almost everything else running up to high treason, the Princess of Wales had to face the Queen, the Duke of Edinburgh and her husband in private. She was fixated by what had gone wrong in her marriage, 'the star in her own private movie' as one observer put it, and had not perhaps realized how deep her treachery seemed to the older Royals. Prince Philip, by the accounts of those close to the family at the time, worked very hard to help the errant Princess and find ways to mend the marriage. He wrote her long and kind, perceptive letters, which she then showed to friends and complained about. The Duke's letters were later stolen and published.

Diana was also involved in a detailed correspondence with the Queen Mother, who had many reasons to understand her plight, having been brought into the royal family as a titled commoner herself, and who had suffered setbacks in her early years. Sadly, the whole correspondence has been destroyed. Princess Margaret spent an entire week burning letters and other papers in an effort, she told friends, to clear out the chaotic and 'hopeless' state of her mother's writing room. It was filled with attaché cases overflowing with letters. Princess Margaret had asked the Queen Mother: 'Do you really want to keep these old things?' and, getting a non-committal response, had set to with the help of rubber gloves, plastic bin bags, and a pinafore, collecting a treasure-trove of royal history and burning it in Kensington Palace's private gardens. Among the items thought to have been destroyed was the manuscript of an ode to the Queen Mother by Benjamin Britten. One writer asked Princess Margaret if by any chance she had found any letters from him? Oh yes, she replied. And had she burned them? Oh *yes*.

Meanwhile, confronted by her heir's broken marriage, the Queen counselled a six-month hiatus. Yet it seemed to her son that separation was inevitable. The final break came over a comparatively minor row over which parent should have the two young princes during rival weekend breaks at Sandringham and Highgrove. It would be unkind to enumerate every twist and tear-stained turn in the months that followed, in what one senior Palace official called 'an unfolding human tragedy', but almost nobody was able to cope. The Palace press officers and officials at the time remember feeling exhausted, beaten down and almost disorientated by the volume of criticism. 'It was a complete feeling of being in the bunker, the original bunker mentality,' says one. A senior official adds: 'It was a wretched business . . . It went on and on. It was worse than 1997. People got a bit punch-drunk and it stopped one thinking positively.' How could things get worse?

On 20 November 1992, fire broke out in a chapel at Windsor Castle and tore through much of the most historic part of the structure, badly damaging the state dining room and three other key rooms. Paintings and other valuables were saved but beautiful and ancient furnishings and fabrics went up in smoke. 'A horrible November afternoon, dull and drizzly and the fire roaring across, heading for the Queen's apartments,' remembers one senior official. 'The next week was ghastly,' says another. 'The Queen was very bruised by the fire. It was her home. It was very close to her, very intimate. I remember going across the Rose Garden carrying Prince Philip's sock drawer.' This was the place where the Queen had grown up as a teenager and where throughout her life she had spent family weekends, entertained friends and received world leaders; it meant much more to her than Buckingham Palace, which has always been 'the office'. She was caught by the television cameras, looking stricken. Prince Philip, who was on a visit to Argentina, did what he could to comfort her by phone. Prince Andrew helped ferry as much of the priceless collection of paintings and furniture out as he could. The fire took 250 firemen fifteen hours to control and eventually damaged a hundred rooms.

After the fire there was an immediate wave of sympathy, but soon the question was being asked, 'Who will pay?' The affable Heritage Secretary, Peter Brooke, prematurely announced that the taxpayer would pick up the bill for the Windsor Castle restoration, since the building had not been insured. The bill would be up to £40 million. As we have seen, both Brooke and Buckingham Palace were taken aback by the hostile public reaction. The problem was not simply a one-off decision to help out the Queen but, yet again, the longer-running issue of her wealth. The public mood was so angry that the cabinet minister Douglas Hurd felt the need to make a speech warning that the British were in danger of treating their constitutional monarchy as 'some trifling toy' that could be tossed about in public debate without causing it harm. The combination had become toxic. 'Sex and money; money and sex,' says one senior figure, 'as in life it always is.' Had the Morton revelations never happened, it is likely public sympathy for the Queen's financial position would have been greater.

What had really rocked the Palace was the Princess's decision to tell all, a tearing-up of habits of royal discretion that had lasted, with the solitary exceptions of the Duke and Duchess of Windsor, for centuries. Throughout the Queen's reign she had struggled to negotiate the boundary between public and private. We have seen how deep she felt Marion Crawford's betrayal had been, upending her childhood in public, and how sensitive the Palace has been to the dangers of eavesdropping staff or bribe-taking footmen. To live under this degree of public curiosity must be a special kind of torment. Yet the monarchy was also in the popularity business, at a time when crowns and sceptres had lost their lustre and human stories were replacing them. So, on the one side she had been pushed by relatives, including everyone from Lord Mountbatten to Prince Edward, for more openness about 'the real Queen', with television companies, authors and journalists demanding to know ever more. Yet, on the other hand, ringing in her ears must have been the words of the great Victorian constitutionalist Walter Bagehot, whom she had studied as a girl and who had warned against letting too much sunlight shine on the magic.

Fewer than four weeks after the fire, on 9 December 1992, the separation of Charles and Diana was announced and John Major blandly told the House of Commons that there would be 'no constitutional implications'. 'The succession to the Throne is unaffected by it ... and there is no reason why the Princess of Wales should not be crowned Queen in due course. The Prince of Wales's succession as head of the Church of England is also unaffected.' Even his own staff were unimpressed. One says: 'They were making statements such as, "She can be Queen," which looking back was complete nonsense. In everyone's mind there was this image of a future Coronation, with Charles and Diana arriving separately.' At a time when the Prince was being blamed particularly for the breakdown, with Camilla Parker Bowles in the background, some MPs were deeply sceptical about his future role as head of the church. Major had worked hard, personally, on trying to bridge the rift sufficiently to ensure that the Prince and Princess still carried out some official duties together. But there was not the automatic and full-hearted support for the battered House of Windsor that would have been expected from previous governments.

This was hardly surprising. On 16 September 1992, 'Black Wednesday', the pound had fallen out of the European exchange rate mechanism and Major had lost his economic policy and foreign policy in one fell swoop, not to mention much of his personal authority. He had seriously considered resigning as prime minister. The Tory Party was at war with itself over the European Maastricht Treaty. As recently as 4 November Major had been contemplating resignation again before winning a Commons division on the treaty by just three votes. A Downing Street observer at the time says,

> You were torn two ways. There was to some extent a normal sympathy in a Conservative government for the monarchy ... but it was a government so battered and knocked about politically that there wasn't spare energy, and a will to go over the top; and there was considerable fear, too much fear, of the media. So because it was a media-driven 'annus horribilis', Downing Street, in my view, pulled its punches and was more responsive to media criticism, for instance on tax, than another government would have been.

There is a crucial point here about the relationship between a constitutional monarch and her prime ministers. From time to time, the monarchy needs cover and support from the government of the day, just as the government of the day needs the authority of the Crown. To a large extent, they hang together. In Britain, their authorities are rarely inseparable. British monarchy is weakened by weak British governments and is given confidence by successful ones. When each week the Queen greets her prime minister, she has a vested interest in that individual doing well. Labour or Tory, it doesn't matter. The politics and the individual policies matter less than the authority of the elected leader and thus the authority of the state which the Queen heads. It was an important piece of bad luck for the Queen that the breakdown of her heir's marriage occurred at the same time that her government, riven by disagreements over Europe and recession, was also unpopular. And the year ended badly too. The Queen's Christmas message was leaked and printed early in the *Sun*. It was indeed her 'annus horribilis'.

This period also showed, however, that the Queen and her advisers had not lost their capacity to learn and change in response to bad times. In 1993 it was announced that to help cover the restoration costs of the Windsor fire – a massive programme supervised by Prince Philip involving rebuilding and improving parts of the ancient building, as well as straightforward restoration – Buckingham Palace would be opened regularly to the public. Tickets were priced at £8 to start with and the scheme was originally meant to last for just four years. It proved a huge success, drawing around 400,000 people a year and necessitating the development of new facilities and a better Queen's Gallery to show some of her art collection. What had started as a stop-gap to raise cash turned into a major new source of income: revenue from Windsor Castle and Holyroodhouse, both run by the Royal Collection Trust, was running at nearly £17 million a year by 2002. More important, though, is the symbolism of opening the great

palaces to visitors, as so many of Britain's country houses have
been opened. What were once rather stern walls and spiked
railings now welcome the curious. Chilly old Buckingham
Palace sometimes now seems almost cosy. The hideous notion
of allowing the public in, which once so affronted Winston
Churchill, has proved uncontroversial and popular.

As the shock waves from the Morton revelations continued,
however, the feud between Charles and Diana proved anything
but cosy and turned even more controversial. The Prince of
Wales decided to hit back through an authorized biography by
his friend the broadcaster Jonathan Dimbleby. Dimbleby had
been given very deep access to the Prince, from his private
diaries to long recorded interviews and state papers. *The Prince
of Wales* threw new light on Charles's strong political views
and his unhappiness about his upbringing. Most of the immediate attention, however, was focused on the admission in the
book and an accompanying television interview of his adultery
with Camilla Parker Bowles and his account of the failed
marriage to Diana. This was devastating and unheard of from
a modern Royal. When the Queen read through the galley
proofs of the book she was observed to be pink with shock
and bemusement. The code of silence, even of dissimulation,
when journalists were around had been central to the monarchy's self-protection. Prince Charles's collaboration with
Dimbleby also did damage by revealing in hurtful detail his
thoughts about the failure of his parents in his own upbringing,
explained in paragraphs felt to be cruel. The Princess of Wales
was shown as unbalanced and paranoid. That too seemed a
dangerous game to get into just at the time when she appeared
to be playing half the British media like saxophones. One royal
servant, who has long supported and still admires the Prince,

described his collaboration over the book as the single worst decision of his adult life. Yet again, the curtain had been ripped aside; but this time by a future king.

At which point, it is worth standing back and considering the forces now ranged against one another. The key advisers at Buckingham Palace were men who had had long careers as royal servants, or in Whitehall, or in the City, but who had little experience of the raw end of modern British life. Their watchwords were tact and loyalty. They saw their job as protecting a discreet and cautious Queen, who had firmly old-fashioned views, and taking direction from her husband, who for good reasons had a deep suspicion and dislike of journalists. During the good years for the monarchy they had become complacent. Nothing in their experience could have prepared them for younger members joining the family and then conspiring with the press to put the most sensitive private matters into the public arena. Yet had they been being paying attention to the fast-changing world of the media, and to the new pressures on more junior members of the royal family, they might have seen the dangers ahead. Against them were the journalists, editors and proprietors of a media world which was in competition for survival and which owed little to the British establishment. The big newspaper companies were often owned by overseas proprietors – that was not new – who did not live in Britain – which was. Their editors had little interest in honours or being associated with the monarchy. Britain had become like America, largely a money-based hierarchy. Journalists had trained on the pursuit and disembowelling of celebrities and were using new technologies to steal information.

The Lightning Strikes

There were four and a half years ahead, before Diana's death in Paris, during which the story of the separation, then divorce, and then her other affairs, screamed from newspapers and magazines, sometimes every other day. And sometimes, every day. The Windsor dynasty was in danger of becoming a sideshow to a soap opera it had spawned and could not control. The Queen and the Duke of Edinburgh had started by trying to reconcile Charles and Diana. Later the Queen and Duke, with the rest of the world, watched and waited to see whether a stable 'separate but allied' life could be sustained by their son and daughter-in-law.

One who was with the Queen at the time says, 'I think she really did go through hell. She found Diana frightfully difficult and was terribly sad when the children were "protected" from her; and then all the tantrums at Sandringham and so forth, which she couldn't really cope with.' The Queen had few illusions about her son: on that subject she has often been, if not salty, then at least peppery. Lord Hurd, the former foreign secretary, said of her during the 'annus horribilis', 'I was surprised by the very great frankness with which she would talk about it – the problems – and how different people were coping with them in her family. She would only talk in a group she trusted.'[4] The Queen was unused to extreme displays of emotion. Aside from her father's famous rages or 'gnashes', before Diana, she had simply not encountered them. Diana, showing an awesome lack of inter-generational understanding, told politicians that the Queen needed to be persuaded to be more 'huggy'. The gap between what the actress Helen Mirren, who played the Queen in that Oscar-winning film, calls 'the noble generation' of buttoned-up public-service Britishness, and the country of the late twentieth century, had never seemed wider.

At any rate, Diana would not be easily controlled. After she moved out of the family home, Prince Charles's Highgrove House, Buckingham Palace could cut her out of most royal engagements and limit her to an apartment in Kensington Palace and a modest office at St James's Palace. They could not make her go away. Her husband's friends and the 'royal set' maintained a frosty, hostile wall of turned backs and unanswered letters. But Diana had her friends too. What remained of wealthy, 'society' London divided into two camps, his and hers. With the boys now at boarding school Diana became isolated, lonely and dangerous. Through it all the Queen carried on with a heavy routine of the usual engagements and the formal turning of the royal year. Meanwhile, Diana's triumphs overseas, including photogenic trips to publicize aid work in Nepal and Zimbabwe, and a notably successful visit to Paris, were rivalling, and upstaging, visits and speeches by her husband. Her office consciously tried to project her as an autonomous, alternative kind of princess, who would speak openly about her eating disorders, weep with the bereaved and clasp the sick, an emotional openness – or exhibitionism – alien to the Queen.

That would have been difficult enough. But Diana, like Charles, was searching for real love. She was furiously jealous of the boys' nanny, Tiggy Legge-Bourke, and, later, obsessively interested in whether Charles would marry Camilla Parker Bowles. She began a series of affairs, some serious, others not, which had to be conducted with cloak-and-dagger secrecy but were in media terms increasingly dangerous. Partly as a result of her own complicity in Andrew Morton's book about her, the rules of the game, always slippery, had changed. She was now considered fair game by tabloids and by foreign magazines, in ferocious competition with one another. She would leak to one journalist or editor, to find the rest of them infuriated and after her. Nobody can win that game.

Diana was a past mistress of the art of being photographed for a purpose. Newspaper photographers who had followed her and other Royals for years – the *Sun*'s Arthur Edwards being the first and best of them – had developed ways of working which allowed them to get good pictures without excessively harassing their targets. But now there was a new private army of freelance 'paps' selling their wares to the highest bidder in a global market. They had no masters who could be summoned for a dressing-down, or pleaded with by phone. Editors could use their pictures and wash their hands of the behaviour needed to get them. They were as competitively aggressive as piranhas, car-chasing motorbike boys, skilled at provocative pushing to get the right expression of rage or fear. Pictures of Diana were soon fetching so much – selling so many copies – that almost anyone seemed to be bribable.

It was a life that many Hollywood stars have coped with; but they were surrounded by regiments of goons, minders and the privacy huge wealth buys. The royal family, similarly, had their palaces and protection squads. Diana had protection officers too, but was relatively exposed. She continued to believe that she could play the media. For a while it seemed she could. She invited newspaper editors, columnists and executives to Kensington Palace, asked their advice, flattered them and flirted with them. When she met the up-and-coming Labour leader Tony Blair, she boasted to him about her ability to manipulate the newspapers and even hinted she would like to help Labour with the forthcoming election. At a dinner with Blair, Alastair Campbell and mutual friends in January 1997, Diana said she had now met almost all the editors. Images were all-important. 'You have got to touch people in pictures. They can take a lot from you, but they can never take away the pictures,' she told them.[5]

For his part Blair explained that 'compassion' would be a key theme of the Labour campaign and said 'we had a lot to learn from her'. He said later that he was wary of her though she offered to advise New Labour – an extraordinary act for someone in her position: 'Occasionally she would phone and say why such-and-such a picture was rubbish or what could be done better . . . she had a complete sense of what we were trying to achieve and why.'[6] It is a bizarre picture of two then glamorous figures who believed themselves to be Mistress and Master of the Media Universe, foot-nuzzling. Alastair Campbell also believed that Diana was after him, or at least bedazzled by him. There was a more important game of self-delusion going on, however, which was to believe that the world of journalism could be endlessly manipulated into giving Labour, or the Princess, flattering coverage. Both would learn the bleak truth about that, Diana before Blair.

Even in 1995 Blair felt the Queen had good cause to be worried about Diana, an 'unpredictable meteor' in the Windsors' 'predictable and highly regulated ecosystem'. Diana was trying to radicalize the image of the monarchy, he thought, rather as he was trying to change the image of Britain: 'For someone as acutely perceptive and long-termist about the monarchy and its future as the Queen, it must have been deeply troubling.' The Queen knew the monarchy had to both stand for tradition and also evolve, but in a steady and controlled way. In Diana's case, manipulating what used to be called Fleet Street was like a child in a pedalo trying to land a shark. She could out-picture and out-smart Prince Charles during private week-by-week competitions for coverage. But when stories of her possessive and aggressive behaviour towards one married man hit the papers, she promptly went to war to defend herself – and lost. Then came a book based on letters to her earlier lover James Hewitt, soon known in press shorthand as Love Rat, and stories about other liaisons.

To try to turn the tables on Prince Charles and those in the media who had decided she was unhinged and dangerously manipulative, Diana decided to allow Martin Bashir of the BBC's *Panorama* programme to interview her in November 1995. It was a decisive moment. She had been advised against it by almost every one of the friends she had consulted. It was kept secret from royal circles; the BBC director general John Birt did not even tell his chairman, Lord Hussey, whose wife was a close friend of the Queen. Birt, who went on to work for Tony Blair, later said that the interview 'marked the end of the BBC's institutional reverence, though not its respect, for the monarchy'.[7] After the recording, Diana informed the Queen that she had been interviewed, though gave no further details. The broadcast went out on Charles's birthday. It was watched by 23 million viewers.

In it, she cast doubt on the Queen's competence in handling her relationship with her people and suggested that Prince Charles might not be able to adapt to being King. Switching between third and first person – always an interesting foible, and one that prime ministers tend to share – Diana said: 'She won't go quietly, that's the problem. I'll fight to the end because I believe that I have a role to fulfil, and I've got two children to bring up.' (Diana had played her good mum card often with photographers, taking the boys to theme parks or films: how she thought it was consonant with displaying her marital woes to the world, while they were left at school to deal with the consequences, is mysterious.) After careful practice, she had a series of devastating one-liners to deliver to the British public, most famously about there 'being three of us in this marriage' and wanting in the future to be 'a queen of people's hearts'. She admitted to her adulterous affair with James Hewitt but was not asked about others. Her private secretary, Patrick Jephson, who had been trying to rebuild bridges with the royal family, resigned from his job shortly afterwards.

The Bashir interview, certainly one of the television events of that decade, was an explosive upping of the ante and a direct challenge to the Queen, as well as to her son. In its immediate aftermath, large majorities in favour of Diana were recorded by polling companies. She seemed to have 'won'. She continued on the attack by libellously mocking Legge-Bourke and refusing to attend the family Christmas at Sandringham. The Queen decided that things had gone too far and that Charles and Diana should divorce. She had talked to the prime minister and to the Archbishop of Canterbury. There followed a struggle over the terms. To start with, Diana refused a divorce. She had emotional support from the Duchess of York, then divorcing Prince Andrew, and the tactical support of a bright young lawyer, Anthony Julius. She demanded a huge, lump-sum settlement of £17 million, plus high annual support, and wanted too to keep the honorific title Her Royal Highness. Though 'HRH' does not mean anything legally, it is a mark of closeness to the Queen, reserved for inner members of the family only. Losing it meant she would be formally cast out and would not, for instance, have to be invited to state occasions. Eventually she won on the money and lost on the

HRH. The settlement, formalized in July 1996, forced the Prince of Wales to borrow money from his mother to give Diana complete financial independence. It also gave them both something they had not had for many years, the chance of personal happiness.

Diana had made clear her ambition to be a rival, unofficial 'royal', and still had plenty of media and public support behind her. She would be able to marry whomever she chose, and of course that person would then have a family link to the British monarchy. The first such lover was an eminent Pakistani heart surgeon, Hasnat Khan, who ended the relationship. The second was Dodi al-Fayed, son of the maverick, foul-mouthed Egyptian owner of Harrods. Diana returned quickly to her high-profile charity work with Aids and leprosy victims and campaigning against landmines in Africa – she had told Blair, with icy calculation, that she had 'gone for the caring angle' – and continued to glow as a global star wherever she appeared. She was ready to make political mischief, telling anyone who would listen that Charles would never be King and that the Royals were in trouble.

At a time when Labour was making much of sinking the Royal Yacht and Blair's 'modernization' theme could clearly embrace the monarchy, this caused real anxiety at the Palace. Yet Diana's position was not as strong as it appeared to nervous courtiers. Charles was now openly being seen with Camilla Parker Bowles, who had divorced. Many felt she could never be Queen. Many felt they could not marry. The Queen herself bided her time. According to one of her advisers, there was a lot of private discussion around 1993–4 about Camilla's future role and 'how much things could or could not be acknowledged.' At all events, it was clear that Charles felt liberated too and that the Windsors felt they had survived a series of devastating shocks. But of those shocks, by far the worst was still to come and Diana would not be there to watch it unfold.

Diana's death in a Paris tunnel was an accident. Human frailty and greed were to blame, embracing the driver of her car and the paparazzi harassing her and Dodi al-Fayed from motor-bikes. She was not murdered. She was not the target of shadowy forces, manipulated from Buckingham Palace, MI6 or the moon. How can we be so sure? It is hard to prove a negative. It is also possible that Harold Wilson was a Russian spy; that the Twin Towers were brought down by the CIA; and that Scientologists are in possession of an important truth. But so much effort has been expended to try to turn the events of that dreadful evening into a conspiracy story, without a shred of evidence, that level-headed people must conclude 'it ain't so'. Nobody who has seen Buckingham Palace actually at work could believe that the Duke of Edinburgh, say, could order any government body to do anything at all.

The conspiracy theories about Diana's death do reflect two realities, however. The first is that she was much loved by millions of people, who had taken her side in the media war with the Windsors. The second is that her death removed a nagging problem for the British monarchy. Had Diana lived, it is likely that her star would have gently and slowly faded and that she would have lived the life of many wealthy and glamorous women who are not members of the royal family. It would have made her former husband's remarriage harder, however, and possibly have prevented it. And on past form, she would been unable to resist taking sly pot-shots at Bucking-ham Palace, or offering unhelpful 'advice'. Marrying a Muslim would probably not have been a problem. Apart from anything

Too much a fairytale to last: Prince Charles and Lady Diana bow and curtsey to the Queen after their marriage in 1981.

The future. 'Granny' with Princes William and Harry, 1987.

The lowest point. The Queen waits to make her 'annus horribilis' speech at London's Guildhall, after the marriage breakdowns of two of her children and the devastating Windsor fire, 1992.

Responding to the eruption of grief: the Queen back in London after Diana's death, when critics had accused her of failing to read the national mood.

One has a website: the Queen goes digital at a school in Brent, 1997.

The Queen Mother waves to the crowds on her hundredth birthday,
watched by the Queen and Princess Margaret. Their deaths, close together,
robbed the Queen of two of her closest confidantes.

The Queen's enthusiasm
for the Commonwealth has
helped her become a successful
head of a state being reshaped by
immigration. London East End
crowds during the 2002
Golden Jubilee.

A genuine triumph, which surprised
media cynics: the Queen's portrait
in a Golden Jubilee-bedecked
Brentford window.

A golden mist:
Cuneo's Coronation
portrait.

Monarchy taken seriously:
a sketch by Annigoni for his
famous portrait has an almost
Renaissance feel.

More informal times: Michael Leonard's popular 1986 portrait of the Queen with her corgi, Spark.

Lucian Freud, the greatest portrait painter of the Queen's reign, insisted on many hours of sitting and was never known to flatter his subjects.

'I think she loves being Queen' – a senior politician. The Queen and the
Duke of Edinburgh at the Braemar Gathering in Scotland, 2008.

A military family, as well as a royal one: Prince Harry, Prince Andrew,
the Queen, the Duke of Edinburgh and Prince Edward watch an RAF flypast
to commemorate the sixtieth anniversary of the end of World War II, 2005.

Above Touchy-feely with new friends: Michelle Obama gets personal with the Queen, 2009.

Above, right One of the most significant and moving visits of her long reign: the Queen with the Irish President, Mary McAleese in Dublin, 2011.

Right All families have troubles; but families mend and grow: the Queen watched by Kate Middleton, the Duchess of Cambridge, at the Garter Ceremony in 2011.

But what does she think of us?

else, there are few white Christians as sympathetic to Islam as Prince Charles himself.

All of which is speculation, because Diana died. Her death on 31 August 1997 shook the British so hard that many became very slightly unhinged. It was a death of such a bright, vivid life; it happened in such a grisly way; and it came so much out of the blue, that it produced anger as well as shock. If anyone was a proper target for the anger, it was the media who had made such a lucrative market in Diana pictures that photographers would do almost anything to get them. Indeed, in the immediate aftermath, photographers were spat on and their editors abused. But it is only a short step from blaming the newspapers to blaming the people who buy them for just those kind of stories; and that means millions of the very people who were angriest. Much the same could be said about phone-hacking.

Psychologically, it was therefore unsurprising that the anger was turned towards a different target. Who had been Diana's enemies in life? Who had stripped her of her royal title? Who had she repeatedly complained of as cold and heartless? The Queen and the Duke of Edinburgh had tried to save their son's marriage. So had the Queen Mother. Diana was hardly guilt-less. No matter. In a remarkably short space of time the Queen herself became the focus of anger. This was something that had never happened in her reign – not even when she had made mistakes, such as not going early to the scene of the Aberfan disaster. We should not overstate this. The anger was felt by a lot of people, who expressed it right in the centre of London to the world's media, who were themselves looking to shift any blame. But away from the flower-bedecked streets, calmer and kinder judgements were being made.

For a while, however, the public mood felt mutinous. The queen of people's hearts had become the anti-queen of the streets. The real Queen was at Balmoral with her husband and their grandsons during those first days. They had taken the children for the Sunday church service at Crathie as usual and the whole inner core of the royal family gathered to help. The boys were talked to, and walked with, and kept well away from television, newspaper or radio reports that would have upset them. Princess Anne was particularly helpful but so was the Duke. A cocoon was put around the grief-stricken children. Throughout her adult life, the Queen had had to put up with people criticizing her for not being an active enough parent. Her critics were often the same people who would have criticized her had she failed to carry out the full round of British and Commonwealth duties. Now she was ignoring media-stoked demands for her presence in London, to join in a kind of state wake, so that she could concentrate on her grandchildren. What was the point of leaving Scotland to go to a closed Palace behind shuttered windows, she asked rather sharply, when she could be looking after the boys?

It should be said that, according to her family, the Queen had taken with great enthusiasm to the role of grandmother, one which had become more important because of the break-down in her oldest son's marriage. Like many others she missed the children who had fled the turreted nest. Princess Anne says of her mother that, having been at the stage 'when you think you can't get the children out of the house quickly enough . . . you suddenly realize how quiet it is, and I think she quite missed that part of having children, so the grand-children were very much enjoyed, all of them'. They, and the various nieces and nephews, had delighted in the same places the Queen had loved as a child and had taken longer than her own children to distinguish between the Queen and the woman who was their grandmother. (Now, said Princess Anne, herself a recent grandmother, the Queen is 'curious and delighted' to have a great granddaughter, 'but I think it may be a little while before we discover what it means'.)

Down in London in 1997 Blair and his media team were watching with alarm. Blair wrote: 'The outpouring of grief was turning into a mass movement for change. It was a moment of supreme national articulation and it was menacing for the royal family. I don't know what would have happened if they had just kept going as before. Possibly nothing, but in the eye of that storm, unpredictable and unnerving as it was, I couldn't be sure.'[8] That is quite something: a prime minister who half-thought the monarchy itself was tottering. Blair identified himself emotionally with people who, when things were done by the book, 'couldn't give a damn about "the book" . . . in fact, thought "the book" had in part produced the chain of events that led to Diana's death . . . Public anger was turning towards the royal family.' Meanwhile the Queen's private secretaries, Fellowes and Janvrin, were in close touch with Blair's Downing Street office as they arranged for Diana's body to be brought back and began to discuss funeral arrangements. During long phone calls about how to arrange a suitable service at Westminster Abbey and what the role of Princes William and Harry should be, the Duke was angrily protective of the boys' interests.

Buckingham Palace still expresses private irritation at the behaviour of Prince Charles's spokesman at the time, Mark Bolland, who seemed to the Queen's advisers to be briefing that, had it not been for the Prince of Wales, there would have been no appropriate or special arrangements made. By then there had been quite a history of bickering and icy silences between the rival courts. In fact it was the Queen's team who arranged a special flight to bring back Diana's body and who quickly realized that any notion held by the Spencers that this might be a limited, private funeral was impractical. Things seemed to be under control. Lord Charteris, that wise old hand, called up his successor, Robin Janvrin, to congratulate him: 'You're getting this about right.' It was not so. The advisers were slow to grasp the scale of public anger. Alastair Campbell, always alert to a new mood in the media, telephoned the Palace to warn: 'I don't know what those journalists are up to but it's something to do with the flagpole.' This was a small but telling issue. Protocol and long tradition spoke with one voice. Only the Queen's flag, the Royal Standard, flew over Buckingham Palace; and then only when the Queen was there. (It shoots up as she passes through the gates, a ritual of careful observation and timing conducted by the Queen's Flag Sergeant, a soldier from the Household Cavalry.) When she was not there, no flag flew. The Royal Standard never flew at half mast – or only in theory, if a dead monarch was in the Palace, and the new one was not yet present. The Union flag was not flown.

This made no allowance for the demands of public grief, 1997-style, given focus by television reports and provocative newspaper headlines. The naked flagpole was held to symbolize a chilly monarch. Tear up the stuffy protocol, ordered the *Sun*. Eventually the Queen asked that the Union flag should go up, and fly at half mast: thus a new tradition has been set, for it flies generally there now, when the Queen is away, and is lowered as a mark of mourning, as for instance after the Twin Towers attacks in New York. If you want an illustration of the speed with which the House of Windsor can change tradition to fit a mood, look no further. As huge crowds gathered from Westminster to Buckingham Palace, and at Kensington Palace too, leaving bundles of cellophane-wrapped flowers, impromptu shrines, candles, teddy bears and handwritten cards, courtiers watched and waited. These were strange, strange days. Sober-looking men who had queued for hours to sign the condolence book at St James's Palace reported that Diana was 'appearing' in a painting of King Charles I. Coachloads of people were arriving from all over the country and simply camping out. An undercurrent of hysteria showed itself in the raw and weeping faces and expressions of anger.

One of the Queen's advisers remembered the sound of the plastic wrapping on the flowers outside rattling in the wind at night; 'it was the most sinister noise'. Another returned from holiday to help and found 'the nearest to a revolutionary atmosphere that I have ever witnessed. The silence of this extraordinary crowd milling around Buckingham Palace was dreadful. It was a difficult time internally at Buckingham Palace, and a terrible time outside it.' Tony Blair had himself made a pitch-perfect emotional television speech on his way to church at Trimdon in his constituency: 'She was the People's Princess and that is how she will stay, how she will remain in our hearts and our memories for ever.' But New Labour did nothing except try to help. At this critical moment, there seems to have been no whiff of republicanism from Number Ten. Today courtiers remain grateful, including to the controversial Campbell. 'It was no part of his job to defend the royal family,' says one.

In his autobiography, Blair recounts a strange scene, the last time he had met Diana, when she had come to Chequers, the prime minister's country house, in July 1997. Blair had invited her to see what formal role she could play for his 'new Britain' – wary he might have been, but he was still enthralled and wanted some of the Diana stardust to rub off. She brought Prince William, and the heir to the throne was obliged to play football with the police, staff and Blair family on the back lawn. 'Poor bloke,' reflected Blair, 'I think he wondered what on earth she had brought him for and he didn't much want to play football but, like a good sport, he did.' Meanwhile, Blair and Diana had walked alone in the grounds while he challenged her about Dodi al-Fayed, whom he had not met but felt 'uneasy' about. Their conversation was in parts uncomfortable, but the visit had ended warmly. It is a rare glimpse of the role that Diana might have been edging towards had she lived and it puts Blair's Trimdon tribute in a slightly different light. Blair used 'the people's' in other descriptions too and clearly felt a strong sense of identification with a celebrity being hunted by media critics. Either you attempt to feed the beast, as he put it, or the beast eats you.

Courtiers were watching from inside Buckingham Palace as the Queen, the Duke and the young princes arrived from Scotland. From upper windows they could see the scene: 'As the Queen came down in a car you could hear the crowd beginning to clap, and it was a bit ragged at first, and then it became warmer.' When the Queen and Duke came inside they were talking about the crowd and the flowers, like anyone else, remarking on the strangeness of the scene and what seemed like so many 'Daily Express readers' – the heart of traditional Middle England royalism, on the march. Almost as soon as the Queen was back, the mood shifted again. A girl had come forward with flowers as she walked through Kensington Palace. 'Are these for Diana?' the Queen had asked. 'No, Ma'am, for you.'

The Queen's speech on the eve of Diana's funeral was

untheatrical, calm, even cool. She does not 'emote'. No gallery
has yet been found she will play to. But she tried to *explain*
in a way she never had before. Everyone had been trying 'in
our different ways' to cope. Among feelings of shock, disbelief
and anger there was also 'concern for those who remain'.
She looked her subjects in the camera's eye: 'So what I say to
you now, as your Queen and as a grandmother, I say from
my heart.' She then did what was needed, with a graceful and
Christian tribute to Diana as 'an exceptional and gifted human
being' who in good times and bad was able to smile and laugh,
and inspire others by her kindness. There were, for those who
listened carefully, slight barbs about the millions 'who never
met her, but felt they knew her'. This was surely both an
acknowledgement of her star quality and a hint that public
Diana and private Diana were not quite the same. The Queen
had been at Balmoral, she said, where 'we have all being trying
to help William and Harry come to terms with the devastating loss that they and the rest of us have suffered'. Yet
the overwhelming message of the short speech was that the
Queen had listened, understood and was doing her best to
change: 'I for one believe that there are lessons to be drawn
from her life and from the extraordinary and moving reaction
to her death.' And she ended with a plea for unity under the
Crown. Diana's funeral was a chance 'to show the whole world
the British nation united in grief and respect'.

Since the speech, there has been a minor argument about
how much help had been given by Tony Blair and Alastair
Campbell, particularly in inserting the phrase 'and as a grandmother' after 'as your Queen'. Senior courtiers at the time
disagree among themselves about who exactly wrote what. In
an interview for this book, Blair himself finally laid the matter
to rest. For the Queen, balancing the needs of her traumatized

family and her national role had been very difficult, he said: 'She had to resolve that dilemma between family and nation in real time, very fast. And she did. There were difficulties straight after [Diana] died and there was a worry about how you deal with this publicly . . . in the end, she moved fast and very effectively.' She took the decisions herself including the words of her speech: 'Those words and that speech were her own.' They had not been ghost-written by New Labour? 'They were absolutely not written by New Labour, no. And the very personal touch was actually hers.' The speech and other small acts of acknowledgement before and after it – the flag, and then the Queen's own, unexpected, decision to bow her head in respect as Diana's coffin passed – were among the most important acts of her later reign. Diana's funeral was watched by 32 million people in Britain (as compared to 19 million watching the Coronation), second only in history – and only just – to the audience for England's 1966 World Cup victory over West Germany. No modern television event can match the effect of the Queen's Coronation, simply because television can never seem so fresh or surprising as it did in 1953 and because the optimism of a country struggling out of post-war greyness cannot be recaptured. But the impact of the funeral was similar in scale – and far bigger, of course, around a more television-saturated world, than any previous event involving the royal family. Some 3 million people are thought to have been in London in person, or on the route of the funeral cortège to the Spencer home at Althorp, with flowers strewing the route.

By that stage, after a remarkable, moving and at times bizarre funeral service, which featured a mutinous speech by Diana's brother, Earl Spencer, that enraged Prince Charles and probably angered the Queen, the cause of the Windsors recovered once more. Princes William and Harry, marching behind their mother's coffin with their father and grandfather, had touched the hearts of the British deeply enough to make the future of the dynasty, in their time, seem secure. The Queen had acknowledged the power and charisma of the most extraordinary woman the Windsors had ever brought into their family circle. Her court style had unbent enough, and in time, to prevent the sub-revolutionary atmosphere from going any further.

Had things been done differently – had the flag never flown, the funeral been done badly and the Queen declined to explain or discuss – then in all probability, despite Blair's worries, nothing dramatic would have followed. There would have been no storming of the Buckingham Palace gates, no anti-monarchy bill put before the Commons, no outward expressions of disrespect to the sovereign herself. But the institution would have taken a terrible knock. The careful opinion polling done on behalf of the Palace would have brought bad news. Prince Charles might have found himself so unpopular that he would ask himself whether he wanted to try to be King. The next time there was an argument about the cost of the Royals, it might well have gone badly for them at Westminster. It would have been rust and rubbing, abrading and verdigris: a dulling of the lustre, a souring of the taste. In our times that is how monarchies decline. So those days in 1997 were very important indeed. Yes, they were in part a collective madness, a form of national hysteria that would never have sustained for long. But they could have weakened the Queen and her cause. Instead she emerged wiser, perhaps; sadder, certainly; but stronger, too.

The People's Queen

What did all this do to the Queen's relationship with Tony Blair, who was, after Margaret Thatcher, her longest-serving and perhaps most controversial prime minister? One insider, who knows Buckingham Palace and Downing Street well, says the relationship with Blair was not especially close. On the simple 'Did he stay for drinks?' test, then, Blair, unlike Major, did not. Blair's view, he admits, was based on relative ignorance and a determination not to create any waves about the monarchy: 'I didn't know much about its internal workings. I didn't really know the Queen or the key players much at all.' Over time, however, watching the monarchy at close quarters, 'I actually became more respectful of how difficult it was for them, and how smart, particularly, the Queen was.' Perhaps inevitably, given the central importance of modernization to New Labour's sense of itself, Blair decided the Queen was a fellow soul: 'She was taking the monarchy on a slow but steady and sure journey of modernization, trying to make sense of how what is essentially a very old-fashioned concept, fitted into a world that is very fast changing and very modern.' The Queen, he decided, realized she had to have a very acute sense of the public mood, 'in times when it would be perfectly natural for people to say, we're getting rid of hereditary peers in the House of Lords, we're making all these changes to the constitution, we're very much a different type of country today than we were decades ago – so why the monarchy? She has always kept very much in her own mind, I think, the ability to answer that question.'

The Northern Ireland peace process, started by John Major and pushed forward by Tony Blair, was an early test of the

Queen's flexibility, as Blair acknowledges. 'It must have been very difficult for them because they lost family members in the IRA campaign, but they were completely and totally supportive of it.' He always wanted, he says, the peace process to culminate in the Queen visiting Dublin, and had talked about it early on. As Blair recalls in his memoirs, the Queen did telephone Blair personally to congratulate him on the peace process, 'I thought, I bet she doesn't do this often, and indeed she doesn't.' A senior civil servant at the time characterizes New Labour's attitude to the monarchy as 'complete ignorance, combined with a cheerful arrogance that they could cope with it . . . they saw themselves as modernizing people brought in to sweep away the old institutions'. There was a fascination with the US presidency and a belief that the prime minister should become a more presidential figure, which must have discomfited a constitutional monarch.

In the early Blair years, the hunger of the Palace for information about this new government reached a special intensity. 'Buckingham Palace didn't understand the Blair regime,' says a former mandarin: 'The Palace is very cut off and it was very hard for outsiders to understand, for instance, the Blair–Brown feud, that cycle of rage and fear.' The lack of understanding was a two-way problem. Ahead of the 2001 general election, then a date still very much under the prime minister's control, Alastair Campbell had been instructed to leak the timing. Civil servants reminded Blair's chief of staff, Jonathan Powell, that constitutionally the prime minister had to go to the Queen and ask for a dissolution of Parliament. There was a startled reaction before Blair hurried off to the Palace. On another occasion, early on, Blair had been reluctant to fall in with the timing of a Commonwealth heads of government meeting and the Queen confronted him: 'The

Queen can be hugely formidable if she decides to be formidable.'

Over time, the Queen impressed her personality more upon her New Labour ministers. On one now famous occasion, the overseas development secretary Clare Short apparently left her mobile phone on during an audience and it started to ring. 'Do answer it, dear,' said the Queen, 'It might be somebody important.' On another, she is thought to have gently put John Prescott, the distinctly non-monarchist deputy prime minister, in his place – quite literally. As he came over to talk to her, she dropped her voice. Straining to hear her, Prescott leaned down; and seemed to everyone present to have bowed low to his monarch. Clever. As for Blair himself, he appeared to enjoy his weekly audiences more and more, to the point where his staff began to tease him about his infatuation. One observer says: 'She has phenomenal charm and I think the charm worked.'

Blair's memoirs, however, went far further than those of any other prime minister in revealing stories about the Queen and what he thought of her. There is a larky element in them, which did not go down well at Buckingham Palace, funny though some of the tales undoubtedly are. Mr Blair discussed the routine of his visits to Balmoral, which he called 'a vivid combination of the intriguing, the surreal, and the utterly freaky. The whole culture of it was totally alien, of course, not that the royals weren't very welcoming.' He gently mocks the valets, the food and the artwork. As for the famous barbecue cooked by Prince Philip, 'This, too, is governed by convention and tradition. The royals cook, and serve the guests. They do the washing up. You think I'm joking but I'm not. They put the gloves on and stick their hands in the sink. You sit there having eaten, the Queen asks if you've finished, she stacks the plates up and goes off to the sink.' Later, Blair ruminated over the night of the millennium celebrations at the 'Dome' in east London, which did not go well. 'I don't know what Prince Philip thought of it all, but I shouldn't imagine it's printable. I suspect Her Majesty would have used different language but with the same sentiment,' the former prime minister wrote. Prince Philip had then pointed out that the acrobats overhead were working without safety harnesses and Blair had a vision of one of them falling and killing the Queen: 'I could see it all. "QUEEN KILLED BY TRAPEZE ARTIST AT DOME" ... "BLAIR ADMITS NOT ALL HAS GONE TO PLAN".'[9]

A joke, a few pages played for laughs: but it has been a long journey from the adulation of Sir Winston Churchill. As with the Queen's other prime ministers, she has kept her opinions about him very private. It was New Labour, badly briefed by the outgoing Major government, which decided not to replace the Royal Yacht and, despite Blair's help when Diana died, it is hard to find evidence of much warmth on either side. At Balmoral, when the family were gathering for afternoon tea and Blair was nowhere to be seen, his wife Cherie was asked where he was. She replied that he was probably upstairs writing his speech on the abolition of the monarchy. It was a joke perhaps a little too dangerous for that company. Since then the Prince of Wales has inveighed about political correctness and the blame culture so many times that it is entirely safe to say that he was not an unadorned admirer of New Labour. The Duke of Edinburgh once denied to the writer Gyles Brandreth that he himself was a modernizer, 'no, not for the sake of modernizing, like some bloody Blairite, not for the sake of buggering about with things', which is crisply self-explanatory.[10] Later he openly complained about the decision to scrap *Britannia*.

Blair's fantasy of a radically modernized monarchy, re-branded with Diana magic, came to nothing. Yet when one considers how many changes his government introduced which posed questions about the constitution or (like the foxhunting ban) infuriated individual members of the royal family, it is remarkable there was so little fuss. New Labour expelled all but ninety-two of the hereditary peers from the Lords in 1999, established a Scottish Parliament and a Welsh Assembly, and incorporated much more European law, as well as wanting to abolish the pound in favour of the euro. The Palace might have its opinions, but there were no circumstances in which, under the Queen, it would get into a fight with democratically elected politicians.

This was partly because, when it came to the milestones that mattered most to the royal family, Tony Blair and his ministers were helpful and supportive. There had been gloomy head-shakings about George V's Silver Jubilee and his grand-daughter's one more than four decades later. Yet again, in the winter of 2001–2 there were plenty of those who predicted a Golden Jubilee flop. The *Guardian* spoke of 'panic at the palace' about the lack of organized street parties, and said the new Buckingham Palace website 'bears a forlorn look. So far it lists a golden jubilee snooker and pool tournament in Plymouth, the planting of an oak in the village of Oxhill, Warwickshire, the planting of a jubilee garden at Cranmore infants' school in Shirley, Birmingham, the placing of small fountains all over London – and precious little else.'[11] Palace officials were quoted downplaying any thought that the numbers turning out would have any bearing on the monarchy's popularity.

This jitteriness was caused by the continuing reverberations of the disasters of the 1990s. Some feared that the 'Cool Britannia' of New Labour, though no longer fashionable, was

still a better description of how the country saw itself than
the ageing monarchy was. Nor did 2002 begin happily for the
Queen. In February she lost her sister Princess Margaret. This
was more of a blow than perhaps it seemed to outsiders. Very
different though Margaret's life had been, the two sisters kept
in close touch, talking almost daily. To this day, the Queen
carries in her handbag a worn gold box for her sweeteners
given to her by Margaret, as a small daily reminder. One of
the mourners at the funeral was the redoubtable Queen
Mother, who died six weeks later, aged 101. Neither death can
be described as unexpected, but it was a tough time for the
royal family. Her family say both women had been essential
sounding-boards for the Queen. To lose both so quickly 'was
very hard and should not be underestimated'. They would
have expected her to cope, and she did. Some Palace people
thought that in due course the Queen came to feel liberated,
finally herself as sole Queen, reaching a new phase of her life.
Prince Charles seemed particularly devastated, however, talking
more openly and emotionally about his grandmother than he
had about anyone else.

The Queen Mother's funeral obliged republicans and royal
sceptics to think again, just as the Golden Jubilee would too.
The *Guardian*, now the dominant voice of Windsor-scepticism,
ran a headline which read 'Uncertain farewell reveals a nation
divided' and its columnist Jonathan Freedland argued that the
crowds outside Buckingham Palace were thin, with the queues
to sign books of condolence almost non-existent. This was no
Diana moment. Freedland questioned the official period of
mourning, which had been cut from thirteen days to nine:
'Perhaps they anticipated the current mood and worried that
the nation's grief would not last a fortnight. But is there any
guarantee that nine days won't also come to seem excessive?'

In fact, the turnout for the funeral was huge and long lines eventually queued to pay their respects. The slowness of the country's initial reaction was perhaps a combination of lack of surprise at the news and its taking time for people to recall just how long Queen Elizabeth had served. A media spat fizzed and crackled around the event, as it would often do around royal occasions, with the *Daily Mail* leading the attack on the BBC for showing lack of respect when a newsreader announced the death wearing a burgundy tie, rather than a black one. Showing one's monarchism as fervently as possible was becoming a media-led dividing line, between allegedly the deep and patriotic on the one hand, and the shallow and meretricious on the other. It was not a division the Palace itself particularly welcomed.

The Golden Jubilee year broke records. As with the Queen's Diamond Jubilee, the only comparison could be with Victoria's Golden Jubilee, so long before that lamentations about British imperial decline seemed meaningless. The echo of the Victorian age was dimly audible, though, because the year involved an early royal visit to Jamaica, New Zealand and Australia, and then later on to Canada. There were huge crowds and despite a few protestors, including Rastafarians in Jamaica and French Canadians in Quebec, the tours showed a vast reservoir of affection for the Queen in what had once been Victoria's Empire. There were gusts of dissent, which may change the world of future British monarchs. In New Zealand the prime minister Helen Clark said the country should become a republic. In Canada, the Queen was welcomed by the deputy prime minister, John Manley, who had said that, after her reign, Canada should end its connection with the monarchy.

In Britain itself there were the now customary rituals. The

Queen addressed both Houses of Parliament, reflecting on the altered world since 1952. 'We must speak of change,' she said, 'its breadth and accelerating pace over these years . . . Change has become a constant; managing it has become an expanding discipline.' Much of her address was devoted to the themes of stability, the importance of institutions, and the nature of the British themselves – 'a moderate, pragmatic people' – which have been constants in her speeches for decades. The jubilee was an attempt to express both sides of the national character. There were the beacons, lit around the world this time, 2,002 of them; a procession with the State Coach down the Mall, where a million people crowded on the jubilee weekend, a service of thanksgiving at St Paul's, and a parade of Commonwealth costumes, and an RAF fly-past, watched by the now diminished royal family from the Buckingham Palace balcony. One of those present said he thought the Queen's expression of relief and pleasure was the genuine reaction of a fundamentally shy woman.

So far, so predictable. Even the thousands of street parties went ahead. This time, though, there was also a classical concert, the 'Prom at the Palace' in the gardens of Buckingham Palace, where 12,500 people heard the BBC symphony orchestra and chorus and a galaxy of operatic stars. It was the biggest event ever held in the gardens. More striking, there was a 'Party at the Palace' celebrating British pop, and opened by the Queen guitarist Brian May playing his version of 'God Save the Queen' from the Palace rooftops, before other veterans such as Paul McCartney, Eric Clapton and Tony Bennett played in front of the royal family and their guests. The evergreen Cliff Richard was there, too. Attempts by the Royals to get hip with the kids have not had a happy record. There is something about the conjoining of state formality and youth-centred musical exuberance that makes the well-adjusted adult cringe. The younger Windsors tend to be grouse-shooters, polo-players and military officers and this does not sit well with the music of black and adolescent revolt. But of all the gambles in taste engaged in by the Queen's advisers during the 2000s, this went off the most happily. Britain was a much more varied, knowing – even cynical – country compared with the Britain of her Silver Jubilee. But the celebrations of 2002, which had also included a major series of visits criss-crossing the country, seemed to have firmly re-established the popularity of the monarchy in general and the Queen in particular. They certainly seemed to have engaged more people and produced more enthusiasm than the secular festivities for the millennium two years earlier.

These were the start of the Queen's quieter years, when there was more looking back in affection and less embarrassing turbulence than over the previous decade. After the white water, the limpid pool. In 2006 would follow the Queen's eightieth birthday celebrations – a children's party at the Palace, fireworks, a family dinner at Kew, a thanksgiving service at St Paul's – and parties for people aged over sixty. By now, inevitably, there was more focus on the eventual succession. In February of that year, Prince Charles had taken the *Mail on Sunday* newspaper to court over the publication of extracts from his personal journals which he had circulated himself to friends, and which were politically highly embarrassing. The previous year he had married Camilla Parker Bowles in a civil ceremony at Windsor after years of speculation. She had been divorced from her husband ten years before but had endured a very difficult twilight status since Diana's death. There was much debate about whether remarriage would be acceptable for the heir and future Supreme Governor of the Church of England; though to keep her as (old, nasty word) his 'mistress' seemed worse. Charles's staff at Clarence House had been engaged in a very careful operation to introduce the idea of Camilla as, first, his 'companion' and then likely bride. Most noticed the happier demeanour of the Prince of Wales and the down-to-earth cheerfulness of Camilla. Many merely felt sorry for them, that they had not married half a lifetime before. A minority were Diana-worshippers who would never forgive Camilla for any role she might have played in the breakdown of the Prince's first marriage, and who were dourly determined she would never be Queen.

One observer says that, in Buckingham Palace, the Camilla question 'was there in the background all the time. There was a lot of private discussion with the Queen about her, and her role, and how much things could or couldn't be acknowledged.' Camilla herself became very nervous when the Queen was likely to be present, as did Prince Charles. He was, however, quietly insistent about Camilla. One senior official, contemplating a move to work for the Prince, was warned that if he was to work for the Prince of Wales he had to realize that three things were non-negotiable. One was Camilla. Another was Charles's press spokesman, Mark Bolland. The third was the prince's factotum and private fundraiser Michael Fawcett, who had formally left his service but remained influential, and was regarded with particular suspicion by Buckingham Palace. In general this was not a happy time between the rival establishments. The Queen viewed Prince Charles's extravagant behaviour, for instance when he was entertaining at Sandringham, with puzzlement and worry. The Palace read stories suggesting that, over private dinners at Highgrove,

Prince Charles was saying his mother really ought to consider abdication before too long. These were vehemently denied by Prince Charles's office but a lingering hurt remained.

The position of Camilla, a strong-minded and grounded woman, was the central question. At Buckingham Palace in the late 1990s, 'there was a very clear view that nobody should be talking about her being the future Queen or even consort.' As to remarriage, 'the Queen's view was that it was probably going to come; she thought it was probably going to be after her lifetime.' At least formally, this was Prince Charles's view too. Even before his divorce from Diana in 1996 his office had said he had no intention of remarrying, a position confirmed in 2000, when complaining about a newspaper article. Since then, the situation had become ludicrous. They were a proper couple. Camilla was living with Charles, supported by him, at Highgrove, a matter which had been publicly acknowledged through his accounts and by MPs. The situation was under-stood and accepted by both sets of children. Yet Camilla was not allowed to sit beside Prince Charles at public occasions and was not, for instance, allowed to join him for the family Christmas at Sandringham.[12] If she was present with him, the Queen was said to be acknowledging her as his mistress. If not, she was the victim of a 'royal snub'. In human terms, it was offensive and probably by the millennium, when Charles was still denying he wanted to remarry, both he and Camilla were determined this would happen.

The Queen's position was delicate and difficult. Like her mother, she had enjoyed a strong and happy marriage and firmly believed in the sanctity of marriage. As Supreme Governor of the Church of England, she would risk offending many of its members, particularly on the traditional and evangelical wings, if she condoned the remarriage of two divorcees. Yet as Queen she knew that it would be more damaging to the monarchy if Charles succeeded her unmarried, while living with Camilla. As a mother, she wanted happiness for her son. How was all this to be resolved? A slow dance began to bring Camilla more into the open. The Church of England itself started to speak out. The Archbishop of Canterbury, George Carey, pointed out that Christianity was about forgiveness and that failure was part of the human condition: 'The natural thing is that they should get married.' His successor, Rowan Williams, not only agreed but said that Prince Charles's remarriage as a committed Anglican would allow him to become the church's Supreme Governor. That removed one huge blockage. Other clerics made similarly supportive statements.

This did not mean that the couple could marry in a conventional church service, and they eventually chose what was by then a familiar route, which was to have a civil ceremony, followed by an Anglican blessing. This produced a second problem: would the marriage be legal under English law? Charles could have got round an obscure-seeming problem by remarrying in Scotland, as his sister Princess Anne had, but he wanted to be married at Windsor. The 1836 Marriage Act allowing civil marriages had specifically excluded members of the royal family and it was not at all clear that later repeals and rewritings had changed that. A long and passionate if ridiculous debate ensured. Eventually the New Labour Lord Chancellor had to intervene to declare that the government believed the marriage was entirely legal. He relied in part upon the same human rights legislation at which Prince Charles in the past had snarled so often. Laws and doctrines which had blighted the hopes of Princess Margaret and, before her, of Edward VIII, were cast away like so much waste paper.

In recent years the Queen had rarely met Camilla. In 2000
she did so at a lunch Prince Charles was giving for the birthday
of the former King Constantine of Greece, but this was
followed by reports denying that this meeting was evidence
that the Queen approved of the relationship. By the time of
the Golden Jubilee, relations had eased a lot and Mrs Parker
Bowles was being seen publicly with the Queen. In the next
few years Prince Charles's advisers at Clarence House ran a
careful media campaign to soften up the public and media to
the idea of a wedding, with choreographed joint appearances
of the couple, and much sotto voce briefing. Nothing in the
preparations for the marriage went entirely smoothly. The
official announcement was rushed out after a newspaper leak.
A plan to hold it in Windsor Castle had to be abandoned
when it became clear that this would entitle other couples to
apply to be married there too. The original timing of the wedding had to be postponed because of the death of Pope John
Paul II, whose funeral Prince Charles attended. And that rather
silly argument about the legal status of the civil ceremony
continued almost until the last moment.

The Queen warmly welcomed the marriage announcement, but on the day itself, 9 April 2005, did not attend the
civil ceremony, which had been moved from Windsor to the
town's Guildhall. This was not a snub. It was a mark of her
own strong and traditional faith and her constitutional position.
We know it was not a snub because at the celebration
afterwards the Queen made a particularly witty and emotionally frank speech. She began with a joke, solemnly explaining
that she had an important announcement to make: 'Hedgehun-
ter has won the Grand National!' She then went on, referring
to her son and new daughter-in-law and the formidable fences
faced by horses in that race: 'They have overcome Becher's

Brook and The Chair and all kinds of other terrible obstacles. They have come through and I am very proud and wish them well. My son is home and dry with the woman he loves. Welcome to the winner's enclosure.' It could hardly have been put better. These were not the words of a chilly matriarch but of a loving mother who battled all her life with the chillier demands of constitutional propriety. In turn, and particularly of late, Prince Charles has spoken with genuine warmth and emotion about his mother – and not simply as Queen but as his mother.

The marriage concluded what had been a very grim time for the Windsor dynasty, the only part of the Queen's reign when it had really seemed that the British might turn their backs on the monarchy. Because this is a family story, it is one that never ends. The gap between the Prince of Wales's office at Clarence House, with its agenda, and the offices of his parents at Buckingham Palace, has not disappeared. There have been indications that the Prince of Wales's marriage has not been quite as happy as the couple had hoped. When the announcement of Prince William's engagement to Kate Middleton was made in November 2010, Prince Charles's somewhat curt response – 'they've been practising long enough' – suggested to some friends that he worried he was about to be overshadowed again, this time not by his parents or first wife but by the next generation.

Yet important lessons flow from the successful negotiation of the 'Camilla problem' during the decade 1995–2005. First, if the weakness of monarchy as an institution is that it depends on the foibles of real families, which periodically fail, then its strength is that families can also learn, grow again, and repair themselves. Second, if the weakness of the British constitution is that it is a jumbled attic of historical offcuts, some of which remain useful while others are antiquated or downright embarrassing, then its strength is that one can rummage and pluck from it whatever one wants – a new view of an old law here, a short cut around an awkward doctrine there. And third, though the Queen is wholly serious about her role and status and the importance of precedence, she is far more flexible, adaptable and understanding than the official poker face of the British monarchy suggests.

The next political hurdle the Queen faced came with the British general election of 2010. It followed the most sulphurous and unhappy period in British politics for many years. Parliament had been shaken by a huge scandal over MPs' fiddled expenses. Eventually some would face jail. Many more decided not to stand again. Meanwhile ordinary people were struggling in an economic whirlwind caused by the incompetence of very highly paid bankers and an addiction to borrowing by both state and families. Britain's elites, in politics and business, had rarely looked so discredited.

The great banking crisis of 2008–9 had plunged the world's financial system into chaos and provoked a long period of slow or zero growth, individual national bail-outs and heartsearching – though not at that time the world recession many feared.

With uncharacteristic public bluntness, the Queen had used a visit to the London School of Economics to ask one of its economists, Luis Garicano, 'Why did no one see it coming?' She followed this by summoning the governor of the Bank of England for a private meeting. Her much reported question had been followed in June 2009 by a meeting of economists and others at the British Academy, who debated, and wrote back to the Queen that, 'In summary, Your Majesty, the failure to foresee the timing, extent and severity of the crisis and to head it off . . . was principally a failure of the collective imagination of many bright people, both in this country and internationally, to understand the risks to the system as a whole.'

The bright man whose failure was mostly blamed by voters, however, proved to be the Labour prime minister, Gordon Brown. The Queen had given him all the attention and personal respect of earlier prime ministers and warmly welcomed his two small boys to stay at Balmoral. One had wondered aloud about where all her soldiers were: she replied that she was well protected by her dogs. At the election of 6 May 2010, Mr Brown's party lost ninety-seven seats and its majority. The Conservatives under David Cameron, however, fell short of the 326 seats they would need to govern alone. The possibility of a 'hung' or indecisive result had already been much debated in Whitehall and at Buckingham Palace because the polls showed it was likely. Memorandums had been drawn up, precedents investigated. But everything hinged on the numbers and the way political leaders behaved. As in 1974 it risked the Queen being drawn into political controversy, particularly if Mr Brown tried to stay on for long, struggling to put together a coalition to keep out the Tories.

Though the Conservatives had won the most seats, 302, they did not have the automatic right to try to form a government at once. This meant Brown not only had the right but the duty to stay in office until it was clear that some stable-looking deal could be arranged. But how long was that to be? The election result showed the prime minister had lost the confidence of voters and the condition of the economy remained horribly fragile. The markets were watching. The prime minister and his team tried hard to tempt the Liberal Democrats into a deal, even offering Mr Brown's resignation as Labour leader in the autumn, though this arrangement still would not have produced an overall majority. In the dire economic circumstances of the time, it looked like an unacceptably weak basis for the hard decisions about government spending to come.

Meanwhile, Mr Cameron had made a generous-looking offer to the Lib Dem leader Nick Clegg and opened talks to form a Tory–Lib Dem coalition, founded on a compromise deal between the parties. Over a long weekend, the haggling on both sides continued, as the markets watched and waited. It was not until the following Tuesday that Brown finally resigned, in a speech of some dignity, having accepted that he could not form a stable administration. The coalition agreement, including a determination to govern for five years, which some thought undermined the Queen's traditional rights over dissolving Parliament, was agreed. The markets recovered.

Courtiers and civil servants exhaled. There had been intensive discussion about how to ensure the Queen was not under pressure to try to fire one prime minister, or to appear to favour the interests of his successor. At Downing Street Sir Gus O'Donnell, the cabinet secretary and a man who had served under successive Tory and Labour leaders, led a group of constitutional experts, alongside Jeremy Heywood, the permanent secretary there. At Buckingham Palace, the Queen's team was led by Sir Christopher Geidt, her private secretary since 2007. A former diplomat, Geidt had taken over from Robin Janvrin, now Lord Janvrin, who had had to negotiate the roughest period of the Queen's life, and he was said to see his job as smoothing the latter part of her reign. Geidt had won the Queen's strong personal confidence and was now being credited for recent successes. He and the Number Ten team worked hard on different scenarios, the constitutional implications of different voting figures, and the circumstances in which it would be necessary to call yet another – no doubt highly unpopular and economically damaging – general election. The press was in the mood to be highly critical of any attempt by Gordon Brown to stay in office, and the Queen could have found this a very tricky time. After it was over, she showed her gratitude with a warm and private visit to O'Donnell's team in Whitehall to thank all the civil servants in person.

In the meantime the Queen had been able to call for Mr Cameron to serve as her latest prime minister. Though a younger man, he was not entirely without royal connections. He attended Heatherdown prep school at Ascot, Berkshire, where he once played a rabbit in a production of *Toad of Toad Hall*. Prince Edward, then eleven, played the part of Mole and the Queen came to watch the performance. Cameron would be the Queen's first Old Etonian prime minister since Alec Douglas-Home in 1963 and the nineteenth to serve in the job from that school. Those who think political life will therefore be blandly smooth for the Queen are probably mistaken. The defence cuts which were a crucial part of the new chancellor George Osborne's plan to reduce the national debt faster and further than Labour would have done produced great unhappiness and argument within the military. No family as connected to the military as are the Windsors could have failed to follow rows about aircraft carriers without aircraft and fighter pilots facing redundancy. Senior military figures say privately they 'hope for and expect' discreet royal lobbying to go on.

Out of the Rapids

Friday 29 April 2011 demonstrated that the British monarchy could still put on a world-class show. The wedding of Prince William to Kate Middleton was pitch-perfect in almost every way, outclassing even that of his mother and father. Whereas the Charles-and-Di nuptials in July 1981 had been a fairy-tale event featuring an uneasy man and a very young, inexperienced girl at its centre, nearly thirty years on there was more experience and also a slight swagger of informality. Instead of grand St Paul's and a long procession through London, Charles and Diana's elder son was married at a Westminster Abbey that had been decorated with lines of trees. Prince William had intervened directly in the planning of the wedding. After the buzz of the announcement, 'Obviously very excited and happy about it all, I walked into the first meeting and literally got presented with a list of 777 names, and I looked at it and there wasn't one person on there I knew and it brought a sort of sense of fear and dread over what was going to happen, and who was going to start running the whole day.' So he decided to start again, 'and I rang my grandmother up for some clarification on the issue and duly got told that it was ridiculous and I should start with my own friends.' There was then a debate about which uniform he should wear, but this time the Queen took a traditionalist stance: 'My grandmother very much decided that the red tunic was very smart and the appropriate one to wear for the day, so I . . . did as I was told.' Overall, in the 'chaos and confusion' before the wedding, Prince William found the Queen gentle and calming: 'her lack of chaos and the lack of panic around her was extremely helpful.'

He describes himself and his wife as 'very traditional' but

said they wanted 'our own personal twist' on the wedding: 'we wanted, basically, everyone to share in our happiness, as anyone does at anyone's wedding day; but it obviously had to be on a slightly bigger scale.' The understatement of the year, perhaps; but he had been mainly worried that his father's car would stall on the Mall as he left the Palace. That was cheekily confirmed by Prince Harry: 'I think William's been trying to drive that car for ages, and the couple of times he has driven it at home, he's stalled it. It is a very difficult car to drive – combined with the fact that he can't drive – but to make it even harder, he obviously had his spurs on, which was very entertaining to see him . . .' And Prince Harry made juddering, car-stalling noises, with a grin. He himself had been 'absolutely terrified' at the wedding: 'I was just as nervous as William. The uniforms we were in were hot, to say the least, so . . . throughout the majority of the service I was sweating, which wasn't much fun.' Mainly, though, he was worried about the ring, which as best man was his responsibility. Dress uniforms, however, come without pockets. Harry had slipped it into his cuff and was half-convinced it would fall out: 'So I was having to check to make sure it was there, without making it obvious.' As to the uniforms, 'my grandmother, the Queen, put us both back in our boxes and specifically told William exactly what she wanted him to wear, and quite rightly so.' The newly minted Duke of Cambridge drove his Duchess away from Buckingham Palace himself, just the two of them in Prince Charles's green Aston-Martin, which had been decorated with an L-plate and various slogans by his younger brother Prince Harry. It is hard to imagine his father doing something so relaxed. (But then it is also hard to imagine Harry's father 'goosing' Kate's younger sister Pippa on the balcony of Buckingham Palace during an RAF fly-past, either.)

As with that earlier wedding, which had been one of the most popular events of the early 1980s, huge numbers of people had poured into central London. Many had camped out overnight for the best spots, just as people had done for the Coronation in 1953 and other royal spectaculars. Despite dire warnings of rain and a cold start to the day, it turned out fine and – apart from an errant Guardsman's horse bolting and a verger caught by the cameras turning cartwheels down Westminster Abbey after the guests had left – everything went according to plan. The police were criticized for arresting a handful of anarchists and protestors ahead of time, but given the very real security risks from Irish republican extremists and others, they could be forgiven as they congratulated themselves on the flawless marshalling of a million people.

With a bigger and better-connected global audience, their wedding was seen by almost three times as many people as had watched Charles and Diana's, some 2.4 billion rather than 750 million. These figures are estimates and must be taken cautiously but, if they are true, this means that around a third of the world's population watched the wedding. In the United States, some 22 million watched the main channels, fewer than had watched the drama of Diana's funeral, though the figure does not include all those – presumably a lot – who watched online. Like Manchester United, 'Mon United' is one of the very few British brands which are still instantly recognized around the world. These royal events are therefore rare national showcases. They are how the British, like it or not, are viewed in China, California and Chile. What message was being sent by this twenty-first-century monarchy? It showed that London could put on and manage a highly sophisticated and complex public event with no slips, and a certain amount of wit, a year before the Olympics. It was filmic. The richly coloured uniforms of the male Windsors and the glamorous, British-made dresses of the bride and her new family added to the Harry Potter effect of swooping television shots in the gothic, leafy and stained-glass-illuminated Abbey. This was hardly an image of the egalitarian, technocratic nation New Labour had hoped for, but had failed to deliver. Nor, however, was it an image of decline or self-doubt.

The British audience on mainstream television peaked at 24.5 million, mostly watching the BBC, while around the country 5,500 roads had been closed for street parties, by now a firm tradition. The great British composer Arnold Bax once told his countrymen they should try everything once, 'except incest and folk-dancing'. Ignoring half of his warning, many streets were filled with Morris dancers and inebriated English people introducing themselves to their neighbours and trying Scottish reels. The day could be summed up as one of grand pageantry, but pageantry with a knowing smile. In the crowds many people wore a T-shirt reading 'Thanks for the Day Off'. Even the *Guardian* cleared most of its news pages for lavish coverage.

This was without doubt a very good day for the Windsors, which showed that the British reacted as enthusiastically as ever to a happy ending and the prospect of a successfully self-regenerating dynasty. Perhaps the only sour note was that neither of the last two Labour prime ministers, Tony Blair or Gordon Brown, had been invited, though all living Conservative ones had been. The excuse, which was that they were not members of the Order of the Garter, seemed thin and some muttered that it was quiet revenge by Clarence House for Labour's banning of foxhunting and the failure to order a new

Royal Yacht. It probably was, instead, a genuine slip-up by Buckingham Palace. At any rate, some found it churlish, given Blair's help after Diana's death.

More generally, Charles and Diana's story had been such a roller-coaster for the monarchy, starting so spectacularly and ending so badly, that one of the questions had been how this wedding would avoid too many obvious echoes of theirs. The real difference, it turned out, was not in the choice of one location over another, but in the demeanour of the stars of the show themselves. Prince William was smiling sheepishly but clearly enjoying himself; Kate Middleton was poised and self-assured; they chatted quietly at key moments about how lucky they were. As they left the Abbey the newly created Duke of Cambridge told his Duchess, 'It was amazing, amazing. I am so proud you're my wife.' Around them Prince Harry grinned and muttered encouragement. These were people at ease in their skins, the same age, who had met at what they would call 'Uni' and who had lived together – in what used to be called Sin but is now known as North Wales. They had split up and made up. At twenty-nine, Kate Middleton was old for a royal bride – nearly a decade older than Diana had been – and she would face the inevitable demands to produce an heir quickly. But that extra experience of life is a golden treasure, and she seems already to have the toughness, savoir-vivre and staying power that Diana Spencer had struggled to find.

In retrospect, the earlier wedding seemed like a naïve explosion of frenetic patriotism at what had been, admittedly, a very tough time for Britain. The journalist Ian Jack reminded *Guardian* readers that in 1981 'British pits still employed a quarter of a million miners, ships still went down the slipways of several dozen British shipyards, the Rolls-Royces that purred to the front doors of St Paul's still had British engines' and yet, at the same time, 'Imprisoned IRA men were dying on hunger strike, urban rioting had erupted in several English cities, 2.5 million people (and rising) were on the dole.' The Falklands war, the revival of the economy and the boom years of Thatcherism were still ahead. 'Di-mania' had come like sunshine in midwinter and, as now seems clear (but was less obvious then), far too great a burden of promise and hope was loaded onto frail shoulders. Then, the political divisions in Britain were more bitter and there was an angrier anti-royal-wedding, republican reaction, with left-wingers taking boats to France to avoid the coverage and more media mockery.

By 2011, Britain still faced plenty of problems. In some respects, they had got worse. With the spending cuts to pay off a too-large national debt hanging over many people, and the complicated war in Afghanistan dragging on, nobody could say these were easy times. But a different Conservative prime minister, David Cameron, was at a peak of his authority. Republican hostility to the spectacle of the wedding was so muted as to be almost invisible. We should not assume any easy division between royalist and conservative on one side, and left-wing and republican on the other. The crowds in London were much more than the hard-core of royalist sightseers. Overall, they seemed relatively young, and from every background. With different banners, many could have been at a summer rock festival or even on a march of trade unionists against the coalition cuts. Many expressed pleasure that a middle-class woman had been welcomed into the Windsor embrace and noted the Queen's expressions of delight as she returned to Buckingham Palace. In an unscientific survey by the author, asked whether one day an Asian or black member of the royal family was possible, most in the crowd replied with a puzzled shrug and a 'Why not?' or 'Of course'.

Kate Middleton was not, as we have seen, the first commoner in modern times to join the core monarchy. Lady Elizabeth Bowes Lyon and Lady Diana Spencer had been, strictly speaking, commoners, since they did not have royal blood. But they were not what most Britons would call commoners. Kate and her parents were genuinely middle-class. They had gone through a long period of testing and apprenticeship in the odd world of royalty, managing to say or do nothing embarrassing despite teasing from twits and snobs. The Middletons were millionaires, but self-made ones who had built up a mail-order business for children's parties. Kate's father had been a flight despatcher and her mother, the daughter of a shop assistant, had been an air hostess. Her mother's family was traced back to coalminers who had worked in pits owned by the Bowes Lyons, the Queen Mother's family. Though Kate had been educated at a private boarding school, Marlborough, and was doughtily learning to shoot, stalk and watch polo matches, her world was that of the aspirational, successful middle, not of landowners. She and her mother were the kind of women millions of other British women could identify with. Girls in the crowd waving signs reading 'Harry's mine' were (mostly) joking but could go home afterwards and feel the joke was not absurd.

The 2011 wedding was only one part of a story, which has much longer to run. But it contained messages and dilemmas, which Prince William will need to think about during what will presumably be a long apprenticeship before he becomes King. The British are now less class-conscious than ever before and far less formal. Negotiating the right balance between the reserve that royal mystique depends on and the openness that people (not just the media) expect has been difficult for his grandmother and it will be difficult for him. What jokes are acceptable? How does he dress? Which television programmes, if any, does he agree to appear on? Should he give interviews to newspapers? Can he go on holiday anywhere other than secure royal estates or remote islands? After he finishes his career as an RAF helicopter search-and-rescue pilot, where will he make his home and how much royal work will he take on in the early years, when with luck he will have a young family to take care of? These are old questions but they never go away, and the answers slowly and subtly change, generation by generation.

Prince William's education at Eton and St Andrews University may have been in some respects more 'normal' than his father's or grandfather's. With his younger brother, he has been a regular at elite London nightclubs and has had a circle of well-off friends that gives him security and support beyond 'the Firm'. It still puts him inside an elite group. At his wedding many of the guests, including the prime minister and the London mayor, had been at his old school; so had some of the commentators describing the event. The future king's wife went to Marlborough school; so did the prime minister's wife. None of this need mean very much at all, so long as care is taken to avoid the impression of a closed ruling class, with morning coats, identical accents and similar views. That would undo the Queen's hard work to ensure she is seen as everybody's monarch – certainly not classless but certainly not politically tilted either.

The good news is that Prince William has so far showed a sure touch and is married to a woman who, having faced a long ordeal by newspaper columnist, starting with the 'Waity Katy' jibes earlier in the relationship, is tougher and more street-wise than her predecessors. Some who know him have said that below the surface of smiling normality, Prince William remains coldly angry about the role played in his mother's death by the media. If so, who can fail to sympathize? There are no other obvious scapegoats for what happened. His father looked after him and his brother warmly and well after her death. Charles and his sons now seem to have a good, mutually micky-taking relationship and Prince William seems to be genuinely pleased that his father found warmth and support from Camilla. So far as the press is concerned, in the past it has been William calming his father down, rather than the reverse. At the ski resort of Klosters in 2005, unaware of the proximity of microphones, Prince Charles had conducted the traditional photo-call with a murmured commentary: 'I hate doing this . . . I hate these people . . .' and, observing Nicholas Witchell, the BBC royal correspondent: 'These bloody people. I can't bear that man. I mean, he's so awful, he really is.' It was his son who urged him to keep smiling and attempted to lighten the mood.

The Duke of Edinburgh was a more open, optimistic man before feeling himself mauled and misunderstood by journalists and closing off. The Prince of Wales is said by friends to have been a funny, loving, open character before hitting a wall of media hostility, and again closing off. The question is, can the same pattern be avoided a third time? Given the appalling blow of his mother's death, at such a vulnerable stage in Prince William's life and in the eye-scorching glare of global publicity, he seems to have emerged as an astonishingly balanced man. Yet part of the reason for that must be the love and care of a grandfather and father, both of whom have been demonized by sections of the press and public. So 'balanced' and 'happy about the media' are likely to be two very different things.

In 2005 Prince William and Prince Harry had had their

mobile phone inboxes hacked into by a private investigator working for Rupert Murdoch's *News of the World*. They were hardly alone: the story of the illegal hacking of phones covered hundreds, perhaps thousands, of targets, including a thirteen-year-old murdered girl, Milly Dowler, the bereaved relatives of victims of the London bombings of 7 July 2005, as well as numerous politicians and celebrities. It pushed Murdoch into closing his 168-year-old Sunday newspaper, which for much of its life had been the biggest-selling paper in Britain. As public revulsion exploded, the scandal rocked the entire Murdoch empire, embracing some of the journalists and titles which had over the years most infuriated the Royals. The fear of being eavesdropped, entrapped or betrayed runs deep in the Windsor family and most of its senior members have been conned or caught out at some time. Greedy or credulous junior Royals had been humiliated publicly and secrets spilled from the highest levels. Even police protection officers upon whom the Windsors depend so heavily have been drawn into the web of suspicion.

Since any senior member of the British monarchy has to live part of his or her life in the public eye, this is not a problem that can be shrugged off. But it is not a problem, either, for Prince William alone. What happened to the Duke of Edinburgh and Prince Charles – the spite and jeering, rather than the reporting – not only did them damage but damaged the monarchy. It made them, and thus the monarchy as an institution, less optimistic and more inflexible. If the British value the monarchy, as they do, then the media grandees who set the tone of some of the coverage at least (Twitter and the blogosphere have democratized much of it) must ask themselves whether they are making the country a better or worse place by hounding a future king. 'Hounding?' the reader might ask, 'Who is hounding Prince William? Are not he and Kate the most popular Royals of all?' Yes, they are. But if the twentieth-century history of the British monarchy is any guide at all, the mood will change sometime, and harder times will follow. Public fury about the behaviour of some journalists and newspaper executives in 2011 may bring to an end the free-for-all behaviour of the past few decades. After the monarchy, the City and Parliament, newspapers themselves have become the latest target of pitiless and unforgiving scrutiny. Painful as it is, this may simply be what democracy feels like in our times. Deference, and a belief in the virtues of privacy and reticence, will not return to make life easier for future kings and queens. And if Prince William has not been warned about that already by his father and grandfather, it would be a great surprise.

The Good Life

It has been a good life. The Queen has moved among beautiful places and interesting people and always known that she was here for a purpose. Almost every year, season by season, almost exactly the same things must be done, said and performed – Garter days, Maundy services, ambassadors retiring, prime ministers and civil servants to be seen, hospital wings to be opened and Commonwealth visits to be retraced. It is a public life of huge predictability and minimal spontaneity. Alongside, it has been a private life with a lot of fun and warmth as well as the odd disaster. She has been an outdoor woman who has bred racehorses, gossiped with close friends, walked, shot and ridden, and been amused, as well as alarmed, by her family.

In her eighties she still rides, still stoutly refusing to wear a helmet: her daughter points out that for this to happen, someone would have to be brave enough to suggest to the Queen that she rides unsafely enough to need to. As the Princess Royal puts it, 'That's a difficult one to get past.' For the Queen, horses have been a refuge because they don't know she is the Queen. They are no respecter of rank, only of ability. The Queen and her sister were brought up to tack their horses and untack them, and brush them and pick stones from their hoofs. The Queen's oldest friends remember horse games from the start of her life. One, Margaret Rhodes, has written: 'We cavorted endlessly as horses, which was her idea. We galloped round and round. We were horses of every kind: carthorses, racehorses and circus horses. We spent a lot of time as circus horses and it was obligatory to neigh.'[13] As a girl, her rooms were full of toy horses.

None of that now, of course. But she keeps in her head detailed information about the bloodlines of racehorses that even professional trainers need to check in books. Sadly because of a lost horseshoe, Carlton House, her much fancied runner in the 2011 Epsom Derby (the only Classic she has never won), finished third; but life always has to offer further challenges. Her husband at ninety still drives four-in-hand carriages with verve, which would be a dangerous sport even for a much younger man. She no longer stalks or shoots, but she takes a great interest in that too, padding by evening into the pantries at Balmoral or Sandringham to check what has been killed.

She stays on top of her papers. Is that fun? Hardly; but the Queen still expresses a great interest in the latest scandals and gossip from Westminster. Former civil servants talk when they retire of the pain of 'information withdrawal'. With 'dine and sleeps' at the palaces, and the constant comings and goings of well-informed people, never mind those secret papers, the Queen has never experienced that. She has been looking down from the top of the mast at the whole ship of state. Yes, in obvious ways she has been out of touch with daily realities, swaddled by the routine of court life, the constitutional job and the scale of the buildings she lives in. Yet by touring and talking endlessly to a wider cross-section of people than most politicians or journalists ever meet, she is remarkably well informed. And she has done her share of sneaking out, sometimes it is said in an elderly, anonymous-looking brown car, chauffeured by that slightly wild driver, her husband. She may not carry the money with her head on it, but she keeps a close personal eye on royal budgets, the salaries and daily running costs of the monarchy. She has seen the effects of family break-up at close quarters – rage, abuse, sorrow, regret. So she isn't swaddled, really. In private she can be spontaneously warm, but she never forgets her destiny and when she needs it she has a terrifyingly expressionless stare that could halt a tank at twenty paces.

Long ago, John Selden, one of the leaders of the other side during the great Crown-versus-Parliament confrontation of the seventeenth century, observed that a monarch was a thing people made 'for quietness sake'. Politically, the Queen has shown there is truth there. Despite economic turmoil, overseas war and terrorist violence, her reign has seen no dramatic breakdown of the political order: switches from left to right, from radical to consensual, have happened with almost boring simplicity.

Critics of monarchy might say that this is precisely the problem. During the Queen's reign, Britain's power in the world, her ability to make things, her productive energy, have declined. Maybe a less stable system would have allowed sharper turns. Perhaps the British needed a bigger shock than they got in the second half of the twentieth century. And perhaps as a buffer, a reassurance-institution, the monarchy contributed to British complacency. This is a plausible criticism. The trouble is that it cannot be proved or disproved. Some countries with monarchies – such as Spain, or Japan – have undergone far bigger shocks than most republics. On the other side, it can hardly be said that key republics such as the United States have been somehow less stable. (The closest rival to Britain, France, has chosen to have the form of a republic hiding the reality of something close to intermittent but absolute monarchy. And if anyone thinks republicanism is a cheap option, they should scan the chateaux, holiday homes, guards of honour, aircraft, wine cellars and army of truculent chefs required to keep the President of the Republic in his comfortable splendour.)

The Queen has certainly thought about all this. She has hinted in speeches over the years that she takes seriously the criticism, as well as the applause, which monarchy attracts. She has personally challenged policy makers about Britain's decline both economically and as a world power. Closer to home, in family discussions several times a year she has over-seen the corporate strategy of 'the Firm', as the Windsor dynasty calls itself. She changes. Her voice has changed mark-edly over the years, becoming less glass-pingingly 1950s, if still 'upper'. She has ditched quite a lot of royal tradition, from 'the Season' to the once inflexible insistence on curtseys and bows. She stopped her children curtseying to her back in the 1960s. She and her husband are well used to being greeted by a democratically fixed eye and an outstretched hand.

Accepting the need for constant change is firmly rooted in the family. Even in his sixties, Prince Charles, the most

conservative senior Royal since his grandfather died, is a restless man, scratching away at the meaning of his life. His
son, Prince William, appears to be what royal insiders fondly
call The Natural – more in touch than his grandmother, less
haunted than his father, and with a reasonably level temperament. By taking into the family its first middle-class recruit he
is continuing the pattern of restitching the monarchy into the
changing social fabric of Britain – the Windsor knit.

In the Queen's lifetime, an Empire has become a Commonwealth; a military monarchy has watched the radical slimming
and shrinking of Britain's military forces; an aristocratic system
has been taxed and legislated out of existence; a firmly Anglican
Christian monarchy has had to adapt to a multi-faith and partly
atheist country; a 'family monarchy' insisting on its role as
upholders of morality has been hijacked by adultery and break-
up; and Royals brought up to show no emotion in public
have struggled to adapt themselves to an exhibitionist, emoting,
celebrity-crowded culture. Yet bizarrely the British monarchy
has emerged from all this not shredded and diminished, but
strengthened. 'The Royals' have been laughed at, dismissed,
harangued, lectured and sometimes even ignored; but under
the Queen, they have always bounced back.

Is she the last of her kind? It is hard to imagine another
monarch lasting so long on the throne of an important country
that has changed as drastically as Britain has. Her life spans
the lost and in many ways unhappy inter-war years of jazz,
depression and empire; the titanic struggle which nearly saw
democracy capsized and fascism triumph; and the decades of
growing material plenty, punctuated by national nervous breakdown. Her reign has lasted through international crises, from
nuclear threat, Suez and Vietnam, to Iraq and the 'war on
terror'. When crowned by the Archbishop of Canterbury, he

said: 'The Lord give you faithful Parliaments and quiet Realms; sure defence against all enemies; fruitful lands and a prosperous industry; wise counsellors and upright magistrates; leaders of integrity in learning and labour; a devout, learned and useful clergy; honest, peaceable, and dutiful citizens.' Over sixty years, she may at times have wondered how hard the Lord was listening. She has had to make the most of the politicians, clergy and citizens on offer.

The year 2012 marks the Queen's Diamond Jubilee. The British are good at looking back. Perhaps a little too good. Nostalgia is the vice of an old nation. Yet the jubilee does allow stock-taking of a useful kind. Britain has been strongly marked by monarchy. Without the Queen, that odd alliance of fifty-four countries – rich and poor, democracies and despotisms – known as the Commonwealth would probably not exist. Without the survival of her dynasty, the Windsors, there would be no slightly mysterious 'Crown' powers used by the British state. It is true that monarchies exist all round the world, from absolute ones in the Arab world to informal family ones in Scandinavia or Spain. But the British monarchy, in its relative wealth and splendour, and its continuing attachment to an important nation, makes Britain a slight oddity among her natural allies and partners – the republics of the United States, France, Germany, India and Pakistan, never mind China, Brazil and Russia.

If we have lived through an American century, then it must have been a republican century too. Passionate royalists play what feels like a trump card, by pointing out various dunderheaded or merely controversial politicians who might have been elected president instead. Would we have been better off with X or Y? We may fantasize about ideal presidents. Alan Bennett, who has written so well about the Queen? Helen

Mirren or Judi Dench, who have played Queens? We would not get them, though. We would have had a failed politician, whom at least half the nation cordially loathed. The British president would be a man or woman also who would soon return to civilian life – to join the board of a bank, perhaps, or travel the world charging £50,000 a time for speeches to conferences of plastics manufacturers. We would know. It would not feel the same.

A fair account of the Queen is likely to end up putting her case, and therefore a case for monarchy. You would have to have an elephant-hide layer of republican resentment to resist. But this author's overwhelming belief is that the question – good thing, or bad thing? – is itself pointless. The scale of reinvention required to turn a monarchy into a republic is only likely after a shattering break with the past. The United States was the exception, as a new nation. France, Russia, Germany and China became republics because of some shattering trauma, involving social collapse and revolution. Since no sane person would wish one-thousandth of such a trauma on a stable country, it follows that republicanism in today's Britain is a sideshow, an intellectually respectable but theoretical position. The monarchy may fall. A future King may make such bad decisions, or have such bad luck, that an infuriated country rises up, tears down the state, and insists on a clean break. But if we lose the monarchy the British will have much worse to worry about at the time. Countries come with history attached, good and bad. What matters is what they make of it. Britain has a monarchy and this means, for most of our lifetimes, we have had Queen Elizabeth II as a kind of mysterious, half-seen shadow-relative of us all.

The British monarchy could yet be radically curtailed. That would happen if a future monarch put himself at the centre of political argument, and then lost it. (Though winning the argument could be just as dangerous.) Britain might then move to the normal position of drawing up a constitution, which formally limited the Crown's existence to a few pages of legalese. Parliament could simply take away the traditional lands and wealth which remain as the Crown Estate. Politicians could easily tax the Windsors in such a way that, within a short space of time, they would find themselves severely reduced. The British monarchy has been impressive and useful because it has been popularly supported – and mostly more popular than the elected government of the day. That has been possible because of its human popularity, and because it is not the government of the day.

For monarchy goes on by acts of individual willpower and choice. Nostalgia makes us very ready to think that 'it' was always like that. Peering a little closer, it was not. From the OBE to the Duke of Edinburgh's Award Scheme, the 'D of E'; from Trooping the Colour to Facebook and Twitter, the Windsors are always on the move. The Queen's Official Birthday, when Trooping the Colour takes place and an Honours List is published, dates back only to her father's reign. The Maundy Service, so ancient, so cobwebbed by medieval history, was revived by her grandfather as long ago as – 1932. Garter Day at Windsor, a splendid ceremony featuring the Knights in their ostrich and heron plumes and swaying blue mantles, is as gorgeous a piece of ceremonial as one is likely to see. It does indeed go back to the reign of Edward III of England when in 1348 he initiated days of feasting and praying for this new order of chivalry. Actually, though, in its current form, after a very long break, it goes back only to the immediate aftermath of the Second World War, when it was revived by the Queen's father. And as the historian David

Starkey has written, the mass investitures, cramming the Buckingham Palace ballroom, 'are the most important and characteristic ceremonies of Elizabeth's monarchy. And they are without any historical roots whatever further back than the Windsor monarchy.'[14] Reinventing tradition is a key tactic of the British monarchy.

She thinks about it. She rethinks about it. When the Queen spoke to the meeting of the Mothers' Union at Central Hall, Westminster in October 1949, she warned against an age of growing self-indulgence, materialism and falling moral standards. Yes, there would be unhappy marriages and there was a shortage of housing for newly-weds, she conceded: 'But when we see around us the havoc that has been wrought, above all among the children, by the break-up of homes, we can have no doubt that divorce and separation are responsible for some of the darkest evils in our society today.' The relationships of husbands and wives were permanent and they ought to bring up their children as Christians, without worrying about being thought priggish; it was important to show disapproval of what was wrong.

This was a speech made in the aftermath of a war that had broken up many families, and in a capital city where many children were still living almost feral lives among the bomb sites and abandoned buildings. Much of what the young Princess said then, the older Queen would surely stand by today. But she could not make the same speech now. Tony Blair, her 'modernizing' prime minister, says, 'She understands the world is changing . . . The family has to be seen to be part of society and part of the modern world, and not some strange collection of people from the past . . . So for her it's not a question of whether she likes it or doesn't like it; she knows it is necessary.' Like millions of other British families, the Windsors found the gap between principle and life too wide. She has not retreated far from this ground, though. Her annual Christmas broadcasts are shot through with a moral idea of the world, which emphasizes forgiveness, reconciliation and loyalty. In recent years, her bishops notice, they have become more religious, not less.

On the broader meaning of her reign the Queen has never tried to assert herself rhetorically, or argue her case. A succession of image-makers, from Cecil Beaton, Pietro Annigoni, Lucian Freud or Andy Warhol in pictures, to Winston Churchill, Richard Dimbleby, Ted Hughes or Gyles Brandreth in words, have provided colour and glitter. But given the amount of time and attention paid to the monarchy, there has been precious little intellectual argument made for it. What there has been has tended to be a rather desperate clutch back at Victorian hand-me-downs. The vivid arguments have been on the other side, from writers such as Willie Hamilton and Tom Nairn. This is potentially dangerous for the monarchy, though it may not seem so. Monarchy is, as we have seen, a perpetual act of reinvention, always behind the times but never very far. The case for monarchy, similarly, needs to be rethought, generation by generation. It cannot afford to become something generally tolerated but privately acknowledged as silly.

What might the Queen say, if she let fly? I think she might say that actually her case was a radical one. Modern democratic society claims to value special talent – for business, sporting prowess, dexterity – and to share out the rewards accordingly. It claims to honour the useful and the gutsy. But this is pious nonsense. Modern market democracies are webs of special connections, riven with unfairness, hidden conspiracies and family deals. The children of successful lawyers, bankers, journalists and so on tend to rise to the top of the money-making professions, apparently convinced they are there 'because we're worth it'. What does this mean for the millions who do not get the leg-ups and do not make it? How humiliating can the rhetoric of this false meritocracy feel? Is it a coincidence that the most fervent Royal-worshippers tend to be the quieter, getting-on-with-it majority, the very people ignored by the elite?

Modern monarchy can be a system which places a family at the top of the social pyramid as a kind of release valve. They are there because they're there because they're there. If they do the job well, this makes many people happy because it doesn't seriously 'put down' or demean anyone else. The little formalities of bowing, curtseying, 'ma'am'-ing, are no longer obeisance to the mighty. They are simple politeness. One man who has worked closely with her says the Queen and the Duke have 'the humility of the hereditary principle; because they know they have done nothing to deserve getting to their position, it poses a huge obligation of duty on them, to fulfil this extraordinary thing that has happened to them. It makes them in a funny way dutiful, almost humble'. The British electorate, adds one Palace servant, is prepared to admire the grandness of the British monarchy because it believes its members understand they are as individuals not special: 'they want a communism beneath the skin, and that is what she gives them'.

This may sound overstated but the more one observes the Queen, the truer it feels. She understands that the respect is first for the sovereign and only second for the individual, though she must realize how much her individual service is now admired. It is a vocation but it is also a job. At eighty-five she always knows where the cameras are. She dresses to stand out. When it rains, she uses see-through umbrellas so she can be observed and photographed. She is acutely aware of the opportunities and pitfalls for picture-making: when in Norway opening a British Council exhibition of large, explicit nudes by the painter Lucian Freud, she told one of the organizers that she had spent some time making quite sure 'I was not photographed between a pair of those great thighs'. She directs her lightbulb-on smiles to where the cameramen are waiting. She loathes being late, not least because punctuality is part of the technique of being seen by as many people as pos-sible. She has never gone looking for personal publicity, given interviews or tried to explain her 'side of the story'. When something hurtful or wrong is reported she bites her tongue. As a young woman she was a global superstar; but she does not play to cameras in a gushing way and certainly does not court the media. She has never 'confessed' or reinvented herself. Monarchy is a parade of images – castles, state occasions, flags, anthems, ritual celebrations. But the Queen, in the modern self-conscious sense, has no 'image'.

Are we then saying that the Queen is ordinary? Of course there is nothing ordinary about her life, circumstances or sense of duty. She is one of the richest people on the planet, attended by staff from her earliest years, whose private pursuits, from breeding racehorses to shooting, are not ordinary. She had no school education, no middle-class friends and has never had to ask herself how to earn money. Nor are her interests middle-class. She may keep her breakfast cereal in Tupperware boxes, watch the same television programmes as the rest of the British and enjoy gossip, but as the 'fount of honour' she is far more interested in titles, orders, uniforms and decorations than most of her subjects. The royal family lives in a world where precise rankings of this Cross or that Order, and the correct buttons, really matter; and this is not perhaps the most engaging feature of the institution.

So – *not* normal. But the key point is that the grandeur, the gilt and the wealth, the history and the pomp, surround people who have been accidentally selected by history to fill a special national position and who are well aware of it. Had ancient battles gone the other way, or now forgotten people changed their faith, or had different marriages occurred, other people entirely would have been the Queen and the Duke. When was the last time in European history that somebody became a monarch purely by virtue of his personal qualities? Napoleon, perhaps – and look how long his dynasty lasted. Chance put this Queen on her throne. In a brutally competitive world, many will find that a kind of consolation. Today, democracy and monarchy are no longer in opposition. Odd as it might seem, they support one another.

The Future

The Queen is blessed with a strong constitution and the calmness of someone who knows they are useful. If she lived as long as her mother, she could reign for another fifteen years. That would make her the longest-reigning British monarch too, easily outstripping that earlier great Queen, Victoria. The British monarchy remains physically Victorian. The palaces and their decoration still reflect the taste of Queen Victoria; the ceremonial uniform of the Guards remains essentially Victorian; most of the grand events of today are modelled on Victorian predecessors. But Queen Victoria was an empress, whose reign saw her small archipelago of damp, sooty towns and newfangled farms stretch its power across the world. She was Great Britain's figurehead during her super-stretched and confident heyday. Elizabeth II was dealt not this royal flush but lower-value cards. She has reigned during the final demolition of empire when the republican United States, formed in reaction to British monarchy, became the dominant world power. She yet may live to see China challenge for that role.

Queen Victoria had to do hardly anything towards Britain's continued expansion. She was more of an executive monarch, in the sense of having more of the state's business to transact herself, than her great-great-granddaughter; but Elizabeth II has travelled relentlessly to keep alive the spirit of the Commonwealth, the legacy of her imperial ancestress. She works at least as hard at her papers as did Victoria, determined to demonstrate her relevance to the politicians and civil servants who rule in her name. Unlike Victoria, who closeted herself on the Isle of Wight and at Windsor and Balmoral for so long she fomented republican feeling, the present Queen constantly shows herself. Queen Victoria, though a doughty woman, would have demanded the smelling-salts and headed for home in a carriage had she faced her descendant's schedule.

Being Queen these days is simply a harder job. The Duke of Edinburgh, who has seen it at closer hand than anyone else, has reflected that it is a life nobody would choose or volunteer for. In a sense, of course, the Duke did volunteer for it because he married Princess Elizabeth when he knew she would become Queen. Since then his role has been to support her and act as the head of the family, working behind the scenes to keep 'the Firm' together.

The central thing which makes monarchy different in kind from republicanism is that it stitches family life into the public realm. Every monarchy has found this difficult. From the archaic struggles of Chinese imperial families or Byzantines, Ottomans, Habsburgs or Mughals, weak characters, jealous children, conniving mothers and star-crossed love affairs have brought political instability, regime change and murder. Life for the Windsors has been, thankfully, calmer than that. Today's constitutional monarchies are lower wattage and lower risk. Yet any danger to the Windsors in the future will come not from political turmoil of the kind that created the dynasty in 1917, but from inside the family. Unlike the bereaved Victoria, Elizabeth has had the great good luck to have a long and happy marriage, which is part of the secret of her success. Like Victoria, she has produced a large family, who have had their share of scrapes. Like Victoria, her heir has had to wait until his own old age for the chance to reign, while struggling to establish an independent role.

What lessons does her success have for her son? Modesty is one. Her view of her role has been that she is a symbol, and that symbols are better off keeping mostly quiet. After the first excitement of her Coronation she was never the centre of a frenzy of national optimism, so she was never in the firing line during a spasm of national self-loathing. If this is a strangely passive record of achievement, one only has to think of what trouble an activist, opinionated monarch might have got into during the 1960s, or the Thatcher years, or when New Labour was going to war in the Middle East.

It goes further. The Queen's style of monarchy has buried much of a sense of self, as we understand that today. Almost everyone who reads this book has been brought up, explicitly or not, to believe that personal development, 'being oneself' in the most vivid way possible, is the highest human good. To develop one's talents, to get on, to be promoted, to end richer than when you started, or at least wiser – we are told that these are what give human lives meaning. Not for the Queen. Socially, there was nowhere further to go. Her life has its meaning through vocation or calling. Not so long ago, many other people defined themselves by their role. If you were a shoemaker, that was your meaning and identity. You looked like a cobbler, dressed like a cobbler and were happy to be known as cobbler. You were, in essence, what you did. Well, she still is what she does. There is only a little space (though an interesting space) between Queen Elizabeth II and the woman who lives her life.

With her heir, the Prince of Wales, it is very different. He has had to carve out a life, a role, for himself. Prince Charles is a puzzle, and one suspects he would agree. Well-meaning, shrewd, ambitious to do good, he is also a more prickly and self-conscious person than his mother. This may be a problem when he becomes King. We have become used to self-abnegation in our monarch. Prince Charles, already summoning ministers to see him, and firing off letters to government departments, is not big on self-abnegation. Indeed, around him there is a new theory of monarchy quietly being discussed. It goes like this. The sovereign's role is to be the non-executive chairman of the national company. The chairman ought therefore to challenge, balance and make up for the deficiencies of the rest of the board – those short-termist, pesky, and often incompetent elected politicians. If Parliament brings itself into contempt by expenses or other scandals; if ministers dodge difficult long-term problems; if the public has lost its allegiance to the old political ideologies – why then, a modern monarch must step forward and help.

Over the past sixty years, as we have seen, the Queen has taken a much more cautious attitude. As a 'non-exec' she has been thoughtful, hard-working, psychologically shrewd and able to offer politicians a great store of memories about the business of state. She is not the real board, but she is listened to, and provides continuity, in the way that a veteran chairman and one-time founder of a global company might be listened to. The more the 'board', the party-political parliamentary government, is in disrepair, or struggling, the more attentive the listening is. Why does she sit for hours each day, patiently reading her red boxes? It is a question of credibility. If she is to be a good head of state, she must know what is going on, just as a non-executive chairman must have read the paperwork before a board meeting.

She is in a long-term role. She thinks back to wartime Britain and forward to a Britain of the 2040s when her grandson will reign. The ceremonies the public notice most are the irregular ones, the marriages and jubilees, but the one that matters most is the complicated constitutional pantomime of the State Opening of Parliament in which the Queen represents the continuing state and therefore also the people who did not vote for the party in power, who loathe the prime minister of the day, or who perhaps did not vote at all. She represents the years and generations before today's government and the prospect of governments to come – a state that lasts far longer than any electoral cycle and whose interests, like its people's interests, last longer than a mere government. This is a truth rarely discussed, but as we have seen, it has had its practical side. Ministers express astonishment and wary pleasure at how much the Queen has thought about their dilemmas. Though she takes no decisions she can be a provoker of second thoughts and a catalyst for deeper thinking.

She responds to the mood of the times. When the banking crisis hit, and the country faced a period of public austerity, the Queen cut the cost of monarchy by £3.3 million, froze salaries and slashed her travel bill. The Royal Flight, despite its name, is mostly used for military purposes and sometimes for conveying ministers around. The future of the Royal Train, which allows the Queen to stay overnight during visits around Britain, and offers rare security, is now in serious doubt; the Queen has already been seen taking an ordinary train seat to get to Sandringham for her Christmas break. When Prince William and Kate Middleton, now the Duke and Duchess of Cambridge, made their first visits abroad, to Canada and the United States, they took a fraction of the staff that used to be thought necessary. Average salaries at Buckingham Palace are lower than in other royal establishments.

What she has never done is to take the lead on a subject,

express her own thinking forcibly, or campaign, even on issues closest to her heart. Ministers may guess her anguish about Commonwealth crises, military cutbacks, countryside legislation, or attempts to reduce royal budgets. But there has not been a single example of her intervening or protesting. The same could not be said of her son. He shares his father's interests in environmental issues, from population growth to genetically modified crops, wildlife to the future of rainforests. The Duke of Edinburgh has strong views but has been very careful about expressing them – mostly as rhetorical questions at private meetings. Prince Charles is more public and more emotive, though he also uses a formidable network of private funding (including from Arab monarchs) and contacts to push his projects. We know about his strong views on architecture, community, science and agriculture. It is a commonly held view that he must repress these views once he becomes King. Speaking out would be a risk, not just for the obvious reason of entering political and rough-and-tumble debate, but because the monarch is supposed to represent the whole community – scientists, radical architects and business people too.

The Queen has been able to cast her net of goodwill very widely. Parts of this role Charles would find easy, and indeed already performs. The Queen has supported the unsung heroines of the health service and the voluntary groups, the successful companies, the well-run towns. The media, in general (so goes the royal thinking), exists to point fingers and criticize: the monarchy must try to correct that balance when it can and celebrate all the un-newsy things that go right. Why does she endlessly visit small towns, industrial estates, colleges and relatively minor firms? Because nobody else does; and as cheerer-upper, that is her job. Her son is a hard worker too, and well practised at feigning interest, week after week, when out and about.

Yet if monarchy has influence, Prince Charles would ask, should it not be used for good? Traditional from her scarf to her Wellington boots, the Queen might agree and gently suggest she has been readier to change than her image suggests. To stay the same, it is necessary to change. Charles is said to have a plan for his first six months as King. The kind of things he might look at include the honours system. Is it any longer appropriate to invest good citizens with the Membership or Order of a defunct British Empire? Are the ancient orders of chivalry really cutting the mustard with the British public any more? Are there now a few too many members of the official royal family? We do not know his opinions on these questions but we can be sure he has opinions, and that he would want to make a mark. As he ages, friends observe, he grows more like the father who once seemed his opposite. The Duke of Edinburgh, says one who knows them both, is a poetic, sensitive man who has spent his life going to huge lengths trying to hide it, while the Prince of Wales is a tough, cut-throat, rather ruthless man who goes to great lengths to hide that, hence the caricature of an agonized cuff-fiddler.

However he resolves these dilemmas, the eventual passing of the Queen will be one of the greatest tests for the Windsor dynasty so far. Outside Britain, there is a sense that other countries of which she is head of state may then want to shift to native presidencies. John Howard, who led the pro-monarchy campaign in Australia in 1999 and subsequently became prime minister, said during the Queen's tour there in 2006 that though he thought his country would keep her as head of state, after her reign 'I do not know'. In Canada, republican feeling is on the rise and the moment of a change on the throne is often cited as an appropriate one. Something similar has been said in Barbados. Even the Queen's role as Head of the Commonwealth, which she has guarded jealously, does not pass automatically to her heir. It has no constitutional standing and is in the gift of the political leaders of the Commonwealth nations at the time. It may well be that none of this leads to a break of any kind. But it probably will.

Inside the United Kingdom, there are other changes which now seem obvious and which surely cannot be resisted for long. An immediate one is the Coronation Oath, which at the moment requires the new sovereign to do his utmost to maintain 'the Protestant Reformed Religion established by law' and the 'doctrine, worship, discipline and government' of the Church of England. Though the proud royal title of Defender of the Faith is an intellectual absurdity, granted by the Pope to Henry VIII before and not after he broke with Rome, it has been taken to mean defence of Protestant Christianity in its Anglican and Presbyterian forms. And under the 1701 Act of Settlement, indeed, Roman Catholics (persons 'who shall profess the popish religion') are barred from ascending the throne. In a study of this the legal scholar Robert Blackburn has amusingly listed some of the 'lost monarchs' Britain might have had had it not been for this disqualification: they include King Henry IX, Queen Amalia and Queen Yolanda, who is described as 'an exiled countess and family beauty'.

Prince Charles has publicly said he wants to be a 'Defender of Faith' in general and not simply one faith. With his sympathy for Islam and other non-Christian faiths, it is hard to see how he could tolerate the current Coronation Oath or the continuing bar on Catholics. Such changes might seem minor, gnats after the camel-sized mouthfuls caused by divorce. They would matter, though. First, the ban on Catholics is simply offensive to a strong and important part of the British people. Second, unpicking the Oath would immediately place a question mark against the continued status of the Anglican Communion as a state church. This has hardly been a good recruitment issue for Anglicanism, which is in severe decline. The business of prime minister and officials busying themselves (however remotely) in the appointment of bishops seems increasingly odd not just to bystanders but the church itself. And in a multi-faith Britain, should the high priests of any one religion be particularly privileged? Again, these are matters almost certain to be revisited after the Queen's reign. A bigger question is whether the monarchy can continue to catch the imagination. If Prince Charles is alive and willing, he will be crowned as an elderly king. If he then reigns for a long time, even Prince William will be a middle-aged figure by the time the throne is his.

Prince Charles has pushed the boundaries of what Royals are supposed to do. He has raised an astonishing amount of money for good causes such as helping preserve rainforests and giving young people a new start. Almost all of this work is done away from the limelight because of his despair about the likely effect of media exposure. Millions of people share his environmental and culturally conservative views, and they are poorly reflected in the ordinary, democratic politics of modern Britain. Here, as in most developed countries, the primacy of economic growth, attended by free-market economics and scientific optimism, overshadows all other debate. It is therefore naïve to claim he keeps 'out of politics'. He is a political man, whose political vision just happens most of the time to be rather wider than the current debates at Westminster. As we have seen, he irritated Downing Street during Lady

Thatcher's time with comments about a two-tier Britain, and did the same again when Tony Blair was prime minister, and the Prince came out strongly for the cause of 'the Country-side', which had become a euphemism for foxhunting. More important than either was his decision to show his disapproval of Chinese behaviour in Tibet by boycotting official visits by the Chinese president.

So here is a man of strong views and considerable energy, albeit not the greatest organizer, who has raised important questions about religion, the environment and human rights, and who has tried to use his unusual position to bring together politicians, business people and campaigners to change things for the better. Thanks to the coalition government headed by David Cameron, the Prince has his wish for much greater financial independence, and possibly greater monarchical wealth, too. He could be, as King, in a remarkably strong position. The problem is that he cannot be a campaigner, in any meaningful way, and also be the above-it-all head of state. As King, his job would not only be to receive a Chinese president but to do his very best to make the man or woman feel genuinely welcome. As King, when his ministers brought him planned legislation involving, say, wind farms which would blight a part of the landscape loved by sportsmen, he would be required to smile graciously and sign. As King, if his government agreed a deal with a South American nation, which meant a further destruction of some invaluable ecosys-tem, or wanted him to unveil the super-modernistic design for a new museum in Abu Dhabi, he could say nothing at all.

Could the man who is now Charles, Prince of Wales, stomach being the man who would be King Charles III, or George VII? If a hereditary monarchy means anything, it cannot break its own rules, so the odds are heavily that he will succeed. Prince Charles long ago distanced himself, physically and emotionally, from the Queen's court. His succession would be followed by a dramatic clearing-out of the current Buckingham Palace staff and the arrival of his own team. One of the more dramatic ideas that has been discussed is for the Royal family in his reign to leave Buckingham Palace entirely, leaving it as a kind of grand official government hotel and centre for events. The King would base himself not in London, but at Windsor Castle. Whether this happens or not, Charles has a strong desire for his reign to be different, and to make his own way as monarch, just as he has in his current life. This is natural, but if it excludes the hard-learned lessons and iron self-discipline of the Queen's reign, it is dangerous too. Assuming he lives longer than his mother – and he has at times wondered aloud if he will – then Prince Charles will become a very interesting king. She is teaching the younger generation still by example, rather than directly. Prince William, serving in the RAF, says he is bad at time-keeping but is watching his grandmother in action, 'who's done this for many years, she's a professional.' A naturally private and careful man, the Prince is also observing how the Queen has learned to move between her private and public selves: 'I think she doesn't care for celebrity ... and she really minds about having privacy in general; and I think it's very important to be able to retreat inside, and be able to collect one's thoughts and collect your ideas ... and then to move forwards and be able to project those ideas and those thoughts.' It is, he adds, 'a very tricky line to draw between private and public and duty and I think she's carved her own way completely; she's not had a blueprint.' Prince Harry says she has generally left the family to go off and find their own way, however: 'If you get it wrong, stand by, you'll be put in your place, quite rightly so.' But, 'guidance-wise, I've never asked for advice much, apart from betting on horses.'

Whenever one mentions the word 'abdication' at Buckingham Palace, faces wince and mouths tighten. 'I don't suppose the Queen has ever entertained the thought,' comes the reply. Or: 'She doesn't know what the word means.' Or, harking back to Uncle David, 'The Queen's view is that you couldn't have two abdications in one lifetime.' It is not quite true that the Queen has not entertained the thought. She has discussed abdication privately with loyal and senior figures, though she has gone on to declare against it. For her, if it can possibly be done, the job really is for life. Yet as we have seen, the Queen is a pragmatist. More and more of her work now will be passed over to her son, and to her grandsons too. She will travel less. As Prince Philip grows very old, she wants to be with him as much as possible. He has retired from some of his jobs. He has said he wants more time to relax and feels his memory is not what it was. For both, the formal duties are becoming a little more tiring all the time. Speaking unusually frankly, Prince Harry says that the Queen would find it hard to keep doing her duties after her husband's death: 'Regardless of whether my grandfather sort of seems to be doing his own thing – wandering off like a fish down the river – the fact that he's there . . . I personally don't think that she could do it without him, especially when they're both at this age.' He expresses awe at her stamina, meeting people she does not necessarily want to, at an age 'when people want to be sitting in front of the television and having a takeaway – couples sitting there on the sofa and very happy having their own time together.' She was on duty, smiling, bringing rooms to life, dressing up yet again: 'You know, these are things that, at her age, she shouldn't be doing, yet she's carrying on and doing them.'[1]

Should the Queen be unable to carry on in great old age –
a more common problem these days – there is a Regency
Act, which some profess 'perfectly serviceable' and others say
'needs revisiting', to allow Prince Charles to dissolve Parliament, give royal assent to bills and read out Queen's speeches.
One source says of abdication, 'I wouldn't actually rule it out,
at the end of the day. If she got to a point where she was
very old, and very tired, it could come to be the sensible view.
A lot depends on the public.'

It always has. So far, the British public's view of the
Diamond Queen is sparklingly, crystal, clear. The longer she
reigns, in good fettle and spirits, the better for what remains,
despite everything, her lucky country.

Notes

What the Queen Does

1. Prince William, interview with author.
2. David Cameron and Tony Blair, interviews with author.

Part One – Dynasty is Destiny

1. Kenneth Rose, *King George V*, Weidenfeld & Nicolson, 1983, p. 167.
2. James Pope-Hennessy, *Queen Mary*, George Allen and Unwin, 1959, pp. 480–1.
3. Harold Nicolson, *King George V*, Constable, 1952.
4. Frank Prochaska, *The Republic of Britain*, Allen Lane, 2000.
5. Rose, *King George V*, see chapter 6.
6. Pope-Hennessy, *Queen Mary*, p. 518.
7. Prochaska, *Republic of Britain*.
8. John Wheeler-Bennett, *King George VI*, Macmillan, 1958, p. 145.
9. Nigel Nicolson (ed.), *The Harold Nicolson Diaries: 1907–1963*, Weidenfeld & Nicolson, 2004, entry for 17 August 1949.
10. Pope-Hennessy, *Queen Mary*, p. 494.
11. Prochaska, *Republic of Britain*.
12. John Gore, *King George V: A Personal Memoir*, John Murray, 1941.
13. J. R. Clynes, *Memoirs*, quoted in Pope-Hennessy, *Queen Mary*, p. 534.
14. Sir Arthur Bryant, *King George V*, Collins, 1936.
15. Edward, Duke of Windsor, *A King's Story*, Cassell & Co., 1951, pp. 132–3.
16. Sir Alan Lascelles, *In Royal Service: Letters and Journals 1920–1936*, Hamish Hamilton, 1989, p. 50.

17. Ibid., p. 88.

18. Ibid., p. 109.

19. Nicolson, *Diaries*, entries for 25 May 1929 and 10 July 1940.

20. King George VI's own words, from a memorandum on the abdication crisis he wrote, and which is reproduced in full in Wheeler-Bennett's official biography, *King George VI*.

21. Ibid., p. 294.

22. Mark Logue and Peter Conradi, *The King's Speech*, Quercus, 2010, p. 62.

23. Dermot Morrah, *The Work of the Queen*, William Kimber, 1958; see also Robert Lacey, *Majesty*, Sphere Books, 1977, pp. 128–9.

24. Kenneth Rose in *Kings, Queens and Courtiers*, Weidenfeld & Nicolson, 1985.

25. Eleanor Roosevelt's diary, 9 June 1939, Roosevelt archives, quoted in Wheeler-Bennett, *King George VI*, p. 382.

26. From the Broadlands Archive, quoted in Philip Ziegler, *Mountbatten*, Collins, 1985, p. 457.

27. Ibid., p. 680.

28. Wheeler-Bennett, quoted in Harold Nicolson's diary, March 1954: see Andrew Roberts, *Eminent Churchillians*, Weidenfeld & Nicolson, 1994.

29. William Shawcross, *Queen Elizabeth, the Queen Mother: The Official Biography*, Macmillan, 2009, p. 167.

30. Ibid., p. 75.

31. Ibid., p. 165.

32. Ibid., p. 187.

Part Two – Lilibet

1. David Cannadine, interview with author.

2. Harold Nicolson, *Diaries and Letters*, ed. Stanley Olson, part 3, Weidenfeld & Nicolson, 1980, p. 338.

3. Marion Crawford, *The Little Princesses*, with an introduction by A. N. Wilson, Duckworth, 1993, p. viii.

4. William Shawcross, *Queen Elizabeth, the Queen Mother: The Official Biography*, Macmillan, 2009, p. 336.

5. Lady Cynthia Asquith, *The King's Daughter*, Hutchinson, 1937, pp. 96–7.

6. See Philip Eade, *Young Prince Philip*, HarperPress, 2011, p. 111.

7. Gyles Brandreth, *Philip & Elizabeth*, Century Books, 2004, p. 181.

8. Shawcross, *Queen Elizabeth*, pp. 523–4.

9. Ibid., p. 532.

10. Robert Lacey, *Majesty*, Sphere Books, 1977, p. 179.

11. See Nigel Dempster, *H.R.H The Princess Margaret*, Quartet Books, 1981, p. 5ff.

12. Taken from Margaret Rhodes, *The Final Curtsey*, Calder Walker Associates, 2011.

13. See David Cannadine, *The Decline and Fall of the British Aristocracy*, Penguin, 2005.

14. Basil Boothroyd, *Prince Philip: An Informal Biography*, Dutton, 1971, p. 24.

15. Michael Sissons and Philip French (eds), *Age of Austerity: 1945–1951*, Penguin, 1964, p. 138.

16. Peter Clarke, *The Cripps Version*, Penguin, 2002, p. 268.

17. Ben Pimlott, *The Queen*, HarperCollins, 1996, p. 170.

18. Elizabeth Longford, *Elizabeth R*, Weidenfeld & Nicolson, 1983, p. 141.

Interlude – The Queen in the World

1. John Wheeler-Bennett: *King George VI*, Macmillan, 1958, p. 722.

2. Robert Lacey, *Majesty*, Sphere Books, 1977, p. 260.

Part Three – The Queen at Work

1. David Cannadine, interview with author.

2. Harold Macmillan, *The Macmillan Diaries: The Cabinet Years 1950–1957*, Macmillan, 2003, p. 140.

3. Private conversation.

4. Lord Moran, *Winston Churchill, The Struggle for Survival: Diaries 1940–65*, entry for 15 May 1954.

5. Macmillan, *Diaries: The Cabinet Years*, p. 208.

6. Peter Hennessy, interview with author.

7. Quoted in Jonathan Dimbleby, *Richard Dimbleby*, Hodder and Stoughton, 1975, p. 236ff.

8. *The Spectator*, 27 February 1953.

9. Asa Briggs, *Sound and Vision: The History of Broadcasting in the United Kingdom*, vol. 4, Oxford University Press, 1995, pp. 420ff.

10. *Time and Tide*, 6 June 1953.

11. *New Statesman and Nation*, 6 June 1953.

12. Dimbleby, *Richard Dimbleby*, p. 246.

13. See the round-up in *Time and Tide*, 13 June 1953.

14. For details, see Harry Hopkins, *The New Look*, Secker and Warburg, 1963, pp. 296–7.

15. *New Statesman and Nation*, 30 May 1953.

16. Macmillan, *Diaries: The Cabinet Years 1950–1957*, p. 208.

17. Moran, *Churchill, The Struggle for Survival*, p. 377.

18. Ibid., p. 399.

19. Macmillan, *Diaries: The Cabinet Years*, p. 150.

20. Ibid., pp. 391, 393.

21. Richard Cockett, *Thinking the Unthinkable*, HarperCollins, 1994, p. 127.

22. D. R. Thorpe, *Eden*, Chatto & Windus, 2003, pp. 124–5.

23. Robert Lacey, *Majesty*, p. 298.

24. D. R. Thorpe, *Eden*, pp. 584–5.

25. Robert Rhodes James, *Anthony Eden*, Papermac, 1987, p. 595.

26. Elizabeth Langford, *Elizabeth R*, p. 255.

27. Ben Pimlott, *The Queen*, HarperCollins, 1996, p. 332.

Interlude – Britannia and the Waves

1. Interview with Alan Titchmarsh for ITV, broadcast May 2011.

Part Four – Off with Her Head!

1. Ben Pimlott, *Harold Wilson*, HarperCollins, 1992, p. 113.

2. Anthony Howard (ed.), *The Crossman Diaries*, Methuen, 1979, p. 283.

3. Philip Ziegler, *Wilson: The Authorised Life*, Weidenfeld & Nicolson, 1993, p. 214.

4. Peter Hennessy, *The Secret State*, Penguin, 2010, p. xxxv.

5. Peter Hennessy, interview with author.

6. Tony Benn, *Out of the Wilderness: Diaries 1963–67*, Hutchinson, 1987, p. 14.

7. Ibid., p. 55.

8. Ibid., p. 232.

9. Richard Crossman, *The Crossman Diaries*, Hamish Hamilton/Jonathan Cape, 1979, p. 30.

10. Richard Crossman, *The Diaries of a Cabinet Minister*, vol. 2, Hamish Hamilton/Jonathan Cape, 1976, pp. 43–4.

11. Ibid., p. 121.

12. Ibid., pp. 249–50.

13. Ibid., p. 510.

14. Crossman, *Crossman Diaries*, p. 346.

15. Ibid., p. 594.

16. Willie Hamilton, *Blood on the Walls*, Bloomsbury, 1992, p. 15.

17. *Guardian* parliamentary report, 15 December 1971.

18. Ian Smith, *The Great Betrayal*, Blake Publishing, 1997, p. 86.

19. Edward Heath, *The Course of My Life*, Hodder & Stoughton, 1998, p. 483.

20. Sir Anthony Jay, interview with author.

21. See Asa Briggs, *Competition: The History of Broadcasting in the United Kingdom*, vol. 5, Oxford University Press 1995, p. 917; Cawston's entry in the *Dictionary of National Biography*; and Elizabeth Longford, *Elizabeth R*, Weidenfeld & Nicolson, 1983, pp. 220–1.

22. *New Statesman*, 17 June 1969.

23. *Spectator*, 28 June 1969.

24. *New Statesman* profile, 27 June 1969. Though anonymous, it reads very like the prose of Mr Alan Watkins.

25. Ann Leslie, interview with author.

26. Harry Arnold, interview with author.

27. Gore Vidal, *Point to Point Navigation*, Little, Brown, 2006.

28. Robert Lacey, interview with author.

29. Edward Heath, *The Course of My Life*, Hodder & Stoughton, 1998, p. 308.

30. Ibid., p. 318.

31. Ibid., p. 394.

32. Interview with author.

33. Philip Howard, the *Times*, 8 June 1977, special edition.

34. Roger Berthoud in *The Times*, 4 June 1977.

35. See Kenneth O. Morgan, *Callaghan, A Life*, Oxford University Press, 1997, p. 511.

36. Timothy Knatchbull, interview with author.

37. Jonathan Dimbleby, *The Prince of Wales*, Little, Brown, 1994, p. 266.

38. Longford, *Elizabeth R*, p. 7.

Interlude – Money

1. Ben Pimlott, *The Queen*, HarperCollins, 1996, p. 534.

2. Dorothy Laird, *How the Queen Reigns*, Hodder & Stoughton 1959, p. 332.

Part Five – Into the Maelstrom

1. Margaret Thatcher, *The Downing Street Years*, HarperCollins, 1993, p. 18.

2. Peter Hennessy, *Having It So Good*, Allen Lane, 2006, p. 235.

3. Jonathan Dimbleby, *The Prince of Wales*, Little, Brown, 1994, pp. 322–4.

4. Lord Hurd, BBC interview.

5. Alastair Campbell, *The Alastair Campbell Diaries*, vol. 1, Hutchinson, 2010, p. 621.

6. Tony Blair, *The Journey*, Hutchinson, 2010, p. 133.

7. John Birt, *The Harder Path*; see Tina Brown, *The Diana Chronicles*, Century, 2007, pp. 350ff.

8. Blair, *The Journey*, p. 142.

9. Ibid., pp. 148–9 and 260–1.

10. Gyles Brandreth, *Something Sensational to Read in the Train*, John Murray, 2009, p. 649.

11. *Guardian*, 24 January 2002.

12. See Robert Blackburn, *King and Country*, Politico's, 2006, pp. 32–3.
13. Margaret Rhodes, *The Final Curtsey*, Walker Associates, 2011.
14. David Starkey, *Crown and Country*, HarperPress, 2010, p. 492.

The Future

1. Prince Harry, interview with author.

Select Bibliography

There is a vast literature about the Queen and her family. Madness and exhaustion would have followed any attempt – at least by this author – to read everything. The various political and other memoirs and general histories I have used are referred to where they are quoted from directly. But the following is the list of books about the Queen and other Royals that I have found particularly helpful.

Beaverbrook, Lord, *The Abdication of King Edward VIII*, ed. A. J. P. Taylor, Hamish Hamilton, 1966.

Blackburn, Robert, *King and Country*, Politico's, 2006.

Bradford, Sarah, *Elizabeth*, William Heinemann, 1996.

———, *George V*, Weidenfeld & Nicolson, 1989.

Brandreth, Gyles, *Philip and Elizabeth, Portrait of a Marriage*, Arrow Books, 2004.

Brown, Tina, *The Diana Chronicles*, Century, 2007.

Dimbleby, Jonathan, *The Prince of Wales*, Little, Brown, 1994.

Donaldson, Frances, *Edward VIII*, Weidenfeld & Nicolson, 1974.

Eade, Philip, *Young Prince Philip*, 2011.

Hibbert, Christopher, *Queen Victoria: An Intimate History*, HarperCollins, 2000.

Hoey, Brian, *Mountbatten*, Sidgwick & Jackson, 1994.

Lacey, Robert, *Majesty*, Hutchinson & Co., 1977.

———, *Royal: HM Queen Elizabeth II*, HarperCollins 2002

Longford, Elizabeth, *Elizabeth R*, Weidenfeld & Nicolson, 1983.

Morton, Andrew, *Diana, her True Story*, Michael O'Mara Books, 1993.

Pimlott, Ben, *The Queen*, HarperCollins, 1996.

Plumtree, George, *Edward VIII*, Pavilion, 1995.

Pope-Hennessy, James, *Queen Mary*, Allen & Unwin, 1959.

Rose, Kenneth, *King George V*, Weidenfeld & Nicolson 1983.

———, *Kings, Queens and Courtiers*, Weidenfeld & Nicolson, 1985.

Shawcross, William, *Queen Elizabeth, the Queen Mother: The Official Biography*, Macmillan, 2009.

Vickers, Hugo, *Elizabeth, the Queen Mother*, Random House, 2006.

Wheeler-Bennett, John W., *King George VI*, Macmillan, 1958.

Zeigler, Philip, *King Edward VIII*, HarperCollins, 1990.

———, *Mountbatten*, HarperCollins, 1988.

Picture Acknowledgements

Listed clockwise by page.

Section One

Page 1: The baby Elizabeth with the Duke and Duchess of York © Mary Evans Picture Library/Grenville Collins Postcard Collection. Princess Elizabeth in 1930 © Hulton-Deutsch Collection/Corbis. Princess Elizabeth with her grandmother, Queen Mary, and her grandfather, George V © Getty Images.

Page 2: The Prince of Wales, later Edward VIII, and the young Louis Mountbatten © Getty Images. 'Uncle David' with his niece, Princess Elizabeth © Getty Images.

Page 3: 'We four' © Getty Images. Princess Elizabeth, with her parents and sister, after her father's Coronation © Popperfoto/Getty Images.

Page 4: An exuberant Prince Philip of Greece prepares to entertain the young princesses © Getty Images. Princesses Elizabeth and Margaret in a private pantomime © Getty Images.

Page 5: Princess Elizabeth with her father, 1946 © Getty Images.

Page 6: Princess Elizabeth dancing with the son of the Marquess of Abergavenny © *Illustrated London News*/Mary Evans Picture Library. Princess Elizabeth playing tag with midshipmen aboard HMS *Vanguard* © Bettman/Corbis. Princess Elizabeth and Prince Philip of Greece at the wedding of Patricia Mountbatten and Lord Brabourne © Popperfoto/Getty Images.

Page 7: The infant Princess Anne with Prince Philip, Princess Elizabeth and Prince Charles © Gamma-Keystone via Getty Images. Queen

Elizabeth II arrives in what is now her kingdom © Press Association Images. King George VI waves goodbye to his daughter at London airport © Popperfoto/Getty Images.

Page 8: Children in the East End get news of a knees-up © Hulton-Deutsch Collection/Corbis. The most solemn moment: 2 June 1953 © Getty Images.

Section Two

Page 1: The Queen and Sir Winston Churchill, 1953 © Getty Images. The Queen and Prince Philip with President Eisenhower in Washington © Wally McNamee/Corbis. The Queen was the first reigning monarch to visit Australia © Popperfoto/Getty Images.

Page 2: The Queen in the streets of Karachi, Pakistan, 1961 © Getty Images. The Queen travels on the London Underground's just-opened Victoria Line © Getty Images.

Page 3: The Queen taking a photograph of Prince Charles driving Prince Edward in a go-kart © Getty Images. Prince Charles's investiture as Prince of Wales © Press Association.

Page 4: The Queen and the Duke of Edinburgh celebrate their silver wedding anniversary (© Getty Images).

Page 5: The Queen with Sir Martin Charteris, her private secretary, 1972 © Lichfield/Getty Images. The Queen at dinner on the Royal Yacht © Lichfield/Getty Images.

Page 6: Harold Wilson and the Queen © Press Association Images. The Queen with the Labour defence secretary Fred Mulley at an RAF review © Press Association Images.

Page 7: A congratulatory postcard is delivered © 1900 Keystone-France/Getty Images. The Silver Jubilee was a much-needed tonic © Hulton-Deutsch/Corbis.

Page 8: The Queen comforts her horse Burmese, after blank shots were fired at her during the 1981 Trooping the Colour © Press Association Images.

Section Three

Page 1: Prince Charles and Lady Diana bow and curtsey to the Queen after their marriage in 1981 © AFP/Getty Images. 'Granny' with Princes William and Harry © Tim Graham/Getty Images.

Page 2: The Queen waits to make her 'annus horribilis' speech at London's Guildhall © Tim Graham/Getty Images. The Queen back in London after Diana's death © Tim Graham/Getty Images. The Queen goes digital © AFP/Getty Images.

Page 3: The Queen Mother waves to the crowds on her hundredth birthday, watched by the Queen and Princess Margaret © Tim Graham/Getty Images. The Queen's portrait in a Golden Jubilee-bedecked Brentford window © AFP/Getty Images. London East End crowds during the 2002 Golden Jubilee © Tim Graham/Getty Images.

Page 4: Terence Cuneo's coronation portrait, courtesy of The Royal Collection © 2011; Her Majesty Queen Elizabeth II. A sketch by Annigoni, courtesy of The Royal Collection © 2011; Her Majesty Queen Elizabeth II.

Page 5: Michael Leonard's popular 1986 portrait of the Queen © National Portrait Gallery. Her Majesty Queen Elizabeth II by Lucian Freud, courtesy of The Royal Collection 2011 © Lucian Freud.

Page 6: The Queen and the Duke of Edinburgh at the Braemar Gathering in Scotland © 2008 Getty Images. The Queen, Prince Harry, Prince Andrew, the Duke of Edinburgh and Prince Edward watch an RAF flypast © 2005 Getty Images.

Page 7: Michelle Obama with the Queen © Daniel Hambury/AP/Press Association Images. The Queen with the Irish President, Mary McAleese © Getty Images.

The Queen watched by Kate Middleton, the Duchess of Cambridge © Kirsty Wigglesworth/PA Wire/Press Association Images.

Page 8: The Queen © Tim Graham/Getty Images.

Index

extracts reading groups
competitions books new
books discounts extracts extracts discounts
competitions extracts
books reading groups
new events
events books
reading groups extracts books new titles reading groups
new new
interviews
reading groups books extracts events extracts extracts
discounts events new
new books events interviews new books extracts
events new

www.panmacmillan.com

extracts events reading groups
competitions books extracts new
books